Safe Passage to Healing

Safe Passage to Healing

A Guide for Survivors of Ritual Abuse

Chrystine Oksana

AN AUTHORS GUILD BACKINPRINT.COM EDITION

AN AUTHORS GUILD BACKINPRINT.COM EDITION

Published by iUniverse.com, Inc.

For information address:
iUniverse.com, Inc.
5220 S 16th, Ste. 200
Lincoln, NE 68512
www.iuniverse.com

Originally published by HarperPerennial

Designed by Laura Hammond Hough

ISBN: 0-595-20100-8

Printed in the United States of America

To my husband and children

Survivors who shared their experiences use pseudonyms, except for one survivor, who had her name legally changed. All identifying details have been omitted or modified, including those in my personal story.

Chrystine Oksana is my actual first and middle name. I chose not to use my surname for several reasons. First, I have struggled many years to gain personal freedom, and I wish to manage my privacy so that I can enjoy it. Second, being a survivor of ritual abuse is *part* of my identity, but it is not my entire identiy. Maintaining a measure of anonymity allows for recognition of my other facets as well. Finally, the family with whom I share my married surname have nothing to do with my abuse history, and I do not wish to cause them any distress.

Contents

Acknowledgments

I would like to thank and acknowledge the courage of the survivors who shared their recovery stories which make up the "heart" of this book. I would also like to recognize pioneering survivors who contributed so much to our healing literature and often remain unacknowledged.

This book evolved through the support, insights, and help of many giving people. I would like to thank the following for their contributions:

Laura Davis, for her steady encouragement, her time, and guidance in mentoring me through this, my first book. My editor, Janet Goldstein, for her belief in this book, her confidence in me, her patience, and care in seeing this project through; HarperCollins Publishers for their continuing support of survivor issues; Charlotte Raymond, my literary agent, for helping this idea succeed; Betsy Thorpe for attending to the many behind the scenes details; Judy Tashbook for her enthusiasm, as well as the many other people involved in the production and marketing of this book.

My husband, Jack, who always believed me, and in me, who continues to be my "life-support system" for his many many hours of assistance. My children who lived with the ups and downs of both my recovery and the writing of this book.

I would like to additionally thank Gail Fisher-Taylor, Pamela Koster, and Susan Mroczynski for their contributions and suggestions in the start-up phases of the book; Kay Hagan, Zachary Kleiman, Mimi Power, and Yvonne Wilder for their advice on the technical aspects of writing and publishing; Robert Shaw, Martin Smith, Caryn StarDancer, and Mitzie West for their contributions to my understanding of ritual abuse; Sheryl Patterson, Jacklyn Pia, and Kitty Riordan for their insights in helping me to appreciate multiplicity.

I would like to express my gratitude to the following professionals for reviewing all or parts of the manuscript: Dnise Dickey, Renee Fredrickson, Mary Ellen Holmen, Cliff Morgan, Suzanne McLennan, Susan Mroczynski, David Neswald, B. J. Smith, and Walter Young; for their time and expertise in providing professional background information for the book: Ruth Alpert, Lynn D. Finney, George Gannaway, Diane George, Michael Moore, Cliff Morgan, Margery M. Noel, Sandy Robbin, Martin R. Smith, Felicia N. Trujillo, Robert Weisz, and Mary R. Williams.

For providing research information and resource material: Carolyn Bemis, Maureen Brugh of Monarch Resources, Dee Brown (Colorado), Dee Brown (California), Christi Calkins, Peter Dimock, Paul Davis at University of New Mexico, Blake French, Kristie Haley at ISSMP&D, Bruce and Dale McCulley at Cavalcade Productions, Mary Morell at Full Circle Books, Pam Noblitt at the Society for the Investigation, Treatment, and Prevention of Ritual and Cult Abuse, the staff at the Sidron Foundation, Michael J. Siegel, and Civia Tamarkin.

A very special thank you to my many willing and insightful readers whose feedback on all or parts of the manuscript helped to define this book: dede Bell, Martha C., Tasha Curtis, Laura Davis, Terry DiGiuseppe, Erik, Donna Fine, Nell Grainger, Margy Hillhouse, Joani, Zachary Kleiman, Janet Linden, Ulana Liskevych, Virginia McNally, Adam Randolph, Dawn Schkade, Robert Shaw, and Caryn StarDancer.

Thank you to Emily for her drawing of Rainbow Place, and thanks to all the people who contributed in various ways, but asked to remain anonymous.

Finally my heartfelt thanks to Donna Fine, Jiivanii, and Mitzie West who embraced the idea of this book, and with loving care witnessed the highs and lows, ups and downs, supporting me through the writing from start to finish.

Introduction

If you know or suspect that you are a survivor of ritual abuse, you are not alone. Thousands of survivors are walking the road to recovery. With each step, survivors are gathering strength and momentum. Survivor poetry, art exhibits, performances, networks, and newsletters speak of the many paths being taken. These paths will converge on the main street of life, where survivors will walk with pride and freedom.

Although you may have suffered alone, you do not have to recover in isolation. There is lots of companionship, survivor to survivor, in these pages. Survivors share the pain and despair of the early stages, and ways in which they found courage and strength.

No matter how severe your circumstances, you will find that healing is possible. There is hope. You will discover your own internal heal-

ing resources and many sources of outside help as well. Most of all, you will discover that you, too, can make it. After all, you are a survivor.

BACKGROUND

In my quest for healing, I tried to learn everything I could about secret societies, the occult, ethics, thought reform, questions of good and evil, roots of violence, effects of abusive parenting, and healing from ritual abuse I researched more than four hundred articles and reference materials. I read or reviewed more than eighty books. I have investigated and/or experimented with every therapeutic lead that sounded promising. I attended seminars and workshops and interviewed experts and therapists. During the course of my recovery I've met many other survivors. I spent close to two years interviewing over thirty survivors in depth.

This book brings together the collective knowledge gleaned from that extensive research. Much of the material takes the form of first-hand accounts and is therefore anecdotal, not scientific. Anecdotal accounts generally serve the purpose of healing best. However, explanatory information has been verified with experts in their respective fields. In the case of varying opinions, I have selected the view that most closely reflects survivors' views and experiences. It is my hope that these accounts will inspire much-needed studies and research in ritual abuse.

WHO CAN BENEFIT

This book is written for adult survivors of ritual abuse. However, survivors of any trauma may find it helpful. If you have been suffering the effects of incest, sadistic or violent abuse, or abuse at the hands of multiple perpetrators, this book may help in your healing. If you have been raised in a negative, critical, or fearful atmosphere, you may find issues in common with survivors. If you are suffering from chronic difficulties such as anxiety, sleeping disorders, food and chemical dependencies, depression, chronic fatigue, or other unexplained chronic difficulties, and have not found relief despite professional treatment, this book describes tools for self-discovery that may lead to healing, no matter what the specific causes of that behavior might be.

Finally, this book is also intended for the partners, caring friends, and extended family who share a concern for and desire to support and understand a survivor of ritual abuse. Professionals such as therapists, clergy, counselors, medical personnel, crisis and hot-line staff, researchers, educators, legal staff, law enforcement personnel,

and support organization staff will find it helpful as well.

CULTIVATING SAFETY

The material in this book parallels recovery in many respects. The book, like recovery, is not meant to be read in a single sitting or over a weekend. You may find the material difficult and at times disturbing or disorienting. Recovery is a difficult, disturbing, and at times disorienting process. One of the most important safety tools to prevent being overwhelmed is to take frequent breaks.

To help readers establish the habit of taking breaks, there are reminders in the more difficult sections. You may need them more or less frequently than suggested. In some parts, you may want to take breaks after each sentence or paragraph. You'll discover that a slower pace accelerates healing.

INTERNAL AND EXTERNAL SAFETY

Violators use fear to control victims of ritual abuse. A key tool both in recovery and in reading this book is learning how to manage your level of safety. There are two types of safety issues for survivors, external and internal. External safety issues are discussed in Chapter 13. However, the vast majority of safety issues for survivors are internal. Establishing internal strength and safety is discussed in Chapters 1 and 2 and addressed throughout the book.

Generally speaking, the most difficult material is contained in Part Two, About Ritual Abuse, Part Three, Dissociation, and Chapter 16, "Getting Through the Toughest Moments." Part Two may contain particularly difficult material. What is helpful to some is unhelpful to others. Some survivors benefit by understanding as much background as possible. Knowing the big picture may accelerate their healing. Others may find detailed information about ritual abuse traumatizing. These survivors may benefit more by *not* reading about ritual abuse.

If you decide to bypass Parts Two, Three, and Chapter 16, or read them only with a support person present, it's a good idea to separate the pages in these parts from the rest of the book. You may want to clip them or place tape or a rubber band around them. That way you have better control of if, when, and how to read the information. As a safety precaution, you may first want to read Chapters 1 and 2 and Part Six before proceeding with the remainder of the book.

STAY SAFE PAGES

Sections of this book contain difficult material for survivors or sensitive readers. As a safety precaution, I have provided a quick reference safety section at the back of the book. Please turn to pages 383–88 and familiarize yourself with them. They are self-explanatory. Please complete them now.

HONORING YOUR FEELINGS

You can expect to have strong reactions from time to time. Your reactions are important. They need to be acknowledged and honored. You may feel excited, optimistic, encouraged, and hopeful. Take time to notice your uplifting feelings and enjoy them. You may want to act on the suggestions or ideas that inspired them. This an important part of healing.

You may also feel angry, upset, ashamed, and in despair. Hearing about the good things that are possible may remind you of your losses. You may feel hopeless about ever getting to a better place. These feelings are common for survivors of extreme abuse.

Each unhopeful feeling is a clue to your healing. There is a reason for your discouragement. By uncovering it, you can transform the underlying beliefs and alleviate the underlying pain. Chapters 15 and 16 talk about this essential recovery skill. Keep in mind that healing is possible whether you are coming from a place of hope or hopelessness.

RESPECTING YOUR NEEDS

There is lot of information in this book. It attempts to cover various areas of potential concern to survivors. Not all sections will be of equal value or interest to each reader. There may be sections that are irrelevant to you. Some suggestions may never apply to you; others may "click" as late as three or four years from your initial reading. Remember to respect your needs and intuition. Take whatever information is useful, and feel free to skip or disregard what isn't.

There may be suggestions you would like to try that don't seem to work for you yet. That's quite common. Everyone's recovery course follows its own timetable. If something isn't working for you now, try it again later. Don't get down on yourself or be impatient. Trust that things happen in their own time and that your own timing, whatever it is, is right for you.

I attended a support group where I heard survivors describe their symptoms, and I used to think, "That's someone else's problem. That's not me. One of the things I gained from that group is the ability to stay on my own schedule. I'm where I need to be. I'm okay not comparing myself to somebody else's recovery and saying, "Well, if she can do this, I should be able to," because it's not about that. It's about what's happening with me. That's part of coming into touch with ourselves. And to me, that's about personal freedom. Suzzane

ABOUT THE SURVIVORS

Ours is a pioneering effort. Early survivors traveled into uncharted territory. There was no information, no road map, no guideposts to say "You are here" in their solitary quest for healing. But as survivors explored new frontiers, they began to map the course for others. By sharing our experience, those who follow will be able to travel a charted course towards healing.

I know that if I can get this far, other people can too. My passion is to lend a hand back to anybody behind me. And to keep moving forward. I want to tell survivors to stay alive. Work your recovery. You'll get there.   Caryn StarDancer

Most survivors I interviewed were well on the road to recovery, while a few were just uncovering their abuse. They are women and men, mothers and fathers, married and unmarried. They come from all across North America. Their abuse spans a continuum from sporadic sadistic abuse to a systematic regimen of abuse and indoctrination suffered from infancy into adulthood. Even though these survivors agreed to be interviewed, it wasn't easy for them. Most were concerned about reprisals for talking. Others were afraid that their comments may be misconstrued. One survivor remembers being taped by her violators when she was a little girl. Her words were played back to her "all twisted." Another survivor expressed the same concern:

I hate to have my picture taken. I can't [keep a] journal. Any kind of writing or recording of my thoughts seems like evidence against me. You never want to leave a trail.   Sunny

Yet one by one, for their own reasons and in their own way, survivors decided to participate. Sunny eventually decided, "Well, the hell with it. I'm going to do it. And if anybody horribly mean and nasty got hold of it and said, 'You said this,' I would say, 'I did. And I meant it.'" For all survivors who participated, sharing was empowering. By pooling our experience, we give each other strength and help one another heal. No matter how great your difficulties, how deep your pain, how impossible your circumstances, *healing is possible.*

I have a favorite vacation spot in one of the most arid regions of Nevada. Desolate is the word that describes it. One year it rained while I was there, and within days I saw grass sprouting. I was astounded. Then I began to realize how you can walk on grass, grind it into the ground with your heel, you can starve it, parch it, freeze it—but at the first opportunity it comes back and keeps coming back. And then it occurred to me—that's exactly like the human spirit.   Josie

This book is written to honor survivors, to acknowledge people doing the hard work of recovery. Although I know that the survivors who participated cannot take away your pain, we hope to be your voice of encouragement. Although we cannot hold your hand, I hope we can touch you through our words. I know the journey is hard, but we can make it. Take good care of yourself. And remember, if ever you need a friend, perhaps you can find one through a voice in this book.

My Story

I HAD A NORMAL CHILDHOOD

If there was one thing I knew, it was that I had a normal childhood. My immigrant parents worked hard to build a better life for my siblings and me. We were a conservative, conventional, church going family. We lived "as God decreed."

I married a wonderful man, had two healthy children, completed an M.B.A., and had a financially rewarding career. Everything was perfect—well, almost perfect. I was constantly sick, a condition I kept secret.

Growing up, I understood one thing; nothing matters more than what other people think. They had to think I was respectable and normal in every way. A deep, unconscious part of me understood something else: that being weak means being destroyed. I had to look healthy and able to take care of myself. Looking "good" wasn't a nicety. It was a necessity. I had to hide my condition from everyone, including my parents. I smiled a lot, dressed well; my hair was always groomed.

IT MUST BE STRESS

I struggled to look normal yet barely made it through each day. "Stress," I thought. "It must be stress." Just getting to work proved overwhelming to me. I had to secretly recuperate before I could begin each day. I'd go to the washroom, put down the lid, and sit curled up on the lid so that no one would see. "Fifteen minutes," I'd think to myself. "They won't miss me."

During the morning, I'd sneak out to "meetings." Safely behind a closed door, I'd shut my eyes again. I spent lunch under a blanket in the back seat of my car. After the hour had passed, I'd get up and try to make it through the afternoon.

The effort it took to get back home was so great, I always headed straight for bed. I would lie there, expressionless. As night descended my body would sometimes begin to tremble and shake. Often my limbs convulsed erratically. My head shook in abnormally quick, rhythmic movements. My kids barely knew me. My husband was both mother and father to them. He did the shopping, made the meals, bought all their clothes, and helped to make them feel that everything was all right with me. I didn't even know their shoe size.

I woke up every morning feeling dead. The hardest thing I had to do was get my lifeless body out of bed. Once I got my feet moving, the daily cycle would begin again. Barely to work, stolen breaks, lunch hours in a darkened garage, back home, and back to bed. That's how it was on days when I wasn't sick. I was running on empty, on back-up reserves. There was nothing left to handle a real emergency. The slightest cold would put me in bed. I would lie there, almost catatonic, the sound of a radio too much to bear.

SUB ICTAL PHENOMENON

I kept trying to find a reason for my illness. I had been such a healthy kid, always on the go, athletic. I almost never got sick. But after the age of eighteen, things began to change. I started getting colds, flus, muscle stiffness, depressions, and just an overall bad feeling. I still looked okay on the outside, but inside I was feeling worse and worse. By thirty-five I was barely making it day to day. In search of a cure, I went from doctor to doctor, from test to test, only to be told, "Everything is normal. Continue to rest." That's what I'd heard for the past seventeen years as my condition worsened.

One day a friend told me about a stress man-agement program at a nearby health clinic. Full of hope, I went for an interview. I explained my problem to a psychologist and filled out a five-page questionnaire.

The personal profile results came back normal in all respects, with just slightly lower than average self-esteem. However, the psychologist detected a condition that he said was the cause of my stress: My brain was overreacting to stimuli, discharging a higher than normal electron stream—a condition related to epilepsy. It was called sub ictal phenomenon.

I sat there in awe. There was a name for what I had! What's more, there was even a cure. It involved placing electrodes on my scalp to monitor and help calm my brain activity, a form of behavioral therapy.

Sub ictal phenomenon. It sounded strange enough to be true. Part of me was ecstatic. Part of me was concerned. I was willing to try anything to get well. But somehow the thought of someone messing with my head and brain unsettled me.

PLEASE DON'T HURT ME ANYMORE

I asked for a second opinion. The psychiatrist who saw me was a kind and gentle man. In our first interview, it seems he touched a nerve. After the session I headed straight for the washroom, where I cried hysterically. I had no idea why I was crying. After all, I believed I was a happy person. I was usually smiling. I had no reason to be sad, let alone crying. The night before my second appointment another strange thing happened. As I lay down to sleep, a message began to take shape in my head. It unfolded like this: Please . . . please . . . please . . . please . . . please . . . please don't . . . please don't . . . please don't . . .

"Please don't what?" I wondered to myself.

"Please don't hurt me anymore," the answer came back.

Once the message came out it wouldn't stop. For the rest of that night, like a broken record, it kept repeating itself. Please . . . please . . . please don't . . . please don't hurt me anymore. I told the psychiatrist about the message, but it wasn't explored beyond that. After my third interview, the doctor suggested, "Behavioral therapy is often successful and might prevent opening up a Pandora's box." The words "Pandora's box" stuck in my head. I wondered what he meant.

I did behavioral therapy as recommended. At the end of a year all the monitors were reading "normal" and I was pronounced "cured." I may or may not have had sub ictal phenomenon, but whatever it was, it was not the source of my problems. After some initial improvement, I was feeling much worse by the end of that year.

I WANT TO TRY THAT

One night I heard a radio special commemorating the anniversary of the German doctor Friedrich Mesmer, the father of hypnosis. It described how hypnosis was used to retrieve repressed childhood memories. I returned to the psychiatrist and with a certain resolve announced, "I want to try that." He referred me to a specialist.

I remember sitting in the chair opposite the hypnotherapist. He told me to look at a spot on my hand, and I was to get more relaxed as he counted down from ten. I think he got as far as three when I blurted out, "Why, why, why are they doing this to me? What are they doing to me?" And then in the voice of a very young child I said, "Why doesn't anybody love me?"

In the sessions that followed I found myself curled on the floor, an infant. No longer could I move or even crawl around. I was a newborn baby. I was kicking at the air; my head kept twisting and stretching back. I was screaming without words—a terrified baby crying.

Then something new happened. I didn't tell the therapist, but I was having intense sensations in my genitals. The same scenario kept repeating for the next several weeks. I didn't know what to make of it. But I did know it was important to stay on this track. And finally I braved saying to him, "I think I was being molested."

I WANT TO KNOW WHO MOLESTED ME

The next session, I said to my therapist, "I want to know who's molesting me." We did the count down, and I heard him say, "Who do you see?"

My eyes were shut tighter than ever. I even cupped my hand over them. In every way I knew how, I resisted knowing.

"Look," he repeated, emphatically.

"I see the torso of a man," I said. It was hairy. The skin was olive. I shut my eyes again.

"Look at the face," my therapist insisted.

I opened and quickly shut my eyes again. From underneath a dark chin I saw extending upward the swarthy face of Malcolm, a family friend who lived in our building when I was a child. It was Malcolm who was molesting me.

Shock and relief swept through my entire being. I felt a major weight lifting. At last the burden I'd been carrying was being shed.

I left the therapist's office with tears streaming down my face, but my body was floating through the air. It was as though I couldn't keep my feet on the ground. Keeping that knowledge repressed had taken enormous energy. And now that energy was being returned to me. It literally felt as though fifty pounds of weight had been lifted. I had an answer to my illnesses at last at the age of thirty-seven.

LOOKING FOR PROOF

Within days, however, the whole incident seemed unreal. This couldn't have really happened to me. After all, from everything I could consciously remember there was nothing extraordinary about my childhood. I needed to learn more, but I was too afraid and confused to bring it up with my parents. I needed to search for answers on my own. I tried to locate people from my past, but most of my leads led to nowhere.

Six months into searching I tracked down an old woman who had lived in the same building with us when I was a child. She was ninety-one and dying. I asked her a few casual questions, but didn't want to upset her. I decided I would just keep her company instead.

Somewhere, an hour into our conversation, she mumbled something about Malcolm and the landlord's daughter. I sat up straight and said, "Would you please repeat that?"

"That Malcolm—Oh, what a man! He had relations—you know sexual—with the landlord's fourteen-year-old daughter." Somehow I took that as a cue. I broke into tears and said, "I have been sick all these years. Please tell me, is there anything else you remember?"

She proceeded to tell me, "I don't know how it affected the children. That building was a horrible place. I got out of there as soon as I could. . . . One night three men who lived on the second floor threw a woman out onto the street naked. . . ." her voice trailed off. Then as if suddenly startled the old woman sat up, eyes wide, and a hand over her mouth. She leaned over and whispered to me—"God protect me—but I didn't say this. That young girl—the landlord's daughter—was developing a belly. I think she was pregnant. One day she left and I never saw her again. No one knew what happened to her . . . " the old woman's voice trailed off again.

Although it was not a lot to go on, it gave me great relief. At least it showed that everything about my childhood wasn't ideal. It was years before my parents could afford to move out of that building. I could feel more memories coming.

I'VE GOT IT!

My therapist said, "We need to stop memory work and integrate this material." Ordinarily, that may have been the correct thing to do, but I knew it wasn't right for me. I knew there was more. Whatever it was, I needed to know it, in order to make sense of what I had learned. I also felt that for this phase, I wanted to work with a woman. I couldn't verbalize a reason. It just felt right. I tried several leads before I found someone who seemed solid, steady, and thoroughly professional.

My new therapist did "mat work," as she called it. I lay down on a mat, relaxed, and gave myself permission to remember. Each week, a tiny piece of an incident emerged. Other times, pieces I already knew repeated themselves. One day, I suddenly sat up from the mat. Snapping my fingers, I announced, "I've got it! I know what this is! It's a ceremony!" I had fit the puzzle together at last. It had taken one year of memory work to figure it out.

Those memories included Malcolm and other robed figures humming and chanting as they manipulated me to orgasms and administered electroshock. At the end, Malcolm would pin down my arms, and with his face only inches from mine, would say, "You are to forget this. If you ever remember and try to tell, you will never again see your family." His words, like his penetrating stare, went right through me. I knew that the most important thing was to keep the secret. This ceremony took place regularly, perhaps even once or twice weekly.

After that, the memories came a little more easily and a little more frequently. However, they grew increasingly more strange and frightening.

DO YOU BELIEVE ME?

As I got through each memory, my therapist and I sat there, dumbfounded and aghast. Often I asked, "What do you make of this material? Do you believe this really happened?" And she would reply, "I'm convinced that you were severely sexually abused. But I simply don't know what to make of the other memories. Do you think it really happened as you remember it?"

I never knew what to think. However, I was sure of one thing. Either both the sexual abuse and the ceremonies happened or neither of them happened. There was no in-between. My memories all felt equally true and equally hard to believe.

I felt very alone, strange, and isolated in this work. My husband totally supported and believed me. But to me it seemed so extreme as to almost be beyond belief. It was nothing I had ever heard anybody speak of. It's as though I was the only one in the world having this bizzare experience. Yet I had no choice except to keep going to therapy. It was my only source of relief. I continued going to work and kept my therapy a secret. I was used to keeping secrets.

VALIDATION

Five years into my bewildering memories, I saw a flyer advertising a forum about sexual abuse. I still hadn't told anyone and felt shy about being seen at a public forum. I wasn't sure if it would help me. But I went.

There was a question and answer period at the end. It was getting very late. I wanted to leave, but for some reason I stayed. The last question of the evening was from a woman. In a barely audible voice she asked, "Have you ever heard of anyone being sexually abused in a ritual?"

I sat forward in my chair, my face expressionless, as usual. Every cell in my being was fixed on hearing the reply. But the answer I wanted to hear so much never came. The speaker said there was no information and then offered a few guesses at potential sources. Could it really be possible? Had it happened to someone else? I'm not the only one in the world remembering this? I approached the woman and said, "I have been sexually abused in rituals. Would you be willing to talk with me?" She seemed a little cautious and afraid, but agreed.

My meeting with that first ritual abuse survivor was a major relief. We were able to share and validate one another's experience, and I learned there was a support group for people abused in rituals. Once I learned there were other survivors, I also heard about knowledgeable therapists, familiar with ritual abuse. For the first time I realized it was possible to work with someone experienced. It took five months of looking and traveling to another city to find the right therapist, but for me it was well worth it.

I BELIEVE YOU

Although my therapy work took nine years, the majority of my healing took place in two and a half years, once I found a therapist who could move me confidently through recovery.

Every time I asked, "Do you believe me?" she

always answered, "Yes!" That "yes" was the sweetest word to me. As a child my violators told me repeatedly, "This didn't happen. You're not seeing this. You saw nothing, heard nothing. If you ever try to tell, they won't believe you. You're not worth listening to."

Once my therapist believed me unreservedly, I began to slowly test the idea of unreservedly believing myself. Denying or questioning my experience was the largest single stumbling block to my healing. My recovery zoomed forward once I learned to accept my own memories. I no longer fought for months over the truth or probability of every detail.

I learned that intuition is my friend, not an enemy. I learned I had feelings, and I learned that they matter. I learned to believe myself instead of others. I learned that what I needed in order to heal was within me. I just needed to trust that.

ACCEPTANCE

Memory after memory emerged. There seemed to be so many. With each one came horror, deep pain, and grief. At times the work was debilitating. Many times I thought to myself, "I just can't keep doing this. I don't have what it takes. I can't go on even one more day." Still the memories kept coming. And with each memory also came relief.

And ultimately, for me, there was no question. I knew I would experience any memory pain once, rather than return to spending lunch in a darkened garage recuperating under a blanket in my elegant business suit.

From time to time I felt major healing shifts from within. At those times I experienced joy, even euphoria. I remember thinking, "It's over. I'm done. I know all I need to know about my past. Now I can get on with living my life." But

more memories kept coming. And still more after that. There is no pain known to me that compares with the pain of reclaiming those early childhood experiences. Yet as more and more pieces from my past began falling into place, I began to feel as though I, too, were falling into place as a human being.

With recovery I came to understand a number of things. All my life I had tried very hard to be happy and normal. I wanted so very much to get this "life thing" right. I focused everything I had on achieving the things which I was told would "get me there." But when I did get there, I didn't feel either happy or normal.

I came to undertand that in focusing on outer things, I successfully avoided focusing on me. When I finally did turn to face myself, what I saw was pain—a lot of it. Too much, I thought, to bear. Facing myself meant facing the fact that for me, it hurt to live.

Slowly it dawned on me that the consuming focus of my life had been on escape. I could no longer spend my life escaping. If I wanted to feel alive on this earth, I had to come to terms with my own reality. I started taking it in small increments. In time I was able to stay with it more and more. In time, and it was a very, very long time, the pain grew less and less. My health took a turn for the better at last. The nightly convulsions were subsiding. The stiffness and depression were lifting. And even though this work took enormous effort, my energy was slowly returning. It continued to increase steadily. For the first time, I began to feel genuine.

THE BREAKTHROUGH

A year into working with my new therapist, I had *the* pivotal memory of my recovery. I saw Malcolm and other people, black robes, and a circle. There was an electric tension in the air. The adrenaline rush was at an all-time high and mounting. Inside the circle, I saw a killing in progress and, at the moment of death, orgasmic release. It was the most horrifying and freeing moment of my recovery.

At that moment many things became instantly clear. I had unlocked the secret. I finally understood the "why" of this insanity. These people were addicted. It was they who were enslaved, not I. The rituals and dogma simply enabled a deviant behavior. This group met to release tension through sadistic sex, torture, and death. They rationalized their atrocities using dogma and rituals.

I realized that Malcolm and my violators were enslaved. Their sadistic dependency ruled. They lived for the ritual release. In that freeing moment, though, my violators lost their hold over me. I realized it was they, not I, who was powerless. I knew it was they, not I, who were entrapped. Malcolm and his group of friends terrorized children in order to feed their addiction, and only weak people could do that. In that moment I gave them back their terror. I had broken free. That was a turning point in my recovery. My memories, once so frightening, turned to neutral information that I continued to integrate. The fears, bewilderment, and helplessness were gone. My need for therapy and support groups gradually lessened. In time I was able to continue on my own.

THE CONNECTION

Recovery had been the process of dismantling the fractured foundation of my childhood. As my foundation came apart, little by little, I was left with the bleakest realization of my recovery: I don't know who I am or if I even belong in this world. After all my recovery triumphs, I still felt utterly alone and isolated. I knew I had people who cared for me, but I couldn't connect with their loving feelings. My earliest experiences with outsiders brought pain, not love. Instead of connecting, my challenge had been to disconnect and survive. My unspoken intuition was that nothing would ever touch the wounded part that was my "self" again.

And now I was faced with doing something I had never done—to go against my very survival instinct and break the rule that sustained me in life. I never cried as hard as when I picked up the phone and asked for help. Sobbing and in tears, I asked a friend, "Do you think you could pretend I'm a newborn infant, and tell me who I am?" As her voice answered back, I cried even harder because I felt the fragile child within, the one who hurt the most. And I let the child listen to the words my friend expressed:

There are many things I love about you . . . about your little child and your infant. One of the things that I connect with the most is that your eyes dance brightly with curiosity, wit, humor, and intelligence. And I can see that in your child's eyes. You are so warm and soft inside and out. You are precious. I will hold your preciousness in my heart. I can see how vulnerable and soft you are . . . and I will protect that softness. It really is good that you came into life. I am so glad that you are here. Your life is very important to me. You know it is good that you are a girl. It's okay to trust now. You know you are safe in the world. You belong to the good people, and I see how good you are inside. I love your goodness and I love your humanness. It's good to reach out with your little hands . . . you're free now. You can touch and feel and explore with safety. You will never be alone again. I love you.

I allowed those words to enter the deepest, most sensitive part of me—the self that I felt had been mortally wounded. Those words hurt as I received them. But as the hurt passed, I felt my wounds closing up. I even felt a bit of joy and spontaneity. For the first time in my life I was feeling welcomed. I was beginning to feel that maybe I belong in this world.

A few weeks later a new feeling swept right through me. I went and cleaned my children's room. And for the very first time I cleaned it not so that things would look good, but because I loved them.

THE BEGINNING

My recovery has been a quest to reclaim all parts of myself and then connect that whole self with the good things of this world. My journey is ongoing. Today, most of my illnesses are gone. Now I know that they were symptoms of my repressed feelings—mostly rage and grief. My emotional pain is leaving more slowly, but it is leaving.

Today I am able to cry freely. And in addition to deep grief, I also feel gratitude. It is my tears, not my smiles, that are healing me. Today my tears speak *my* truth and reveal *their* secrets. It's through my tears that I am breaking free, and so today I cry triumphantly.

The main thing that helped me through my recovery was accepting my humanity, with all its wonders and shortcomings. I learned to love myself in my suffering and to honor the ways I coped. I understood that, as a child, I acted based on my perceived choices. I understood that, until I began my journey, I was not acting freely. Free choice is only exercised by a soul which is free. Recovery is allowing me the freedom to go forward with awareness and so to act consciously.

It has been a long journey, which brings me not to an end but to a beginning. There's a grin on my face from time to time as I realize that I'm free to be me. At this very moment, as I write, I am looking forward to the rest of my *own* life. Each day I know more and more that I exist, that I am good, and that I do belong in this world.

Ritual Abuse in Perspective

I am an optimist. As one of my friends recently observed, you have to be an optimist to be a survivor. And with that comes a basic belief in people. I subscribe to the idea that all people are good and, given the opportunity, will always try to do the right thing. I draw my inspiration, my observations, and my conclusions from looking at the face of a newborn child. People are born blameless and innocent. Babies are full of wonder and they are the keenest mimics in the world. Children live what they learn. They would not grow up to be adults who injure unless they themselves have been hurt. So how does a child turn from innocent to victim, and when does a victim become a victimizer in turn? How can something as aberrant as ritual abuse, which is systematic violence aimed at breaking the will of a victim, usually a child, ever come to exist?

PURSUIT OF POWER

As I began my healing journey, I made one rather surprising discovery. My issues as a survivor of ritual abuse paralleled issues faced by survivors of other types of abuse. What's more, I found that several recent, popular books seemingly unrelated to abuse (*Chalice and the Blade, Revolution from Within, Earth in the Balance, The Power of the Myth, The New Peoplemaking,* to name just a few) hit my own issues head-on. If ritual abuse is such a rare phenomenon (as most people led me to believe), why do my recovery issues coincide with issues of society at large?

In the hopes of gaining insights, I pored through books on philosophy, sociology, anthropology, psychology, and religion. I learned that despite rhetoric to the contrary, what our society values most is not the person but power. While our social principles overtly condemn abuse, it is in fact tolerated, even justified. People are routinely deceived, negated, and violated in pursuit of power. I found the single common denominator that links survivor and societal issues in Alice Miller's *Thou Shalt Not Be Aware.* She writes:

> The advice regularly given in the old pedagogical manuals was to "break" the child's will at as early an age as possible, to combat his "obstinacy," and always to impart to him the feeling that he is guilty and bad; they stressed that one should never allow the impression to arise that an adult might be wrong or make a mistake, should never give the child an opportunity to discover adult limitations, but that the adult should, on the contrary, conceal his or her weaknesses from the child and pretend to divine authority.

When a loving parent hurts a child, the child begins to associate love with pain. Significantly, in *Spare the Child,* Philip Greven describes how traditional child-rearing practices are the roots of sadomasochism. He shows that sexual violence is not an aberrant, but rather inherent part of our society.

> The breaking of the will is often a primary aim of sadomasochism. Shapiro recognizes, as few others have, the centrality of the will to many forms of sadomasochism. Absolute authority and total obedience are the usual goals played out in S&M [sadomasochistic] games and rituals, and pain and punishment are the means by which these goals are obtained. This is why the insistence on the breaking of children's will, generation after generation, century after century, has been the foundation for sadomasochistic forms of feeling, thought, and behavior—private and

public, social, religious, and political—for time out of mind.

VIOLENCE

People are often baffled at the level of violence in our society. "Where does it come from?" a confounded public asks. The answer is really quite simple. Our society is ordered by power, and allows or forgives violence in order to achieve it. The violence can be physical, mental, emotional, or spiritual. The pedagogical manuals Miller quotes would likely endorse many of these.

Violence is the by-product of our power-ordered society, which itself is rooted in violence. It starts with traditional child-rearing practices using negative conditioning (learning). Negative conditioning stresses inadequacy, condemnation, and blame and is reinforced with punishment. Deception is often justified as well.

Traditional thinking dictated that children must never express anger at their parents or authority-invested adults. Holding the power structure inviolate, societal "rules" also forbade expression of anger at those in power but allowed expression of anger at those in one's trust. Several years ago I saw a cartoon that illustrates how this rule gets played out. It goes something like this: In the first frame, the boss yells at his employee; in the second frame, the employee argues with his wife; third frame, wife punishes her son; fourth, son smacks his baby sister, and so on. The net result is that the weakest, most vulnerable members of our society feel the brunt of misdirected anger, which is expressed as violence.

Displaced rage is repeatedly acted out, often by those least privileged in our society. The media describes gang abductions and rapes, drive-by shootings, and mass killings of unsuspecting patrons at fast-food restaurants as senseless violence. It is only "senseless," however, in that it is disconnected from its source. As in the cartoon, everything is connected somehow.

EVIDENCE

Displaced violence in our society is all too common, and all too often denied. According to ChildHelp USA, a referral help organization for abused children and adult survivors, in 1990, 2.5 million cases of child abuse and neglect were reported in the U.S.; over three children in the U.S. die each day from child abuse; and 25 to 35 percent of women and 10 to 20 percent of men in the United States were victims of sexual abuse as children. They also estimate that over 40 million people (or one in six Americans) have been sexually abused, and that every fifteen seconds a woman will be abused by her husband or boyfriend. Battery is the single major cause of injury to women, and two to four thousand women are beaten to death annually.

These crimes do not exist independent of one another but on a continuum that ranges from punitive parenting to ritual abuse and includes spouse battery, violent crime, prostitution, pornography, child abuse, incest, and hate organizations. In every case the underlying principle is the assertion of power, or expressing misdirected rage by usurping the will of someone less powerful.

RITUAL ABUSE

The far end of a continuum that aims to break the will of a child and allows expression of displaced rage toward the powerless is the practice of ritual abuse. Here, abuse is systematically rather than randomly applied. Ritual abuse is not an unheard-

of perversity. Everything found in ritual abuse collectively (physical abuse, emotional abuse, sexual abuse, incest, sadistic violence, murder, drugs, deception, manipulation, conditioning based on punishment, and unbridled veneration of power) is known to occur independently in our society. We also know that it is tragically common for people in our society to organize to abuse others in pursuit of power. (Think of neo-Nazis and the Ku Klux Klan.) Ritual abuse combines all of the above. It is organized abuse carried out by a group for the purpose of achieving power. The abuse aims to break a victim's spirit and to gain the ultimate in power—absolute control over another human being.

To stop ritual abuse, we need to acknowledge it. As with incest, ritual abuse can only thrive in secrecy. Both ritual abuse and incest depend on it. Through awareness both can be stopped. Moreover, to recover, survivors must be recognized and validated. When society denies that ritual abuse exists, it literally denies survivors permission to heal.

THE QUEST FOR HEALING

The search for healing from ritual abuse is similar to a pilgrimage in many ways. Pilgrimages are journeys of self-discovery that lead to transformation. They are often long and difficult journeys, but with worthwhile results. And while it is still a struggle to gain society's acknowledgment of ritual abuse, there are positive signs of change. There is a great recovery movement under way—recovery from alcoholism, drug dependency, eating disorders, sexual and other addictions, from battery, familial abuse, emotional and sexual abuse, and incest. In this climate of acceptance and recognition, survivors of ritual abuse can, at last, find hope.

Modern-day pilgrims are recovering their past and so claiming their future. In reclaiming our truth, we claim something of value for others. Each pilgrim leaves an impact that goes beyond her or his own footprints. Our footprints make a path.

RECLAIMING OUR INHERITANCE

In walking the road to recovery there is much pain to be healed. We carry the pain not only of our generation but of preceding generations. As we each heal our own pain, it heals the world.

The issues of survivors are the issues of a recovering society. In large measure, both survivors and nonsurvivors are trying to accomplish the same thing. Although our paths may vary in their routes and challenges, our final destination is the same. Therefore this book is not about judging or blaming. There is no "us" and "them." We are all in this together. By joining hands, we join forces. Anyone who has suffered is welcome to walk with us through this book. Together we are reclaiming a world where every soul is loved and honored. Together we are reclaiming our inheritance.

Part One

Preparing for the Journey

Going Forth Empowered

A lot of us don't realize the power that we have to heal ourselves, which is kind of amazing when I think about it. It should be the most obvious thing in the world. Mentally, we are extremely powerful human beings. If we had the capability to protect ourselves and keep ourselves alive, then we've certainly got the power to heal.   Sunny

By definition, survivors are exceptionally strong people. The strengths that you used to survive the abuse will also sustain you through healing. To benefit from the chapters that follow, you need to feel supported and safe. Safety is an issue for most survivors but can become more or less significant an issue at varying stages of recovery. Some survivors have always felt unsafe, while others become concerned about safety as they start to identify their abuse. Some may feel unsafe from time to time while reading certain passages in this book. This chapter will help you get in touch with the many resources already available to you, both internal and external. Identifying these strengths and resources will help remind you that you are strong; you are safe, and you made it. By making your strengths and resources conscious, you can draw on them as you read this book and work through your recovery.

There is a lot of information in this chapter. Give yourself permission to skip sections that seem irrelevant for you. If you decide to follow all the suggestions, remember to take lots of breaks so that you don't feel overwhelmed.

INNER WISDOM

The ability to establish safety comes from within. It comes from our internal resource system. I call it "inner wisdom." You may prefer to call it by a different name. Feel free to replace "inner wisdom" with your own term throughout this book. Every person is born with inner wisdom—it is what guides us through life. It got us through our abusive childhood, and it contains the answers that will help us heal. Inner wisdom is our greatest resource in recovery. When you are in touch with your inner wisdom, you experience wholeness and knowing. There is a sense that things are unfolding as they should. You feel at one with yourself. Life flows from the center of your being. Every person's inner wisdom looks and feels different—it may be a feeling, a knowing, a color, gut instinct, a sense, a presence, a dream, or a voice. It may be a combination of things. It can change over time. For many survivors, it feels like the original self, before the abuse. For some people it may not have any name at all. Whatever it is for you, it is the right thing. Trust that. Trusting it is what matters most in healing. When you're in touch with your inner wisdom, you will know what to call it.

It is something intangible and yet it permeates everything and your every interaction with every human being. I think of it as being at home on earth.   CeeCee

For others it feels more concrete:

I think of it as kind of a globe. It is made up of millions of tiny droplets, each droplet mirroring a rainbow. It contains life and beauty and truth and permanence. Although it moves and changes, it is always whole. It has integrity. I can tap into it whenever I want. It contains everything I need. I feel it is me.   Roxana

For some it is harmony:

I think there is a certain harmony in the way I was meant to be. We all know our natural harmony. We just have to uncover it. I feel it's like the bass line of a song. It's there—always. You can add instruments, and chords, and whatever melody you want on top of it. But if you lose the bass line, your song is messed up. A lot of times it's easy to lose that bass line. I can get caught up following people—going in directions that don't feel right. A big part of recovery is not losing touch with that bass line. And if I can just wait things out, things will clear away to where I can hear it—the natural order of things. And then I'm all right.   em

For some, it's the "I" of their being:

If there is a "me" that's completely in touch with God and the world, and I walked up to this person and asked, "What do I do?" she would tell me. And she does. It's like someone handing me an answer, and all I have to do is go inside and get it. It's not something I had to manufacture or get out of a book. I just have to let her talk. And I know it's right. I can bank on it. It's me.   Sunny

For some it's a color:

I've never had that inner sense of knowledge. But I have a feeling within me that is absolutely good. The cult didn't get it—my yellow part connected to my Heavenly Father.   A survivor

Inner wisdom is always with us. It cannot be destroyed. It is our life-affirming, positive guide. Inner wisdom comes from the core of our being. To protect it, many survivors had to separate from it or hide it. Others felt its presence but were forced to ignore it. Reconnecting with inner wisdom is the first and most important step in taking back our power.

RECONNECTING WITH INNER WISDOM

Inner wisdom can be accessed in many different ways. Most people begin by focusing inside. However, if "going inside" feels frightening to you, perhaps you can think of "checking with yourself" instead. If you feel you do not have an inner guide or wisdom, it is perfectly all right to imagine it. You can ask your imagined wisdom for help when you need it. Then you can imagine its answer. Sometimes survivors are concerned about whether they can trust the answer that comes from within. Here's a suggestion: When you hear the answer, ask yourself, "Does that feel right? Is it in tune with my well-being?" If it is, go with it. Trust it. In all things, trust yourself.

Following are some suggested exercises that may help you connect with your inner wisdom. If you have other ideas on ways to connect, try them. Some survivors may prefer to do these exercises with a therapist present, or with the help of a supportive friend.

1. Think of a time when you felt good. Stay in touch with that experience. Do you feel a presence? A color? A sensation? See a being? Whatever it is you experience, trust it. You can have access to that goodness whenever you need to call on it.

2. Have a little dialogue with yourself. Ask to get in touch with your inner wisdom (or whatever you prefer to call it). Feel your own stillness as you wait for an answer. How does it feel? A voice? A knowing? A texture? Sound waves? An expansiveness? Trust your response. Now describe it. Can you draw it? You will be able to reach it whenever you need it for support or strength.

3. Imagine a marble staircase. It has several flights. As you walk toward the top, you will breathe fresh mountain air. At the top of the staircase is a door. Behind the door is your inner wisdom. Prepare to open the door and meet the guiding part of yourself. Does it have a sense? A sound? A feeling? An attitude? A connection? A shape? Whatever it is for you, trust it. Call it up when you want it. It is there to offer help.

4. If a good and kind person were to give you a gift, what would it be? A locket? A ball of different colors? A pet? An exquisite vase? A gem? Hold the gift in your mind. It can be your source of strength. It is yours whenever you want it.

5. Imagine that you are a tree. Your legs are the trunk. Your toes are the roots. Sink the roots far into the ground. Send up nourishment from the roots into your body. How does the nourishment feel? Can you describe it to yourself? Call on it whenever you need it. It can help you feel strong and secure.

6. Think of a spiritual being, such as God, Jesus, an angel, a good spirit, Mohammed, Buddha, or a sacred being. You can also think of nature, the universe, the ocean, or a tree Connect with that presence. Bring that presence (or feeling, knowledge, etc.) into the center of your being. If you do not feel the center of your being, then bring it into each part of yourself. Feel its goodness, wisdom, and strength. This is an eternal source of guidance.

Develop a friendship with your inner wisdom. Call it up often. Hold it in your mind. Touch it, feel it, explore it. Greet it. Talk to it. Enjoy it. Become one with it. Have fun with it. The closer your relationship to your inner wisdom, the more you will benefit.

It's like religion. It takes a leap of faith. It doesn't always make sense. Often I can't know if it will work out. But every time I've followed my inner wisdom, it was always the right thing to do. I just had to have faith, and it has never let me down. It's been one hundred percent right. Sunny

Some people's inner wisdom is very shy. It takes a little coaxing to come out of hiding. In some cases it has been hidden so well that it will take longer to find it. But in time you will feel it. Connecting with inner wisdom is connecting with yourself. Your inner wisdom is always at work, even if you don't know it:

I read Journey to Ixtlan, *and in it the Indian said to Carlos, "You have to follow the path of your heart." And I remember thinking, "My whole world is just a big mish-mash, but I want to remember that. I want to keep saying that to myself over and over again. I don't know what it means. I don't know how you would do that, but it sounds like that's what I want to do." That really changed my life. CeeCee*

For many people inner wisdom isn't static. It changes over time. At times you may feel in touch with it; other times you may feel you have lost it. That's okay. It hasn't really gone anywhere. Inner wisdom comes to the rescue without your even knowing it. The key is to ask for its help.

When things feel nuts, I yell "help" silently to the universe. I always get help. My help comes from what some people call God. But it feels more personal than that. It feels like helpers, angels, spirits . . . I believe in all of them. Jane Linn

In all things be guided by your inner wisdom. It got you through impossible odds. As you read, some things will feel right to you, and others won't. They may be wrong for you, or the timing may not be right. Listen to that inner knowing. Now, more than ever, trust it to help you through

healing. Trusting your inner wisdom means simply trusting yourself. No matter what is said in this book, the final authority is you. If it doesn't feel right, don't do it. Make positive decisions on your own behalf.

RECOGNIZING YOUR STRENGTHS

Our childhood revolved around messages of how inadequate and helpless we are. Nothing could be further from the truth. After all, it is we who made it out. We're the ones who beat the odds. Every survivor found her or his own way to do it. Now is the time to find out how. By taking an inventory of your special strengths you will be giving them their long overdue acknowledgment.

You may have survived through your intelligence, ability to handle crisis well, or just an uncanny ability to stay alive.

There were those parts of me that I saved, and I didn't let anybody touch. They were the protectors. Sunny

It may have been your imagination, creativity, great instincts, reliable intuitive sense, or spirituality.

I think it's my soul. My soul just won't give up. Sophia

You may have drawn on your idealism, integrity, persistent optimism, or special connection with God.

I do still have faith in God, amazingly. I think faith in God keeps me going. Jacques

It may be through your sense of justice, dedication to the truth, unshakable desire to right a wrong, or faith in your own goodness.

We're still innocent, you know. There is still a part of us that's innocent that they could never touch. Mike

The possibilities go on. Many survivors have found that identifying their strengths has been an important resource during the toughest parts of recovery. If you would like to develop your own list, here are a few suggestions.

Take an inventory of your own strengths. What are they? Everybody will have at least one. Write down anything positive that comes to mind. (Disregard any shyness, modesty, or humility which may come up while doing this exercise.)

As a child, you may have been told that you have no strengths or good qualities. But the very fact that you are reading this book and undertaking recovery is a testament to your strength, optimism, and resilience. If you cannot think of any wonderful qualities you have, then write down qualities you would like to have. Now in front of each quality write "I am" or "I have" wherever it is appropriate.

You do not have to believe any of it for now. The important part of this exercise is to state these things as if they were true. Gradually, you will accept more and more positive things about yourself. You should add to this list every time you recognize or want to develop a new strength.

AFFIRMING AND USING YOUR STRENGTHS

Acknowledge and affirm your sources of strength regularly. Ask your friends to remind you of them often. If that feels too scary or presumptuous, then ask if they would remind you of them

from time to time. Your special strengths and qualities provide the building blocks of recovery. In time, they will become the foundation of your recovery.

Here's how one survivor does it:

It's really easy for me to get into a spiral of hopelessness and shame, and so I made myself a hope jar. I got a jar we used to use for canning and pasted gold stars on it. Then every time something good happens or I get a new breakthrough in recovery, I write it on a piece of paper and throw it into the jar. It's amazing how quickly it can start to fill up. Then every time I'm feeling particularly depressed, I dump out the contents of my hope jar, and read some of the papers. It's kind of fun— almost like reading fortune cookies. Sophia

As you connect with your inner wisdom and inner strengths, you can begin to exercise them by taking positive steps in you own behalf. The rest of this chapter will give you the opportunity to exercise these internal resources in privacy and safety. As you continue to read, stay in touch with your own intuition. As different suggestions are proposed, check in with yourself and ask, "Does this feel right for me?" Every survivor is unique and each person will have different needs.

EXTERNAL SUPPORT—SAFE FRIENDS

As you read through this book or try to heal through recovery, you can expect difficult material or strong feelings to come up from time to time. It is important to share your discoveries or feelings with safe, supportive friends. You had to bear the pain and grief of your childhood alone. You do not have to go alone through recovery. Being heard and comforted by caring people can be a deeply healing experience.

As hard as it is for survivors to rely on their own strengths, it is even harder for most survivors to rely on others. As a child you may have been told that no one could ever love or care about you, that no one is to be trusted, and that you should never count on others for help. As result, you may believe that people find you a burden, that you're not worth helping, and find it hard to ask for and accept emotional support. But violators tell children many lies in order to control them. The truth is that people like to help people.

It's been so important to have a few other people I could call when I'm down and out—people who have loved me for who I am, and told me that I'm wonderful, and told me that I'm okay—and being able to take in that love and acceptance has been crucial. Bea

Support friends can help you in many ways. By reaching out to safe others, you no longer bear the secret burden alone. You break the isolation. A friend becomes a witness to your pain and, in doing so, helps it to heal.

What works for me has actually been pretty straightforward and simple. The worst times have been utter and complete despair, a feeling like there's no hope for me . . . there's no place for me . . . I'm nothing . . . I'm worthless. And those are the times when I needed to call somebody. I don't try to get through that alone. They don't even have to say anything; they don't have to try to fix it, or have any great analysis. Just to have someone on the other line who cares about me and can hear me breaks the cycle. It has done it every time. Sometimes it takes longer than others, but it works every time. Lynn

FINDING SAFE AND SUPPORTIVE FRIENDS

An ideal source of supportive friends may already be available to you. You can connect with other survivors through workshops, exhibits, newsletters, or conferences on incest or ritual abuse. Another excellent source is through various support groups. These are discussed in detail in Chapter 24.

I call people that I know will believe me and also people who know what I'm dealing with. Not just someone who'll say, "Well, did you take your vitamins this morning? Maybe it's PMS." Lynn

Some support organizations offer opportunities to pen-pal with another survivor. This may be a good way for you to begin building outside relationships in a safe way. (See the Resource Guide for a list of potential resource organizations.) Many survivors find healing and meaning by getting directly involved with some of these organizations.

ASKING NONSURVIVORS FOR SUPPORT

Another source of support is your existing nonsurvivor friends. Telling them about your abuse background may initially feel strange or awkward.

When I did start to tell, I expected nothing but rejection. But people weren't rejecting me—just the opposite. They supported me. Then it slowly dawned on me that it was my parents who rejected me, and made me believe that the rest of the world would reject me too. But the rest of the world isn't doing that. It doesn't mean that every time we tell the truth or take a risk, we won't get rejected. But if we can just take that leap of faith and test the waters, we can start to change a whole lot of things. Erik

It's wonderful to get support and validation from nonsurvivor friends. However, some people feel uncomfortable hearing about abuse. It's a good idea to ease them in slowly. Share your past with them in stages. Perhaps start by telling them that you were physically or emotionally abused. Make a note of their reaction. If they don't ask questions, give supportive feedback, or show any interest, chances are they may not make a suitable support friend. If they do respond with concern, interest, and caring, in time you can tell them about sexual abuse or incest, and eventually about the ritual abuse as well.

If you live in an area without established support networks, it may be a little more difficult to find support friends. That was the case with me. I had kept my abuse secret for so long, even from myself, that even when I admitted it to myself, I still couldn't admit it to my nonsurvivor friends. Today I know that as long as I was keeping the secret, I was also taking the blame and responsibility for it. Once I broke the secret with my closest friend, she helped me put the responsibility squarely where it belonged—on my violators. Telling my friend didn't come easily, but over time, the more I was able to risk sharing, the stronger and closer our friendship grew.

ASKING FOR HELP

Some sections of this book may be painful, or bring up frightening memories. For some people it is important to read with a support friend present or readily available by phone. You might want to call your support friend before you begin, and when you've finished particularly intense sections of this book. Give them an idea when to expect your return call. That way they can be assured that you are okay.

Getting to the point of being able to pick up a phone and ask for help is an important step for many survivors. Sooner or later, recovery means being able to reach out, unashamed, and ask for help.

Thanks to AA, I've developed a new skill. Now I reach for the phone instead of reaching for the bottle.   A survivor

OTHER SOURCES OF SUPPORT

Until you are able to reach out to supportive friends, you can accept nurturing and support in other forms—through books, newspaper articles, and documentaries offering hope and help for survivors. The written word can be a powerful source of healing.

I can't think of anything much more powerful for me as a survivor than picking up a book and going, number one, I'm not alone; number two, I'm telling the truth; number three, there's something that can be done about it; and number four, I can have a rich and full life, no matter what they said or what they did. There's nothing more powerful.   Lynn

A lot of cult messages worked to undermine survivors' ability to reach out. Survivors often feel that it's unsafe to ask for help. But as survivors begin to risk reaching out to safe friends they find the opposite is true.

IF YOU NEED A SUPPORT NETWORK

For many survivors, safety is a central issue in recovery. If personal safety is an issue for you, it makes sense to have a more organized and reliable safety support system in place. This section gives detailed suggestions for establishing a formalized support system for yourself.

BUILDING A SAFETY SUPPORT SYSTEM

One of the most powerful messages of the cult is, "No one can ever love you like we do. No one will ever take care of you like we do. You can never be a part of anybody like you are a part of us." Bullshit! I have a support system that loves me tremendously, that takes care of me. So it breaks that essential message of the cult. I know I'm not alone in any sense of the word.   Alicia

Make a list of people you could approach as part of a support network: a friend? your partner? a safe family member? (See Chapters 13 and 20 for a discussion of safe family members.) A clergy person? Another survivor? Friends from one of your support groups? Write down as many possibilities as you can think of. The broader the network of safe support people, the better the chances of success. There may be times when your support needs will be too great for one person to handle. Some people you approach may not feel up to the task. Some may be willing to help but may not always be available. Having a number of people to choose from gives your safety system flexibility.

If you cannot think of anyone, you may want to contact helping organizations such as a local rape crisis center or the American Association of Pastoral Counselors. These organizations may have volunteers who would be willing to be a part of your support system. Remember to check inside to make sure that you feel comfortable with any individual who offers to help you. You are not obliged to accept help if the person doesn't feel totally supportive and safe to you.

Ask each potential candidate if she or he is willing to help. If someone is unable to assist you at this time, respect that. Do not take "no" as a reason to feel unworthy or hurt or to get down on yourself. Don't give up.

IF IT'S HARD TO ASK FOR HELP

Asking for help is difficult for many survivors. Maybe you haven't told anyone of your abuse. Some survivors have unresolved issues with trust or fear (see Chapters 17 and 19), so it may take a little while before you are ready to ask for safety support. If you're really shy, maybe you could ask a support friend to help you make some calls. Once you are ready, it may take a little trial and error.

As a start, try asking a close friend for one small favor. Do not prejudge the outcome. Watch how the request is met. Did your friend object? Make excuses? Was she or he eager to help? Did you feel good at the outcome?

If it didn't turn out well, maybe you need to try a different friend. If it turned out well, acknowledge the success. Make a point of affirming for yourself, "The friend was glad to help. My request was honored. Everything turned out well. I feel I can count on my needs being met again." It is important to give yourself many affirming messages after each success. This is an effective way of counteracting the negative messages that may be running through your head.

Once you have some willing friends, it is important to discuss several things. Be clear on what your needs are. Encourage your support person or people to express their needs as well. Give them permission to refuse any request. Thank them for being open and honest about their own needs and abilities. This will prevent burnout, unconscious build-up of resentment, and feelings of being overwhelmed. Here are some suggestions for your discussion. Add to the list or modify it to suit your own needs.

Your Needs, and What Is Helpful to You Do you need someone to drive you to and from therapy? Someone to babysit while you take time out for working through your feelings? Someone to hear your retrieved experiences? Someone who can give you unqualified emotional support? Someone to assure you that you are loved, and okay? Someone to listen and not offer any feedback? Someone who can help you to feel safe? Someone to be a regular "time-out/fun-time" friend? These are just some ways in which support friends can help. Make your own list of needs and review them.

Type of Support the Person Is Willing to Provide Telephone support? In-person support? Direct assistance with locating a therapist? etc.

Times When Your Support Person May or May Not Be Available Be specific. If your support person says, "Call me any time," see if that includes 4:00 A.M.

Amount of Time Your Support Person May Be Willing to Spend Specify hours per week, days per month, etc.

Their Needs They may need notice if your therapy sessions are canceled or rescheduled so that they can adjust their plans to be available for you. They may have certain days off and may or may not want to be available on those days, even for emergencies. They may wish to know about your progress. (If they do, share what feels comfortable for you to tell. You are not obliged to share everything or anything.) There may be times when they feel inadequate. How can you help them feel competent in helping you? Can you suggest things they may notice as signs of a potential problem with you (e.g., isolating, being noncommunicative, being overly reassuring that everything is okay)? If they notice these problem, can you suggest how you would like them to respond?

POINTS TO KEEP IN MIND

1. Common courtesy and common sense are a good guide. For example, when you call your friend for support, it's a good idea to ask, "Is this a good time to talk?" However, when you're calling for help in an emergency, be direct. State simply, "I'm in a crisis. Can you help?"
2. The more informed your support friends are about dissociation, ritual abuse, healing, and building support, the more helpful they may be. Ask if they would be interested in reading sections of this book or other related literature.
3. Schedule regular reviews with your friends. Recovery is a dynamic process. Your needs may change. Your support friends' circumstances may change as well. It is important to keep the lines of communication open. Modify your agreements as necessary. Be sure to review them at least once a month. Review them more often in times of crisis. Reviewing your support system will help keep it working for both of you.
4. Each person has to take responsibility for understanding, communicating, and meeting their own needs.

Remember that your support friend is not a therapist. In an emergency they can help you seek professional help, but the responsibility to ask for help and stay safe ultimately rests with each survivor. You should ask how your support friend feels about helping you through an emergency. Some people do not feel comfortable handling emergencies. Do not take a "no" as a personal rejection. Respect the ways in which your friend *is* willing to help:

1. Consider asking several people to share emergency support. It may take a little more effort to put a workable system in place, but it is important to establish one.
2. Complete and review all emergency-related sections of this book with this person(s). This

includes the emergency section on the back pages and Chapter 16, on getting through difficult situations. The more understanding your friends have, the more confident they will feel.

3. Review how your support friend(s) can help you reach professional help. Ask your therapist to assist in putting together a "stay safe" plan.

4. Have a practice emergency drill with your support friend(s). Make sure that your plan works. For example, I called the rape crisis line listed in my phone book. I got a recording saying that the number was no longer in service. I finally got the right number by calling Information. This scenario is not uncommon. You don't want to learn midcrisis that your system doesn't work. Check out every number and procedure in advance. Know what kind of assistance you can expect from the different services in your area. You can also learn which ones offer the best help. This will help both you and your support friend(s) feel more competent in a crisis.

5. Emergencies are a frequent cause of burnout. If you are experiencing a steady series of crises, check with your friend(s) about their continuing ability to provide support.

6. Your support person(s) may also consider getting support, much as therapists have their own support systems to prevent feeling overwhelmed.

IF YOU'RE HAVING PROBLEMS WITH SUPPORT

If you have followed the above suggestions and your support system isn't working, ask yourself some of the following questions:

- *Did I communicate what I needed clearly?*

- Does this person always feel safe?
- Does this person always feel willing?
- Is this person respecting my needs?
- Am I respecting her or his needs?
- When offered help, was I able to receive it?
- Are there healthy limits in our mutual give and take? How are we each following them?

Balancing the give and take may be especially difficult for survivors. Some survivors have difficulty asking for and receiving support; others need to develop the part of them that is able to give. When there is an imbalance in the give and take, you can expect that sooner or later the relationship will break down.

One problem I had at first was with a couple of survivor acquaintances who called me whenever they were in crises, but I never felt like they were there for me. One of the hardest things I've done in recovery was to tell them that I just wasn't comfortable being used like that. I don't want to be the therapist. I want to be a friend and get support in return. Bea

Recognizing and addressing problems is a skill that develops through recovery. Accept that both you and your support friends may experience problems—even severe problems, from time to time. If you run into problems, do not be discouraged. Discuss any relationship difficulties with a therapist, if you have one. It may be a problem with communication. It may be changing circumstances that haven't been recognized or addressed. It may be that you or your support people are not yet adept at maintaining well-functioning relationships. That's okay. It takes time and patience. Check out Chapter 20 on working through relationships and maximizing healthy behaviors for additional clues to the possible source and resolution of a problem.

Problems can be solved and relationships can be saved. The key is to recognize when things aren't working and address them. The earlier, the better. Don't wait and hope the problems will go away; most often they only get worse. The main thing is to accept that even the best of relationships needs help from time to time.

A MESSAGE FOR SUPPORT FRIENDS

If your friend or partner tells you that she or he is a survivor of ritual abuse, it may bring up many feelings. You may feel honored that your friend risked sharing this very sensitive information with you. You may feel grief, sorrow, and pain. At the same time you may be feeling frightened, helpless, overwhelmed, resentful, or panicked. All of these feelings are normal. The following messages from survivors may help:

— Do not be afraid of us or for us. We are strong and we have survived. Mostly what we need is simply for someone to listen.

— Do not take on our pain. It will not help us get better faster.

— If you are feeling overwhelmed with feelings, seek outside support for yourself, or counseling.

— It's okay to express your pain without blaming anyone.

— Remember that you are important and you matter. You cannot be there for us unless you are also there for yourself.

— Healing from ritual abuse takes a very long time. It's important to try to live life in the meantime.

— It's okay to say "no" to any request that does not feel comfortable to you.

SUMMARY

Now that you are in touch with your internal resources and are aware of possible external resources, call on them often. Remember to read this chapter when you need encouragement or moral support. You may want to refer to this chapter before and after other readings in this book to help remind you of your resources and strengths.

2

A Course in Safe Passage

*It seems that there are two main ways to per-
ceive things in this world—through the eyes of love
or through the eyes of fear. Although fear often
seems to have the upper hand, it is always love
which triumphs in the end.* Roxana

If you have been abused as a child, you grew up
in fear. Often, the fear was intentionally reinforced with pain. Most survivors have split off
some of their pain and fear and surrounded it
with a barrier of amnesia. This process is called
dissociation and is described in Chapters 5 and 8.
As healing begins, the amnestic barriers may
begin to dissolve, and so the repressed fear and
pain may resurface or intensify. Sometimes it
makes survivors feel unsafe.

Survivor reactions vary widely. You may have
few, if any, safety concerns while reading this
book or working through recovery. On the other
hand, you may feel tense and agitated. Many sur-

vivors go through periods of constant vigilance;
some may feel panicky. All of these reactions are
quite common and normal in survivors of childhood abuse and are discussed throughout the
course of this book. However, to benefit from the
healing information, each survivor needs to learn
how to feel safe.

Whether or not you are currently experiencing anxiety, it's a good idea to know how to manage it. The tools you will learn address a range of
reactions experienced by survivors. Once you
learn how to handle any possibility, you can
move through recovery more confidently.
Although a fear may feel real and present, it most
often stems from the unresolved pain of childhood. Unresolved pain is often held by split-off
parts or inner children (see Chapter 8). These
inner children can become frightened. In order
to overcome the fear, it first must be calmed. The
first part of this chapter will help inner children

learn ways to stay safe. The rest will address other safety issues for survivors and ways to manage them.

This chapter will help you begin to appreciate the wealth of internal resources you have to keep yourself safe. In addition, you'll learn how to handle emergencies. By becoming skilled with these techniques, you can go forth in charge of your own recovery rather than being overwhelmed by it. As you read, stay in touch with your inner wisdom. As different suggestions are proposed, check in with yourself and ask, "Does this feel right for me?" Every survivor is unique and each reader will have different needs. Learn to exercise your power by deciding what feels right and what doesn't, and respond accordingly.

ESTABLISHING SAFETY

What is safety? How do we know what is safe? Some survivors live in constant fear; others are so out of touch with their feelings that they never feel afraid. It is helpful to establish not so much what is safe but what is safe enough. Your reactions may change over time. It's important to regularly check your own responses. You should ask yourself the following questions: Am I able to read this book or work on recovery without being in danger of hurting myself or anyone else? If not, what do I need to be safe enough?

— should I only read in the presence of a therapist?

— should I work out a "stay-safe" plan with my therapist?

— should I only read in the presence of another supportive adult?

The following pages offer suggestions to help each survivor feel safe enough. A solid founda-tion of support may include safe places, safe things, safe thoughts, and safe people, as well as know-how in an emergency. The importance of establishing safety was initially developed in the *Courage to Heal Workbook*, by Laura Davis (see Bibliography). In addition to the ideas mentioned below, you may want to refer to it for other helpful suggestions. Not every option works for all survivors. Choose the ones that work best for you, or combine them with ideas of your own.

CREATING A SAFE PLACE IN YOUR HOME*

Many survivors like to have a Safe Place in their home. Perhaps you can choose a special corner that has cuddly toys, pillows, and soft blankets. Maybe it has your favorite books. Put things that feel healing in this corner. For example, one survivor put a rug in the corner of her bedroom. The rug outlines her special space, and no one else in the house can go there without permission. On the rug she has placed gifts she has received from her friends while working through recovery. It has a turtle named Sarah, a seashell from a survivor friend, a clown with funny red hair from a support friend, and a magic wand she bought for one of her inner children, among other things. Whenever she's feeling particularly sad and abandoned, she goes to her special corner. It helps to remind her that there are many people who care for her and want to help her get better. It also helps her remember that today she has a place that is totally her own—where no one unwelcome can ever come in. It helps her remember that today she has control.

Some directions regarding safety in this chapter are in child-like language. Survivors usually have "inner children" or "a child within." Often it is not the adult, but the child within that becomes unsettled. These child-like comments are directed to the inner child.

Sometimes making space for yourself isn't easy.

I've been best at being superwoman all my life. I could run six acts at once. I have a large family, and I was constantly putting out for them. My challenge has been to learn to slow down, learn to let stuff go, learn that I don't have to be perfect. I've found that I can have a busy life, have a business and a big family, and still create space for myself. I've set up this little space—it has special things, like crystals and empowering things for me, and my desk, and my dresser. And I know it sounds kind of funny that I should say that—but I never had clothing, I never had jewelry, I didn't have my own dresser. I used my bedroom to store things that didn't fit in the rest of the house. So there was always this closing in on me—there was no space for me. Now part of my recovery is that I have my music, I have my dresser and my own place for my clothes. And the other day I cleaned the closet and I put my clothes on one side of the closet and my husband's on another side, and it really felt good to have that. And one of my kids actually yelled at me and said, "Mothers are supposed to be for their kids." And I told her, "That one's going to change. I'm forty-three years old, and there's a space in this world for me now." I'm still there for my kids more than ever really, but I'm there for myself too. Suzzane

If you have a special place, you may want to use it while reading this book. Visit this place often. Affirm that it is safe, and that it is yours.

ESTABLISHING INNER SAFETY

Visualization can be very powerful and healing. Think of a Safe Place. It can be real or imagined. In this place you are loved and protected. Here there is no abuse.

Your imaginary place is filled with healing things. What things give you joy? What things help you feel safe? A magic pony? Cuddly lion friends? Running water? A rock? Your place is filled with these real or imagined things. These things are yours and will help you heal. This place is always waiting for you. No one has the power to remove you from it. No one can enter without your permission. You can come and go as you please—when you need to feel safe, or when you just want to play and feel good.

I think visualization really works for me. I used to get these massive migraine headaches. My friend used to have me come to her apartment, and lay me down on the couch. Then she would talk about running water and forests. I used to visualize all these beautiful butterflies and unicorns, and it would really help. Annie

SAFE THOUGHTS

When inner children become frightened it is helpful to remind them that they are safe. Safe thoughts could include:

No one is hurting me now.

The bad people are gone.

This is just a memory.

I am a big person now.

Today I can protect myself.

I love and I am loved. (Sometimes it helps to write down names of people or pets that are loving and loved.)

Think of things or affirmations that feel comforting or safe and write or draw them on your Safe Page.

YOUR SAFE PAGE(S)

You can create a special page called "My Safe Page." It can be used to remind you of your safe places, safe affirmations, safe pets and people, and safe things. It might be fun to color this page with pens or crayons. You can add more pages if there isn't enough room and store them inside the back cover of this book or make your own notebook.

Turn to your Safe Page(s) whenever you're feeling frightened or just want to feel good. Some people may want to begin and finish each reading in the book with their Safe Page. That way they can start and end by feeling good. Now is a good time to take a break from reading, and begin creating your Safe Page or Pages.

RAINBOW PLACE

Maybe you're having a hard time thinking of a Safe Place, safe thoughts, or safe things. That's okay. Until you decide on safe things of your own, you're welcome to go to an imaginary Safe Place. Imagine that it belongs to a very kind and gentle lady, the best mother a kid could ever have. I've named her Sarah.

Sarah cares for any children who are hurting. Some children feel they don't belong anywhere. These children belong and are always welcome at Sarah's place. Some children feel they are so bad that no one could love them. Sarah knows that no child is bad. In time Sarah helps every child learn that they are good. Her Safe Place is called Rainbow Place.

On rolling green grounds stands Rainbow Place. It is clear as glass, but strong as granite. Inside the glass palace is a rainbow. When people who want to hurt you look at Rainbow Place, they have to turn away. When you are hurting or scared, you can go into Rainbow Place. There is

one Rainbow Place for each hurting child. Walk into the rainbow. Feel its softness. Notice how your pain is absorbed by its colors. Cool colors will soothe your pain. Warm colors will bring comfort and nurturing.

You can stay inside Rainbow Place as long as you want. No one can see you, but you can see out. When people look in, they see only rainbow colors. When you look out, you will see other children at play. These children will always be there. When you're feeling better you can come out and play too. They will play safe and happy games with you.

Rainbow Place is on page 385, next to other information on safety at the back of the book. You can color it or add to it in any way you want.

If ever you or your inner children feel sad, lonely, or frightened, there are many places you can go to feel better. You can go to your Safe Place, your Safe Page, or Rainbow Place. There are also many things you can do. You can imagine a fun and Safe Place in your mind, you can remind yourself that you are safe by reading the statements on page 16, you can hold your pet if you have one, or you can call a friend and reach out for comfort from her or him.

The next section will talk about other things that will help to keep you safe during recovery.

BASICS OF SAFE PASSAGE

If a healing journey is similar to a pilgrimage, then every pilgrim needs to learn the basics of safe passage. Whether you're taking an internal or external journey, it's important to know your environment. Once you gain familiarity with it, you will know how to read its signals and make the right choices. In an internal journey, the environment is our body and mind. With attention and practice, you'll learn how to recognize and benefit from the wealth of information they offer. The skills you will learn in this chapter are important in two ways. They will help to keep you safe and significantly advance your own progress in recovery. Once you gain these basic skills, you become a navigator in charge of your own healing.

The first step is to recognize your own early detection "radar" systems. Whether you know it or not, you do have them. Everybody does. With their help, you'll be able to avoid danger. And even if you miss the early signs, you'll learn how to exit quickly to safety.

YOUR EARLY DETECTION RADAR SYSTEMS

In order to gain control over children, cult violators teach them to suppress and ignore their own protective warning systems. These include feelings, emotions, thoughts, and behaviors. As a child you may have been punished for responding to them. You may have coped by learning to suppress your instinctive responses. In time this may have become an automatic reaction to stress. You may have found safety in ignoring or denying your own needs.

The first step, therefore, is to unlearn the old learning. For some it means reversing their concept of what is safe. It's very important to understand that your feelings, emotions, instincts, and intuitions are the guardians of your well-being. These are our natural protectors that direct us to respond in our own best interest. The most important safety precaution you can take is to recognize and use your own early detection radar system. You can no longer afford to ignore it, or act in opposition to it.

It may be a while before you learn your body/mind signals, but don't be discouraged. You will learn to recognize them over time.

Maximizing safety involves three things: learn-

ing to recognize a feeling or body signal when you are having one; understanding how to interpret it; finding what works best in attending to it.

Once I started paying attention, I noticed this faint sort of vibrating feeling in my body. It felt kind of like crawling ants. Then one day I was able to connect the vibrations with my feelings. I realized that it was anger, and that my body was seething with rage. Once I realized what it was, I took out my art pad and began to draw furiously until my rage dissipated, and the vibrations stopped. Janes

Learning to allow and identify feelings may not come automatically. It may take time, patience, and some trial and error, but it's well worth the effort. In fact, it can be a rewarding experience. It's being in touch with yourself. I remember how awed I felt the first time I allowed myself to have a feeling. It was like discovering a lost treasure. For the first time in my life, I felt wealthy from within. (For more information on recognizing and connecting with feelings, see Chapters 18 and 19.)

UNDERSTANDING HOW YOUR BODY/MIND COMMUNICATE

The first step in staying safe is learning when you are being signaled by your radar system. No matter how faint or insignificant the signal may seem, it is important to pay attention to it. Each person's system of communication is unique. However, there are patterns of response that can offer you some indication of what to monitor.

As you go through this book, try to be aware of your feelings and sensations, both physical and emotional. This will help you get more in touch with yourself and allow you to understand how you are being affected by the information you are reading. You may immediately recognize a reaction. That's an important stepping stone to healing. On the other hand, you may not be aware of any reactions. The challenge here is to give yourself permission to feel.

When was the last time you were hungry, tired, scared, happy, angry, sad, or lonely? If you cannot remember, or it's been a few days ago, then you're probably not in touch with your feelings. Keep checking inside. It may take a while before any feelings come. (Charts of typical survivor reactions and their possible indications are given in Chapters 15 and 18.)

A good way to begin getting acquainted with yourself is to make a list of feelings. Make them simple: mad, sad, glad, bad, hurt, scared, lonely. Check the list every day to see if you are feeling any of those things. Make a note of the bodily reactions you associate with them. For example, if you think you're feeling sad, you may notice that your body feels cold; if you think you're feeling fear, you may notice that some parts of your body feel paralyzed and others parts are trembling. After a while, you will begin to notice a pattern that will help you recognize that you are having feelings and know what they are.

If you notice dizziness, drowsiness, changes in body temperature, emotional reactions, any pains, discomforts, skin reactions, need to urinate, or any other reactions, stop reading and ask yourself, "What do I need to do to take care of myself?" You may know instinctively what it takes, or you may get some ideas from suggestions mentioned throughout this book. You may want to reinforce some positive strengths by re-reading Chapter 1. Practice recognizing, interpreting, and responding to your body/mind signals until the process comes more naturally.

Once this idea becomes instinctive (as it was meant to be), you will have aquired the basic skill of safe passage through recovery. By learning to recognize and react to these responses *as they come up,* you can prevent difficult, intense, overwhelming reactions. Later, you can learn to use your body/mind responses as avenues towards association and healing (see Chapter 18).

I've lived in my head so long . . . it's like living in a penthouse. It's disconnected from where the real living is. Real life is in the whole body. It's from the feet and legs and pelvis and belly and chest and head. It's not just the head. I want to own my whole body, with all of its feelings and abilities. CeeCee

PACING YOURSELF

As a child, you were conditioned to ignore your needs. Life was a series of unbroken crises. The harder we could push ourselves, the safer we felt. In typical survivor fashion, you might say to yourself, "I know my skin has broken out in hives, and I have a migraine, but I'll make it through one more chapter." This worked for us during our abuse, but it works against us in recovery. You cannot heal while on "emergency alert." If your head is pounding and your skin is irritated, your body is trying to get your attention. Healing requires honoring, not ignoring, our needs.

Pacing yourself is important. You may be comfortable reading half a page or half a chapter a day. Acknowledge your needs and honor them. They are your protection. You may choose to arrive at your therapy session early and read certain sections of this book. Your therapist is then available to help you through any issues that may cause you distress.

By practicing the above techniques for recognizing your feelings, you can avoid the vast majority of difficulties that may arise during the course of recovery. Your safety hinges on being self-aware and responding with care to your body/mind signals.

QUICK REFERENCE IN AN EMERGENCY

Some survivors experience difficulties as the body/mind try to heal. You may sometimes feel as though you are losing touch with the present. Some survivors experience impulses to hurt themselves or sabotage their own recovery as they begin to heal. The important thing to realize is that these reactions are actually signals of recovery. They will begin to disappear as you heal. If you are experiencing any of these currently, you may want to familiarize yourself with Chapters 15 and 16 now. Intense or overwhelming reactions that persist over weeks may indicate a need to slow down your pace.

Some sections in this book and parts of recovery may be particularly difficult for survivors or sensitive readers. If you unexpectedly find yourself overwhelmed, help is available. The back page contains the most immediate information that may be required in an emergency. Turn to the back page and follow the procedures you have prepared for yourself. The several pages preceding the last page can be helpful to read while waiting for outside assistance. If you have not completed these yet, please do so now. The pages are self-explanatory.

YOUR BEST CRISIS PREVENTION—NURTURING YOURSELF

I always begrudged myself the time to heal. I don't anymore. Right now, fifty percent of my time is spent in healing. I maintain my support system. I spend a lot of time with myself and with caring people. Now I wake up and work out if I feel like it; I linger over breakfast, I eat right again. My life has gotten much, much better. The biggest difference is I've learned to love myself.   Alicia

When asked how to measure progress in recovery, Laura Davis, author of *The Courage to Heal Workbook,* replies, "How often do you nurture yourself?" Every person deserves nurturing, just for being alive. Nurturing yourself is not only a measure of recovery, it is also preventive maintenance. Being good to yourself is your best insurance against becoming overwhelmed.

I am healing myself with kindness.   Roxana

Make a list of things you enjoy: hiking? gardening? singing? drawing? going to a pet store? playing sports or a musical instrument? talking to a friend? visiting a gallery? Make the list as long as you can.

I knew it was important to take breaks, and have fun, but I could never manage to do it. There was always something more pressing. One day, I decided to schedule my "fun time" on my calendar. I felt silly doing it. But I kept my appointment to have fun. That was the best silly idea I've ever had.   Jeanne

Have you made a long list of things you enjoy doing? How about picking four of them to schedule on your calendar? Now is a perfect time to start honoring a commitment to nurture yourself.

3

Overview of Recovery

SNAPSHOT OF RECOVERY

Browsing through my family photo album, I often noticed a picture of me at the age of three. I was sitting in some tallish grass with a ribbon in my hair, holding a toy machine gun. As I remembered the story behind it, I came to think of it as representing my recovery. One day a man came over to our house and brought my cousin a toy machine gun. The instant I saw it, I knew I had to have it. I wrestled it away from my cousin and escaped into our backyard. I staked out my territory and began to fire rounds of shots, as loud and as many as the gun could discharge. The thought in my mind was that with this gun, no one could ever get near me. That man, impressed with the incident, took a picture of me.

Recently, I found a way to get that picture back. As I studied the photo, I began to understand why reclaiming it was so important to me. I had always thought I was just a rambunctious, tomboyish child. Today I see things in a different light. Today I see the fight for the machine gun as a fight for my life. The little girl in the picture was being abused by every significant adult in her life. By six, through predetermined, abusive rituals, my anger and any thought of fighting back were gone. Although I never lost my fighting spirit, I did lose touch with that original, whole, alive child. To protect her I hid her so well, that nobody, not even I, could find her. In time, I forget who she was. By losing touch with that still alive child, I lost my sense of self.

For me, recovery has been about rescuing my three-year-old, forsaken child. She has been waiting, frozen in time, to be told that the abuse has stopped. And I'm beginning to see her more clearly now. Today I see the toy machine gun, and behind it a broken heart. It was broken many times, and in many pieces, but it still kept beating somehow. She is making her way home to me, the hurting and waiting adult. A Survivor

Recovery is the search to find and heal each hurting part of ourselves. Each part, like the three-year-old, is waiting to be found. As the split-off parts are reunited, survivors feel increasingly healed and whole inside. Our healing proves an enduring truth—that the human spirit cannot be broken. It will survive impossible odds.

Of all pilgrimages, the greatest is to relieve the sorrow-laden heart.

Abdu'l-Baha

SEARCH FOR THE CHILD

Life is sacred, and every child is a sacred child. Infants contain our human potential. That potential unfolds through love, nurturing, and guidance. Abuse interfered with that process. Instead of thriving, our sacred child withdrew and hid. It found many ways to stay protected and safe. The purpose of recovery is to find that original child. By recovering and healing the child, we heal the adult. A healed adult is in touch with her or his true self and human potential.

The search for the sacred is always difficult. Like the Odyssey, the journey seems an unending series of Catch-22's, double-binds, and impossible challenges. That's how it was for me. Years into recovery, I thought I'd been making good progress, only to find myself in an impossible bind. Here's an entry I found in my journal:

It feels as though I've been wandering in a forest of monotonous trees, meeting challenge after challenge for seven years. One day

recently I thought I saw a clearing. But when I got to the sparsely growing trees, I found a bog. And the thing is that I have to make it through that fog. With each step, I find myself being dragged down deeper and deeper. I can't go forward, I hate it where I am, and I've come too far to turn back.

One survivor described the familiar feeling:

It feels like I'm on a treadmill called recovery. It's not an option to get off the treadmill. The only thing I can do is keep moving. I feel like I'm a numb being, walking in slow motion and being carried backward by the treadmill. Deborah

There may be bewilderment, confusion, and terror. Often it's hard to get your bearings, to know what's happening, to know if you are coming or going, or even if you're on the right track.

It feels like I'm in a labyrinth of trick mirrors. I never know what's real and what's not. I can't tell if I'm going forward or moving backward, and more often than I care to admit, I think to myself, "My God, am I ever going to make it out of here?" Roxana

THE FORMULA

Yes—you can make it through. Here's how survivors are doing it:

It requires that leap of faith initially. You know, when you think, "I just can't do it. I can't go on another day." That's when we really need to have some faith, or just a little willingness to be open to the fact that maybe there's help for us. You don't have to do it alone. There's all kinds of help, and it'll come in all kinds of forms. You just have to put one foot in front of the other and there's a natural momentum in this life bringing help to anyone who wants it.   Lynn

For some, abandoning faith is what gets them through.

Faith was something I hated, as was trust. The idea that my life sucked and I was suicidal, and had absolutely nothing to lose by trying this process on a month by month basis got me through the first year.   Adam, survivor of satanic and KKK abuse

The formula for successfully completing a pilgrimage has always been the same. No matter how complex and confusing the entire process seems, the formula doesn't change:

Trust in *your own* process. You will need to find some guides. Others will appear when you need them. Gather up your special talents and strengths. You will need all of them to complete the journey. Listen to your inner wisdom. And remember, the hero always makes it home.

The important thing is that we remember that the keys to our freedom are simple things. They don't lie in esoteric things that are beyond our comprehension. The key to the door is a very simple key. And once it's found, you're going to sit there and go, "How could it be so simple?" And it is that simple.   Suzzane

How are you doing? Are you all right to continue?

If not, you can turn to Rainbow Place or spend some time in your Safe Place.

CYCLES OF RECOVERY

Going through recovery is like running laps. You pass the finish line many times, only to have to run the course again. At times it feels like a marathon with no end. But just as marathon runners go through recognizable phases during the course of the race, recovery has its special rhythms. Following are cycles survivors have described. You may discover others.

PEELING THE ONION

To keep from being overwhelmed with all the information at once, our body/mind have protective mechanisms that reveal the abuse to us in phases or layers. The layers may be grouped according to the age(s) when the abuse took place, according to type of abuse, certain perpetrators, or difficulty of the material. Survivors have compared this process to peeling an onion. With each phase a layer of information is revealed. As each layer is peeled away and healed, you experience a wonderful sense of completion. This feeling can last for weeks, months, even years. Another layer may begin to emerge, and you are surprised to learn that there is more. However, the good news is that with each layer, you are becoming more healed.

THE SPIRAL

The Courage to Heal, Third Edition, by Ellen Bass and Laura Davis, describes the spiral cycle as follows:

You go through the same stages again and again, but traveling up the spiral, you pass through them at a different level with a different perspective. You might spend a year or two dealing intensely with your abuse.

Then you might take a break and focus more on the present. A year or so later, changes in your life—a new relationship, the birth of a child, graduation from school, or simply an inner urge—may stir up more unresolved memories and feelings, and you may focus in on it again, embarking on a second or a third or a fourth round of discovery. With each new cycle, your capacity to feel, to remember, to make lasting changes is strengthened.

THE SEESAW (OR TEETER-TOTTER)

Dr. Pete Danylchuk of the Restoration Therapy Center in San Mateo, California, observed the up/down cycles of recovery. His description made me think of a seesaw. Most of the early stages are spent on the low end. You may be feeling depressed, terrified, dissociated, suicidal, and ashamed. As you work through each experience, you take some of your burden and place it on the other side. And slowly the balance begins to shift, until one day you're on top. You may feel invincible, like you've conquered all obstacles to recovery, and sitting on top of the world. However, a new wave of unassimilated events, a quarrel with a friend, a financial crisis, or disappointment at school may send you plunging down again. As you hit bottom, it may feel as though you've never left. It can be the most devastating feeling in the world, especially because you now know what it's like to be on top. However, now it takes less time and effort to make it to the top again, because the burden you've placed on the other side through recovery gives you more leverage.

In between there will be times when you may feel stuck. You feel caught midway, frustrated with no movement. Even though you may feel stuck in limbo, trust that there is something important going on inside. As you gain strength through recovery, fewer and fewer things can plunge you back down. You remain on top for increasingly longer periods of time. From the high vantage point, you gain a better perspective on your history. In time, you will feel like you've come to terms with your past. You are no longer riding the highs and lows on the seesaw of recovery. More and more you begin to feel balanced, or "centered." You are able to get off the seesaw and get on with life. You may return from time to time, but you are no longer riding a seesaw, with recovery as the consuming focus of your life.

THE JIGSAW STORYBOOK

Making sense of repressed experiences is like putting pieces of a jigsaw puzzle into place. It takes a while before the full picture emerges. At times you get pieces that don't seem to fit. It's important not to throw them away. Every piece has its place. Sometimes you want to give up on the puzzle altogether—it seems too complicated. But with a lot of hard work and patience a picture begins to emerge. One day you feel you "get" the picture, and experience a great sense of relief.

As new pieces continue to emerge, you begin to work on the next picture. Every picture is self-containing and complete. You become more proficient in putting together succeeding puzzles. In time you have a book with many pages. One day, as you flip through the pages, you find they tell a story—your story. The book is complete.

STAGES OF RECOVERY

Recovery follows many paths and courses. No two paths are alike. The events occur in their own time, place, and order. Internal journeys are not linear but multidimensional. There is movement on many levels and in many directions. You usually cannot recognize a stage until you've moved beyond it. However, looking back, survivors have identified certain landmarks.

Most survivors do not complete each stage with a single pass through. You may return many times, completing many visits. As one survivor remarked, "I had to go through these over and over again with new information before it actually started to 'take.'"

While the stages are numbered for convenience, they do not imply an order. Survivors can be working on stage eight all along. You may start at stage six, and then move to stage two. You may be in stages three and four at the same time. You may have moved through all the stages with one experience and at the same time find yourself in the beginning stages of the next. All of these are common. The important thing is to recognize the similarities and respect your differences, while charting your own course.

1. SOMETHING IS WRONG

This is usually a time of searching. For some it's because "life is hell, and always has been." You may find yourself in and out of abusive relationships; unable to hold down a job for more than two months; perplexed by violent, uncontrollable behaviors; or a victim of sex, drug, or other addictions.

The other extreme is also common. Many survivors lead "model" lives except for the occasional depression. You may have graduated from school with high marks and have a successful career; you may be raising an exemplary family, go to church regularly, have a wonderful circle of friends; you may be a contributing member of your community. But something's not right, and you just can't put your finger on it.

Many survivors try promising solutions. Some, understandably, are drawn to cults or cult-like groups offering *the* answer. Many survivors report having been attracted by new age religions, guru-oriented groups, or organizations such as EST (Erhard Seminar Training), offering crash courses in belief and attitude transformation. Many survivors are avid readers of self-help books. It seems that all the ideas apply but that, long-term, nothing works.

2. I THINK I NEED HELP

Things get out of hand, become unbearable, or you run out of self-help options and seek outside help. You may find a therapist, join a support group, or check into a treatment center. You may find yourself establishing close relationships with other survivors while remaining certain that you are not one of them.

It's like before I realized I was a lesbian. I started hanging out with lesbians and felt really comfortable around them. One day it hit me that I was a lesbian, and so with great anxiety I "came out" to one of them. I was stunned when she said casually, "I just assumed you were one of us." It's the same with the ritual abuse. I found myself hanging out and feeling really comfortable with other survivors. I was drawn to learn more about it and found myself reading everything I could lay my hands on. My partner knew I was a survivor long before I did.   Jeanne

3. GROWING AWARENESS OF YOUR TRUTH

If you've found a therapist familiar with post-traumatic reactions, you may begin to get in touch with underlying issues that have affected your life. You may identify unhealthy patterns, including addictions. As you stop behaviors that helped you to repress your trauma, you may begin to get flashes of unresolved events. It may be sexual abuse by a family friend, molestation by a coach or teacher, sexual encounters with your siblings, or incest by one or both of your parents. You begin to see through the myth that yours was a perfect family.

As you grow stronger through recovery, new information begins to emerge. You may remember other people, candles, robes, and rituals. You may get in touch with experiences in which you or others were abused. Later you may uncover rituals in which you abused. Later still, you may recall cult dogma and how you exited the cult.

When I came into recovery, I used to say, "The truth will set me free. Seek the truth and the truth will free you." And I'm very much aware that the truth does not set us free. Once we know the truth the fear can put us back into denial, and if we do, we can be used by our cult perpetrators. Freedom is found in how we process the truth. That is what sets us free. Suzzane

4. RESPONSES TO THE TRUTH— RELIEF/DISSOCIATION/EMERGENCY STATE

There are many reactions survivors have upon discovering their ritual abuse past. You may have a single reaction or, more likely, a combination of reactions. You may experience immediate relief— "At last I know what's the matter with me. This sure explains a lot of things." Relief may be followed by confusion and disbelief. "That couldn't have happened. I must be making it up." You may find yourself in an emergency state: dissociation, terror, hopelessness, feeling overwhelmed. At the same time, messages to injure or kill yourself if you begin to remember may get activated. No matter how strong the thoughts or impulses, DO NOT ACT ON THEM. Turn to the back page and follow the steps you've outlined to keep yourself safe. In time you will recognize these impulses for what they are: a stage of recovery that you will learn to overcome.

That's when all the feelings came. I wanted to be dead and I was willing to kill myself. But I had a lot of good friends who knew right away that I was starting to weird out on them and they wouldn't let me. Grace

Some survivors resort to old behaviors in response to the truth. You may turn to tried-and-true coping habits such as drinking, drugs, creating havoc in your life, double- and triple-booking appointments, provoking arguments. Some, believing themselves to be helpless, return to a cult.

Whatever the initial reaction or reactions, many survivors journey on.

It's been off and on for many, many months— just back and forth about believing it or not. And I was using that word "hallucinate," saying, "Well, you know, either it's real or else I'm really fucked up. I'm either in denial or I'm falsely accusing my parents. In either case I can no longer bear the shaky ambivalence of the middle ground." Deborah

5. DECISION TO HEAL

Survivors begin to come to terms with what's happened and make a commitment to heal their pain. You read everything you can get your hands on and bring reading material to your therapist. The "work" begins to take on a rhythm: retrieving repressed experiences, examining unhelpful behaviors, discovering deeper emotions and feelings. What used to be a constant fear may now be felt as constant terror.

Instead of feeling better, you may actually feel worse. You can't see an end to the pain. As things come together in one area, they seem to fall apart in another.

What I keep learning is that the better I get, the worse I feel. Now I find myself saying, "Things are getting worse, I must be getting better." Amiee

Each "falling apart" eventually brings a coming together. Despite the pain, and unbearable feelings, there is healing. Life, at last, begins to make sense. You're committed to recovery. You're seen wearing the "recovery uniform," warm-up pants and a sweatshirt—as one survivor put it, "survivor fatigues." You feel out of place in the "regular" world. Conversations about the news, politics, or brands of good tea no longer interest you. Your life feels consumed with recovery. You only feel comfortable with other survivors and wonder if you'll ever relate to "normal" people again.

6. LEARNING YOUR OWN SYSTEM

As recovery progresses, you begin to recognize your own patterns and behaviors. You become aware of your defenses, how your body communicates, and how you respond to it.

What's been the most liberating is to catch the little things—like when someone says, "Hi, how are you?" and I want to hide under my desk. I can recognize that that's an overreaction. Before, I couldn't do anything about it because I was not aware of what was happening. But now I can recognize when I am having an irrational thought pattern or behavior. So I don't act. I stop and ask, "What's really going on with me?" It's knowing when I'm having a feeling, what to call it, why it's

there, and if it's a bad feeling, knowing how to deal with it. Sunny

You discover simple truths that other people have always taken for granted, or, as one survivor put it, "You have BFOs: Blinding Flashes of the Obvious." For example, one survivor realized, "I am alive." You discover split-off parts or selves. You worry, "But who am I, really? Will the real me please stand up?" At the same time, you despair of ever getting through it all. As one survivor told me, "I just sat on the couch all day, staring at the rug and telling myself, 'I just can't do this anymore. I can't have even one more memory. I just can't go on.'" But in time your strength and resolve return, and you journey on.

You learn to let go of the struggle and accept what comes. In time the splits begin to heal and you feel more whole. As you feel more in control, you begin to appreciate yourself and respect the ways in which you've coped. You feel there may be a life after recovery. You assure newly aware survivors that there is hope.

7. DEMYSTIFYING THE RITUALS AND THE CULT

Through continued examination of the past, you begin to gain perspective. You uncover negative thinking and discover how to break it. You discover ways in which you were manipulated and set up. You discover the lies. In *Out of Darkness,* Dr. Walter Young, medical director of the National Treatment Center for Multiple Personality and Dissociation, observes: "The production of illusions suggests that the cult members have extraordinary powers that the child cannot possibly confront or challenge. . . . The task of treatment is to recover from tricks and brutal indoctrinations perpetrated by sadistic humans, not evil 'deities.'" You begin to break free of the lies and manipulations. You may begin to see your abusers as addicts—powerless, not powerful. You gain freedom from the pain and fear. Your healing takes on a new momentum. You now have the skills to handle whatever else may come.

8. TAKING BACK YOUR OWN POWER

You take charge of your own recovery. You experience more good days than bad days. You have come to terms with fear, guilt, shame, and blame. You can accept yourself and what happened. You can take responsibility for things within your power and let go of things that are not—and you know which is which.

Slowly you begin to take action on your own behalf. You may decide to go back to school, change careers, relocate, or break off an unhealthy relationship. Where once secrecy was a sacrosanct rule, you may suddenly find yourself wanting to tell. You may join a survivor advocate group, initiate workshops, display your art work, or tell your story in other creative ways.

As you feel increasingly whole, you're surprised to find that the "real you" hasn't changed but now has more freedom of expression. You realize that you had always put your best foot forward, but now it feels like it's your foot and not someone else's. You begin to experience your spiritual self and your healthy, wholesome sexual self. You are able to be playful and spontaneous. Others see you and find hope for themselves.

It seems like the most important thing we can do at the outset of recovery is take back some power—and that's nothing more than exploding the myth that we're powerless. We're strong individuals or we wouldn't have made it. We're just out of touch with that strength. Sunny

* * *

How are you doing? Remember the feelings list? Mad, glad, sad, etc.? (See page 19.) It's a good idea to check the list at break times, to help you get in touch with yourself. It may be helpful to keep a bookmark at that page.

HOW LONG BEFORE I'M HEALED?

Healing times can vary widely. It also depends on when you start counting. A significant amount of time is saved with a proper initial diagnosis. In my case, it would have saved eighteen years. I've heard of survivors being misdiagnosed for thirty years or longer. Prompt diagnosis is usually the single biggest factor in advancing your recovery.

Many survivors work on other issues before discovering their ritual abuse past. This is an important period that lays the foundation for the work ahead.

I always felt so frustrated because it took me so long to get to the place where I'm having memories and dealing with this—six years of hard work and recovery before I had my first memory. And I just thought, "God! I'm retarded." I felt like I was defective in some major way. But I tell you, it takes every ounce of recovery I have to do this. I've never had to call on my repertoire of tools like I do with this. I'm taxed to the limit. And now with hindsight I can see the brilliance of it all. From my experience, I really trust the wisdom of it, and everyone has to find that out for themselves. Lynn

One of the hardest things about recovery is that while each milestone seems enormous, overall progress often feels imperceptible.

I never forget how hard recovery is. Never. The worst part of it was nine years of hard work. We're talking twenty-four hours a day working our rear ends off in order to get well. Year after year of struggling, struggling, struggling. And I saw no possibility of it changing. I just knew I had to keep crawling. Looking back, it doesn't look like it took all that long, but going through it, it felt like it was endless.   Caryn StarDancer

Every time a new issue begins to emerge, survivors tend to think, "I haven't made any progress at all." However, if you go to a support group and listen to newcomers, you'll immediately recognize how far you've come.

If you discover and then can accept that there is ritual abuse in your background, you can begin to experience immediate results in healing. The most remarkable changes often occur in the first few months or years. No one can know in advance how long your overall healing will take—not even your therapist. Length of recovery is affected by many factors: your age when the abuse began; length of time you were abused; type of abuse you suffered; whether the abuse was overt or covert; your relationship to the violators; the types of defenses you employed; your ability to get good professional help; number of years spent reinforcing dissociative behaviors; amount of time you can devote to recovery.

Some survivors make immediate leaps in recovery. Others take a long time to get their bearings and then make excellent progress in the later stages. Almost everyone experiences ups and downs, great strides and then greater frustrations, moments of hope and moments of hopelessness, and plateaus of no movement at all. Some survivors stop therapy, thinking they are fully healed. However, months or even years later, they return for more. If this happens to you,

do not blame or shame yourself for having "failed." Appreciate the breathing space. You need it. The key is to stay in touch with your own process and trust it.

There's a beauty to getting to the plateau that I'm at. Even though I've got the summit of the Himalayas up ahead of me, I feel like I'm at a plateau where I can look back and know how perfect the wisdom has been—the timing and everything.   Lynn

WHAT RECOVERY MEANS

Survivors talk about "recovery" and "being recovered." For some, it is a process in which we become increasingly healthy. For others, the idea of "lifelong recovery" is unimaginable. They need to know that there is an end. The two ideas are valid and complementary.

Caryn StarDancer, survivor, leading educator on ritual abuse, and editor of *SurvivorShip,* defines being recovered as follows:

Being recovered means completing a critical mass of healing. It is a given amount of healing after which the feeling of well-being is self-sustaining, and the process takes on a momentum of its own.

It used to be my therapist, my support system, and books that kept me going. Now it's something inside that keeps me going.   Jeanne

Because of the goal-oriented thinking in our society, many survivors feel pressure to be recovered. But for most, recovery is a lifelong process.

It took a lifetime to get me this sick, and my approach is, it'll take the rest of my life to get well.

*But every day gets better, and I'm going forward.
Dave*

*My goal used to be to become "normal." Now
it's to become more who I am—to be more sensitive, more aware, more alive. Jeanne*

Many survivors feel relieved in simply accepting the process without goals or expectations. As
one survivor put it,

*One day I realized that I wasn't going to be
happy every day for the rest of my life, and that
was okay. I found a lot of freedom in that thought.
Janes*

Letting go of certain expectations can enhance
your recovery:

*Maybe there are things that you don't recover.
It's really valuable to know where to cut your
losses. It's never going to be the way it should have
been. My inner kids will never have a "Mrs.
Cleaver Mom." And there's a certain freedom in
facing it—being able to say, "I know what I can do
and what I can't." So if I can base my recovery on
what can be helped, then I'll get further faster em*

Recovery is the point when the aftereffects of
ritual abuse no longer define every experience
and dominate day-to-day. It's the process of
achieving selfhood through healing. Therapist
Mary Ellen Holmen at the Recovery Center in
Albuquerque, New Mexico, suggested the following signs of recovery.

BAROMETERS OF RECOVERY

1. You believe and trust yourself.
2. You take delight in your own company and in
   the company of others. You are as content
   being alone as you are being social.
3. You feel whole within yourself. You do not
   need something outside of yourself, such as
   approval, a job, wealth, spouse, academic credentials, slim physique, social status, etc., to
   feel complete. You are neither made superior
   nor diminished by these things. You do not
   judge your own or other people's worth
   according to these things. As Mary Ellen
   remarked, "It must be awful to be one's credentials."
4. You don't change who you are to conform to
   who you're with.

*As I recover, I realize more and more how my
life's been about following "ought to's" instead of
"want to's". And I realized that the inescapable
result of that is that my epitaph will read, "She
lived someone else's life." And that would be horrible. Sophia*

5. You love yourself and so can love others.
6. You feel a connection with our universe. You
   experience the oneness of this planet, its people, plants, and animals.
7. You intuitively know where you end and
   where others begin (often referred to as having "boundaries"). You understand that we
   are all separate yet a part of this planet, and so,
   connected.
8. You are responsible for your own thoughts,
   feelings, and behaviors. You also know that
   your thoughts, feelings, and behaviors affect
   our planet and all things in it.
9. You live in the present more than in the past
   or future. You are conscious of your history,
   but you do not dwell on it. You may have
   goals, but you are not driven or possessed by
   them.
10. You feel at home with yourself. You are com-
    fortable in your body, with your emotions,
    mind, and spirit.

11. You are spontaneous and find excitement in living. You experience things as they occur through feelings.

12. You engage in regular activities that enhance and deepen your experience of yourself in the universe. You may find these through prayer, meditation, communion with nature, laughter, joy, and playfulness.

13. You accept the human condition. This means living a full life while accepting human imperfections and limitations; you accept your joys and disappointments, health and illnesses, accomplishments and shortcomings. You are able to come to terms with each as it occurs.

Many people are afraid to die because they have never really lived.   Erik

14. You do not wonder what "normal" is. You live according to rules and rhythms that are in keeping with your self and the universe.

Recovery means experiencing your own self and enjoying your full potential. One reader summed up recovery with, "I heal, therefore I am."

Today, for the first time, I feel alive in this world. To me, that's clearly nothing less than a miracle. For me, I know that healing is not only possible but miraculous, in spite of how difficult it tends to be. Because, my God—I was a mess. In any way that you could look at it, I was a mess.

And I may not be perfect now, but my life is pretty amazing. It was something I never even dreamed could happen. The most important things have been restored to me—the ability to give and receive love and trust. Trust was a biggy. And I want everybody to have at least this much.   Caryn StarDancer

The journey is difficult, but you have what it takes to complete it. Every answer is inside you. The simple key is *TRUST YOURSELF.* Remember that as you read this book and as you walk your own road to recovery.

Now that you have established some recovery essentials, remember to exercise them while reading through this book: Proceed empowered. Check often with your inner wisdom. Pace yourself. Take breaks from reading. Be willing to ask for help. Pay attention to your body signals and try to catch them early. Attend to them. Remember to have fun, and, most importantly, nurture yourself.

May your healing journey begin.

The remainder of the book deals with difficult material. This is a good time to take a break and complete any safety suggestions that can be of help to you. You can have some fun making a Safe Place for yourself, or coloring Rainbow Place.

Part Two

About Ritual Abuse

Cults and Ritual Abuse

When I was first having ritual abuse memories, I was very confused about what in the world these people were trying to do. Why would someone go to these lengths, and what are they getting out of it? They take healing and bonding rituals and twist them. They take everything that's sacred and warp its meaning. To deliberately disorganize and tear apart and damage was unfathomable to me. And I was just in tears, saying, why, why would they do such a horrible thing? Bea

The bewilderment surrounding ritual abuse comes as much from the mystery and secrecy as it does from the abuse itself. Although much is still being learned, much is already known. Stripped of secrecy, ritual abuse is being demystified.

DEFINITION OF RITUAL ABUSE

A ritual is an established procedure or series of steps followed in order to achieve a transformation. There are many different types of rituals, ranging from secular to religious. For example, a person's morning routine could be referred to as a ritual: Awakening at the same time each morning, washing, dressing, eating, and traveling to work in precisely the same order. A religious ritual is usually a service in which a cleric follows a prescribed format or series of steps in order to achieve spiritual enhancement or renewal.

Abuse is anything that injures, damages, or interferes with a person's healthy or normal development—physical, emotional, sexual, mental, or spiritual.

Ritual abuse, therefore, is methodical abuse, often using indoctrination, aimed at breaking the will of another human being. In a 1989 report, the Ritual Abuse Task Force of the Los Angeles County Commission for Women defined ritual abuse as follows:

> Ritual abuse usually involves repeated abuse over an extended period of time. The physical abuse is severe, sometimes including torture and killing. The sexual abuse is usually painful, sadistic, and humiliating, intended as a means of gaining dominance over the victim. The psychological abuse is devastating and involves the use of ritual indoctrination. It includes mind control techniques which convey to the victim a profound terror of the cult members and of the evil spirits they believe cult members can command. Both during and after the abuse, most victims are in a state of terror, mind control, and dissociation.

In *The Power of the Myth,* Joseph Campbell describes a ritual associated with the men's societies in New Guinea which "actually enacts the planting-society myth of death, resurrection, and cannabalistic consumption." His example contains both ritual and abuse, as well as many of the elements found in ritual abuse (repetitive sounds, prolonged ordeals, exhaustion, sexual orgy, killing, and cannibalism). However, the term "ritual abuse" as used within the context of Western society has a different connotation. It is first a crime of secrecy practiced underground to "benefit" or further the power of a group, and in rare instances of an individual. Group members are often people addicted to sadistic violence. The group's aims contravene the stated values of society and the group promotes its values as preferable and superior to those of society. The purpose of the abuse is to subjugate a person's will to the wishes of the group. The victim is not honored, but degraded.

The practice of ritual abuse can take many forms.

It is practiced by different groups for different reasons. It may be done for one or more of the following: religious reasons, as a preoccupation with the supernatural and the occult, to achieve power, for financial gains, or to satisfy sadomasochistic drives. It is often associated with the underworld of prostitution, child prostitution, pornography, and international drug trafficking.

Ritually abused children who survived into adulthood found a way to cope. Most developed extraordinary coping skills relying primarily on creativity and imagination. Each child instinctively knew to protect her or his core self, and find a way to hold onto hope.

> *I've always had these incredible dreams that would sustain me. I'd be somewhere where there was so much love, it was like air. It would move right through you. You'd breathe it, and it would be really, really healing. I'd hang onto those things.* Jane Linn

> *How are you doing? Time for a break? Stand up, take a stretch, have a cup of tea. Are you feeling okay to continue? People often accelerate or stop breathing when in distress. A good idea is to check if you're breathing normally after each section. Remember, it's safety first.*

SUBVERTING THE POWER OF RITUAL

Although ritual abuse is practiced in many ways, it likely originated in religious beliefs and practices. Understanding the probable roots of ritual abuse may help shed some light on its forms and practices today. Many religions have public rituals for the congregation and additional secret rituals that are the privilege of the "holy people"—medicine people, shamans, priests, priestesses. Secret rituals often involve psychic and supernatural powers. These powers are accessed through the unconscious while subjects are in a trance or altered states of consciousness. These trance states are achieved by use of hypnosis, drugs, rhythmic sounds or movements, frenzied movements, use of special herbs, etc. Altered states also result from extreme pain.

In these altered states, some people achieve extraordinary feats, such as lifting enormous weights or suddenly speaking in tongues. Spiritual leaders believed that people in altered states of consciousness were "possessed" by spirits or the gods. The secrets that gave holy people access to "gods" were closely guarded and passed along as tribal or religious mysteries from one generation to the next.

This same knowledge was likely usurped and used by people who coveted power: religious, political, military, personal, or sexual. Over time they studied and perfected methods of gaining control over others, through use of ritual, altered states of consciousness, psychology, and extreme abuse. This knowledge, too, was closely guarded and passed along from generation to generation.

Because both established religious groups and covert groups used ritual to access power, there are a lot of similarities between the two. Both might use symbols such as circles, triangles, pentagrams, and crosses. In tribal communities these symbols may be feathers, beads, pearls, and stones. Both may use mood-enhancing aids such as candles, incenses, chanting, humming, drugs, or potions. Both are known to have secret writings, Scriptures, special dates, and numbers. Both may have a special calendar designating "holy days" or holidays. Both might use special trappings such as robes, headdresses, vestments, containers, chalices, ceremonial knives, and masks. Both might have specially designated places of worship and altars. In both, a foundational idea could be that of sacrifice. In both, there may be either symbolic or literal consumption of flesh and blood. Both may attribute special significance to excrement.

There is a good discussion of various ancient, unconventional, secret or antisocial religions and belief systems in a video entitled "Cult and Ritual Trauma Disorder" by Randy Noblitt, Ph.D., LCDC. Another source describing unorthodox groups and beliefs is *Encyclopedia of the Unexplained,* edited by Richard Cavendish, with consultant J. B. Rhine.

THE ADDICTIVE NATURE OF RITUAL ABUSE

While much discussion has focused on understanding violators' motives for practicing ritual abuse, it is also useful to understand the behavioral needs that underlie them. Ritual abuse may be practiced by people or groups who feel powerless in a society that venerates power. Just as ancient rituals are rooted in superstitious beliefs, which in turn are rooted in fear, much of the practice of ritual abuse may be rooted in superstition for the purposes of gaining special power as an antidote to fear.

Survivors often describe their perpetrators as people who are preoccupied with power. It is often the case that people preoccupied with power are preoccupied with fear. Like the classroom bully, they may prey on defenseless, weaker people to reassure themselves of their own potency. No matter how impressive or tough their exterior, it may mask cowardice and fear.

We're talking about people wanting power out of powerlessness. At some point they were helpless, and I think they never quite get rid of that deep, deep inside. So they create this facade and all these rituals. But they wouldn't have to do that if they didn't feel so powerless.   Ann Seery

Violators' need for power may be insatiable. It likely stems from unmet emotional needs for security, which were denied to them in childhood, probably by their own abusers. This unmet need results in fear, shame, and grief. It also carries with it intense levels of rage and hate. The rituals may be used to discharge the members' emotional tension in an artificially manipulated atmosphere of heightened power. Rage and hate are discharged through violence, sadistic attacks on a victim, humiliating sex, and killings of animals, children, or adults who may or may not be members of the group. This may temporarily restore violators to a sense of security, control, and power. In *Rediscovering Childhood Trauma,* Jean M. Goodwin, M.D., writes:

> Sadists are addicted to these activities; their sexual discharge is profoundly dependent on being seen by each other, cleverly designing and ruthlessly executing sadistic acts. They plan together; anticipate together; are sexually kindled by each other's excitement, erection, or ejaculation; and boast to each other afterward. They are assisted by paid professionals acting from financial as well as sexual and power motives.

As long as violators do not address the root cause of their rage and hostility, it never leaves. It continues to resurface following each release. This may become a compulsive/addictive need, which is met through repetitive rituals. These ritual assaults may be supported by dogma allowing violators to rationalize their atrocities.

Profound altering of reality may help to keep members out of touch with their feelings of fear, pain, and helplessness. In some cases members may inflict sadistic acts of violence on themselves. It is theorized that the body produces adrenaline and endorphins, a reality-altering narcotic and opiate, to counteract extreme fear or pain. The "better" the members are made to feel, the more it may serve to intensify the addictive/compulsive drive and the need to repeat the "good" feelings.

When the ritual is over, the members may be faced with a profound sense of shame. To keep their pain and shame at bay between rituals, violators may be openly or secretly addicted to alcohol, drugs, sex, or other aids, which serve to keep them out of touch with their own truth.

TRADITIONAL RITUAL ABUSE

Ritual abuse is practiced with varying degrees of conformity, dedication, and intensity. In some cases it is practiced haphazardly and sporadically; in other cases it is practiced with strict adherence to custom and rigorous attention to detail. The degree and type of abuse varies as well. The description below, from survivor accounts, appears to represent the most common, traditional form of ritual abuse, sometimes referred to as "orthodox." Variations will follow later.

OVERVIEW

Ritual abuse is most often practiced in a group. A group practicing ritual abuse is called a cult and usually refers to a group dedicated to an idea that deviates from societal norms. While not all cults practice ritual abuse, all groups practicing ritual abuse are part of a cult.

A closed cult community may address the members' primary unmet needs for power and emotional release. Ritual abuse cults may offer a sense of belonging to people addicted to violence, who may feel disenfranchised from society. The group may function as a secret society, with its own hierarchy, rules, and conventions. It is believed that these secret societies, propagated through cult families, go back not only for generations but for centuries.

Abused from birth, cult-raised children lose their sense of autonomy and power. The ritual assault destroys children's sense of self, sense of reality, trust in self, intuition, ability to make decisions in their own interest, and ability to nurture themselves. The systematic abuse aims to render a victim totally dependent on the cult. This may assure a cult's power and continuing membership.

Adults, most often parents, may initiate a child into cult ceremonies at a very early age—usually well before five. Children are taught the cult's beliefs through repetition and negative reinforcement. They may be abused by every member of the group. Violators usually include parents, aunts, uncles, grandparents, and extended family members. They may also include close family friends and neighbors. People may also be abducted into a cult by strangers.

In traditional groups victims may be prepared from birth to assume special roles within the cult. These may be predetermined according to bloodlines. The roles may fulfill the needs of a secret organization. In smaller groups one person may assume several roles. Victims may gain more privileges and suffer less abuse as they take on their designated roles within the group (see Chapter 6 for specific examples).

These children never have their own developmental needs met. They, too, may grow into adults with intense levels of unresolved fear, shame, grief, hate, and rage. As adults, these children may repeat the pattern of learned behavior. In this way, the members' emotional deprivation may be passed along from generation to generation.

Ritually abused children may marry partners who carry intense levels of unresolved pain. The rituals may appeal to these spouses as a "sanctioned" form of release. This helps continue the unbroken cycle of abuse, which is known as multigenerational (or generational, intergenerational, transgenerational, and intragenerational) ritual abuse.

THE ABUSE

The abuse may begin at birth and appears to be concentrated in the earliest developmental years. This ensures maximum group control over the victim. Parents may "prepare" a child for cult rituals by "training" at home. Here the child is physically and sexually abused and forbidden to cry out. She or he is conditioned to never express emotions, no matter how extreme the pain. This ensures "proper behavior" in the rituals, where members do not wish to have ceremonies disrupted by the bothersome protests of a victim.

In addition to being trained in proper ritual protocol, children are trained to believe certain "truths," such as: Cult members are all powerful; You are one of us; There is no escape; You do not belong in the outside world; Only we can love you; You have two choices: join us or commit suicide.

CONDITIONING

These training lessons are systematically and relentlessly applied until they are learned. Violators use reliable manipulations to achieve their aims. For example, children may be taunted into anger but not allowed to express it. When they reach the point of rage, a "victim" is provided, allowing the child to discharge. At this point the event is interpreted for the child: "You are bad. You are guilty. You are responsible for what happened." At the same time, the child is "saved" by a "loving and nurturing" cult member.

My father and my uncle tormented me to the point of rage. Then they gave me a club, a police-type billy club, and taunted me to into hitting this guy. I ended up battering this guy—just beating his face to a pulp. Then this good cop/bad cop thing happened between my uncle and my father. My uncle saying, "Oh—you killed him. You'll go to prison if anyone ever found out. I'm not going to prison for you, kid." And then my father would stick up for me. And that's how it always went after the abuse. He would always be there to clean me up and take me out for a chocolate milkshake and wrap me up in a warm blanket. David Gabriel

With repeated set-ups, the cult lessons of "You are bad; You are one of us; There is no escape; and Only we can love someone as bad as you" begin to take hold in a child's mind. (Conditioning is explained in greater detail in Chapter 6.)

DISSOCIATION

Children are indoctrinated into two belief systems: that of society and that of a cult. However, the conditioning is meant to convince them that their real place is in the cult. As with incest victims, children may have a sense of two or more realities: a day reality, a night reality, a school reality, a home reality, a cult reality, and so on. Ritually abused children are able to keep their worlds separate through a process called dissociation (see Chapters 5 and 8).

I was totally unaware of what I was like. I was all locked up on the inside, but I was thinking to myself, "I'm having a good time." I had no idea even of what a good time was. Samantha

USE OF RITUAL

A group's power may be reaffirmed in many ways. Use of special trappings such as robes, symbols, altars, special sites, and ritual give the cult an aura of mystique and suggest supernatural powers. The power may be further enhanced through mood- and mind-altering drugs, manipulation of psychic phenomemon, and many set-ups (for examples, see Chapters 5, 6, and 22).

SECRECY

Ritual abuse is always practiced in secret in Western society. The element of secrecy carries with it profound negative consequences. The victim, usually a child, knows that something bad has happened and is told it must be kept secret. Children commonly assume responsibility for abuse inflicted on them and are explicitly told that it is their fault. As a result, the child carries both the secret and the responsibility for it.

The feelings of guilt and shame may result in a child's self-imposed isolation from society. The child may live in terror of being found out. This, in turn, prevents any possibility of the child ever exposing the secret, and so getting a "reality check" (i.e., it's *not* your fault). Ritually abused children may grow into adulthood carrying their secret and assuming they are at fault.

There was a teacher in the fifth grade and my aunt who seemed to want to reach out to me and help me, but I couldn't reach back because I loved them and I knew that if I let them help me, they would get close enough to see how horrible I am and begin to hate me. I couldn't risk losing them as well. Sunny

In summary, ritual abuse is organized abuse, usually practiced in secret, using conditioning and indoctrination to induce feelings of guilt, shame, fear, and rage and ultimately to destroy the will of a victim. This ensures total control over another person and descendants for a cult.

DIFFERENCE BETWEEN RITUAL AND RITUALISTIC ABUSE

In their paper "A New Clinical Syndrome: Patients Reporting Ritual Abuse in Childhood by Satanic Cults," Walter Young, M.D., Roberta Sachs, Ph.D., and Bennet Braun, M.D., distinguish between ritual abuse ("part of specific Satanic rituals") and ritualistic abuse ("ritual-like"). Some perpetrators incorporate ritualistic elements into their abuse. For example, a mother may always silently turn the knob, turn off the lights, stand in the moonlight, take off her clothes and hang them up neatly before committing incest with her son. Pornographers and child pornographers may incorporate ritual into their assaults.

The use of ritual during abuse does not necessarily constitute ritual abuse. Ritual abuse, as defined in the above paper, includes the idea of indoctrination into a deviant belief system for the purpose of breaking down one's sense of self. The above example would be ritual abuse if the mother systematically instructed her son, "You are the Master's child, and He has commanded me to be your wife. When you get the really good feelings (orgasm), it's a sign from the Evil One, that we are one—."

Whether abuse fits the definition of ritual or ritualistic, its effects should never be minimized. All abuse is destructive.

I'm not a survivor of ritual abuse, but I recognize that my abuse was very ritualistic. It was consistent, predictable, and repetitive. I can relate to fifty percent of the symptoms of ritual abuse.   Paul

The only way to stop ritual abuse is through recovery. Until that happens, the domino effect of perpetration, raising emotionally damaged people who may in turn violate, is likely to continue. Survivors are breaking the cycle.

Human beings can become monsters, but on the other hand maybe it's possible to become angels. If we can go that far down, how high can we go? We can make this world into the most peaceful, beautiful place in the universe.   Jane Linn

How are you doing? Is it time for a break? Maybe you'd enjoy going for a walk, or calling a friend. Take as much time as you need.

VARIATIONS OF RITUAL ABUSE

According to Caryn StarDancer:

You hit your kid—that's abuse. You hit your kid and say, "God wants this to happen," and if you do it every Friday at a specific time, then you've got ritualized abuse. The more complex the dogma, the more ritualized and elaborate the rationalization, the more it resembles generational [ritual] abuse. Because basically generational abuse is a highly systematized, very elaborate rationalization system that is supposed to distract you from the fact that it's just one person taking power away from another.

There are many variations of ritual abuse that do not meet the orthodox definition. It is not possible to describe every instance. However, do not use strict definitions as a way to invalidate your own experience. It is important to recognize, validate, and heal from any form of abuse that took your power. For example, the following does not appear to be traditional ritual abuse, yet it has the same elements of abuse, training, and manipulations in order to break a child's will that constitutes ritual abuse.

I wasn't in a group. I was abused by my nanny, who wasn't a family member. And I have some memories of being in her room, and a knife that was used as a threat to me. And I think it involved some sort of training. Like I am supposed to understand a certain sequence of events. There was a certain kind of progress that involved being mind-fucked with seduction, like "I love you," or "You love me, and this isn't going to hurt, and this is because I love you." And then there would be some pinching and slapping and then pinning me down. And I have a lot of memories of trying to flail. Then there's like a teasing, "You don't like this? You're trying to be strong? Let's see how strong you can be." Then putting more pressure so I'm even more frustrated. Or baiting me, like, "If you really want me to stop, you need to get really angry." Then when I got angry, I would be slapped even harder. So it kind of progresses into sexual perpetration, and at some point I shut down. I mean I don't even resist or fight. And I think that is probably the point of all that— and also for me to recognize that she has all the power. But it took me a long time to figure out that, "Well, of course, it's ritual abuse!" CeeCee

JONESTOWN

Jonestown, Guyana, gained notoriety in 1978 when cult leader Reverend Jim Jones of the People's Temple commanded his followers to commit suicide. More than nine hundred cult members were found dead. The People's Temple started as a religious group promoting charity and racial integration. However, as Jim Jones became more obsessed with power, he introduced increasingly abusive practices in order to break down and control his followers. Shiva Naipaul recounts a survivor's experience in *Journey to Nowhere,* which shows Jones introducing the types of practices found in ritual abuse.

After 1970, the Temple seemed to lose sight of individual need. It abandoned affection and turned to terror. . . . The main victims were the children. They were mercilessly punished for any infringement of the rules. Their screams were magnified by a microphone put close to their mouths. The beatings began to get really bad. No one was allowed to cry.

The more abusive Jones's practices, the more secretive he became. While the People's Temple did not begin as a secret society practicing ritual abuse, increasingly horrendous reports of violence, human degradation, sexual abuse, and secrecy indicated that the People's Temple was evolving in that direction.

PORNOGRAPHY

Many survivors recall being used for prostitution or child pornography. Both contain the elements of ritual abuse without dogma and indoctrination. They may involve costuming, props, and paraphernalia, staging scenarios, ritualized events, and prescribed scripts. In pornography frightened, cowardly violators, most often men, assert their power and vent their rage by humilaiting powerless others—mostly women and children.

In traditional ritual abuse, dogma suggests the idea of a higher purpose and so rationalizes the abuse. In pornography, there is no suggestion of a higher value or purpose—simply degradation of a victim. Without a framework within which to rationalize the pain, a child may assume total responsibility and feel even more shame.

The first memories I had was of this man who I think was the cult leader who was also a child pornographer. I remember him very clearly. There was nothing that I forgot about this guy. I started having memories of being molested by him one time, then I started having memories of the camera and me being photographed. They would tie me up . . . I guess it arouses people. There's just no limit to what they do. I started having memories of being raped by a lot of different people and having shit rubbed all over me. And it feels like that was the beginning of my ritual abuse memories because pornography is so tied in with ritual abuse. Lynn

SATANISM AND RITUAL ABUSE

There is a mistaken impression that all ritual abuse dogma is based on the worship of Satan. Ritual abuse may exist as the shadow or underside of Christianity. However, while elements common to Satanic doctrine are reported in other types of ritual abuse, many survivors report little or no focus on

Satan. Ritual abuse can also be the underside of other belief systems besides Christianity such as vodun (commonly known as voodoo), Santeria, or certain kinds of witchcraft.

Satanism and ritual abuse may be manipulated by organizations with completely different aims. Rituals can create an environment in which participants can satisfy extreme addictions. The most common addictions are to sex, drugs, power, and sadistic violence. Here members may participate in an underground where they can perpetrate aggression and violence without ever having to account for it.

My sense is that my father really wasn't involved in a Satanic thing. He got hooked up with a bunch of other guys who were doing pornography. There was definitely Satanic-type stuff going on—a woman being crucified, with demons being called up; demons torturing the kids. But they didn't really give a shit about robes or chanting. They didn't even attempt to rationalize it with any kind of philosophical or religious bullshit. They wanted to do their sex and their pornography and their torture and their violence. And it was just really clear that "We're here to rape and torture and film women and children." They were really specific about that. David Gabriel

There was some part of me that just held watch and said, "You're not getting any further with me. You're not getting my soul." Lynn

Are you feeling okay? Remember to stay in touch with your reactions and take care of yourself. If you need to cheer up, it might help to turn to Rainbow Place near the end of the book, or your own Safe Pages.

DOCUMENTED CASES

Reports of cult practices are as old as recorded history and as recent as today's news. Human sacrifice is well recorded throughout history. Until it was outlawed, ritual cannibalism was practiced by groups as diverse as some early Christian sects, the Mayans, and the Aztecs. The worship of destructive forces was recorded as early as 7000 B.C. by the Azidis of Mesopotamia. An example of a criminal and commercial ring practicing ritual abuse in France in the 1680s is cited by Martin H. Katchen in *Out of Darkness*. Catherine Deshayes, known as La Voisin, combined astrology, Satanism, and black magic in the running of her abortion and infanticide rings. The children were sacrificed to Astaroth and Asmodeus during the Guibourg Mass.

In *Painted Black*, Carl A. Raschke gives an example of a political/military group practicing ritual abuse in Germany in 1776. A renegade Jesuit Mason named Adam Weishaupt founded an order called the Illuminati, the illuminated ones. (There are other, nonrelated religious groups who have also used this term.) The Illuminati had initiation rites that used skeletons, corpses, and crosses painted with blood and involved drinking blood. Initiates were told that they had entered "another dimension." The oath of allegiance demanded willingness to kill or be killed. Initiates were taught the art of poisoning and urged to assassinate princes. Illuminati secret societies spread all across Europe during the late eighteenth century.

The late 1700s Spanish painter Francisco Goya documented sexual sacrifice cults in his painting *Witches' Sabbath*. In 1836 Maria Monk wrote a book called *Awful Disclosures of the Hotel Dieu Nunnery of Montreal*. She described her escape from a cult that bred babies for sacrifice. In the 1980s, two books, *Michelle Remembers* and *Suffer the Child*, documented experiences of ritual abuse survivors. Both describe practices that parallel accounts of ritual abuse spanning the centuries.

WHO PRACTICES RITUAL ABUSE?

Ritual abuse is most commonly practiced by the following:

1. Multigenerational families. Since children currently in families practicing ritual abuse are terrorized into silence and otherwise helpless to act, most reports of multigenerational abuse come from adult survivors. Some multigenerational family members may own, operate, or work in establishments that give them ready access to potential new recruits or victims. These may include homes for disabled or mentally retarded people, child care services or organizations, and church organizations running youth activities or summer camps, etc. When victims outside the family are targeted, there may be an increased chance of detection and disclosure. The majority of disclosures by children have come from extrafamilial ritual abuse.

2. Self-styled groups. Ritual abuse may spring up spontaneously. This may occur when a person or group feels overwhelmed, powerless, or disenfranchised and perceives society or another person as the cause of their pain. The Charles Manson "family" is an example of an apparently nonmultigenerational, self-styled ritual abuse group. The People's Temple was adopting ritual abuse practices. There is a possibility that each leader had a history of childhood abuse.

3. Lone operators. There is evidence of ritual abuse among lone operators such as some serial killers. They hold captive, indoctrinate, then desecrate the bodies of their victims. These may be cult-

abused persons who are estranged from their multigenerational families. They continue to practice alone.

4. Dabblers in ritual abuse. These may be adults or teens. They may fit one of two profiles: 1) troubled, disillusioned people looking for answers; or 2) people experimenting with power, the supernatural, and the occult. While these are most in evidence in the media, they tend to be the least extreme of the four profiles.

CHARACTERISTICS OF CULT VIOLATORS

There are many misconceptions about people who practice ritual abuse. The most frequent misconception is that "respectable" people are not involved. I put "respectable" in quotes, because respectability is judged almost exclusively by external things in our society—employment, education, family, a pleasing personality, appropriate behavior, and good grooming. The last two in particular are easily mimicked. Few people examine internal characteristics such as emotional, mental, and spiritual health. Therefore, perpetrators may appear quite normal in all respects, and so exist undetected in our society.

We need to keep dispelling stereotyped beliefs that people who practice ritual abuse are tatooed, beer-drinking bikers. My father was a leading pediatric surgeon nationally and internationally renowned. He had lots of access to young children. Adam

In *Trauma and Recovery,* Dr. Judith L. Herman writes:

Authoritarian, secretive, sometimes grandiose, and even paranoid, the perpetrator is nevertheless exquisitely sensitive to the realities of power and to social norms. Only rarely does he get into difficulties with the law; rather, he seeks out situations where his tyrannical behavior will be tolerated, condoned, or admired. His demeanor provides an excellent camouflage, for few people believe that extraordinary crimes can be committed by men of such conventional appearance.

In order to avoid detection, orthodox multigenerational families may try to blend in with conventional society as much as possible. Their external appearance would rarely divert attention or cause suspicion.

My parents pretty much considered themselves to be liberals. They were both commercial artists. They had a close friendship with another artist who happened to be black, and they would not have anything to do with a racist group. We had a couple of big lawn parties for congressmen at my house when I was really little.   Brice Roweland

While there are no hard and fast rules for who practices ritual abuse, there are common patterns. Abusers may show signs of emotional underdevelopment.

DEVELOPMENTALLY IMMATURE

Cult perpetrators are hard to detect, because the clues are subtle and hidden. People capable of inflicting such unimaginable damage may be damaged themselves. They may be suffering mental, emotional, or spiritual damage, or most likely all three. Some violators may hide their damage through rigid emotional control, humor, extreme politeness, and so on. Survivors often describe their violators as intelligent but emotionally immature. During psychological testing, one priest accused of child molestation was found to have the emotional development of a four-year-old child. Although usually masked, sometimes these clues are seen quite readily.

My father was an architect. He's hard to describe. He was violent in a childlike way. Pretty impulsive, out of control, whiney, and emotionally very immature.   Lynn

EXPLOITER OR DEPENDENT: MUTUAL DEPENDENCY

These people may find security by either taking power or aligning themselves with someone powerful. Some may look to control; others may look to be taken care of. At times, the characteristics are interchangeable. Cults attract charismatic people looking to fill their need for power by exploiting others. The dynamics played out in the cult may resemble those of a strongly patriarchal family. Some members take on a child role in relation to their charismatic leader. She or he is seen as perfect and infallible. The dogma and the leader's statements are never questioned. In exchange for "taking care of them," the "children" will give the "parent" leader whatever she or he wants. These "children" will often defend their charismatic leaders against clear proof of wrongdoing in the same way that a child will show undying loyalty to an abusive parent.

This relationship is seen repeatedly in examples such as David Koresh and the Branch Davidians in Waco, Texas, where followers held out with him until death; and in countless obscure cults around the country, last estimated to number 2,500.

POLAR OPPOSITES

Pat Graves, clinical director at The Life Healing Center of Santa Fe, New Mexico, observes:

There's the potential for good and evil in all of us, and it's blended, like a molecule of water. But in some people it's polarized—as if someone took a magnet and split apart the molecules.

I might really like my sister, but when she gets the ice cream which I wanted, I get angry. But that anger is mediated by the fact that I like her, and both of those are going on at the same time and moderating one another. It's never pure. But with some people, like certain preachers or politicians, those things are polarized. And you can bet, if there's this much purity over here, there's this much evil over there. When we talk about this we talk about what Jung called our shadow side. When we deny it we lose our ability to control and mediate it.

Human beings aren't monsters. It's when we don't give constructive expression to all aspects of our humanity that monsters may be created. People practicing ritual abuse may see themselves and others as all good or all bad. They may disconnect or dissociate "unacceptable" parts of themselves and repress them. Denied or repressed feelings seek expression. This sets up a conflict that may result in splitting into polar opposites: the conscious "extremely good" competing with the repressed "bad" for expression. The greater the conflict, the stronger both energies may become. The ultimate conflict finds expression in classical literature in Robert Louis Stevenson's *The Strange Case of Dr. Jekyll and Mr. Hyde.* The exceedingly good doctor and the monstrous Mr. Hyde were discovered to be the same person.

Jeffrey Dahmer is a modern-day example of Dr. Jekyll and Mr. Hyde. He was described as a polite boy who "didn't have a mean bone in his body." This very polite boy was a serial killer. It appears that he was unable to find nonharmful expression for his socially unacceptable "bad" urges. He seems to have perceived his options in terms of polar opposites. The apparent inability to mitigate his feelings produced monstrous results

The following excerpt from the transcript of the television journalism program "Day One" illustrates his struggle with his perceived choices—one all good, the other all bad.

He constantly fought urges to kill by attending church with his grandmother, by reading the Bible, and by trying to live life in an orderly fashion. . . . He stopped drinking. . . . He tried to suppress any sexual thoughts at all. For two years Dahmer did manage to stop drinking and he found work. . . . But once again his work was poor and once again he was released. . . . Dahmer stated that he believed he had blacked out and killed [a man] . . . and at that point, [he] stops fighting [and] begins to believe it's his destiny to do this. [It] . . . was a kind of surrender.

These "strange" cases of polar opposites are in fact quite common. Serial killers have been variously described by their shocked neighbors as nice, quiet, and polite. Many cult perpetrators may be exceedingly "good" people who live in terror of being perceived as "bad." Therefore, their "good" is pure and uncontaminated by any trace of badness.

My father is this well-respected businessman who belongs to the Kiwanis Club and has this high-paying executive job. He was this hero kind of guy. He was also unbelievably, insanely, violently crazy, but he had it split very neatly so that he was able to maintain this veneer of respectability. David Gabriel

Another familiar example of polar opposites may be seen in evangelical preachers such as Jimmy Swaggart. He zealously denounced "sinful" sex, warned his congregation against "licentious" thoughts, yet was discovered in sexual relations with prostitutes. Polar opposites may be found in religiously fundamentalist families who practice generational ritual abuse.

Part of the family lore is that when my father was a little boy my grandfather would tie him to a post in the basement and try to beat the devil out of him. On my father's side my grandparents were both born-again fanatics. No alcohol use in the house, no dice, no art, no television, no radios, no records. My father was a minister brought up during the Depression, and, being a minister, they had what was known as a poor box. People in the community would contribute clothing or food or whatever. My grandfather's theory was that you fed and clothed everyone else and if there was anything left then that was used for your children.   Matthew

RITUAL ABUSE, CULTS, AND ORGANIZED CRIME

Groups practicing ritual abuse may have the combined profile of coercive cults and organized crime. The following comparison and contrast may be helpful in putting ritual abuse into a more familiar context.

Traditional ritual abuse groups may share the following characteristics with coercive cults:

- they are usually based on dogma
- dogma is more important than people
- there is a radical separation of good and evil
- there is a demand for purity
- members are ceaselessly monitored, and their loyalty may be tested
- accusations establish members' guilt and shame
- the dogma is enacted through rituals
- the group convenes regularly to observe the rituals
- rituals frequently invoke supernatural intervention
- there are staged events such as planned spontaneity (where, for example, existing member "plants" are responding on cue, to "spontaneously" convert to a group's beliefs)

- similarly, there are mystical manipulations
- cults capitalize on members' fear and ignorance
- they promote a sense of separateness through an "us" and "them" mentality
- there is a siege mentality with a paranoid view of the outside world
- humor is forbidden
- resistance of members is worn down through physical and emotional manipulations
- a person's identity is destroyed in order to create a new one
- members give up autonomy in exchange for approval and acceptance
- mind control is used to indoctrinate the victim into the group's belief system
- individuality is uniformly suppressed
- there is a well-defined hierarchy
- members are exploited for the benefit of the leader(s)

Ritual abuse cults may be similar to organized crime in the following ways:

- both engage in criminal activity
- perpetrators consider themselves above the law
- the group operates as a secret society
- the secrecy protects criminal activity and the criminals
- both are expert at hiding or disposing of evidence
- both are often well-connected to people of influence
- they are rarely discovered or prosecuted
- they are often organized within the context of an actual or conceptual family
- the family expects offspring to continue the family practice
- the group often loosely associates with other common interest groups
- the group may include nonrelated "outsiders"
- outsiders are less trusted and more expendable than "family"

- members live a dual existence; they maintain a veneer of respectability to divert attention from their true activities
- the leadership is totalitarian and ruthless
- rules are followed unquestioningly
- transgressions are punishable by death

Ritual abuse may differ from organized crime and cults in some respects. The main points of departure are as follows:

- abuse is the organizing principle of the group
- the abuse is extraordinarily cruel and extreme
- abuse is used to achieve power
- victims live in constant terror of death
- abuse usually begins in infancy
- the abuse follows a systematic course of mind control

Mind control is used not only to convert the victim to the group's belief system, but also to ensure secrecy (much of the mind control is aimed at ensuring secrecy) and to carry out cult instructions. In addition, ritual abuse may both create and satisfy an addictive need.

CULTS AND SECRET SOCIETIES—WHERE ARE THEY FOUND?

Wherever there have been societies, there have been secret societies in opposition to them. Cults practicing ritual abuse exist as a secret society. While all secret societies undermine the establishment to some extent, not all secret societies exist to pervert or destroy it. Arkon Daraul states in *A History of Secret Societies:*

> Secret societies are generally considered to be anti-social: to contain elements which are distasteful or harmful to the community at

large. . . . None of them can be regarded as good from every point of view. But all of them can be considered evil, from one standpoint or another. . . . When, however, their beliefs become those of the majority, they cease to be considered anti-social.

He cites as examples: "Communism and Fascism function as secret societies where they are prohibited by law. Christianity was a secret society in Rome, and was considered . . . to be a dangerous innovation."

Secret societies compete for membership with established organizations. Therefore they have to offer something not accommodated by the establishment: wealth, power, fame, sex, drugs, security, promise of salvation or eternal life. In some cases the aim of the group may be to pervert or destroy a particular society. A tactic may be to operate secretly within the structure of that very organization. There can be secret societies within secret societies. Ritual abuse does not appear limited to Western society or North America. Reports have come from China, Southeast Asia, Africa, and from as far away as Australia. The organizations cited below as harboring cults have been mentioned in newspaper articles, studies based on survivor accounts, and directly by survivors. It is important to emphasize that the vast majority of members *do not* participate in ritual abuse. Furthermore, currently there are no studies formally documenting the extent of ritual abuse activity. The abuse is practiced in secret, likely without the knowledge of legitimate members of the faith or group.

RELIGIOUS

Few religious institutions seem to be exempt from ritual abuse activity by some of their members. Survivors have reported religiously motivated ritual abuse within the Catholic Church, Protestant congregations, the Penitentes, fundamentalist groups, Judaism, the Mormon Church, the Greek Orthodox Church, the Mennonites, Native American religions, groups practicing witchcraft, (Wiccan, paganism, neopaganism), Druid, and Celtic rites, and "legitimate" Satanism. Some cult members subscribe to both belief systems. Others, it appears, simply pretend to be members of a religious faith as a cover for their real beliefs.

CRIMINAL

Crime rings may use ritual abuse as a means to break down, desensitize, dehumanize, and control their membership. Ritual abuse has been cited within the multibillion-dollar pornography industry; it has also been reported within child and adult prostitution rings and within the human trade industry (illegal child adoption rings, supply of victims for rituals, white slave trade, etc.) and drug rings. One survivor I spoke with reported being abused by a group involved in an underground bootlegging/prostitution ring during Prohibition.

POLITICAL/MILITARY

This is reportedly the most highly organized, sophisticated, and clandestine of the three groups. It appears to consist of multigenerational upper- and upper-middle-class families. Many of these are reported to be well-educated and well-connected politically, professionally, and socially. Of the three broad categories, this group appears to be most oriented toward exerting influence—political, military, or economic. Members may be "strengthened" through withstanding extreme levels of torture. The ritual abuse is used to indoctrinate the victims to a worldview. They are reported to network at local, national, and international levels. However, not all of them may cooperate. Some may also compete with one another.

Many survivors have reported that at least one of their violators was involved in a secret society or a fraternal order other than the ritual abuse group. In some cases survivors believe that the organizations in which the violators were members were directly involved in the ritual abuse.

All three categories of ritual abuse groups reportedly network much the same as business organizations loosely associated for mutual benefit and exchange of ideas. For example, one survivor recalls an incident where her cult group engaged the KKK to provide them with a victim. The KKK abducted a black person. The black person was then used as a human sacrifice by the cult group.

The same persons or families may be involved in more than one category of ritual abuse. There may also be considerable crossover among the three main categories. For example, one survivor was ritually abused by her family, which included a priest as well as a former Catholic brother. Some members of her family also participated in a Nazi cult. Some of the Nazi cult members used the survivor for child prostitution.

Some groups may recruit members from other groups for special assignments or purposes. Services are exchanged for money or reciprocal favors. For example, one survivor was abused within her own family. She was also loaned out to a religious order of men who wanted a "subject" for experimentation with various tortures. A nine-year-old child was given money in an envelope after her ordeal. The envelope was turned over to the head of her cult family.

MUTUAL DEPENDENCY AND UNDERGROUND INDUSTRIES

People who have inordinate addictive/dependency needs may be easily manipulated. They are marks for exploitive people—either from within or from outside of the cult. Underground businesses and ritual abuse groups trade in the same basic commodities: drugs, prostitution, slaves, weapons, violence, and pornography. Exploitive business manipulators may cash in on cult members' childlike neediness by offering them what they want: security, protection, and new ways of reaffirming their own power. These opportunists may have no interest in dogma. Their main interest may be in exploiting the secondary opportunities offered by ritual abuse cults. Cults and business opportunists may form a symbiotic relationship. The opportunists may create neediness and dependency in the cult members by manipulating levels of fear, tension, and release. Caryn StarDancer explains:

> Their dysfunctionality is managed by the cult dynamics. A cult functions as a relief valve. That's what the bacchanalian activity is about—control and release, control and release. You have all the strictures of threats, fear, and torture to manipulate and control, but you also have sanctioned activities such as ritual revels or access to illicit sex and drugs, which are set up by the cult to indulge and let stuff out.

Both cult violators and big business operators may deny that ritual abuse exists—each for their own and different reasons. Cult violators may be ashamed and afraid of exposure for legal reasons. However, many cult violators may be damaged, relatively powerless people.

> *The high priest in the "Brotherhood" was a medical doctor who went off the deep end with prescription drugs. I saw this all-powerful man become a weak and confused child during a period of six months. In the end he committed suicide.   Susan*

Survivors report that the real power lies with exploitive manipulators who control cult members and exploit them for profit. Cult members and activities may be used in pornography, prostitution, and the drug underground. These industries may have a vested interest in perpetuating ritual abuse and denying that it exists. They have both the money and the power to mount convincing campaigns discrediting survivors and their therapists.

> *If you are being seriously ritually abused, you will try every single capacity that you have for survival—your basic genetic strength, intelligence, imagination. Imagination goes a long way toward helping you survive—it's one of the biggest qualities that allows you to survive. So I think it's a combination of luck, coincidence, love, and having enough material to draw from which got us through this.   Caryn StarDancer*

> *Would you like to take a short break? Here's a relaxing breathing exercise you might enjoy. Deep-breathe in to the count of four; deep-breathe out to the count of four. Repeat this cycle four or five times. If the exercise works for you, you can use it during other breaks from reading.*

HOW CULTS ESCAPE DETECTION

The highest emphasis in cult indoctrination is placed on secrecy. Victims may be threatened with their own death or the death of a loved one for disclosing. This has a powerful hold on keeping the abuse secret. In addition, cults typically prey on the weak and helpless. These may include children, ill or retarded people, derelicts, the homeless, troubled teens, and illegal immigrants. Some cannot risk disclosure; others would not be believed. Violators may use blackmail to keep members quiet. Members may be forced to participate in illegal activities. To disclose means risking prosecution. Victims may be made to believe that there is no way out.

Violators may create dependence of members

on the cult. This may be emotional dependency, feeding an addiction, or guaranteeing privileged employment. To disclose would mean hardship on the member. Violators may be expert in avoiding detection. Cult professionals such as doctors, psychiatrists, lawyers, judges, politicians, morticians, and police may cooperate to mask or dispose of evidence and sabotage prosecutions.

Secret societies have existed, undetected, throughout recorded history. Until recently, the public was not even aware of the practice of ritual abuse. Evidence cannot be accumulated when there is no one looking for it. Organized crime offers a good point of comparison. Many people find it hard to believe that ritual abuse exists. However, many people agree that organized crime exists and that crimes, including murder, are committed by its members. Yet for decades the FBI denied the existence of organized crime citing "no evidence." Today the FBI denies the existence of organized ritual abuse citing "no evidence."

Finding objective evidence is not without its challenges even when people agree that a crime is being committed. On January 8, 1993, the NBC television journalism program "20/20" reported on the Air Interdiction Program intended to stop the smuggling of drugs across the United States/Mexico border. It is estimated that 70 percent of drugs entering the United States are smuggled across this border, and the times and locations of the transfers are generally known. At the time of the report, not a single smuggler had even been arrested, yet alone convicted. At air time, two billion dollars had been spent on the program.

Adult survivors are reporting crimes committed many years ago. In addition, a lot of ritual abuse may involve manipulation of reality. So while the terror and effect of the abuse are absolutely real, the crimes in some instances may have been staged (see Chapter 6). Getting proof of ritual abuse is like finding tangible evidence of incest and organized

crime combined. They both disappear under the spotlight.

SUCCESSFUL PROSECUTIONS OF RITUAL ABUSE CASES

Although various jurisdictions are increasingly passing laws prohibiting ritual abuse, this is a relatively recent development. Because ritual abuse was not illegal in most jurisdictions, it could not be prosecuted as such. Instead, ritual abuse was and still often is prosecuted for crimes committed within its context, such as murder or sexual abuse. However, victim accounts indicated ritual abuse practices in the following cases. All have been successfully prosecuted:

- The Manson murders in the summer of 1969 (Bugliosi, *Helter Skelter*)
- The Son of Sam murders in New York in the late seventies (Terry, *The Ultimate Evil*)
- The March 1987 sexual abuse and neglect case in Hamilton, Ontario, Canada (Marron, *Ritual Abuse*)
- The April 1989 murders in Matamoros, Mexico (Raschke, *Painted Black*)
- Country Walk Daycare (Hollingsworth, *Unspeakable Acts*)

I think cults have been here forever. And a lot of them had to do with fear and trying to please gods that you didn't understand and so you'd sacrifice your children. I feel like we have a huge culture behind us that says this is the way to do it. And I want to believe that we're coming out of that. I want to believe that my relationship with whatever life force there is can be more direct. I don't have to sacrifice some other being to win the favor of some god or of my boss, or the minister of my church. I don't have to hurt someone else to get to where I need to be. Part of me really believes that there's a growing number of people who want to heal and be part of a healing that's universal. And there's a surge of that energy now. We can break things and we can fix things. There are a lot of people on their way to fixing things right now. Grace

THE NATURE OF TRAUMATIC MEMORY

If there is a substantial number of survivors in North America, one may well ask why they haven't been identified as such. There are many reasons. The first is that survivors typically use repression and denial to distance themselves from the abuse. In addition, multiplicity and dissociation are coping mechanisms designed to make traumatized survivors function as normally as possible. These mechanisms protect survivors from knowing their own truth. Additionally, violators use a person's natural survival defenses of repression and denial for their own purposes. Using mind control, violators program survivors to not know, see, hear, or remember what has happened to them.

Violators who practice ritual abuse may be expert at leaving no physical scarring or evidence. They may also use extensive conditioning to prevent survivors from trusting their own perceptions. If survivors do begin to remember, they may doubt their own memories. The lack of physical evidence may reinforce their belief that this couldn't have happened to them.

Debate about the validity of repressed memories complicates the challenge of recovery for survivors. Some people promote the idea that survivor experiences can be explained by "false memory syndrome." This implies that such a diagnosis exists. A syndrome is a condition based on identifiable signs or symptoms. At this writing, no such syndrome is identified or documented in empirically validated clinical literature.

If there were such a syndrome, then supposedly anyone could be stricken by it, including violators. Typically, people deny the truth when it is either inconvenient or too painful to remember it. There is far more incentive for violators to forget abuse than for survivors to remember it. Survivors have much to lose, including their family. Violators, on the other hand, have much to gain by suffering from false memory.

When survivors do suffer memory distortions, it's more likely in order to deny, not fabricate, abuse. As one therapist observed, "Psychotics will try to convince you that they were abused; survivors will try to convince you they weren't." A study by Linda Meyer Williams, researcher and associate professor at the University of New Hampshire, bears this out. She found that out of one hundred women whose sexual abuse was documented in hospital records, "Thirty-eight percent of the women were amnestic for the abuse or chose not to report the abuse to our interviewers seventeen years later."

Leading Harvard trauma researcher professor Bessel van der Kolk also supports this point. In a video entitled *True/Not true* (see Bibliography), he explains that the most common "false memory" survivors suffer is imagining they had a happy, even perfect, childhood, when in fact the opposite was true. The idealized illusion helps them survive the unbearable reality. He therefore points out that often the greater the abuse, the more likely a child is to invent increasingly utopic illusions.

Although there is no documented false memory syndrome, this is not to suggest that all memories are accurate. Trauma can cause distortion of perceptions and alterations of consciousness (Chapters 5 and 6). Denial itself is a distortion of truth caused by traumatic circumstances.

Recall may also be affected by factors such as number of occurrences. In her study "Childhood Traumas: An Outline and Overview," Lenore C. Terr, M.D., describes Type I and Type II traumas and the coping strategies associated with each. Type I trauma typically involves a single overwhelming event and is often associated with "full, detailed memories," "omens," and "misperceptions." Type II trauma follows "long-standing or repeated exposure to extreme external events" and is typically associated with "massive denial, repression, dissociation, self-anesthesis, self- hypnosis, identification with the aggressor, and aggression turned against the self."

A study by trauma researchers Judith Lewis Herman, M.D., and Emily Schatzow, M.Ed., entitled "Recovery and Verification of Memories of Childhood Sexual Trauma," suggests that the greater the trauma, the earlier its onset, and the longer the duration, the more likely it might be repressed. It follows that ritual abuse which is severe, may start as early as infancy and typically continue throughout a child's developmental years, may more likely be repressed than other types of trauma.

While some trauma may result in massive denial and repression, other types of trauma can make recall more accurate. In a 1991 study by Goodman, Hirschman, Hepps, and Rudy, *Children's Memory for Stressful Events,* the authors found that "when stress was very high and children became nearly hysterical with fear, stress was associated with enhanced memory."

The degree of accuracy and number of details recalled varies from survivor to survivor and from memory to memory. Once in recovery, one survivor who had suffered type II trauma, began to remember not only the abuse, but also background conversations between the violators almost word for word. As recovery progresses, many survivors are able to recall the key event accurately, even if the surrounding details are distorted or forgotten. For example, a child may have witnessed her or his dog dying in a car accident. The child may remember or repress the event. However, whether the pain is healed in childhood or through repressed memory therapy in adulthood, in both cases the main event—the dog died in a car accident—is likely recalled, even if details such as model and color of car are distorted or forgotten. Therefore in general, memories are reliable for purposes of healing, but may need external or additional validation for purposes of courtroom testimony. (For more on dissociation and programming see Chapters 5 and 6. For more on denial and reliability of memories see Chapter 14.)

WHY ARE SURVIVORS REMEMBERING NOW?

Cults have counted on, and traditionally received, society's disbelief and denial. Survivors were variously diagnosed as paranoid schizophrenics, manic-depressives, and mentally ill. Instead of getting help, most survivors were condemned to mental institutions or otherwise ostracized.

Cults did not count on the return of Vietnam War veterans and, with them, the diagnosis of Post-Traumatic Stress Disorder (PTSD). Clinicians observed soldiers having nightmares and flashbacks of trauma suffered in the war. These veterans were not paranoid schizophrenics. They were reliving actual events. Clinicians realized there was a similarity between these soldiers and certain patients describing horrible deeds. For the first time clinicians began to pay attention to survivor accounts of ritual abuse. Cults did not count on survivors being believed or finding help.

Cults also did not count on the loosening of the nuclear family. For the first time in centuries children were going away to college and settling away from home. Children no longer remained "on the land" (in effect, landlocked) in family-controlled communities. Cults did not count on disclosures, prosecutions, and convictions or on children telling and being believed. They did not count on our coming into the age of information. Instant and widespread access to news and findings poses a threat. Their dogma thrives on ignorance. Information challenges the dogma. Cults did not count on the programming breaking down. Most of all, they did not count on our coming into the age of healing. Adult survivors are healing from alcoholism, sexual abuse, incest, emotional abuse, and other legacies.

This heightened awareness is helping ritual abuse survivors awaken to their own truth.

This stuff has to stop. It's so barbaric. There's so many wasted, wasted people. At some point, maybe we can help to heal others, but first I've got to heal me. If there are enough people healing themselves, it will heal the world. Jane Linn

5

Programming and Indoctrination

*I want clinicians, therapists, mental health work-
ers, and survivors to understand that for ritual abuse
survivors breaking the silence constitutes breaking
the bonds of mind control and programmed messages. The ritual torture, cannibalism, the dismemberment were all used specifically, repeatedly,
systematically over an extended period of time to
indoctrinate me to the sick and harmful worldview of
someone else.   Adam*

*This chapter deals with difficult material. It
describes a type of traumatic learning called
programming. Remember to go slowly and take
lots of breaks. If you are feeling overwhelmed,
it may be a good idea to first familiarize yourself with the tools and support systems described
in Part Six.*

There are many similarities between victims of
ritual abuse and prisoners of war (POWs) sub-
jected to rigorous thought reform. As with some
of these prisoners, ritual abuse survivors are primarily indoctrinated through the three T's: torture, terror, and threats. The difference is that these
victims are not trained soldiers but usually young
children. The war zone is not a foreign country but
the child's home, school, or other "safe" environment. The tormentors are not a recognized
"enemy." They are the child's primary caregivers.
There is no escape and no end to the war.

Ritual abuse differs from traditionally described
mind control in one key respect. It includes dissociation. Ex-POWs know that they were tortured
and brainwashed. Because of dissociation, adult
survivors of ritual abuse do not. Dissociation is a
central issue in recovery

"Mind control" carries the notion of a fixedness

or finality. This is what violators promote and want survivors to believe. However, mind control is based on learning theory using negative reinforcement, or traumatic learning. What is learned can be unlearned. In *Out of Darkness,* Dr. Walter Young points out: "The tendency is often to get lost in a 'Manchurian Candidate' syndrome of complex programming or implantation, which can create a sense of helplessness and victimization. . . . It is helpful to remember that the general task . . . is to gradually reduce the dissociative defenses, allow information that has been dissociated to be retrieved into the psyche, and counter the conditioned responses through self-awareness."

DISSOCIATION: HOW IT WORKS

Dissociation has both a general and a clinical meaning. Dissociation in its broadest sense is defined by Bennett Braun, M.D., an authority on dissociative disorders, as our ability to "sever the association of one thing from another." It is a way to escape overwhelming stimulation or unpleasantness by creating a different reality.

It is both normal and healthy to dissociate. A person lost in a mystery novel "shuts out" surrounding noise and conversation. Absentminded professors seem unaware of their surroundings, as if in a different dimension or time zone. Car drivers pay attention to the road signs but not all the buildings they pass. To try to do so would be overwhelming. The conversation, the surroundings, and buildings that are seen but not consciously noticed are dissociated and go into the unconscious. The unconscious holds our dissociated or unassimilated experiences.

Young children dissociate readily. Common forms of dissociation observed in children include daydreaming during class, playing "pretend" games, even denial, as in, "I didn't do it—Elsa did it."

In the last case, the child creates a different reality to protect herself against punishment—a natural response to fear.

All dissociation exists on a continuum. In the above examples, both the adult and the child remember the conscious as well as the dissociated events. The reader remembers reading a book and tuning out the noise. The child remembers daydreaming and tuning out the drone of the teacher's voice.

When children are tortured, they may dissociate to create a different reality. A child convinces herself, "My mother is good; this doesn't hurt, this isn't happening to me, this is happening to Elsa." However, once the danger has passed, children are unable to comprehend or assimilate what has really happened. Without outside help, they have no means of processing a life-threatening event. The event not only goes into the unconscious; a second important step takes place. The overwhelming event is split off from the child's conscious awareness and encapsulated in a barrier of amnesia. This is a self-protective survival mechanism known as dissociation in the clinical sense. It is defined, according to Brendan O'Regan, Vice-President for Research of the Institute of Noetic Sciences, as "an unconscious defense mechanism in which a group of mental activities 'splits off' from the mainstream of consciousness and functions as a separate unit." For all intents and purposes, it is not a part of the child's life or experience—not a part of who she or he is.

There are many ways to split off trauma. Some children split off the knowledge, emotions, and feelings. Coping this way may be called dissociative experience. An extreme form of splitting happens when a child creates different "selves," or "alters," to survive the trauma. The selves hold as much abuse as each can tolerate. A self may split even further to create additional fragments or selves to survive one abuse event. Each self or alter has her or his own personality.

Splitting off by creating selves or alters is called dissociative identity or multiplicity. Survivors who survived in this way are described as having multiple personalities and may be called multiples. In *Multiple Personality Disorder: Diagnosis, Clinical Features, and Treatment,* Dr. Colin A. Ross defines a multiple as "a little girl pretending the abuse is happening to someone else."

This natural body/mind defense protects children and allows them to survive into adulthood. It allows the child to learn, grow, develop, and carry on an apparently normal day-to-day life. The amnesic barrier stores abusive events in their unassimilated active form, awaiting resolution. (Part Three discusses clinical dissociation in greater detail.) As long as the child cannot deal with an event, it remains split-off. This saves children from having to face what really happened to them. If children didn't dissociate, they would die or suffer total psychological collapse. However, unassimilated traumatic events create problems for a child, and if not resolved, these problems continue into adulthood. Although the traumatic event is negated, the fear remains. It controls a child's thinking and behavior from behind the scenes.

I'd come to in the morning, open my eyes, and look out the window. I was always happiest when I'd see the color blue—because I knew I would see the sun that day and that proved to me that I was still alive. Janes

In ritual abuse, the dissociative defense may be manipulated by a cult and used to its advantage. Normal, healthy dissociation may be manipulated to form abnormal dissociative patterns. These dissociative patterns are used for purposes of programming and indoctrination. A "program" is an instruction which is activated by a specific cue. Indoctrination is forced "learning" of cult beliefs, rules, and dogma. Some cults may rely primarily on programming to control their victims; some may rely primarily on indoctrination, and some may use a combination of both. The following sections illustrate how violators may combine mind control methods with dissociation to "train" victims. Programming and indoctrination may be done by the group as part of, or apart from, cult rituals. It may also be done at home by caregivers.

PROGRAMMING: HOW IT WORKS

A tremendous amount of attention is focused on manipulating dissociation in victims of ritual abuse. To achieve this, violators make use of human learning and developmental patterns. For example, it is known that most lifelong beliefs and resulting behaviors have their roots in the crucial early developmental years. It is also believed that dissociative learning happens more readily at this time. Therefore cult indoctrination is likely concentrated before the age of six. Dissociative training may start at birth. Some survivors and therapists sense that dissociative training may even begin during pregnancy (see below).

There are many different types of programming. The following outline is based on information initially discovered by pioneering survivors who often contributed their findings anonymously, and by advocates and educators such as Jaimee Karroll of the Westword Institute. In addition, it draws on the following articles and research papers: "Obedience to Insanity: Social Collusion in the Creation and Maintenance of Dissociative States," by Martin R. Smith, M.Ed.; "Overview of the Dynamics of Ritual Abuse Programming," by Caryn StarDancer; "Working with Primal Dissociative Experiences in Adult MPD Survivors of Satanic Ritualistic Abuse," by David W. Neswald, M.A., M.F.C.C.; "Ritual Abuse, Multiplicity and Mind-Control" by Catherine Gould, Ph.D., and

Louis Cozolino; and "Common 'Programs' Observed in Survivors of Satanic Ritualistic Abuse" by David W. Neswald, M.A., M.F.C.C., in collaboration with Catherine Gould, Ph.D., and Vicki Graham-Costain, Ph.D.

THE FIRST STEP: PRIMAL DISSOCIATION

A body that is threatened with overload may instinctively use dissociation as a survival mechanism. To encourage the survival instinct, violators may overload an infant or possibly even a fetus with sensory stimulation. Cult programmers may use trial and error in order to find the right amount of overstimulation without killing the infant. They then may stimulate the infant at predetermined intervals. The stimulants may be feeling (pain, hot/cold); sound (loud noises); sight (scary faces, masks); smell (bad odors); taste (harmful chemicals, bad tastes, including blood); breathing (suffocation) and primitive reflexes (tossed in the air); deprivations (abandonment, lack of sleep, darkness, isolation); and drugging. Survivor accounts indicate that pain is frequently administered via electric current, since it does not leave scars or other noticeable evidence. The infant instinctively reacts with physiological numbing and psychological dissociation. These preliminary learned responses may later enable full body/mind dissociation.

THE SECOND STEP: DISSOCIATION TRAINING

This intial training may become the foundation for future, more complex dissociative experiences. Between eighteen and thirty months of age, children develop the ability to process information (cognitive abilities). At this point perpetrators may introduce fear, threats, and Catch-22 or double-bind experiences. These are new types of painful experiences from which there is no escape. The infant may resort to the learned option—she or he dissociates. David W. Neswald gives the following example:

A young child might be strapped to a table to have the bottoms of his/her feet cut—an extremely painful experience. The child might be told something like: "If you hold very very still it won't hurt." The child would then be cut and no matter how still the child was, he/she would nonetheless experience great pain. The child might then be told, "You weren't still enough! Next time you must be even more still." Having no other option to escape the pain, the child will then focus even more intently upon immobilizing him/herself. In so doing, the child will in effect be attempting to cut off from his/her painful sensory environment—and thus dissociate.

The double bind of "you didn't hold still enough" reinforces the idea that there is no escape. Among other things, the child may learn that she or he is completely alone; there is no outside help. Here, again, the child may learn how to cope by shutting down or splitting away from the painful feelings. Once this capacity is developed, instruction may take place. One survivor whose violators abused him using needles commented:

I remember waking up in the mornings and one of the first things I'd do is look at my hands and feet. There would never be any marks. Having no marks made it worse. Erik

THE THIRD STEP: PROGRAMMING— SECONDARY CONDITIONING AND DISSOCIATION

Programming uses dissociation and a basic principle of mind control—secondary conditioning. Famed

Russian physiologist Ivan Pavlov noticed that every time food appeared, dogs salivated. This is an example of stimulus/response, or primary conditioning. Appearance of food stimulates saliva. Pavlov next introduced a third factor. He rang a bell every time food appeared and the dogs salivated. In time, whenever Pavlov rang a bell his dogs would salivate, even if food did not appear. They learned to associate the bell with food, and their saliva appeared in expectation of receiving it. This is an example of classical, or secondary, conditioning. A normal stimulus/response (food and saliva) is paired with a secondary random cue (bell) to produce secondary conditioning, or paired association learning.

Programming builds on learning by association and adds trauma into the equation. Trauma produces amnestic dissociation, which ensures that a victim will respond predictably to a cue without conscious awareness of the associations. For example, the normal stimulus/response in a child is pain/escape. But most cult-conditioned children have been taught that there is no escape. Instead their stimulus/response becomes pain/dissociate. For example, a child may be suffocated every time she starts to cry. In this way she will be conditioned to dissociate and not cry. At each instance, a random cue such as a bright light may have been introduced. Now the child will not cry every time she sees a bright light. The child automatically makes the associations (bright light, suffocation, no crying), and therefore learning has taken place. In the future, the bright light becomes a cue that will produce the desired action (no crying). The child will never cry in the presence of a bright light, even if she or he is in distress. However, the child will be at a loss to explain why she or he cannot cry.

Clinical specialist Stephen Ray, M.A., R.N., identifies the types of cues usually used with an acronym, PACEM. It stands for pain, auditory, context, emotion, and medication. Cues can be sounds, rythmic notes, ringing sounds, snapping of fingers, a light touch on parts of the body, sometimes in a design pattern, special handshakes, special signals such as holding up three fingers, and so on. Other cues can be any object or picture of an object. It can be almost anything—a piano, a lamb, a bottle, a pattern, etc. In addition, cues can be smells such as perfumes, cooking odors, scent of burning leaves, etc. These represent the possible components that may elicit a learned response.

I can remember being a child and when they did a lot of electric wire torture and combined it with programming and hypnosis. I can remember inside my head screaming "No!" to the things they were saying and also being out of my body and thinking, "You idiots. Don't you know you can't even touch me? No matter what you do to my body you can't touch me." They thought they had me just because I was little and they could tie me down and hurt me and get me to say what they want me to say. But they couldn't touch the part inside.   Jane Linn

How are you feeling? Time for a short break? Here's an exercise you can try. Lift your shoulders and roll them back in a circular motion. Repeat several times. Now reverse the direction, rolling them in a forward motion. Check and see if it's time to stop reading for a while.

While cults may prefer to keep their methods secret and create an illusion of having special knowledge or powers, it's often a matter of applying a learned formula. You don't need to have invented soup to know how to make it. The following survivor was abused by "plain folk" parents who were unsophisticated and had little formal education.

JOSIE

The following is taken from a taped therapy session detailing an account of traumatic learning by a previously dissociated four-year-old child alter named Miranda. The survivor, Josie, is in her twenties. The words are spoken by several selves: Josie, Miranda, and an alter named Josephine. The point of this ritual, among other things, is to "prove" to Josie that she is bad and evil, just like her violators. The material has been condensed and put in chronological order for clarity. The excerpt starts before the actual traumatic incident in order to illustrate the way in which dissociated, traumatic material might surface.

> *The material that follows may be distressing to some readers. This might be a good time to take a short break or get in touch with reminders of your own safety. You may prefer to read this with a support friend present, or skip this example altogether, and continue at page 6 1, "The Aftereffects."*

I'm scared, I'm always scared. The one thing that I am all the time is scared. Sometimes it's just stark terror where you just feel like everything is going to fall apart and you're not going to live anymore. Don't go. Don't go—don't come near me. I'm afraid of you. You're hurting me. I don't know what she's doing. They're hurting me again. I can't move. I can't walk. I can't go anywhere. I feel totally boxed in. I'm in jail. I'm in a great big white twisted jail. That's where I am. They're hurting me . . . seems like they're sending shots of something into my palms and into my soles. I had to feel it. Other pain—I could get away and didn't have to feel it. But this time, I don't know, somehow I don't run away from my body. I couldn't run away from it. They somehow wouldn't let me, as though they knew if I was or wasn't there. They made sure I was there. I had to look them in the eye—then if I just slightly swerved

or anything, they increased the pain, and so I had to keep looking, and they said, "Be big bad wolf. You are a wolf." I don't like it. I don't like life. I don't like living. I don't like pain. I don't know what's living. I don't know what's dying. I don't know, I don't know, I don't know. They're making me horrible. They tell me that dirty evil things are now me. That I'm dirty. I'm evil and they're giving me another name—Josephine. Then they're going to call me by that name and they're gonna want me to behave a certain way. They say that on a full moon Josephine returns for special wolf ceremonies. They put something in front of me. My stomach wants to explode all the way. Who? Where am I? Who am I? They told me I'm not me . . . I'm me, I'm me. They said I'm not me. But I am me. Don't hurt me, don't hurt me, I can't stand anymore pain, I'll be whatever you want me to be—just don't [painful screams]. I don't wanna be the big bad wolf. Okay, okay—I'll be the big bad wolf [horrible animal crying sounds]. Big bad wolf had to go and he had to take a kitten with his teeth and he suffocated it with his teeth. Like I had to do that. Josephine is a wolf. Big bad wolf kills animals. I don't like it—I don't like it—I don't like pain, I like it, like it. I love it. Give me more. It's good. It feels good. They hurt me so much and I don't know anything except to be a big bad wolf and I did it because I didn't want to hurt anymore. I lost my kitten. I like kittens. Kittens are so nice. Can't make me kill kitten. Please. Please. I'll be the big bad wolf, but I don't want to kill kitten . . . and then I think they made me eat the kitten. It was gray, like the wolf. Wolves eat the things they kill and I had to eat the kitten. I don't want to be a big bad wolf. I'm just a little girl.

Toward the end of the session Josie remembers the following:

A few years ago I used to have these fits at night where I was having these strange body motions. In one of them I got down on all fours, jutted out my tongue and wanted to growl. It was really strange, to say the least, but I remember thinking to myself that I was a wolf. I didn't know what that was all about, but it's beginning to make sense to me now.

THE AFTEREFFECTS

The amnestic effect of dissociation minimizes the chances of detection or disclosure. Knowledge of the torture is dissociated, but the message and the fear remain. It ensures that a victim becomes indoctrinated without any conscious awareness of the event. In the above scenario, the child dissociates during the pain. She can pretend it is not happening to her but to another child—four-year-old Miranda. When the ritual is over, she doesn't remember any of it. It is now being held by a dissociated part of her called Miranda, as well as a cult-created part called Josephine. (As it turns out, Miranda holds other experiences as well.) However, learning has taken place. The child learns that Josephine is connected with great pain. She also learns that if she becomes a wolf and kills, she can bypass the pain. She now is responding in a predictable manner. When Josie hears "Josephine" in a commanding tone especially at or near a full moon she knows it's time for a ritual in which her role is to be a wolf and kill an animal. On some level, her violators have succeeded in convincing Josie that she is bad, just like them.

The message "You are a wolf" carries with it many other meanings. These messages may come directly from the violators, or they may be conclusions drawn by the child herself. The damage is the same, regardless of the source. Based upon the above incident Josie also believes the following: "I am bad. I am subhuman. I can lose control and then terrible things happen. I am not to be trusted. I cannot trust myself. I destroy the things I love. I am

unable to protect myself or anyone (or anything) else. I am powerless. I am guilty. I am unlovable. No one must ever know about me. If anyone finds out who I am, they will hate me. I will be punished for what I did. Only the cult knows what I did and still 'loves' me. Maybe I do only belong in a cult."

Messages such as these may be verbally reinforced by caregivers in day-to-day family life. Although no mention is made of a ritual, cult-raised children may receive enormous amounts of verbal/emotional abuse, which reaffirms negative messages. Another tactic may be to call the child "Josephine" in a denigrating voice, to reinforce the original programming and keep the child "in her place."

Traumatic learning may serve other purposes. For example, survivors talk about feeling as if all their internal wires are crossed. In the example, Josie's full name, Josephine, is associated with something vicious and violent. Instead of feeling pretty and nice, as all four-year-olds have a right to feel, Josie believes that her real self, Josephine, is someone bad. Even though Josie does not want to be a killer, at some level Josie knows that she has killed and that maybe she even liked it. ("Liking" it is simply a defense against the child's true, unbearable feelings. However, after repeated manipulations some children may become used to "liking" pain, thus being conditioned toward sadism. Conditioning toward sadism is another form of abuse.)

Although all children are completely good and innocent, Josie is made to feel bad and guilty. In similar fashion, violators may purposely make children associate good things with their opposites. They may teach children to associate love with hate and abandonment, trust with attack and betrayal, joy with catastrophe, and so on. The number of crossed associations and their variety are infinite (these are illustrated in Chapter 6). The confusion serves to isolate a child by making her feel like she's hiding secrets, and so she must be bad and different. This reaffirms a cult's message that she does not belong in normal society. It also causes children to avoid seeking outside help.

Because Josie believes she is bad, and bad children should be punished, she does not believe that she is entitled to the naturally good things in life. If children were allowed to follow their natural inclinations, pursuit of pleasure would compete with the designs of a cult.

They really got me from time to time, but even when I lost it, I still kept coming back. They didn't count on that. A part of me never forgot who I am. Josie

Years later, the incident and the pain remain dissociated in Josie's unconscious. Dissociated events rarely resolve themselves spontaneously. Now if Josie sees a gray kitten, she breaks into a sweat and feels panicky. Unless she is in recovery and connecting, or "associating" her experience, she has no idea why. The kitten is a reminder of her painful ordeal, and this reminder is called a trigger. Triggers can be anything—sights, smells, sounds. Breaking into a sweat and feeling panicky is called "being triggered." Josie is being triggered by reminders of her unresolved, dissociated pain.

If she hears her full name near the time of the full moon, she is being cued with the specific stimulus "Josephine." If she had found a way to escape the cult, her fear and panic are likely to be even stronger. Unconsciously she may fear punishment or death for not obeying the cue to kill. Cues are often everyday, common objects, sounds, words, etc. Violators may prefer to use ordinary items because they serve to constantly reinforce the traumatic learning. In addition, they can be given as easily in public as in private. Cult messages may be reinforced through nursery rhymes. Every time Josie hears the children's song *Who's Afraid of the Big Bad Wolf?* her crime and guilt are reinforced.

* * *

A lot of things that you learn as you're growing up, you take for granted. You never look at how you learned them, or if they were accurate, which is one of the things generational occultists take advantage of. They plant all these seeds which they know you will fill in later, but they plant them in such a way that you will fill them in to the occultist's advantage. I learned a lot of stuff. I learned about history and its occult meanings through nursery rhymes and stories from a teeny child. I just thought everybody knew them. I had to go to therapy a long time before I realized that everybody doesn't learn these things. Caryn StarDancer

The taped session provides another example of how cues may be reinforced. It has to do with names. During traumatic learning children may be called by a name similar to their own. For example, Richard may be called Richie or Rick. Catherine may be called Cathy or Kitty. Every time the child is called by her or his "nickname" the learning is reinforced, but outsiders perceive nothing unusual going on. Names may also be given an unusual spelling during rituals to reinforce the learning. So for example, Sylvia may be spelled Silvya, or Roger may be spelled Rogr. Many survivors have issues with their names—wanting to change them or spell them differently.

OTHER ISSUES

As seen in the example, during dissociation, violators may "create" bizarre events. This may play into their designs to have survivors be disbelieved. Josie did not physically become a wolf, but her pain and experience were real. The example shows how at the point of dissociation, cultists can implant any number of experiences. A tactic may be to induce more pain in the alter and cause the alter to split further. Cultists intend, and survivors may experience the pain as absolutely real, even though no further physical torture may be taking place.

In the same way that Josie can have an animal "self," a wolf, a victim can have selves of the opposite sex, older or younger selves, and selves with completely different attributes. For more on attributes of alters, see Chapter 8.

As Josie begins to connect with her experience and declares emphatically that she is a wolf, she may test the belief of even the most steadfast and supportive therapist. Some uninformed therapists, helping professionals, or people may use this piece of information to discredit Josie's entire experience. It is understandable, yet tragic, that many survivors are disbelieved. Dissociated events are hard enough to accept without having to test one's own credibility. This common questioning and denial act as powerful deterrents to recovery and healing. The details of this memory initially caused Josie to doubt her own experience. However, once she was able to accept it as real, permanent healing began to take place.

I never felt crazy. I always knew I was sane. But at the same time, the thoughts popping into my head during therapy were so weird, like outside the realm of human experience. My immediate reaction with every thought was to reject it. It took a very long time before I learned to accept my thoughts as somehow rooted in my experience, and so important to my healing.   Josie

Issues of denial and credibility of traumatic accounts are discussed in Chapters 4, 6, 14, and 15.

DIFFERENT TYPES OF TRAUMATIC LEARNING

There may be many ways to impose traumatic learning, some more complex than others. They are limited only by the knowledge and imagina-

tion of the violators. New methods discovered by Nazi's may have been introduced after WWII. It is likely that approaches and methods keep changing. Therefore it is impractical to focus on any one approach as being either representative or prevalent. The best way to break free of traumatic learning is to develop tools that will give you access to your own experiences. These are described in Parts Four, Five, and Six. Nevertheless, it may be helpful to learn about specific types of traumatic learning being discovered by survivors as possible validation for your own experience. It is also useful to know how traumatic learning may interfere with some survivors' attempts at healing.

Are you remembering to check in with yourself? How is your breathing? Are you having any feelings? A fun break may be to imagine following a leaf downstream.

RECOGNIZING CUES

As survivors move away in an often unconscious bid for freedom, they may continue to be cued through letters or phone calls. While they cannot put their finger on why, they often have a strong negative reaction to these letters or calls. While at a treatment center, one survivor received a cue to leave therapy. Here's how she discovered and broke free of its influence.

I was in the treatment center and uncovering ritual abuse when I got a letter from my mother. Immediately after reading it, I got up calmly and proceeded to Admissions and requested that I be released. The release procedure normally takes several days, and on the day of my scheduled departure my therapist approached me and asked why I felt I needed to leave. I couldn't give her a reason, I just knew that I did. We finally figured out that it had to do with the letter. I went to my room and reread it. It was a totally normal, two-page letter. Here's an excerpt:

> So happy to get your address from Bob. I just called Rita and she wants you to call or write.... Thursday I took time out to see what K-Mart had on sale. Did good on a few items. Then I found your dress behind the glass display. Only one left in the store—had to have a young man and a ladder to get it! Naturally after that—it followed me home! Soooo—happy. Easter Bunnies to you! Please let me know if you need anything else from here.

> I kept rereading it, and finally, with the help of the therapist, I realized that the phrase "followed me home" was triggering me. "Follow me home" was a message that I had to get back to the group. As soon as I got it, I no longer had to do it. But until I realized it, I was playing straight into their hands, without even knowing it.   em

The key in dismantling cult programming is to work with the internal system created for protection and survival. This, of course, will require learning to trust ourselves, our instincts, and learning to trust others, all of which may take some time.

> They can kiss my behind because they have no more power over me. I can feel when mind control is coming in. There is this tingling around my head and I start praying and it goes. They can't get in anymore.   Dave

INDOCTRINATION

In addition to programming, ritual abuse cults may use a wide variety of mind control methods, some known, some relatively obscure, for purposes of indoctrination. Methods used to indoctrinate prisoners of war in Communist China, in the former Soviet Union, and in Korea may also be found in ritual abuse. These were studied and described by Dr. Robert J. Lifton as "thought reform." Thought reform may include physical torture, manipulating and inducing guilt, alternating threats with kindness, constant surveillance, extracting confessions, and controlling information and communication.

> I would read the reports about the Salvadoran torture, about the effects of torture, and the part of a technique they learned from the CIA. You take a member that you want to destroy, and you destroy that person's family by torturing that person in front of them. My older brother and I were used in that way for each other. I just had a memory a couple of weeks ago of a German doctor torturing my brother. He had to watch me being tortured; I had to watch him being tortured. He had to watch my grandfather use me sexually. And so it has made our connections as fucked up as you can imagine. I think my brother was given this idea that I belonged to him. And so by the time I was an adolescent he acted on it. And I'm angry at him for it, but at the same time, it feels like a logical outcome of what happened to us.   Grace

INDUCING STATES OF HEIGHTENED SUGGESTIBILITY

The mind control methods illustrated above may also be supplemented by more commonly known forms of indoctrination, equally if not more difficult to undo. They may be implanted while a victim is in a state of exhaustion or relaxation and so can be more insidious. Hypnosis, drugs, humming, chanting, soft drum beats and repetitive messages, boring long lectures, or physically exhaustive ordeals can lull our instinctive, self-protective radar system. This, in turn, relaxes our defenses. With relaxed defenses, messages that normally would have been evaluated and possibly rejected are allowed through. In this state of heightened suggestibility cult messages are more easily accepted.

One survivor who had successfully overcome several intense impulses to commit suicide noticed a different quality in her most recent thoughts. Although she could see it as programmed thinking, it seemed almost more difficult to resist.

It's such a blah feeling. It's hard to describe. It feels more inevitable than it does traumatic. With the other there was always a build-up of tension and fear. But with this there wasn't any panic. There was no fight, there was no struggle, and I accepted it completely. I began to look for an opportunity for an accident in almost everything. I could be driving along the highway and begin imaging the oncoming cars smashing into me. And as long as I saw things that way, then it's inevitable—like an accident waiting to happen. Except that there was one part of me that said, "Wait—stop—let's figure this one out." Sunny

ILLUSION-CREATING TECHNIQUES

Cults may derive considerable power and authority from using various illusory techniques to call up and manipulate supernatural phenomemon. Without an understanding of how this is possible, violators may appear to have supernatural powers, especially to a child. In his paper, "The Utilization of Hypnotic Techniques in Religious Cult Conversion," Jesse S. Miller, Ph.D., reviews the findings of Milton H. Erickson in clinical hypnosis. Erickson shows how a series of indirect techniques can lead people to fulfill or "see" their own expectations.

The subjects are told in advance what is going to happen, so that an expectation or vision is already established in a person's mind. The next series of steps takes the person from expectation to fulfillment. This fulfillment is more certain in a context of heightened suggestibility and traumatic learning. A key event in achieving fulfillment is called pacing and leading. Miller writes:

. . . the hypnotist acts like a biofeedback machine, verbally commenting on every behavior of the subject. He will note that the subject is seated, that there is noise outside the room—perhaps a bus that is slowly moving farther and farther away. By continuously feeding back verifiable descriptions of the subject's reality to him, the hypnotist slowly moves into synch with his subject. He follows each breath, in and out, and notes them. Very slowly he paces his words to the subject's breathing, and then slightly alters his feedback. If he slows down, he may notice an appreciable slowing in the subject's breathing. . . . The lines between the subject and the operator become increasingly blurry as the subject allows the operator to describe more and more of the subject's experiencing of reality.

Once boundaries, which help to establish our own reality, are blurred, people may begin to "see" things that are described to them but aren't really there. This phenomenon may be even more successful when applied in a group setting. Group pressure and reinforcement act as powerful reality inhibitors. Here a person may lose her or his own reality and assume the consciousness of the group.

Two helpful articles describing specific programming and indoctrination techniques observed in some ritual abuse cults are Caryn StarDancer's "Sibylline Shackles: Mind Control in the Context of Ritual Abuse" and Dr. John D. Lovern's "Spin Programming: A Newly Uncovered Technique of Systematic Mind Control."

How are you doing? Would you like to stand up and have a stretch? Are you okay to continue? Remember that a slow, gentle pace works best.

PROGNOSIS

There are two important things to be aware of about mind control and traumatic learning. First of all, they do work. Studies done on ex-POWs and controlled experiments show that it isn't a matter of IF but WHEN most victims are converted. Even hardened, seasoned officers, who themselves may be well versed in mind control techniques, are usually unable to resist their influence. Traumatic learning evokes primal human survival reactions that have little to do with our will or voluntary processes. Recognizing this, POWs are generally not held accountable for acts committed under coercive influence.

However, it has also been found that once the "enforcer" leaves, a victim will strive to dismantle the learning and break free of it. In other words, mind control is conversion through coercion. Without coercion, traumatic learning begins to disintegrate. The body/mind strive for health, wholeness, and spirituality. Ritual abuse programming runs counter to all of these. It acts as an unwelcome foreign body within the body/mind system. A healthy body/mind system will fight to expel this "foreign body." (This does not mean destroying parts of self. See Chapters 10 and 11.) As a result, survivors have an excellent prognosis for recovery.

HOW TRAUMA MAY INTERFERE WITH HEALING

A number of factors may interfere with survivor attempts at healing. These include programmed messages, self-protective defenses, and trauma reenactment. Knowing how quickly programming begins to lose its hold, violators may try to counteract a survivor's attempts at healing. To maintain a cult "presence" within a survivor, they may create internal programs that work to ensure that coercion and therefore cult indoctrination remain intact.

The most serious types of interference are impulses to self-injure or to commit suicide.

I was inculcated with messages which were what I call mental booby traps—messages which were designed to prevent me from being able to reason my way out, from being able to see a glimmer of hope, to see any light anyplace. The messages that are implanted in us are designed to make us self-destruct rather than be able to escape the system.   Gerald

However, survivors themselves may unconsciously block the healing process. Certain selves or parts may resist help that might be perceived as interfering with their established survival system.

Sometimes too much emphasis is placed on programming, thereby overlooking fundamental psychological responses. Abused people regularly reenact trauma and victimization in cycles until the trauma is resolved. Repeated attempts at suicide and self-injury may be signs of incomplete resolution rather than separate sabotage programming.

Some people speak of "cult-created" alters that try to sabotage recovery. However, it is misleading to say that violators "create" or "implant" alters. Although violators manipulate the dissociative process, it is always the child/survivor who creates alters in order to survive. Therefore, ultimately alters are within the control of survivors. Regardless of where the interference is coming from, it delays healing. Being aware of potential problems, identifying and addressing them early in recovery, can spare survivors years of needless suffering.

COMMON TYPES OF INTERFERENCE

Sometimes victims may be allowed to leave a cult, especially during the typically rebellious teenage years. However, they may have instructions to return at prearranged times, such as on a specific birthday, on a certain cult high holiday, or during a specific year. The alternative is to commit suicide. Desire to commit suicide may escalate for survivors at the full moon, on or near their birthdays, on or near the four seasonal solstices, or after contact with their estranged parents or family members.

In addition, survivors often grapple with the following impulses:

— to not see, hear, remember, or believe anything that happened during rituals

— to doubt their every intuition or recall

— to develop inertia in seeking help, connecting with others, or nurturing themselves

— to update violators on strategic personal developments such as job changes, address changes, pregnancies, marriage, or enrollment at school

— to call in advance of important decisions in order to get "permission"

— to report to someone in the cult, if they begin to remember; this may be done by immediate confrontation with parents

I remember when I first started getting in touch with some strange experiences from my childhood. I was furious and confounded. I needed to know what was going on. I called my mother and demanded an explanation. She said she had no idea what I was talking about but offered to go to the therapist to help straighten things out. I didn't know why, but I had an immediate and very strong reaction inside that said, "No!" The image that came with the "No!" was that of an injured lamb, and a wolf offering to perform surgery.   Sophia

CONFOUNDING THERAPY

Survivors have typically been indoctrinated against seeking help from societal helpers, such as doctors, clergy, teachers, social workers, police, etc. How-

ever in earlier decades these people did not probe if an adult assured them that everything was fine.

I told the teacher that my mother was hurting me. The teacher called my mother in and they had a nice chat. I heard Mother tell the teacher that she misunderstood my poor English. But I could tell Mother was furious with me. As soon as we got home, she tied my legs over each shoulder, and my hands around my legs in back. It hurt the worst. Even though I wasn't supposed to, I cried. She locked me like that in the closet for a long, long time. But what I remember most were her words: "See? I told you no one will believe you. Don't you dare ever try that again."
Janes

Starting with the sixties, in addition to the above societal helpers, survivors may have been conditioned against seeking help through therapy as well. Because therapists are trained to probe, it appears that violators go to even greater lenghts to confound the therapy process. There may be a concerted effort to discredit therapists or interfere with their ability to work. One tactic may be to charge that therapists are suggesting ritual abuse experiences to their patients, thereby "creating" survivors. Other tactics may include harassing therapists with frivolous lawsuits. This works to interrupt the therapeutic process and depletes a therapist's financial and psychological resources.

The following are ways in which violators may try to interfere with progress in therapy.

1. Children may be set up in "sessions" with actual or mock therapists in which the therapist rapes or otherwise hurts and betrays them. One survivor was sent to a psychiatrist by her parents when she repeatedly hid behind the fish tanks at the back of the room in grade one. The psychiatrist was a member of her cult group. In his sessions he retraumatized and raped her. He used

therapy to reinforce cult lessons and teach her not to behave "abnormally" in public. Her behavior did "improve." This survivor has had great difficulty establishing trust with therapists.

2. Survivors may be taught to believe that therapists are in fact cult members out to trick them into disclosing cult secrets and will punish them for betraying the group.

3. If survivors begin to remember, their existing protective amnestic barriers may be lifted as "punishment." These survivors are then flooded with pain and emotions beyond endurance. They are expected to believe that this is the outcome of therapy and quit.

4. There may be internal impulses to "scramble" or otherwise jumble a therapist's words. The survivor hears only a jumble and is unable to understand what the therapist is saying.

Along the same lines, there may be other automatic or self-protective responses that initially ensured survival and today interfere with healing. For example, when a multiple changes personalities, it is called "switching." Sometimes survivors find themselves in a "revolving door" scenario with one alter appearing after another throwing the entire system into confusion and disarray. Infrequently, as survivors begin recovery, certain amnestic alters or dissociated parts may still be "unconverted" and so may continue to report back to a cult well into initial therapy. These alters may report on what direction therapy is taking and be given instructions on how to confound it. In addition, survivors themselves may unconsciously try to stall therapy. Some have become aware of the following patterns:

1. Alters may be set up to prevent the therapist from accessing various layers of traumatic learning. (In each of these examples "alters" may instead be compartmentalized impulses, thoughts, or feelings.)

2. Alters may come out in therapy and have fake "memories" or say confusing and outlandish things, causing the therapist to wonder if they have a "fake" survivor on their hands. They may also present a part of the problem as if it were the entire problem, thus blocking access to the key issues. Alters can sometimes misdirect the course of therapy by focusing the discussion on irrelevant issues.

3. Some alters may give survivors counteracting information as soon as they begin to disclose sensitive information. The survivor may experience these as self-spoken messages saying, "I am a liar. I am just making this up. None of this really happened" (for more on denial, see Chapter 14).

4. There may be alters who specialize in reindoctrinating inner parts, setting up new traumatic learning once the original learning has been neutralized through therapy. Until these are found and also dismantled, they may continue to confound a survivor's progress. One survivor became increasingly panicky as he worked on an article for a magazine detailing some of his abuse. In therapy he connected a traumatic memory where he had been horribly punished for "telling." He experienced immediate relief, but within days the panic returned. Eventually, he and his therapist discovered an alter who was retraumatizing other alters and renewing the "don't tell" learning. By working with this alter and befriending him, the survivor was at last able to complete his writing (techniques are discussed in Chapters 10 and 11).

I used to think I was fucked up and maybe someday I'd be able to fix myself. Now I can see that I was always okay. I was struggling to overcome incredibly difficult abuse.   Jane Linn

SELF-INJURY AND SUICIDE

In general, people consider suicide when life feels hopeless. However, survivors may feel suicidal or have impulses to self-injure after a particularly successful therapy session. In addition, when considering suicide, people generally need to figure out how to do it. Survivors reenacting their trauma or acting on internal impulses may already know how. With the impulse come automatic thoughts such as "with a gun; with a knife; with an overdose." (Remember to turn to the back page if you are having these impulses. Overcoming these impulses is discussed in Chapter 16.)

Self-injury can be severe or mild. Some survivors report wanting to scratch themselves, slap themselves, or bang their head against a wall upon disclosing cult experiences. Others punish themselves by eating harmful foods or ingesting chemicals, refusing to eat and sleep, suddenly having a series of accidents in which they cut or burn themselves, or destroying cherished personal items.

During the day I'm all stressed out. I keep getting images of ripping myself apart. I'll wake up in the morning and my pyjama sleeves will be soaked with blood. I'd find grooves in my upper arms where I've been scratching myself at night. I'd never thought of that as self-injury. Maya

THINGS TO MONITOR

It is important to keep a few points in mind. There may be more than one type of impulse counteracting therapy. Until there is clear and steady progress in recovery, you need to examine the possibility of interference, especially at anniversary dates (see Occult Holidays, page 132) and after major memories. You also need to be on the lookout for interference if therapy is proceeding too smoothly. You need to consider the possibility of interference if

you regularly find fault with each therapist you've tried, if you become more suicidal the more you progress in recovery, or if you have to keep reworking successfully covered ground.

It is harder to counteract these impulses if you are still in contact with your violators or if you have anmestic dissociated parts. These issues are resolved in time through recovery.

I think the biggest clinical breakthrough will be in the area of hypnosis and trance—seeing the extent to which we are hypnotizable or self-hypnotic, learning about people who live in trance or just go from trance to trance. Basically their life is just tranced out. We have to learn how to support people around being in their bodies, about being their genuine selves, learning what their God-given gifts were versus their programmed shame messages or intentionally indoctrinated messages, helping people to differentiate for themselves, so that they know who they are. Adam

BREAKING FREE

For the human spirit is virtually indestructible, and its ability to rise from the ashes remains as long as the body draws breath.

Alice Miller, *For Your Own Good*

People who get into recovery typically have a strong survival instinct and/or retained a strong sense of self. Staying in touch with that sense of self is one of their strongest assets in healing. Once in recovery, it becomes increasingly difficult to cause people to act against their will. At the same time, simply moving away from abusers may not guarantee freedom from early learning influences until they are addressed.

While the many mind control techniques may seem overwhelming, it's important to remember that they all represent conversion under coercion. Traumatic learning begins to lose its hold once you uncover and confront your abuse. Once the coercion is brought to conscious awareness, you can choose not to act on it. You can refuse to play their game.

Fear often prevents survivors from recovering their experience, and violators count on that. However, there are many ways to overcome fear. Initially, you may require the help of a competent, experienced facilitator. The tools and approaches to break traumatic learning are described in Parts Four and Five. Finding the right help is discussed in Part Six.

Survivors are exceptionally strong, creative people. If you survived the original abuse, you have what it takes to make it through recovery. Each survivor is a testament to human resourcefulness and the quest to live as free human beings.

I think life is tough, but extremely worthwhile. No matter how disastrous, overwhelming, overloading, demanding, challenging, tricky, confusing, or scary it is, there's life and I wouldn't want to miss it as long as I'm here. The tools are there and it was worth reclaiming all parts of myself. Today, for the first time, I feel alive in this world.   Caryn Star-Dancer

6

Cult Conditioning

They go for the soul. But souls are so resilient. People can do the most horrible things imaginable. But we can also overcome just about anything and still be striving for health and wholeness and spirituality. Jane Linn

The following chapter describes the nature of rituals that, using traumatic learning, form the backbone of cult conditioning. The survivor quotes may be especially difficult or triggering. To minimize being retraumatized, you may want to read only the text and omit the survivor quotes altogether. You may consider limiting your reading to one paragraph or one page before taking a break. You may want to have a support person present or readily available. There will be a sentence describing the nature of the subject matter preceding certain quotes. You can then decide to bypass the quote and continue reading at the next quote or paragraph.

Some survivors are concerned about "remembering" things that were not from their own experience. They may wonder if they are incorporating something they have read or heard from others into their own history. If this is your concern, you may decide not to read this chapter at this time. Once you are at a point in recovery where you are more able to trust your own experience, you may wish to read it for validation.

HISTORICAL FRAMEWORK

Some people find it hard to believe that cultists are "so devious" and "so sophisticated" as to figure out the many complex levels of indoctrination described in this chapter. However, the events described occur in many familiar contexts, ranging from the child bully who delights in terrorizing smaller children, to cruel hoaxes played by sorority/fraternity groups on their initiates, to familiar conversion tactics applied by various cult groups as described in Chapter 5. As mentioned in Chapter 4, much of the activity stems from reenactment needs of the violators. It doesn't take superior intelligence or insight to follow another's lead or a script, or to reenact one's own abuse.

In her paper "Sadistic Abuse: Definition, Recognition and Treatment," Jean M. Goodwin, M.D., writes:

As we access earlier research about sadism, recent accounts of perpetrators' attempts to gain mind control over their victims come into contextual focus. As Krafft-Ebing noted, emotional terror and successful deception are as important to sadists as is the infliction of bodily harm. One study found that the victim's facial expression of pain and terror, achieved by whatever means, provided the sadist's most direct source of satisfaction (Heilbrun and Seif, 1988). As a sadistic serial killer put it: "The pleasure in the complete domination over another person is the very essence of the sadistic drive" (Dietz, Hazelwood, and Warren, 1990). Careful interviewing of sadists and their victims indicates that many methods are used to achieve total domination or "soul murder" (Shengold, 1989) of the victim. Such methods, used by political torturers as well as by criminal sadists, include: control of basic bodily functions such as eating, sleeping, and elimination; physical beatings; physical torture; pyschological torture; control of information and misinformation; confinement and sensory deprivation; rape and genital mutilation; witnessed violence and threats; forced labor and poisoning. Gelinas (1993) has used the term "malevolence" to describe the emotional abuse found in these contexts. Induction into violence is an ultimate

technique and test of this process in which an initial victim recruits new victims and eventually becomes a co-perpetrator.

In *Rediscovering Childhood Trauma,* Goodwin recounts the specific types of abuse recorded by the Marquis de Sade in *The 120 Days of Sodom:*

What passions are detailed in story and deed? To mention a few: locking in cages, threatening with death, burying in coffins, holding under water, threatening with weapons, drugging and bleeding, tying upside down and burning, wearing robes and costumes, staging of mock marriages, defecating and urinating on victims, killing of animals, having victims witness torture, having them witness homicides, pouring or drinking blood, and taking victims to churches and cemeteries. I mention these acts in particular because these are 15 of the 16 types of allegations found characteristically in children and adult psychiatric patients complaining of "ritual abuse" in the 1980s and 1990s (Findlehor et al. 1988; Hudson 1989; Snow and Sorenson 1990; Young et al. 1991). The only one missing from de Sade's (1789/1987) inventory is photography. Clearly, its absence is due simply to lack of technology; its place is taken by use of peepholes and use of stages at the orgies, where each libertine could be seen to perform with his entourage of victims.

The abuses described by the Marquis de Sade openly were and are being used secretly as elements of traumatic learning in ritual abuse cults. A single event of traumatic learning is relatively straightforward to undo once the trauma and cue are identified. However, conditioning, which involves repeated instances of traumatic learning, takes more time and patience to neutralize.

CONDITIONING

The process of raising children is a process of conditioning. Through repetitive responses (approval/disapproval) and learning (when I skin my knee, Mommy will make it better), children become accustomed to certain ideas and values. They may be conditioned to expect three meals a day or to go hungry. They can be conditioned to expect support and success as an adult or rejection and failure. The sum total of a child's experiences conditions their response to life events and determines who they are.

A healthy society tries to raise children to become self-sufficient, independent, autonomous adults. Cult-abused children are conditioned to be dependent and subservient. Cult conditioning uses traumatic learning with or without cues in order to indoctrinate a child into a negative, destructive view of themselves and others. Through repetition, violators try to ensure that a lesson is not only learned but ingrained. Conditioning is a form of training.

Cultists are able to accomplish this training for two reasons. First of all, they usually have access to a child in a totally controlled environment—most often in the home, sometimes in child care settings. Secondly, tremendous indoctrination and energy are focused on silencing a child or a victim about the abuse. Fear, torture, humiliation, and lies are used to coerce children into surrendering their free will. Conditioning is used to shape and interpret a child's experience of the abuse and the adult survivor's recollection of it. Intense brainwashing prevents remembering, knowing, or telling. It also creates confusion that undermines survivors' belief in their own perceptions.

In traditional cult families the rituals are predetermined. The onslaught of abuse is intense and continuous, because it aims to override a child's basic drives and instincts. This training may start at birth and continue as long as the victim's caregivers are cult-active or the victim remains in the cult. The indoctrination follows a prescribed regimen which is usually carried out meticulously and with regularity. The program is designed to destroy a child's sense of self and to redefine it to suit the aims of the cult. The more violators succeed in creating splits, or alters, the closer they get to their goal. In other words, they try to destroy who *you* are, in order to make you who *they* are.

Although the traumatic learning described in Chapter 5 sounds horrendous beyond belief, many survivors report that their worst abuse did not occur within a cult context but at home. Most survivors are regularly abused at home, because the violators' addictive need for violence escalates over time. Violators need "fixes" in between cult rituals, and increasingly intense violence for emotional and sexual release. At home there are no protocols or rules, and so violators are free to do as they please.

At the treatment center they had a formula for determining and helping us to look and see how much abuse there really was--to try and determine how many times a month you were abused, or how many times a week or a day. And then you multiply that by the amount of years, and for me it ended up being something like 7,723 times. And it was the first time that I owned up to how badly abused I really was. I had always minimized it. I don't anymore.   Alice

People are often surprised at the detatched way in which some survivors recount horrendous events. This may be mistakenly interpreted as lack of empathy or emotion. It in fact may speak of the opposite. It may indicate that emotions and feelings were so overwhelming that the child had to disconnect from them to survive. A parallel example is found in POWs or survivors of political torture who recount the horrors of their experience with the same characteristic, telltale detachment.

How are you doing? For a break it may be fun to think about trying to catch a snowflake.

REAL OR STAGED?

Many factors may affect a child's perceptions during cult rituals. In every case, there is trauma that causes dissociation. Reframing an unbearable reality through dissociation helps a child to cope. This reframing may affect a child's interpretation of an experience. As Alice Miller points out in the afterword to the American edition of *Thou Shalt Not Be Aware*, "Fantasies always serve to conceal or minimize unbearable childhood reality for the sake of the child's survival; therefore, the so-called invented trauma is a less harmful version of the real, repressed one."

A child's experience is further confused by cult tactics to manipulate a child's perception, interpretation, and experience. Violators may use various ploys such as starvation, sleep deprivation, and prolonged isolation in enclosed spaces with rodents, spiders, or snakes to exhaust a child physically and mentally.

As explained in Chapter 5, when children mobilize their energies for survival, they abandon their critical faculties. In this state of heightened suggestibility, cult violators instruct their victims. In addition, violators may use drugs and hypnosis to further distort a child's experience. In this manipulated environment, cult rituals take place. Some are real, some are staged.

It is not very difficult to deceive a child. As children, we naturally trust adults and look to them for direction and explanations. Children believe it when they are told that storks bring babies and Santa Claus brings Christmas gifts. Whether an event is real or not hardly matters. Children accept the meaning of abuse as interpreted for them by their caregivers on faith. A recently enacted Illinois law prohibiting ritualized abuse states in part:

(a) A person is guilty of ritualized abuse of a child where he or she commits any of the following acts with, upon, or in the presence of a child as part of a ceremony, rite or any similar observance:
(1) actually *or in simulation* [author's italics], tortures, mutilates or sacrifices any warm-blooded animal or human being;
(2) forces ingestion, injection or other application of any narcotic, drug, hallucinogen or anaesthetic for the purpose of dulling sensitivity, cognition, recollection or resistance to any criminal activity;
(3) forces ingestion, or external application, of human or animal urine, feces, flesh, blood, bones, body secretions, nonprescribed drugs or chemical compounds
(4) involves the child in a mock, unauthorized or unlawful marriage ceremony with another person or representation of any force or deity, followed by sexual contact with the child;
(5) places a living child into a coffin or open grave containing a human corpse or remains;
(6) threatens death or serious harm to a child, his or her parents, family, pets, or friends that instills well-founded fear in the child that the threat will be carried out; or
(7) unlawfully dissects, mutilates, or incinerates a human corpse.

Whether events happened exactly as recalled or not is irrelevant. What is relevant is the experience of the child. Sometimes it is not so much the torture and horror of an event as the meaning that is repeatedly given to a child—e.g., "It is your fault." The way the experience is interpreted by the violators and resulting trauma shape a child's self-image and remains until it is refuted through recovery.

THE REAL UNREAL

In some cases a ritual is staged. Knowing an event may have been staged helps to diminish its traumatic aftereffects for some, but not all, survivors. However to heal the trauma, the event usually needs to be recalled and understood exactly as it was experienced. As survivors gain perspective—usually towards the final stages of their healing—some begin to see some rituals in the light of additional possibilities explained below. These explanations are not offered as excuses or rationalizations for the pain, which is not diminished, but as possibilities for a deeper healing in some instances.

Many violators leave nothing to chance. Every event may be carefully orchestrated and manipulated. In looking back, some survivors see the ways in which a few of the events were in fact staged. Some survivors today recognize that in some instances the rituals were actually rehearsals for the real event. This is especially true for rituals involving extreme violence or human sacrifice.

(The following example of giving birth is common but very traumatic. You may wish to skip the next paragraph.)

Violators may inject a very young child with drugs or give her powerful laxatives that produce strong abdominal cramps and simulate labor pains. After much commotion, cultists may produce a fetus telling the little girl it is her baby. The fetus is then consumed by the group. The child is crazy with rage and grief. With several repetitions of this scenario, a child begins to respond with withdrawal from the reality of the experience and emotional numbness. This plays directly into the aims of a cult. Now the child has been properly "trained." When an actual delivery and sacrifice occurs, the child is already numbed to its horror. She or he reacts with conditioned dispassion, keeping the solemnity of a high cult ritual undisturbed

while an actual killing takes place. In some cults, even the "training" may be done with actual victims. In either case, the cues and triggers implanted during these preparatory rituals may be repeatedly invoked. As a result, the "reality" of the traumatic experience is continually being reinforced.

Sense of time may be profoundly altered in dissociative states. Very long periods may seem very short, and vice versa. Children may be in a ritual for an hour but be told, and believe, that three days have gone by. This again challenges the credibility of children who may try to tell. A violator may perform "psychic surgery" by telling a child that she or he is implanting a scorpion inside the child's stomach. The scorpion will bite if the child tries to think bad thoughts about the cult. The child is then blindfolded, and a pin is run across his stomach while ketchup or another red substance is applied. The child is told he is being cut open with a knife. When the blindfold is removed and the child sees the red "blood," he is convinced that a scorpion was indeed implanted. To further convince children of their power, cult members often feign supernatural abilities, producing a god or spirit during a ceremony. Children invariably experience these manipulations as real. However, sometimes during recovery, the manipulation is found out.

I started having flashbacks and I'm crying, "This thing is going to get me." And I curled up in a ball and I just started crying and shaking and reliving the memories of being sexually abused by this horrible, grotesque monster with devil-like eyes. And my therapist didn't know what to do. To this day she believes that it was divine intervention, because she really didn't know what to do, but she says, "I want you to look away from the mask and look down." And I kept looking down, and it was all black—black, black, black. And she says, "Keep looking." And I get down to the bottom, and there were these black shoes and white socks. And she goes, "It's a person." And I say,

"No, it's not a person. It's a monster." And she kept making me look, and there was a black robe, a black cape/robe thing, white socks, and regular black tie shoes, like men's dress shoes. Then as he moved towards abusing me part of his robe flew open and you could see the hair on his legs and he had no clothes on, and I saw that it was a man. Alice

The list of similar set-ups and manipulations is unending. More are described throughout the course of this book.

There is something inside that just won't give up— ever, ever, ever! Janes

THE UNREAL REAL

As a baby I was given shots between my toes so the needle marks wouldn't show. Sasha Trillingham

Very often survivors are baffled by lack of scars evidencing their abuse. This plays into their chronic self-doubt, doubts of the general public, and purposes of cult violators whose aim it is to prove survivors delusional. Some events that seem impossible from our culturally protected and shaped experience are in fact possible. For example, some survivors who are multiple have the ability to heal more completely and quickly than the general population (see Chapter 8). In addition, it is possible to cut a child along the dermatome line (going with the "grain"), resulting in less scarring.

My father was a teacher in the cult. He taught and trained great young minds on how to do ritual surgery. Adam

Violators may know that genital lacerations can heal very quickly. While more research is needed, preliminary studies seem to bear this out. In their paper "Genital Injuries Resulting from Sexual Abuse: A Longitudinal Study," Drs. McCann, Voris, and Simon found:

Wound healing by regeneration may be complete within 48 to 72 hours, while further differentiation of new epithelium [new cellular layer of tissue] may take 5 to 7 days. Final restoration of normal tissue may take up to 6 weeks. Deeper injuries usually involve the process of "repair" [and] subsequent development of scar tissue. . . . Most scars will mature in 60 days. . . . In summary, the genital injuries of these children healed rapidly. Over time the jagged, irregular margins of the hymen created by these acute injuries smoothed out and became difficult to detect without use of a multimethod examination technique.

Some survivors are baffled by memories of repeated rapes, yet they also remember bleeding during their first conscious experience of intercourse. This would seem to imply that their hymen had not been broken. Like other genital tissue, hymens can heal and regenerate very quickly. While they may not return to their original intact shape, the regenerated hymen and scar tissue may bleed after a period of sexual inactivity.

Many survivors report giving birth at extremely young, "medically impossible" ages. However, it is interesting to note that according to Muslim law, a nine-year-old girl may be married provided she has begun menstruation. This would imply that some girls are menstruating before the age of nine.

Furthermore, a child can be given hormones to prevent pregnancies or to advance puberty, encouraging premature ovulation, menstruation, breast development, and pubic hair. Although studies are needed, this information suggests possible explanations for "impossibly young" pregnancies.

The credibility of survivor accounts is often challenged by the sheer number of reported victims and the often posed question, "But where are the bodies?" Goodwin cites a study of thirty criminals whose acts of excessive violence included such hallmarks of sadism as bondage, imprisonment, and torture:

> In view of the difficulty of finding bodies to document ritual abuse, it is of interest that concealment of the bodies of victims was admitted by 20 of the 30 offenders (67%) . . . (Dietz et al. 1990). Of the known murder victims of these offenders, 28% were discovered in situations where the body was so destroyed by fire, burial, or decomposition that identification of the victim was initially impossible. . . . How dangerous are these 30 sadistic offenders? Only 22 of the 30 had killed, but those 22 had logged 187 known murder victims. . . . Of those who had killed, 5 of the men accounted for 122 of the murders.

Survivors report that sometimes bodies are buried in excavated grave sites. The violators dig deeper, bury a body, and cover it to the point of the original excavation. The designated body is then buried on top. Bodies may also be disposed of by cremation at mortuaries or in furnaces.

Survivors also have witnessed "superhuman" feats performed by people in altered states of consciousness. In *The Serpent and the Rainbow,* Wade Davis, a Harvard scientist, witnessed the following at a vodun ceremony: "The initiate, a diminutive woman, tore about the peristyle, lifting large men off the ground to swing them about like children. She grabbed a glass and tore into it with her teeth, swallowing small bits and spitting the rest onto the ground."

Not all such feats are performed in altered states. An August 9, 1993, letter to the editor of *Newsweek* reads:

Your reporter says of fire walking, "Even having walked the walk, I can't explain it." There is, however, an explanation: It is nearly impossible to get blisters or singed toes in five short steps over wood coals because of their extremely low heat conductivity. Scientists have performed fire walks with Band-Aids on the soles of their feet. The paper and plastic of the bandages are unchanged by the 1,200-degree coals. The explanation for fire walking lies not in mind control or chanting but in elementary physics.

Some survivors report being repeatedly bitten by rattlesnakes, but not dying or becoming critically ill. However, it is possible to "milk" venom from snake glands, rendering the bites nonpoisonous. The glands can also be surgically removed.

WHAT'S REAL, WHAT ISN'T

The real tragedy is that the actual circumstances of abusive childhood events may never be known. The child, however, believing every staged event to be real, has been traumatized. Until the event is recalled and healed, the aftereffects continue to shape and affect a survivor's life. Except where a child noticed the manipulations, the event has been experienced as real, it is dissociated as real, it is stored as real, and so it is relived as real in recovery. Survivor quotes in this chapter reflect the way in which ritual experiences are recalled. The uncertainty makes dealing with these memories even more difficult. It results in more, not less, pain. The fact that the trauma and suffering were needless makes the entire result all the more tragic.

It's hard to know how to describe just how much trauma and pain there is to be a survivor. It shatters your faith in people to have lived this shit. And I have trouble believing that anyone would want to hear what they did or want to help. But I'm working on having more faith in people.   Bea

I hope you're remembering to go slowly and check in with yourself often. The next section deals with more difficult and intense material. This may be a good time to take a break.

NO WAY OUT

To ensure compliance, violators may stage events to convince a child that the cult is all-seeing and all-knowing, controls supernatural phenomena, and is omnipotent. Events may be staged to convince a child there is no possibility of outside help and never will be. Children are taught to never reach out to anyone—no matter how nice they seem.

I was three years old. A man came to our house. He seemed very kind and very nice. He picked me up on his lap, and when no one was looking, he said, "Sometimes they are not very nice to you, are they?" And I nodded. It meant so much to have somebody know. But at the next ritual I got punished extra hard. They told me they knew I that I told someone things I shouldn't have—that they know everything. As punishment for telling, they made me eat shit. Roxana

Many "no way out lessons" are reinforced with terror. Children are repeatedly threatened with death and convinced that those who disobey cult commands, die.

(The following quote describes killing and dismemberment. You may chose to continue at the text following.)

I'm inside an old abandoned house that used to be part of a large estate. It has a room which has shackles that are attached to the wall, literally embedded in

the concrete in the wall. It was the scene of a ritual. A man and his wife were to be disciplined for betraying the cult. The man looked to be in his late twenties. He had dark hair and blue eyes and was very thin and gaunt. He begged me to help him escape. He was hog-tied. It's a way of tying people where they are lying on their stomach and there's a rope that's attached between the legs, the wrists, and the throat, so that if you struggle too much, you're strangled. It was real clear to me that he was afraid for his life. At the same time the woman was being tied up on the altar. Her breasts were cut off and thrown into the ceremonial fire. A man shoved a knife into her and proceeded to cut out her heart. This woman was dismembered. A crazed man pummeled me with one of her limbs, forcing me to eat a part of it. Meanwhile the man was tied to a chain and the end of the chain was flung over a tree limb. They hoisted him up and as they did so he was positioned over the fire, and his hair caught on fire first, which was followed by the rest of him, and I can still hear his screams.   Matthew

Children in fear of their life are extra careful not to disappoint or disobey their violators.

My childhood was spent walking on eggshells. Erik

There is a major "investment" in training cult-abused children. Children-in-training are likely not meant to die but to be terrorized into subservient compliance. Survivors who try to die may be saved against their will.

When I was three years old, I tried to drown myself in the lake. I went under several times. My father was watching me and dove in and swam across the lake and hauled me out. I had gone unconscious, but when I came to, I remember feeling angry that he'd pulled me out. He wasn't saving me for me. He was saving me so that he could keep abusing me.   Bea

Children are prevented from committing suicide by threats of killing or destroying their pets, loved ones, siblings, or friends. Some have antisuicide programming. One survivor remembers going unconscious and reviving. He was told that he died and that the cult brought him back to life. This happened many times. He "learned" that he had no control over his own life. There indeed was no way out.

They continually threaten death but never let you die. They took my ultimate power. I believed I had to live—like it or not.   Janes

Like it or not, children-in-training continue to live. Many have no idea how they made it through. Even after abandoning hope, from out of somewhere strength comes to them.

I'm sure I dissociated, because I see most of my memories from a distance. And I always prayed to die, but I just never got my prayers answered. But I got some kind of strength and comfort instead. I learned how to hang on just a bit longer, just a little bit longer, just one foot in front of the other. I don't know—I guess I was supposed to live.   Jane Linn

How are you feeling? The remainder of this chapter continues to address very difficult material, so remember to take care of your safety needs.

CRITICALLY TIMED MANIPULATIONS

An essential formula for cult conditioning is summed up by the thief Fagan in Charles Dickens's *Oliver Twist.* Fagan needs a child to commit a robbery. He tells another thief, Sikes, to recruit a young boy named Oliver Twist for the job. Fagan offers Sikes the following advice: "Once let him feel he's one of us. Once fill his mind with the idea that he has been a thief, and he's ours—ours for life."

Violators aim to irrefutably establish several ideas in a child's mind: I was born bad; my life is in danger; the cult has total power; there is no way out. As shown in Chapter 5, each traumatic learning event carries countless negative messages, verbal and nonverbal. The following examples show patterns of abuse taken from a wide variety of ritual abuse cults. (For simplicity, only a few negative messages are discussed with each abusive event.) They cover the most comprehensive patterns of abuse starting from before birth and progressing into adulthood. Not all ritually abused survivors experienced all of these. However, the more traditional (multigenerational) the family, the more likely that the child was assaulted at every stage of development. Such a child would have experienced hundreds of the types of set-ups described.

Virtually every child resists and fights assaults on their selfhood. Children who somehow managed to find a way to persevere have a chance to reclaim their identity during the course of recovery. Those who could not find a way to persevere through the assaults begin to identify with a cult. Even then, some look for a way out after reaching adulthood.

THE BASIC APPROACH

Children have developmental needs that ensure their survival, growth, and maturity. These needs were first identified as a hierarchy by psychologist Abraham Maslow: basic/physiological, safety/security, love/belongingness, self-esteem and self-actualization. Each of these fundamental needs is denied or manipulated at critical stages of a child's development. The categories are loosely based on several models of child development. They do not represent a particular child training strategy but rather serve to illustrate common patterns of abuse. The examples of the rituals can overlap defined stages or be applied at more than one stage.

Prenatal The introductory page to *The Secret Life of the Unborn Child* states:

Long before they're born, your children are thinking, feeling, and even acting. What happens to them before—and as—they are born may profoundly shape the people they will become.

The authors Thomas Verny, M.D., and John Kelly write:

Today we know that from the sixth month of pregnancy onward and especially from the eighth month, memory templates are laid down that follow recognizable patterns. . . . The fact that memories retrieved from this period have a recognizable shape and form tends to confirm the notion that the brain is operating near normal adult levels by the third trimester.

At a time when an unborn child is enjoying the safety and security of the womb, cult-abused children may experience their first threat.

At one point [the therapist] did regression work. I became like a fetus, and I could see something coming up and poking. I have no idea whether my mother was trying to abort me, whether she was being abused as part of a cult ritual, whether she was being raped. I just know something was going on.   Matthew

Several survivors sensed something like the following:

It's like they intended to do all this [to me]. It seemed like this was planned from before I was born. Katharine

This is only the first step in lifelong training to deny children their right to self-affirmation.

Birth to Six Months This should be the happiest of occasions. Children are supposed to be welcomed into the world, loved, held, and nurtured. The messages they need to receive are, "You're special and important. You are alive. You have a right to be here. I am glad you exist." A cult-abused child at this time may be experiencing the following:

The very first impression I had was that nobody loved me. Nobody looked at me or smiled at me. I was never held or enjoyed. I was usually left to cry for hours—hungry, cold, or wet. When Mother did come to feed me her milk tasted sour. Today, when I think about it, I want to vomit. The first ritual memory I have is three very hideous old hags standing above my crib. They had hoods on that looked like old torn rags. I couldn't move, but I remember feeling really frightened. They each held a candle and were chanting. It feels as if I was six months old.   Erik

The first, most basic physiological needs may be denied or manipulated. At a time when children need human contact, they may be starved for touch. Their basic life needs of food and drink may be provided by default. Breathing may be manipulated through intermittent smothering. The messages a cult-raised child receives are: I do not belong to anyone. I do not exist. No one cares for me. I am not loved. Something is wrong—with me. The infant begins life ashamed, enraged, and fearful.

Some cults may place a high premium on physical strength and endurance. In these groups the abuse is used for conditioning and also as a weeding-out process to ensure "survival of the fittest." Children who do not thrive at each stage of the assaults may be allowed to die.

Six to Eighteen Months At this stage children begin to explore their environment. They delight in sounds, colors, objects, tickling, and playing peek-a-boo. A cult-abused child may be experiencing variations on the following:

I have body memories and visual memories about lying on a table in a room with ceiling fans, and I had memories about being shocked with electric voltage. I can see what's happening, but I can't see who's doing it. It's painful for me to look up and see that these are people that I know.   Matthew

A cult-abused child learns: The world is dangerous and hostile. It's scary to explore. I always need to be on guard. I belong to people who hurt me. I am bad. I am afraid.

Eighteen Months to Three Years Children begin to interact with the world around them. They begin to form a sense of self. They begin to think and feel for themselves. They may delight in saying "No!" The "No!" helps them separate themselves from others—affirming that they have some control. They begin to form their own thoughts based on testing reality.

Cult-abused children are not allowed to express their own thoughts or feelings. Thoughts and feelings may be continually manipulated and controlled.

I had a favorite puppy. He was brown and white. They killed him. I cried. Then they killed my big gray cat. They told me it was because I cried.   Sophia

At this critical time a cult-abused child's feelings may be twisted or denied. Anger is usurped:

(The following quote describes a ritual of physical pain combined with emotional manipulation. You may want to skip down to the second quote.)

The Brothers put me into a stream and stood around me in a half circle. I stood with my wet panties clinging to my skin. The rest of me was naked. Mr.

B. said that I was to be rebaptized. He then took his finger and with blood from the cuts on my face (from a previous ceremony) drew a circle on my chest, with twelve spokes around the circle—four longer ones and eight shorter ones. I think the spoked circle was to represent the sun. Next he took a needle and pricked the end of one of the spokes in a way so as to taunt me. It was uncomfortable and it hurt and I hated it. As he poked me, I got angry. I was horribly punished for that. Then he poked me on the next spoke. I got less angry but still had some anger. I was punished even worse for that. At the third spoke, as he pricked me, I stood silent. I was commanded to show rage—to hit anyone and lash out at the big people around me. I did. When I was through, every adult I hit, hit me back twice as hard and twice as many times. At the fourth spoke, Mr. B. didn't prick but pushed the needle in and kept pushing. I dissociated and was gone. I think I was told to, and did, smile. So he continued through the twelve spokes. By the twelfth spoke, I'd totally stopped trying to figure out what was going on. My legs felt brittle and numb in the cold water. I was theirs. My will was gone. I don't think I ever tried to analyze things after that day. I stopped trying to figure these people out. I learned that the very best strategy was to look to them for directions on how to act, and hope for the best. They toweled me off and we all piled into one of two cars. I sat on someone's lap on the way home. My brother sat on someone else's lap. He had been watching the whole ceremony. No one spoke to us. We were forbidden to speak to one another during the ride home and never allowed to talk about that ceremony or any cult ceremony. These were "high order" secrets. The Brothers talked to one another as we drove home. For them, my brother and I did not exist.   Janes

I've tuned in to a time when I think there were something like angels which have probably been with me since I was a child and have helped me survive. I think that as child I saw things—really beautiful things in the garden. And I feel like the beautiful things are still there. They're just a positive force or influence that saw me through some really hard times, and now they're more like a background presence. I feel it, but I don't have to do anything. CeeCee

As developing children are testing their own reality, cult-abused children may be having their reality confounded:

I saw a man in a cage. I watched them "kill" him. Later I saw him walking down the street. Sunny

Children may be confused with statements such as: What you see isn't true. What we tell you is true. You cannot trust yourself or what you see. You can't trust anything. Rely on us. You are nothing without us. We know and see everything. Having no way of knowing that the event was staged, children gradually begin to abandon their own reason and instincts. They may also be taught dogma that inverts societal values. Many cult-raised children are indoctrinated with edicts such as: Black is white; white is black. Good is evil; evil is good. Up is down; down is up. Love is hate; hate is love.

(The following quote describes cannibalism. You may want to continue reading at the next paragraph.)

There was this big celebration over Easter and we were celebrating death instead of life. And they stimulated me to give birth to a child. And that child was put on my abdomen and killed. And communion was served—the baby's raw flesh and blood. Christi Joy

Easter can be a particularly difficult time for some survivors. One survivor found a journal entry years before she had the memory:

I too was crucified, nails in my palms. The only difference is nobody cared. Sophia

Constantly threatened and abused, cult-raised children may become outer-directed instead of being inner-focused. When other children are delighting in their experience of self, cult-abused children may grow to hate and so abandon their self. Instead of flourishing in their environment, their focus may become survival. Survival means, "I have no thoughts, I have no feelings of my own. I must watch and learn what my guardians want. If I 'get it right' I might survive. Nothing in life is certain." These lessons continue to be reinforced and usually become ingrained for life.

Repeatedly confounded and confused, a child is afraid to trust her or his own perceptions. Most turn over interpretations and directions to their violators. Some act out their usurped feelings in apparently bewildering ways. They may become angry and hostile and go into a rage for no apparent reason. Others may become exceedingly compliant. They no longer even conceive of saying "No." They learn how to become what others expect and want. These children are often praised for being exceedingly polite and well-behaved. The credit for such "model" children invariably goes to the parents.

How are you feeling? If a break feels right, you might want to go for a short walk. If you feel like screaming or crying—do it! Remember to keep checking with yourself often and honoring your own needs.

Three to Six Years This is one of the most critical stages of child development, when foundational ideas about self and the world are formed. Many cult manipulations may be concentrated here. Children are beginning to explore their sexuality. They want to know the difference between girls and boys and may even fall in "puppy love." They may play at being Mom and Dad, having babies, and socializing. Violators may confuse a child about love, marriage, and sexual responsibilities. Children may be married in secret ceremonies to other cult members, often their own relatives, parents, or siblings.

The joy of love and innocent attraction are denied a cult-abused child. "First love" unions may be orchestrated to be failures. Children may be set up to "fall in love" with another, often older cult member who will abandon and betray them. Cultists may kill a child's first love, blaming the death on the child.

(The following quote describes torture, dismemberment, and humiliating assaults on sexuality. You may choose to continue reading at the next paragraph.)

I was five and this little girl was five. I really liked her tons. I was crazy about her. I thought she was the greatest. She and I were to be married. I was being trained to fulfill her sexually, which was very important, because we were to be some sort of special couple— like the perfect cult couple. So my grandmother and her girlfriends did the sexual training, which was a lot of sexual torture and humiliation. My mother was to be a test case for me—like priming me for this marriage through a series of rituals—to see how good I was sexually. I failed my mother, because I was unable to fulfill her sexually. And the whole thing was like, I have no sexual needs. Only she had sexual needs, and I was unable to fulfill them. I was embarrassed and humiliated. I was a failure. And because I failed, my mother was killed and tortured and skinned alive. They put hooks through her ribs, her bones were exposed. I knew later that it wasn't my mother that they killed but some other woman made to look like my mother. They tortured and killed and dismembered the woman. Then I had to watch the little girl pleasing all the older men in the cult sexually. She and they were all laughing at me about how unsuccessful I'd been, about how stupid I was. Because she could do it, and these men could do it—so what's wrong with me? And I had to kill the little girl because I had failed her. And we cut her skin off and hung her onto these hooks, and then they had sex with her corpse

. . . stuff like that, in front of me. And what I didn't understand at the time was that the whole thing was set up so that I would fail.   Adam

At a time when some children go through rites of passage such as First Holy Communion, a cult-raised child's rite of passage may be sexual union and/or marriage with the devil. The meaning of marriage and family may be completely warped for a child through cult-sanctioned incestuous relationships and marriages.

I had two uncles who were my mother's brothers, but they were my age so I was raised with them as my brothers. Later I married one of them in a satanic ceremony and he fathered my daughter. So my family was very much into the incestuous part of keeping things all within the family, and keeping the world confused, if not us.   Christi Joy

Instead of being a haven, a cult family is a place of terror.

I remember being taught to sit at my father's feet. And there was this altar there, and it's the first time I remember my mother actually walking away from me, actually placing me on the altar and walking away. And I remember crying and screaming, "Mommy Mommy, Mommy, don't leave me." And she just said, "You don't belong to me anymore. You belong to the devil. And the devil was this tall man who was my father, but I didn't know it. He wore a devil's mask. For years I thought that my father was really the devil and that when they had those ceremonies, the devil part in him came out. And I know today I still struggle with men, because of that fear that the devil part of them will come out eventually.   Christi Joy

Violators may assign children a special mentor/companion who both helps them and betrays them:

I have images of being awakened and carried out of the house in the middle of the night through this wooded area to this quarry. I was being held by a bearded man who was very, very gentle and nurturing with me. And we stood on the sidelines and we watched what was going on. That night, people were cutting cult symbols into their chest and foreheads and being threatened with death. And this bearded man kept telling me to watch closely. That everything was okay. That I didn't need to be afraid. But next time, he took me to a ritual and the next thing I know, he's handing me over. I was tied to the altar. There was chanting going on, and the bearded man disappeared. This group of men was gathered around and one at a time would try to penetrate me anally and everything just went into a frenzy. Then the bearded man came and removed me from the altar, and then I went back with him to his house, where he just nursed me. I was frozen. I mean I was so badly traumatized I was nonverbal. I was just in a state of shock and he very gently nursed me back to health. I have a strong attraction for bearded men who are both abusive and also nurturing. Matthew

The child's right to love and select loving partners is confounded. Since the trauma, disappointment, blame, and failure are reinforced rather than resolved, the idea of doomed relationships may play and replay its themes and continue into adulthood. Many survivors repeatedly find themselves in tension-filled, conflict-ridden partnerships. Some are drawn to people who have no capacity for emotional intimacy. Some routinely break off a relationship if their partner is ready for commitment or tries to get "too close."

This is also a time when children begin to test their skills in the world. They develop personal pride based on their accomplishments. Where children at this stage may be learning how to skip rope, play catch, write their name, help Mommy with the dishes or Daddy fix the car, cult-abused children

may be learning different things. If a cult-raised child is given any chance at self-esteem, it may be for "accomplishments" such as these:

(The following describes training in abortion. You may want to skip to the next paragraph.)

They called my great-grandmother the witch doctor, and she performed abortions on cult people. They used the fetuses and the babies for the rituals. She used to do abortions in the house, in the kitchen, and I remember being taught at three and four years of age how to do these abortions. I had to actually take my hands and put them inside and pull the baby out. Christi Joy

As children are beaming at their accomplishments and developing healthy self-esteem, cult-abused children are feeling increasingly sabotaged and incompetent. Their lessons in life may amount to messages such as: I am bad. I am a failure. I have let down important people in my life. I have done horrible things. The only pride some are allowed to feel is for committing antisocial acts. This leaves the child believing, "If anyone ever learns what I have done, they will hate me. Maybe I do belong in the cult."

This learning may show up later in failed careers and relationships.

The bottom line is that I do not have any type of successful, fulfilling relationship, emotional or sexual, with myself or anyone else, outside of the cult, for the rest of my life. And so the message to me was that the only way I can ever have that is to return to the cult. Adam

I know I was made to believe things would never get better and it was hopeless so I would stay or come back to them. It's a method of breaking down someone's psyche so that they give up, and a lot of that was done to me. I have part of me, fortunately, that is still hope-

ful and does believe that my life is going to get better all the time. And my therapist used to tell me almost every session that I deserved to have a good life and that things were going to work out.   Bea

Six to Ten   Children are using their thinking and feeling skills to determine who they really are and what they believe. They begin to develop social skills, try to assert themselves, test their assumptions, and experiment through trial and error. They may get interested in chemistry sets, find their first "best friend," try out for the volleyball team, or develop a passion for baseball. This time of trial and error helps to shape a child's life choices as an adult.

Cult-abused children are not offered choices, even though often they are set up to believe that they are. Starting from about four years of age, children may be made to kill. An adult usually holds a child's hands and kills an animal or another child. The child, who is starved for approval and affection, may receive praise from their parent or cult guardian for a job well done. As children grow older they are made to believe that they are killing by choice.

There were two children there. They said one was a bad soul; she was dressed in black. One was a good soul; she was dressed in white. They told me to choose one. I chose the one in white. That's the one that died. They told me I chose the one that Satan wanted—that I went against God.   Josie

Whether a child kills or not, the blame for the killing is always laid upon the child. One survivor resisted killing. With each refusal, another infant was killed as punishment for disobeying. Here is a condensed version of a poem trying to resolve the young child's torment.

2 killed not 1 cause of me
3 killed not 1 cause of me

4 killed not 1 cause of me
they say it's cause of me
cause i'm bad
they say it's my fault
they say they kill cause i'm bad
cause i'm not what they want
cause i can't do anything right
rightwrong rightwrong rightwrong
cause there's something wrong with me
badgood badgood badgood
they take the knife and put it in my hand
i dropped it on the ground
very bad
they put me in the pit
snake pit
they say i hurt the group by being bad not do
    what i'm
supposed to do
they say it's my fault 4 killed not 1
they have to kill more to make amends for bad
    me
i feel so bad i tell my pillow i want to die wanna
    die now
i tell the angels i want to die and live with them,
i tell God make me dead so no more babies have
    to die
                                    Jane Linn

There is no choice. The cult-raised child is told in no uncertain terms what is expected of her or him. As adults, some survivors may have difficulty making choices, or being decisive.

(The following describes an initiation ritual and the killing of an infant. You may want to skip down to the next quote.)

I remember standing alongside my father, who was dressed in a black robe, and I was naked. There was an infant on the altar and a knife was put into my hand, and at a certain point in the ritual I was supposed to kill the infant by stabbing it. When that

point came, I froze and wasn't able to do it. This was an embarrassment to my father. He killed the infant and poured her blood on me and told me that her blood was on my hands, and now I was Satan, and was one of theirs. And that my fate was sealed. Matthew

I think I was doing yoga or meditation and all of a sudden I stopped and I started like shaking my fist and yelling and I could see all the adults in my family and all the jerks in the cult one after another. And I yelled, "Who are you to say there's something wrong with me?" Because you know, who are these people? Child molesters, murderers, slime buckets, and they were saying something was wrong with me? And all of a sudden I realized I don't have to believe that—look at the people who are telling me this. And it felt good. Jane Linn

Cult children may be used in drug and prostitution rings. As with killing, the initial experiences often start at four. Children are taught how to sexually please adults and are praised or shamed accordingly. Children of nine or older are often considered undesirable. Many are told they're "too old." This may give violators occasion to shame and humiliate a child. The following event happened to an older child but is typical of what can happen to a nine-year-old.

They put me in a cage that had like a wall halfway up all the way around it. It was full of snakes, and they put me in this cage and suspended me in the cage. And the high priest kept saying, "Well, you know, you're not too bad sexually, you've finally come into your womanhood. You will be enough to please me, but I want you to beg. And I lasted up there for hours and hours, and one of the snakes bit me, I think, and scared the hell out of me. And finally I begged and pleaded to get me down. And he said, "I want to see you on your knees." And this was almost

like a decision I made, saying to myself, "I've been fighting for all these years, and I've never really consciously given in. Even if I had to physically, inside I've always fought." And that one time I said, "Okay—I can't take it anymore. I'll give in. I'll beg and I'll bow down and I'll do what you want me to do." He made me bend down and kiss his feet, and he had me suck on him and I did that, and he said, "I think you're going to pass." And I said, "I will do whatever you want me to do from here on out." He turned around, started to walk away, then he turned around again and slapped me across the face, and he said, "You're not good enough. Get out of my sight." Those words indelibly marked me for the rest of my life. They were more devastating than the physical abuse. I have this drive to be perfect, to do something more. That no matter what I do, it's not good enough, and that has affected me in every area of my life. Alice

Survivors may feel deep shame accompanying each realization. After connecting with a similar experience, one survivor's first words were, "Do you think I'm bad? Are you going to hate me now?"

It really helps to hear words that counteract those messages, especially when I get little and express that pain. Sometimes therapists don't understand that need and I get frustrated because the little child inside really needs to hear it over and over—not only from me, but from someone who sees her pain. Jane Linn

"Training lessons" may be accompanied by cult indoctrination. The messages may revolve around the either/or option of obedience/suicide: Either do what we say—or kill yourself. These "choices" are programmed under duress. The pain and the training event are usually forgotten, but the force of the message remains. Cult-raised children may be trained never to act independently or independently find success. For example, some may be commanded to visualize a rewarding achievement or financially secure career. During the visualization they may be tortured and given a suggestion that this is a time to commit suicide.

I notice every time I begin to do well at a job, I leave. In this last job, I decided to break that pattern. But the more successful I get, the more I can't stand it. I just got promoted to management, and I'm petrified. It feels like a time bomb—the longer I go, the more I know it's coming. I'm supposed to prepare this projections/planning report, but all I can think about is, It's time to bail out—the only question is when and how to commit suicide.   em

How are you doing? Is it time for a break? Remember that in recovery the slower pace is often more productive.

Ten to Fourteen Years This is a pivotal time in a child's development—the threshold to adulthood. Hobbies and interests may be pursued in earnest. Friendships may become all-important. Children may assert their own place in the world by establishing their place within groups, teams, and gangs. They enter puberty and may begin to experiment with a budding sexuality. Some may have their first date and first "real" kiss.

When children are exploring their own potential for creation and regeneration, cult-abused children may be forced to experience the opposite.

(The following quote describes birthing and cannibalism. You may want to skip down to the next quote.)

The memories got harder and harder for a long time, until finally I remembered what I considered the most horrible things a year ago. My most horrible memory is having to have a child and kill it, and then the cannibalism that followed after that. I remembered my mother being there, actually doing the injection to induce labor—she was there. There's

been a lot of horrible things that go on in the cult, but for me, that was the most horrible. It just had the most lasting impact on me. A year later, I'm still grieving the loss of that child. And I think it's the most horrible too because it was the most intensely uncontrollable. There was absolutely nothing I could do. I didn't want it to happen in the worst way. You know, I didn't want to be raped, and I didn't want to be thrown into a hole crawling with spiders, and all those things I didn't want to happen. But I really didn't want to have this child and kill it. After they take your child, kill it, and make you eat it, there's not much else they can do to you after that. My therapist reassured me that it doesn't get worse than that, you know. I spent twenty-one days in the hospital totally wiped out, and it doesn't—it doesn't get worse than this.   Alicia

When I was being abused, whenever I would see a butterfly, I knew that God was out there somewhere. I knew that somehow, some way I was going to be saved. Somebody was going to get me out of this.   Alice

For some survivors this is the very worst experience. For some what feels even worse is learning that a part of them "switched" and became "one of them," a violator. At a time when children are asserting themselves and their own views of the world, cult-abused children may be feeling utterly hopeless. They have negated their feelings, ignored their thoughts and intuitions, assumed guilt and blame for deaths of loved ones and Catch-22, double-bind situations. Knowing that the child feels isolated, strange, and clearly different from other children, violators may offer the child "salvation"—an identity and a place to belong. Violators may reinforce this rite of passage with death and rebirth rituals.

(The following describes a killing and burial. You may want to continue reading at the next paragraph.)

I was brought into the room. Everything was dark. The people stood around in their dark hoods. Their faces were painted all black, so that you couldn't make anything or anyone out. They killed a man, and cut him from the throat to his pelvis, and placed me inside the opening. Then they placed both of us inside a coffin and shut the lid. I was in there a very long time— maybe twenty-four hours. I don't know. But when they finally opened up the lid, it was extremely bright. Everyone was dressed in white and smiling. I was told that I had died and was reborn into the world of the dead. And there was a big party. Erik

The child is "honored" with a new role. There is great jubilation and celebration. The child may receive her or his own official cult robes. To make this forced choice more palatable, and perhaps help ensure more dedication to the cause, the exceedingly deprived cult child may now be offered promises of wealth, happiness, special privileges or powers. Where she or he had been denigrated and humiliated, the child may at last receive recognition. Much of the abuse and torment may now stop. For the first time ever, the child may get relief and some sense of accomplishment from her or his caregivers.

Having never established a firm sense of self, cult-abused children assume their cult-imposed roles. In fact, they have no choice. Ten-year-olds are still dependent on their parents. They must remain in a cult. Whatever role the child is assigned, she or he never reclaims control or autonomy. Even those groomed for power (high priest/priestess) remain powerless. Abductions, rapes, and tortures continue to follow the same proscribed course. The only difference is that these are now done in the name of the child.

Children slated for leadership may gain access to cult dogma and secrets. Children groomed for teachers/trainers/programmers may receive special training in psychology or education; children groomed for security roles may receive special training in forensic sciences and knowledge of criminal investigations. Other roles may include that of caregiver to newly inducted cult children; custodians to store and transport cult paraphernalia. These people have the critical role of cleanup without leaving evidence of a ritual. One survivor recalls learning how to erase traces of blood with a toothbrush, coated with saliva. The more sophisticated the group, the greater the variety and specialization of functions. In small groups a child may assume several roles.

Some difficult roles for survivors to resolve may include breeder, recruiter, slave, and slayer. Breeders are routinely impregnated to bear infants or fetuses for cult ceremonies. Recruiters are taught to entice new recruits for the group or victims for cult ceremonies. (Recruiters may also be young children who are used to entice other young children for abduction.) Slaves are used for continued torture, degradation, and humiliation. The slayer's job is to perform cult killings.

Violators may go to great lengths to force these roles upon unwilling children. They discover and remove every source of support a child may have. They then may torture, taunt, or humiliate the child to the point of murderous rage. At a studied, exact moment, they provide a weapon and a victim. Before a child has realized it, she or he may have killed. Here is one ten-year-old child's memory as excerpted from an adult survivor's journal after a particularly difficult therapy session.

(This quote describes a long series of tortures and killing. You may decide to continue at the next section, "Fourteen to Twenties," page 90)

They're all coming towards me and they're going to hurt me. My best friend Robin is there too. I had told Robin something in secret—about the way they were hurting me. Maybe she tried to help me out and told. They stripped me naked, and I ran for the corner of the room, because they were all in an angry mood. I curled up and tried to protect myself as they all came towards me, their nails outstretched. They all were screaming at me, that I was a liar—that I said things that never happened, and they were all going to teach me to never lie again. Robin was at the front of the group. That's what mattered most—my only friend had now turned against me. Now I knew that absolutely no one was ever safe. No one could ever be trusted. And it hurt so badly that it was Robin who was doing this to me. They uncurled my naked body and lay me flat on the floor. Then they started to scratch me from the forehead to the ends of my feet all along my body. They scratched till they drew blood and then they scratched right inside the open wound, so that it hurt far more. And they kept scratching inside the open wound, telling me over and over again that this will teach me not to lie.

At this point they took Robin out of the room and pulled out what looked like a rat. They forced it down my throat—deep down my throat. As it tried to escape it scratched me really bad. I threw it back up. It seemed that then, anyone who wanted to could have sex with me, and several did. Then this priest from our church—he was one of the more pious priests in our parish and I'd always kinda thought well of him—he's beginning to have intercourse with me. I can't believe my own memory. It can't be Father J. Maybe it was just someone dressed up to look like him. Then the really bad memory begins.

They're putting electrodes in my brain. I feel I'm going to go mad. They put electrodes in my head from temple to temple and shot something through that made me feel as though everything was blowing apart—my world was going to pieces and I was totally out of control. The pain was unbearable. They made me say I loved God and gave me this horrible shock. Then I had to say I loved Satan, and I got this wonderful sexual feeling from this man who looked like Father J. And then I say, "He is Satan. I

love being fucked by Satan. I love Satan." Then again I had to say, "I love God," and the shocks and the madness come. And then I said I loved Satan and the nice sexual feelings come. They continued these two modes back and forth, and then I hear myself saying, "Satan, Satan, I love Satan, am Satan." I laugh this ugly laugh. I feel glee. No pain. I do as Satan does. I kill. They put two knives in my hands and urged, "Kill! Kill!" My name is Rex and I kill little girls. The littler the better.

I sold out to them. They got me. I became one of them. They were cheering me on, and I became initiated into my role in the cult. I killed two girls that day. One was a baby, one was three years old.

Yes, I survived. I sold out to them. The pain was too great. And Robin—even Robin had abandoned me, so there was no one to hold out for. Oh God! Why did I want to live so much? Why?

I hear they groom people to be priestesses. I wasn't groomed to be a priestess. I—Oh my God—I became their killer. I know it's true because of how I feel inside when I say it. That's what I've denied for so long. After that, they would just bring out the torturing needles and I switched my personalities on sight of them. And after a while, they didn't even have to bring out the needles. I just automatically knew when it was time to kill. And when I switched, I began to kill like one of them. I did it with feeling, with purpose, like I meant it. I was taking the initiative to kill. They weren't forcing me to do it anymore.

What am I going to do? How could I have done it? I've killed so many people. How can I ever be forgiven? Why did I let them get to me? I know I could have hung on. Why didn't I let them just keep torturing me? Why did Robin turn against me? Why did I lose everything that mattered, and still want so badly to live?

I felt different things driving home from that therapy session. I had a feeling of calm and relief in my chest and shoulders. I knew that I'd finally touched *the truth that released my body but imprisoned my soul. There was overwhelming despair on one hand, and a desire to get dressed up and crack jokes on the other. I wasn't hungry, but I went to eat, because I didn't know what else to do. As I stood in line ordering a pizza there was a woman with a little girl, about six or seven years old. The little girl kept walking around her mother and looking at me with incredibly bright black, direct eyes. My face and eyes were swollen, my hair a mess. I wasn't paying too much attention to her. Then she planted herself next to me and said affirmatively, "Hello!" I smiled and said "Hello" back. I felt accepted by this little innocent child whose eyes seemed to know it all.   Rex*

After two months of lying sick in bed, this survivor finally began to experience some permanent healing.

Fourteen to Twenties The child is becoming an adult. Having established their identity, interests, and values, children are building their own life. They may find their first job and a life partner and may begin a family of their own. For many cult-abused children, this is a turning point. Some may assume their designated place within a cult. Some may try to leave and still make a life of their own. These children may be let go but with programmed instructions to return at a designated time or times or, failing that, to commit suicide. Some, who despite all the coercion remain unpersuaded, may be scathingly dismissed through a series of expulsion rituals where they are told to "unlearn" or forget all they have been taught. They may be jeered as failures and a disgrace to the family and denounced

as traitors. Next may follow a series of incantations cursing them and predicting they will never be happy, healthy, or successful outside the cult. Even through the expulsion ceremonies, the cruelties may continue:

I know this sounds crazy, and I can't explain how it happened, except to say that it felt totally, absolutely real. Mr. K., the head of our group, called a meeting. It wasn't a cult ceremony setting, but most of the cult group was there in regular clothes. Mr. K. announced that he was severing my membership in the group. But before that, he wanted to see that part of me which had resisted all these years. And once he met her, he would let me go. I guess I sort of think of that part as my soul. So I called her forward, and when she appeared, he became really sweet. He said, "I have a little child here who needs lots of care," and he placed a half-dead baby in my arms. Then he shot us full of holes, and my soul died. And then he said, "Now you are free to go." I left. It feels to me like I carried on in life using my mind but without my soul.   Sophia

Regardless of which group survivors find themselves in, all will suffer the aftereffects of years of coercive conditioning. Some will be battling their internal pain through compulsive/obsessive life patterns; some may find themselves in prison or mental institutions; and many begin the long, slow, but rewarding road to recovery.

I always knew I wasn't one of them. In the end they didn't get me.   Annie

7

Destructive Family Systems

On some level I sensed that Father would love to just absolutely grind me into the ground with his heel. He used to stand over my bed at night and I would be pretending to be asleep. And he used to always say, "I will break you!" And in a lot of ways, that's what kept me fighting. I think that's where my strength and my spirit came from. Because I would say to myself, "No, you won't, you bastard. You're just not going to do it."   Sunny

Ritual abuse does not always occur within multi-generational family systems. However, if a child was being ritually abused outside the family, some problem within the family may have prevented the child from telling or the parents/caregivers from noticing that something unusual was going on. Some parents may have been brought up not to show love or emotion. They may have been taught to avoid rather than address problems. In such a family, even caring parents would not take action or ask questions if they noticed that their son came home from school with torn underwear. Gerald, who remembers ritual abuse outside his family, shares the following about his mother:

I had always thought that I was really loved by her. But I go back and I don't have any memories of really being held by her. I don't have any memories of being close with her. In looking back on it I see that the ritual abuse could not have taken place if my mother had not had some ambivalent feelings that allowed me to be placed in a lot of danger. Gerald

Some survivors have always known that their families were troubled. Knowing there is help through recovery is a welcome option. However, others remember their families as "perfect." Their parents may have had extremely rigid standards or religious beliefs. These survivors are often confounded by their emerging reality. They have to recognize the extent of the problem before they can appreciate that there is help.

I grew up believing that mine was the perfect family. My parents kept emphasizing how perfect we were. I took their statements on faith and even repeated them. I still have a hard time admitting things weren't perfect. Erik

Parents or caregivers seem God-like to a little child—all-knowing, all-powerful. If your caregivers abused instead of protecting you, you probably grew up fearing for your life. It's important to let any frightened inner children know that people who abuse little children are not all-powerful but likely feel powerless. It's important to realize that today, because you are in recovery, you may be stronger than them.

If you know that you are a survivor of ritual abuse, the following descriptions may be validating. On the other hand, if you are not sure but suspect you are a survivor, the following accounts may offer you some clues. They indicate unhealthy family patterns in general and include patterns found in families practicing ritual abuse. The profiles are neither exhaustive nor exclusive. There may have been other patterns in your family as well. Although some characteristics overlap from one category to another, they are generally mentioned only once.

If you recognize the patterns, it does not necessarily mean that you are a survivor of ritual abuse. You may have been raised by emotionally immature or unenlightened parents. In this case, you may have suffered some damage in your emotional, mental, physical, or spiritual development as well.

The newly emerging picture may feel unreal. It may also seems at odds with the carefully constructed reality of your family and society. Some-

times the more ill the family, the more they may strive to hide it. Often the weaker the inner family system, the more rigid and brittle the outer shell. The slightest crack may create havoc and panic. Each new realization may shake the old foundations a little. Stop and wait till the tremor has passed before looking further. It's okay to go slowly. Remember to take care of yourself.

Things may feel confusing. For now there is nothing that you need to do except recognize your own experience. You do not need to figure out, explain, report, confront, judge, or blame. Trust that in time a fuller picture will emerge. Once you have more of the pieces, you can decide what to do.

CHARACTERISTICS OF DESTRUCTIVE FAMILIES

A basic rule of multigenerational cult families is to appear normal at all costs. Normalcy may be stressed outside the home and often within the home as well. There may be typically no clues to ritual abuse involvement in day-to-day family life.

Ritual abuse families come from many backgrounds. There is no standard socioeconomic profile. The following two descriptions reflect different ends of the spectrum.

We come from old money—generations of it. My grandparents and parents have been very high in politics—senators, governors, mayors. We own big houses on the East Coast and in the West. The kids went to East Coast boarding schools, prestigious law schools and colleges. We moved in upper-echelon, high-society circles. Amy

My mother was the first one in her family that moved into town off the farm. A lot of them were farmers—not wealthy midwestern kinds of farmers but poor, hardscrubble dirt farmers or just living in little teensy towns. Baptists—Southern Baptists and

hard-core Baptists. Hard-shell Baptists is what they called themselves. They were hard-shell Baptists and yellow-dog Democrats—you know, they'd vote for a yellow dog if he was a Democrat.   Jeanne

Many families that ritually abuse their children may maintain a veneer of respectability and demand that their children appear "perfect" too. This plays into the commonly held belief that people of status, education, or money are hardly likely to be practicing ritual abuse. (See "Characteristics of Cult Violators" in Chapter 4.)

We were a devout Catholic family. Everyone loved my mother. She was nice and she was sweet. She was just a saint for putting up with my father, who was an alcoholic, and abusive, and never came home at night. She had nine children. People would say, "Oh, poor Mrs. T. She's at home with these children and he's out drinking, and she's just a saint." And in actuality she was a very evil person.   Alicia

Outward appearances of diligence, respectability, and benevolence can be misleading. Destructive families can better be characterized as being somewhere on a continuum from rigid to chaotic, showing symptoms of immaturity, dissociation, violence, control, humiliation, and secrecy.

How are you doing? Is it time for a break? You might want to loosen up by swinging your arms from side to side. Or loosen your feet by running in place. Are you ready to go on on? If not, come back when you are.

RIGID TO CHAOTIC

Some survivors seem to come from rigid families with more deliberate ritual abuse and less commonplace familial abuse. Other survivors seem to come from chaotic families with more day-to-day familial abuse and less systematic indoctrination. Many families do not fit into a single category but fall somewhere between the two extremes of rigid to chaotic.

RIGID FAMILIES

Rigid families are controlled and structured. Day-to-day routines may be carried out with almost military precision. There may be great predictability and adherence to rules. The feeling is that everything is run by the book. There is little or no spontaneity. Information may not be allowed in or out of the family, so a child has little opportunity for normal comparisons. In highly rigid families, family reputation may be of paramount importance. There may be absolutely no clues to the familial practice of ritual abuse. Events don't naturally flow, one from another, but are split off and separated. They coexist side by side, like Dr. Jekyll and Mr. Hyde—each unaware of the other. Compartmentalized events may be three separate realities: respectable "day" life, incest at night, and regularly scheduled ritual abuse at a designated site. Survivors in this category may also be very split and find it more difficult to believe that their family could ever have done anything out of the ordinary. These families may appear quite normal in all respects to outsiders as well.

I grew up in a "perfect" household. My parents had a great relationship. They cared for the family and they tried hard to make things good. We believed that, you know. When I showed old family photos to the therapist, she said the family looked so good, she would have voted for my mother for president of the PTA. What the therapist didn't know was that my mother was president of the PTA.   Jonathan

CHAOTIC FAMILIES

Chaotic ritual abuse families may result when both parents are too damaged to maintain the required protocols of self-splits and dissociation. These parents may or may not be formally involved in a ritual abuse cult. However, elements from their ritual abuse past may burst through on the home scene and are reenacted sporadically. One survivor recalled the following:

At four and a half I went to live with my grandfather, who was a very violent alcoholic. He was cruel and out-of-control violent. He used to grab a cat, swing it by its tail, and smash it against the wall to kill it. He was beaten to death over a gambling debt and lay in the house three days, dying. Samantha

Samantha does not recall ritual abuse, but in piecing together events from her past, she recalls ritualistic reminders of costuming and ingestion of feces/urine.

I wasn't in kindergarten yet and my father took care of me during the day. He used to cross-dress into these ladies. He became these very wicked kinds of ladies, and what I would do is just try to not make them angry. So we would have tea parties and he would serve urine and feces at the tea parties. Each lady had a purse and in the purses there were always knives or glass or objects that could hurt you. And that's how he would entertain me. Samantha

The parents may be openly violent, alcoholic, unpredictable, or psychotic. The children may be regularly raped on the living room floor. One or both parents may incorporate ritualistic elements into the abuse. However, there seems to be little structure, rhyme, or reason. One day the child is made to be a "Nazi" and the parent "kills" her. Next day, the parent is a "crown prince" of the KKK and the child is made to "worship" him, and another time he's Satan. The parents may be on welfare, in prison, part of a biker community, or constantly in transit without any community roots. In these families the children may be completely neglected.

The girl I adopted was environmentally deprived. Those kids lived in a hell hole. They lived day and night with parents who revictimized them. There was no furniture, there were no vacations, there weren't any clothes. There were rags and hunger. Every single person she lived with sexually abused her. She was ritually abused, and didn't have anything positive in her experience of growing up. Suzzane

It's believed that these children rarely make it into recovery. Consistency and dependability are necessary for a child to develop normally. Even negative consistency (I know I will get beaten every day at 6:00 P.M., when my mother comes home from work) is better than chaos (Mother may bring me a new tricycle when she comes home from work, or she may lock me in a closet). Without consistent patterns, a child is unable to form protective reactive patterns to defend against the abuse. If these children survive into adulthood, they may end up in prisons or psychiatric facilities. Some may find the predictability and consistency they lacked in childhood by joining rigidly structured organizations such as the army.

BETWEEN RIGID AND CHAOTIC

A number of survivors described families that seem to fall in between rigid and chaotic. For example, there would be constant tension in the home, interrupted with outbursts of violence. The incest would include elements of ritual. Often one parent appeared quite normal, the other almost psychotic.

My mother did everything she could to try to make things look normal. But I don't think my father looked normal to anybody. He was more the passive one, and the one who was out of control. My father was just really violent. He wasn't an alcoholic, but he would just sort of lose control and beat the shit out of one of my brothers to the point where they would have to be taken to the emergency room and get stitches in their head. There was so much tension between us all the time. I don't think we totally hid it, but I don't think people had any idea as to the extent of what was going on.   Lynn

However bad the family circumstances, children often find signs of hope:

There was this old lady who lived about four blocks down the street—a Catholic older lady, a holy roller. She was for sure going to heaven. She was very sweet. She was probably in her sixties at the time and she seemed real old to me. As I was walking to school every once in a while, she would pick me up and drive me to school. And somehow in her way, she would touch me on the shoulder or she would say, "You look pretty" or "How are you doing in school?" Those maybe ten times that I was with her—not even that— is the only sense of love that I ever experienced. And that old lady—some day when I meet her in heaven, she will know what an incredible impact she had on my life.   Alice

Are you staying in touch with your feelings? Can you name what you're feeling? If it's a sad or angry feeling, what can you do to make it feel better? Remember to be kind to yourself.

EMOTIONALLY DEBILITATED

Families practicing ritual abuse share characteristics with incestuous and alcoholic families. Although recognition of these patterns may indicate abuse, it may not necessarily be ritual abuse. Adults who practice ritual abuse are typically emotionally needy, immature people. As a result they find unhealthy ways to escape their pain, discharge their rage, manage their fear, resolve hate, and avoid their shame. The quotes below show how some of these problems are experienced by survivors of ritual abuse. In structured families the symptoms may be more repressed and harder to detect. In chaotic families they may define day-to-day existence. However, whether evident or hidden, the underlying problems are the same.

IMMATURITY: UNMET DEVELOPMENTAL NEEDS

Immature people are unable or unwilling to take responsibility for their own feelings, thoughts, and behaviors. Instead, they "assign" these feelings to others, often their own children. The children are expected to be out of touch with their own feelings and in tune with the feelings of others—in this case their parents. These children often know their parents' feelings better than their own.

Here the parents may use an all-inclusive "we" instead of "I" when referring to themselves. They may buy their children "gifts" that in no way reflect what the child wants. Children may not exist, except to please others. It is the children's responsibility to make their parents look and feel good. And no matter what the child says or does, nothing is ever good enough.

Therapist Mary Ellen Holmen compares this type of family to a piece of taffy. "It's sticky. It may stretch, but it's hard to break free." If you try to pull any one family member away, it becomes impossible to know where she or he ends and the others begin. The child may move from New York to Los Angeles or Australia, but the thread and the stickiness remain. In other words, people do not have independent boundaries. No one knows who they are. This is called codependency: the learned inability to take responsibility for oneself, one's feelings and one's actions. These people constantly look to others to fulfill their own needs.

My mother and my aunt have two frames of reference. One is "mine" and the other is "what I need." They're really needy people. And really greedy people. I think that they have such low self-value that they keep trying to get more and more and more from other people, as if thinking, "What I take from you is going to be mine and make me better."   Amiee

To make up for their feelings of inadequacy, these people may be boastful, with an exaggerated sense of their own achievements and importance. Everything revolves around them. Their need for attention and admiration is an insatiable black hole that will never be filled.

I have some weird things with my mother. She was an alcoholic and I think she did something sexual in the bathtub with me. They were narcissistic types of things, like, "I'll feel good if I do this to her." I think the damage comes from being very hurt that she would never see me as different from who she was. Like I was there for her needs. Always. I mean, I didn't exist except as how she needed me. I think I was raised in that kind of a slave mentality.   CeeCee

DISSOCIATION: ESCAPING THE PAIN

Like many troubled families who abuse their children, cult families find ways to avoid dealing with the pain of their own truth. Use of mind- and mood-altering aids or other "distraction" techniques may be used to help keep the abusers dissociated from their own reality. The rituals themselves are one form of addictive dissociation (see "The Addictive Nature of Ritual Abuse" in Chapter 4). However, violators may need other aids to keep them dissociated in between. Food, drugs, and alcohol are typical dissociative aids. In his paper "The Addictive Nature of Perpetrators of Ritual Abuse," Martin R. Smith, M.Ed., writes:

Alcoholism in particular seems to be cited most often by researchers as a component of ritual abuse. It is a profound disinhibitor of the central nervous system which allows violence to be easily expressed and then becomes an equally profound sedative which is used to forget the events which have just taken place.

Multigenerational ritual abuse parents find many ways to avoid reality and stay dissociated. They may avoid pain through workaholism, constant busyness, or obsessive/compulsive preoccupation with cleanliness, food, money, and religion. These are the hyper-churchgoing or hyper-housecleaning parents who are never "there" for their children.

My father is an alcoholic, and my main memory of him, before I started having abuse memories, was that when he was at home, which wasn't often, he spent all his time at home passed out or with his eyes focused on the TV. But you couldn't talk to him. He didn't hear you. He was like there, but he wasn't there. My dad really had nothing to do with me when he wasn't abusing me. And that was pretty much just in the rituals. He wasn't abusive on a daily basis. He was too passed out.   Jane Linn

Some ritual abuse violators keep their various worlds separate through multiplicity or dissociation (see Chapter 8). They may have violent mood swings or sudden, unexplained changes in behavior.

When I had memories of sexual abuse with my father, it was like sometimes he'd come in and treat me like a little girl and sometimes he'd come in and treat me like a prostitute. Sometimes he'd come in and treat me like he was some kind of religious person that I had to be worthy of. I hear survivors say, "Oh God, sometimes my dad was a totally different person." My dad was more than one different person—that's scary.   Susan

Destructive families regularly deny or rationalize problems such as alcoholism, chemical dependency, or sexual improprieties. There may be a remarkable tolerance for tension, violence, pain, and abuse. Ritual abuse families may routinely minimize the horror or severity of intolerable situations.

One of the things that helped me wake up to how deep the denial was, was when I was trying to protect my granddaughter from going back into an abusive environment. Three psychiatrists had said her mother should not have custody. My extended family minimized it. They said, "This couldn't be that bad. Why don't you let her go back?" Her worst abuse happened after she was returned to her mother's custody.   Suzzane

VIOLENCE: DISCHARGING RAGE

Ritual abuse perpetrators likely carry excessive levels of hostility and rage. Parents/perpetrators may rationalize violence as necessary discipline. Punishments may be out of proportion to the transgression. For example, one survivor was severely beaten as a child for watching cartoons. In chaotic homes, the violence may be so bad that a child may be taking her life in her hands every time she enters.

My father was a highly intelligent attorney. He was also an extremely violent and abusive alcoholic. He used to shoot at me when I would come home from school. Most of the parents wouldn't let my friends come over. I had one remaining friend that could. One day, we went to the basement to hang up our wet swimsuits. He was in the living room, and started shooting through the floor. After that, she never came over either. It always kind of amazed me that all the parents around our neighborhood knew enough not to let their kids come anywhere near our house, and yet they would let me and my sister walk into it every day.   Sunny

Behind closed doors the violence may be freely expressed.

My mother was really physically violent. She would go into rages and hit us. One of the things I would remember really clearly is she would grab our arms and dig her fingernails into our flesh, then shake us or scream in our face. If Mom was in a bad mood, we would know to lay low, cause that meant that there would be violence, or just like this cold, cold coldness that was almost scarier than the screaming.   David Gabriel

How are you doing? Ready for a break? It might feel good to take a short walk around the room or around the block. Come back when you're ready to continue. As always, take your time.

CONTROL: MANAGING THE FEAR

Much of the tension in destructive families may stem from extraordinary levels of anxiety. Simplistic thinking is one type of safety net. Violators may prefer to think in black and white terms with little tolerance for ambiguity. This "all or nothing" mindset is called exclusive thinking and is very similar to polar opposites (see Chapter 4). Violators may read and quote from the Bible, branding as "evil" anything that deviates from their inflexible set of beliefs.

Certainty helps to minimize anxiety. Some violators may support any existing order and rail against changes. Some cult violators may be strong proponents of discipline, order, and an authoritarian establishment. They may be attracted to hierarchical institutions such as the armed forces, fundamentalist religions, and dictatorship governments. Making others feel powerless helps make them feel powerful. Violators may also be attracted to groups such as the Ku Klux Klan and neo-Nazis.

The family structure is often patriarchal. Parents may emphasize control and perfectionism. Instead of sharing and chatting, family communication may consist primarily of interrogations. Interrogations may also be used as a cruel means of manipulation:

My father used to play mind games with me called "interrogation." It was a no-win situation. He would ask me questions and questions and questions until I ran out of answers, and so I lost. The punishment was incest. But if I tried to resist, he told me he would kill Mother. My life is totally fucked. Today, the closer I get to winning, the more I make sure I fail. Sunny

Violators may pursue things symbolizing power. They may try to develop psychic powers, seek influence through political office, stockpile weaponry, or train vicious guard dogs. They may be obsessed with status, politics, and money. They may prostitute their own children and force them into pornography as a way of earning money for themselves or the cult.

Children are usually taught to control, not express their feelings. They are criticized, punished, or ridiculed for crying or showing anger. Family members coexist physically, but are emotionally disconnected from one another.

We couldn't show any emotions. We couldn't be exuberant playing. We couldn't argue with my broth-ers and sisters. It was like—you were just supposed to be really quiet and any kind of life was quickly snuffed out. So it was weird, because everybody kept to themselves and nobody talked and everything was superficial. Jane Linn

The cult system of exploiters and dependents (see Chapter 4) may be mirrored in the marriage. The dynamics of the relationship may be that of dominator and dominated. Survivors have observed that while both parents are usually (not always) involved, one may participate enthusiastically, the other reluctantly. Although one person appears to be powerful and the other one powerless, both may in fact feel utterly powerless. The emotional need to pair dominator with dominated seems to override other factors and may result in strange alliances. Parents may be often incompatible temperamentally and in other areas as well.

My parents were an odd couple, very mismatched. They had nothing in common. My mother was from this middle-class, snobbish, Episcopalian Protestant family. She is a schoolteacher—very high-functioning and very intelligent. She was controlling and domineering, not passive by any means. My father was from this real working-class Catholic family. He is a very bizarre person with very few social skills. He wasn't alcoholic. He just acted drunk. And he wouldn't wash his clothes or comb his hair. He looked like a street person. Lynn

HUMILIATION: UNRESOLVED HATE

Parents/caregivers may try to resolve hatred toward their own violators by humiliating their children. It can be physical humiliation through beatings or unnecessary enemas or emotional humiliation through verbal needling, ridicule, and unrelenting putdowns.

I remember being poked, being poked by my dad. My dad just being in my face and poking me. So my therapist asked, "Well, how many times do you imagine that happened to you as a kid?" And I said, "I don't know. Probably a thousand times."   David Gabriel

Although all children in ritual abuse families are likely abused, sometimes one child may be singled out for special humiliation. This sets up the dominator/dominated paradigm among the children as well. A son (or the oldest child) may be conditioned to assume a "dominator/violator" role against a daughter (or sometimes younger child). The girl may be forced to assume the "dominated/victim" role within the family system. Grace played both roles in her family. She was the "victim" to her "dominator" older brother and was given her younger brother to dominate in turn.

I have a very confusing relationship with my brother. My whole headset on my brother is that he's mine. And I think that's a cult thing—that people belong to you. And that no one else is going to fuck with him at all. He was mine to protect. But I could mess with him, you know, this is my little brother. And so he has some shit about me, too.   Grace

SECRECY: AVOIDING SHAME

While secrecy prevents detection and prosecution, it also hides enormous levels of shame. Ritual abuse families may have an abnormal amount of discomfort about public displays or discussions about sex. A sexually abusive violator may masquerade as the puritanical matron, condemning displays of sexuality in others. In some families the word "sex" is never mentioned.

Some violators are afraid that any clue at all may betray their activities. Since dirt is considered "bad," cult violators may be preoccupied with cleanliness.

One of the things that really struck me about my mother was her sense of cleanliness. Everything had to be museumlike quality in our house. If my room wasn't clean, if I didn't do my chores, or if we kids didn't fall in line behind her authority, she would fly into a rage where she would scream at me, and that was when a lot of my beatings would occur. Janes

Any family harboring secrets uses many tactics to guard against exposure. A powerful "control and secrecy" tactic is manipulated through a cult community. The community is bound together by tension, secrecy, and fear. To maximize control and minimize exposure, cults manipulate children to believe that they are bad and different and will never make it on their own in the outside world. It may be taboo to seek independence. The family may create a mentality of us and them, making it clear that you do not belong to them. Them is the rest of society, outside the defined circle of extended family and friends.

There may be an understood no-talk rule regarding family matters. The family may move frequently to ensure that no long-term outside friendships are formed. Outsiders such as school friends may be discouraged or made to feel unwelcome. Peer deprivation is one of the most painful and damaging effects of this imposed isolation.

I never would bring friends over to my family's house because it would just embarrass me. I mean my parents would act weird. And I think that by isolating myself, starting at an early age, that was hiding secrets. You know, not dealing with them and not dealing with the world at all in a lot of ways. I don't think I thought of them as secrets, but they were thoughts that I had that I thought must be really bad. And so I wasn't going to talk about them or reveal them.   Amy

To ensure that the secrets aren't exposed within

the family, perpetrators may manipulate hostilities among the children. They may pit children against one another to prevent bonding and trust.

To help avoid suspicion, the family may be concerned with *looking* respectable rather than *being* respectable. This emphasis on appearances is conveyed to the children, who may feel enormous pressure to keep up appearances as well. Some children are made to understand that if they ever slip up, even slightly, it will ruin the family. A child will often lie to cover up rather than risk "ruining" the family.

Children raised in generational cult families may repeat the behaviors they were taught. However, given the chance, a healthy person will opt out. Today, as never before, the opportunity is there.

Survivors are coming out. Many of us, like Sunflower, found a way to survive and break free of the "perfect" family.

I SURVIVED

the perfect family
the perfect church
the perfect community
model parents
upstanding citizens
nice neighborhood
prominent church members
nice and loving parents
cleanliness.

Sunflower

Part Three

Dissociation

8

Surviving Through Dissociation

There's this game I played as a kid called Mousetrap. There's an enclosure with a start and a finish and a maze of obstacles in between. You put a marble at the entrance, and as it goes through the maze, it sets up a whole series of chain reactions and then exits at the other end.

Our conscious mind is like this system set up to handle different types of marbles. The marbles represent expected life experiences. As the marble negotiates the obstacles in the maze, learning takes place. If the marble is oversized for the system, there is no way it can get through. That's how I think of overwhelming trauma. It doesn't fit our existing system. So if we get a weird marble which doesn't fit, we have to modify our system. Until then, we have to drop it into our unconscious. Dissociation is like rerouting the marble into the unconscious—it takes anything that gets dropped into it. There are no restrictions on what fits.
Maya

COMMON DISSOCIATION

The unconscious is like a great holding area or reservoir of unprocessed events. Anything we don't or can't assimilate consciously goes there. The unconscious holds irrelevant things such as images of strangers we see on the street. It also holds important things that need to be brought into conscious awareness but may be too big to fit our existing system (conscious mind). There are times when people are unable to fully assimilate the significance of an overwhelming experience such as a car accident. One of the passengers calmly calls an ambulance, administers first aid, and reroutes oncoming traffic. Once the ambulance arrives, she falls apart and cries hysterically. In order to take care of the immediate priorities, she dissociated her feelings and emotions temporarily. The dissociation allowed her to break up the oversized experience into manageable pieces.

These were assimilated as soon as it was safe to do so. If the accident survivor didn't assimilate the dissociated part of her experience, she would suffer the PTSD symptoms described later in this chapter.

SHAPING OUR CONSCIOUS

Children are commonly seen to dissociate—not because of trauma, but because every time they get a new type of experience, they have to modify or expand their faculties in order to assimilate it. In the meantime, the experience is dissociated and held in the unconscious. There, they "play with it," using their imagination until they work out a way to make a fit. Children go through a very high rate of new experiences and may frequently dissociate as a normal response to an unfamiliar event. They are continually modifying and expanding their system, or conscious mind. This is the process of growth and learning. As they mature, children may dissociate less and less, because there are fewer and fewer experiences that don't fit their conscious system.

Children rely extensively on adults for interpretation. Their developing comprehension is largely fashioned after that of their parents or caregivers. If caregivers are emotionally damaged, their own skewed view of the world is imposed upon their children.

Parents in destructive families have unresolved emotional issues that are being held in their own unconscious. They couldn't or wouldn't find a way to make these emotions fit their conscious system. Instead, the unresolved issues are offloaded onto their children. As children expand and develop their consciousness, they take in experiences that don't belong to them—emotional baggage that belongs to their guardians.

Unresolved issues in the parents' unconscious are misinterpreted for the child. This is a common phenomenon known as projection. For example, if parents feel shame but cannot admit it, they may deny it, separate themselves from it, disown it, dissociate from it, and project it onto their children. They then condemn their children as being shameful. In psychology this is described as retaliatory defense. In other words, the shame the parents have within themselves but cannot accept is expressed by shaming the children. In fact, the less parents are able to accept the "monster" within themselves, the more readily they are able to see it in their children.

I had no idea what a weight and emotional burden I'd been carrying all these years until one day in therapy, I was lying on the mat, and I could feel this massive exodus of negative emotions leaving me. And when it was over, what I realized was that most of it was their shit. I had been carrying it for them. It felt like ninety-five percent of my burden had gone. I could easily handle the remaining five percent—the stuff that actually belonged and was mine. Janes

Emotionally damaged people cannot or will not take responsibility for events in their life. Instead, they assign the responsibility to others, usually their children: "It's your fault." As a result, children assume responsibility for negative events in the family's life. A powerless child is never responsible for problems or bad events. The adults in charge are responsible. However, because these lies are reinforced consistently during a child's developmental years, skewed interpretations become increasingly molded and ingrained. The more the lies are reinforced, the more the children get set in their view of things. Over time, the views become very hard to change. The child spends the rest of her or his life learning how to live with their alien legacy.

Emotionally troubled parents frequently reinforce skewed interpretations with abuse. If the abuse is extreme, as praticed by destructive families, a child's conscious world becomes overwhelmed. The extreme abuse is dissociated into the unconscious, but it cannot be made to fit, even in a misinformed way. The trauma remains dissociated. To survive, children tap into extraordinary coping skills, fashioned from within their own unconscious.

How are you doing? The following section can bring up painful feelings for some people. Remember to go slowly and to attend to any inner children who may be hurting as you read. Remind them that everyone is safe and that you want to help them through healing.

CLINICAL (AMNESTIC) DISSOCIATION

Our instinctive reactions to an assault are fight or flight. However, neither works when children are abused by sadistic adults. The only option left is to freeze, and take flight through the mind. A common initial coping mechanism is to escape the body:

I began to remember some really specific things from my childhood, like being over my father's knee in the kitchen . . . my sister and my brother, you know, everyone watching. He pulled down my pants and beat me. And seeing spots on the floor, and going into the spots. There were gold and red and blue spots on a white background. That was the kind of pattern it was. And so I found that very interesting that I could do that—just be that little spot. Now I understand my first memory of dissociation. Jeanne

This is an example of dissociating an experience, which many children use to survive overwhelming trauma. It is the beginning of clinical (amnestic) dissociation, which allows a shutting out of an unbearable reality. It is held unassimilated—in effect, frozen in time. A dissociated experience can be split up to store the emotions separate from bodily sensations, and the sensations separate from the knowledge of an event. In dissociating an experience, children split off a part of their self to hold the trauma. One survivor said these dissociated aspects of self feel like "compartmentalized intelligent energies." Another said she felt "fragmented." In some cases the dissociated aspects of self, immediately or over time, form their own and separate sense of self.

My system tries to look at everything and make sense of it. If I have a feeling coming, it has to fit. But if the feeling is too big or grotesque for my system, my unconscious goes, Okay, great big rage coming. I'll make a person who's ten feet tall to handle it. It's like a dream world—anything goes. Next time the great big anger comes, my ten-foot-tall person comes out to hold it. If I have to keep calling out my ten-foot person, I may give him a name, like Ogre. Ogre is mean and nasty and he can protect me. If the big rage comes at me a lot of times, Ogre has to "stay out" more and more often. The longer Ogre stays out, the more he has to interact with his surroundings. He begins to develop a memory of his experiences, a pattern of behavior, and his own identity. Pretty soon, I have an alter personality called Ogre. Maya

Because Ogre holds overwhelming trauma and feelings, his existence is kept from the child's conscious awareness. Now Ogre "comes out" to handle the abuse. A dissociated identity, like a dissociated experience, can hold the entire event or parts of it. Alters may hold only a bodily feeling, only an emotion, or only the knowledge. One hundred abusive incidents may be held by one identity or by one hundred or more identities. People are often perplexed about hearing that someone has a hundred alter personalities. However, it may be helpful to think of each identity as holding an abusive experience. In this context, one hundred, one thousand, or ten thousand alters make sense. Taken together, the identities hold a person's overwhelming traumas and express a survivor's entire life story. The possibilities and combinations are virtually limitless. The world of imagination has no bounds.

(The following quote contains some graphic examples of abuse. You may want to skip down to the paragraph following.)

Some of the really traumatic memories come in groups of three or four alters. I'm thinking in particular of when I was having my second child who was killed. And there was this alter who had just a tremendous amount of grief over the loss; one who hated the baby and just thought, "If it weren't for this baby, none of this would be happening"; a third that was totally confused—"Where do babies come from? It's not mine. What's going on?"; and then a fourth one who was very straightforward—"Okay, if this happened, let's just take care of it." So if it was real traumatic, it split into four. But some of the common, everyday sort of things like being in a pit or in a box, or being raped in a particular way, one alter took that kind of abuse for a period of time, then somebody else came and took it. Alicia

I've found fragments of children with names and I had started to realize that there was a difference between a fragment and a fully developed personality within myself. There were parts of me that were associated just with certain traumas, and there were some who had fully developed personalities. Some of them look like me, some of them don't. Suzzane

When the abuse is over, the original self "returns" and resumes "normal" life, having no

awareness of what has just transpired. If severely abused children were forced to experience the trauma they just lived through, they would probably not survive.

Some children maintain a complete split between their everyday life and the abusive episodes. They may be seen smiling when posing for family photographs. Violators often use such photographs to prove there is nothing bad going on.

Someone once asked me how it feels to be a survivor, and I tried to explain it like this. Pretend that you just witnessed your family and entire extended family executed, and you have to go to a party. You've repressed the experience, so you can't tell anybody what happened. Instead, you keep smiling and making small talk, while inside you know that something is terribly wrong. And the question that keeps running through your brain is "How long can I keep this up?" Josie

As abused children grow, their problems typically begin to mount. The load on their unconscious becomes increasingly great, and they feel overwhelmed. As some identities stay out more and more, they may begin to take over and operate in the child's day-to-day world. If the abuse continues or increases, the original self may stay out less and less and, in time, stop coming out at all. The survivor is then functioning through identities who "switch" to cope with day-to-day life.

I don't control who comes out. When someone asks a question, the one who knows the answer comes out. A survivor

In the November/December 1992 issue of *The Sciences* magazine, Dr. Frank W. Putnam writes the following about survivors with dissociated identities: "The (presenting) personality is almost never the (survivor's) original personality—the identity that developed between birth and the experience of trauma. That self usually lies dormant and emerges only after extensive psychotherapy."

In the same article, Dr. Putnam describes multiples from other parts of the globe. Their similarity to many ritual abuse survivors suggests that children use similar coping strategies in the face of overwhelming trauma:

I have encountered a number of such cases (of multiple personality) among children and adolescents from war-torn regions including Cambodia and Lebanon. In each instance the victim had witnessed the massacre of family members by some military faction. One girl said she had seen her parents blown to bits in a mine field. . . . In the face of such ghoulish circumstances, the dissociative response can be commensurately extreme. Some children create a system of imaginary companions—dwarfs, genies, angels, animals, superheroes. Those companions may at first be experienced as distinct from the child's true self, only later to become internalized as alter personalities—or they may be internalized from the start. In any event each dissociated state acquires a specific sense of self, a set of behaviors and biographical details that are elaborated over time as the child repeatedly escapes from traumatic reality. When those alter personalities begin to trade off control of the person's behavior, MPD (Multiple Personality Disorder) has taken hold.

Amnestic dissociation may be used for other purposes as well. Some identities are created to protect fragile, delicate, or creative and expressive parts of the child. The cult can manipulate dissociation to have a child create identities as shown in Chapter 5. Identities can create other identities if a task becomes overwhelming for them.

Are you doing okay? Remember to turn to the emergency pages at the back of the book if your inner selves begin to feel frightened. Or you can reassure them by going to your own Safe Place.

THE REALM OF POSSIBILITIES

I think we're probably some of the highest functioning people in the world, because we do function. Most of us are superachievers. Mainly because we're always trying to climb up on top of the pile so that no one will notice we're crazy. When I was nineteen I was a TV news anchor. I just threw myselves into impossible situations to prove to someone that I could do it. And I think that offered me some sense of safety. If I was in a really high position and doing really well, no one would dare look at me and say something was wrong.   Amiee

Fear and resistance are typical initial survivor responses to learning about dissociated parts or selves. Multiplicity can feel frightening if a survivor doesn't know what it is. Dissociated experiences/identities are frequently greeted with awe. It's natural to fear the unknown. However, once survivors understand the ingenuity of their own system, most develop admiration and respect for it. They no longer see it as awful but awesome.

There's a saying that "necessity is the mother of invention." Pushed beyond normal limits, people have discovered extraordinary abilites. These abilites are in evidence by survivors who used their powers of the mind to survive. Multiples are introducing the world to new realms of possibilities that have yet to be fully understood. With knowing and understanding comes appreciation. Regardless of an identity's name, description, or personality, its main and common purpose is always to protect the child. Alters can manage extraordinary feats in their determination to keep the child safe. Sometimes these feats are beyond the range of normal human experience or comprehension.

The way I feel pain is different than a lot of people. Like I don't feel pain. I'm doing canning [preserves] now, and I can put my hands in boiling water or take something out of the oven without a mitt. And this friend of mine was there and it really freaked her out. So I try to be in my body more—I really try to feel pain. My therapist is so thrilled when I feel pain. I even got a blister recently. And I'm not sure I like it.   Annie

Annie isn't unusual. Initially for survival, and later for managing day-to-day life, some survivors have developed extraordinary coping skills. Although these abilities may be wonderful in some respects, they have come at an exhorbitant price. While no two survivors are alike, some of the more commonly observed abilities in multiples are perfect memory, ability to heal unusually fast, ability to tolerate extreme levels of pain, and ability to self-anesthetize. By "switching," some survivors are also able to work almost continually with minimal rest. Some report the ability to perceive paranormally.

Each identity within the same person may have unique neurological and physiological responses. For example, some identities may require glasses, while others have perfect vision; some identities are allergic to smoke, while others may be chain smokers; some identities are almost deaf, while others have exceptionally good hearing; different alters within one person will register unique electroencephalogram, electrocardiograph, blood pressure, and pulse readings. Alters may have different allergies and different ailments and unique responses to medications. One identity may be diagnosed with an ailment, but a different identity may be "out" when the medication is taken. In this case, the original alter isn't helped, and the receiving alter may have unfavorable side effects. Prescribing medication to survivors who are multiple should be done with special care and extra monitoring.

In the same way that alters protected the child, once survivors get to know their inner parts, most develop a strong reciprocal protectiveness and appreciation of them.

They've got their own personalities. They've got their own talents and their own little quirks and stuff like that. So they're family, and I learn from them. I don't use my alters. I won't exploit them. Jackie Bianco

Professionals who work with multiples often remark on their high level of creativity and awareness. In *Noetic Sciences Investigations,* Tom Hurley echoes an often repeated observation: "Multiples . . . tend to be highly intelligent, perceptive and sensitive." In the same issue Brendan O'Regan writes:

If it is true that most of us are using only 10 to 20 percent of our capacity, then it would seem that multiples . . . may well be using much more than the rest of us. The possibility of tapping into these potentials in a healthy context could have enormous impact for our knowledge. . . . If we do not take these phenomena seriously, and consider their implications for our understanding of the cognitive system, our evolving model of the mind may be led seriously astray. . . .

CLINICAL DIAGNOSIS

Aftereffects of trauma are still being researched, and diagnostic terminology continues to evolve. Some existing terms are being retired and new terms are being proposed. In keeping with evolving trends and thinking, I am using the term post-traumatic reactions to indicate the overall condition; and the terms post-traumatic fear, dissociative experience, and dissociative identity to indicate the most prevalent reactions. (Descriptions and explanations follow.) Professionals are recognizing that post-traumatic reactions exist on a continuum, and many survivors use more than one coping strategy to survive. Trying to arrive at an exact diagnosis using existing terminology can be complex. It is sometimes more confusing than helpful to try to find the right "label."

The current list of specific diagnoses includes but is not limited to PTSD, also known as Post-Traumatic Stress Syndrome (PTSS); various dissociative disorders, which include depersonalization disorder, derealization disorder, psychogenic fugue, psychogenic amnesia, and dissociative disorder—not otherwise specified (DD—NOS); Multiple Personality Disorder (MPD); and catatonia or catalepsy. [For specific term definitions, see the *Diagnostic and Statistical Manual of Mental Disorders,* third edition, revised (DSM—III—R)]. Regardless of which way or ways a child splits, the mechanism of repression and dissociation and therefore the basic approaches to treatment are the same. Recognizing this, the current trend among professionals is to group survivor post-traumatic reactions under a single umbrella that may soon get its own name.

Nancy J. Cole, Psy.D., Clinical Director, Adult Program, at The Center for Trauma and Dissociation, observes the following in the center's June 1993 newsletter:

Traumatic events result in a state of mind that is characterized by mortal terror, helplessness and chaos. . . . As a consequence, the person's entire sense of self becomes organized around the fear of retraumatization. . . . Why do we call it "stress" when we are, in fact talking about fear? . . . If we are talking in the language of "stress" and the client's experience is one of terror, do we increase the likelihood of empathic failure and dysconnection? . . . When I think of the issues in this context, I begin to consider the notion of referring to a person as suffering from "chronic fear syndrome."

In keeping with Dr. Cole's observation, it makes sense to change PTSD to Post-Traumatic Fear (PTF). MPD is being changed to Dissociation Identity Disorder (DID) in the DSM-IV. Following the logic of dissociative identity, it makes sense to change DD—NOS to Dissociative Experience (DE).

Survivors have mixed reactions to the proposed changes. Many survivors have difficulties with change because there are so many selves affected, and each self has a unique reaction. Some worked a long time to accept and feel comfortable with the term multiple personality and so may be reluctant to change. Others prefer the term dissociative identity because it describes the coping strategy rather than the symptom. Some survivors also feel that it sounds less extreme than multiple personality, which has often been given sensationalized treatment in the media. The terms dissociative ident ty and dissociative experience help to desensationalize and normalize the survivor experience.

Many survivors take issue with continued use of the term "disorder." For one thing, it inadvertently perpetuates a core problem for survivors. As children, survivors were repeatedly told that they were deficient, abnormal, crazy, faulty, or inadequate. Believing that there is something inherently wrong with them is one of the most difficult challenges for survivors to overcome. Inadvertently reinforcing cult indoctrination through diagnostic terminology hampers the recovery process.

Disorder also implies maladaption rather than adaption. Having survived is an indication of extraordinary order, not disorder. Sneezing or shivering are not disorders but normal survival responses. They are not called "sneezing disorder" and "shivering disorder." One hopes that post-traumatic reactions will soon be understood in the same way and that the word disorder will be eliminated from the diagnosis.

I want people to realize that we reacted normally to abnormal events. I think of us as extremely normal because our normalcy was challenged to the limit—and we made it. Maya

Regardless of which terms are eventually adopted, use the terms that feel most right to you. If you are uncomfortable with terminology used in this book, feel free to cross it out and substitute it with your preferred term. The most prevalent official diagnoses are PTSD, DD−NOS, and MPD. They correspond to my adopted terms post-traumatic fear, dissociative experience, and dissociative identity, respectively. In many cases these are not discrete conditions but they exist on a continuum. Survivors generally suffer from one or more.

PTSD

The DSM−III−R defines PTSD as "development of characteristic symptoms following a psychologically distressing event that is outside the range of usual human experience. . . . The characteristic symptoms involve re-experiencing the traumatic event, avoidance of stimuli associated with the event or numbing of general responsiveness and increased arousal." This group of symptoms was initially recognized in conjunction with other types of trauma. Professionals noticed that some survivors of car accidents had reactions similar to those of soldiers returning from combat. In the past this group of symptoms was alternately called shell shock, battle fatigue, or combat neurosis.

In the *Journal of Family Medicine* 36 (February 1993), Richard W. Jones and Linda W. Peterson described the PTSD aftereffects of an accident on a three-year-old child.

After the accident, the child experienced nightmares every 3 or 4 nights and would repeatedly scream, "Watch out!" until she was awakened and consoled. In an awake state, the child would cry and tremble whenever she saw large trucks, cars, or motorcycles. She demonstrated reluctance to get into a car, especially when required to sit in the right rear seat. She would often tell her father to drive carefully. When a television program contained car chases or violence, the child would immediately ask her parents to change the channel. The parents also noted that the child's play was more violent: She would occasionally run at her 5-year-old sister and hit her repeatedly. She had never exhibited these behaviors prior to the accident.

Aspects of the event are dissociated, but the event is not forgotten. The soldiers knew they were in a war. The child knew there was an accident. Treatment focuses on processing the unassimilated parts of the trauma by giving expression to it, thereby healing the aftereffects. The trauma may be reexperienced through dreams, behaviors, emotions, and bodily responses. Sometimes the trauma or aspects of it are reexperienced through flashbacks (see page 131).

Post-traumatic fear is usually the least severe of reactions suffered by survivors of ritual abuse. Although symptoms may feel frightening and are a cause of great distress, they are the body/mind's attempt to heal. The trauma is breaking through into conscious awareness, where it can be assimilated and healed. As survivors suffering from amnestic dissociation progress in recovery, they may experience more symptoms. In the meantime, their energies are focused on coping and maintaining a semblance of normalcy through dissociative experience and dissociative identity.

DD–NOS

The DSM–III–R defines DD–NOS as a "dissociative disorder which does not fit the criteria for a specifically identified Dissociative Disorder." Dissociative disorders are generally defined as "a disturbance or alteration in the normally integrative functions of identity, memory or consciousness."

I feel as though I exist in pieces held together by an idea named Erik.   Erik

Survivors with a dissociative disorder are generally more numb and dissociated from the reality of their personal pain. In amnestic dissociation, the experience of trauma is not reconnected, even when memories of the trau-

matic events are retrieved. In other words, survivors feel as though these experiences do not belong to them. Treatment focuses on reconnecting with the traumatic event and assimilating the experience, thereby healing the aftereffects.

MPD

The DMS–III–R defines MPD dissociative disorder in the following way:

A: The existence within the person of two or more distinct personalities or personality states (each with its own relatively enduring pattern of perceiving, relating to, and thinking about the environment and self).

B: At least two of these personalities or personality states recurrently take full control of the person's behavior.

It's as though I'm a ball of mercury that's been dropped on the floor. All the pieces are me but they're separate and different and all going in different directions.   Suzzane

These separate identities or alters can be co-conscious—where a survivor is able to keep track and continous awareness of each alter's activities—or they can be amnestic, or both. Again, there can be any number of possible combinations.

I began to have experiences where I'd be driving along and not know how I got to where I was. Or I didn't know how I spent the last few minutes. Didn't know where I'd been, what I'd done, what I'd said, and that began to really intensify during the course of therapy. I was having some very embarrassing things happen at work. Like people telling me that I had already told them something previously. Or a co-worker will say, "You sounded just like a baby when you said that." Or telling me I'd done something and I'd hotly deny it, because I couldn't remember doing it. It's embarrassing, you know. Jeanne

In the vast majority of cases, dissociative identity is not readily detectable by other people. You may know someone who is multiple but not be aware of it. The popularized portrayal of multiples leading divided lives with radically different personalities and appearances only represents a tiny percentage of situations. Dr. Cliff Morgan, formerly clinical director at Cottonwood de Albuquerque, and currently clinical supervisor at the Life Healing Center of Santa Fe, New Mexico, explains: "Earlier diagnoses emphasized the necessity for external, more dramatic cues such as those found in books about multiplicity—take for instance, *Sybil* and *Three Faces of Eve*. However, not all multiples are alike. For most, multiplicity is an inner experience—often fairly invisible."

It's important for survivors to access and develop the healthy, functional part of themselves. Before recovery, life feels like running a race with a broken leg. Some of us can run forever because we can function and aren't disabled from our past. We are just running on broken legs. Suzzane

Treatment focuses on "association" (as a counterpart to "dissociation"). This involves recognizing dissociated self-states, reconnecting with repressed experience(s), assimilating them, and thereby healing the aftereffects. (Signs and symptoms of post-traumatic fear, dissociative experience, and dissociative identity are discussed in greater detail in Chapter 9.)

AVOIDING MISDIAGNOSIS

The most frequent misdiagnosis is identifying secondary symptoms as the primary problem. Because most survivors are not aware of their traumatic past, they rarely seek help for post-traumatic reactions. However, the aftereffects of trauma often include a variety of symptoms, which survivors usually identify as "the problem." Related secondary diagnoses include depression, physical ailments, chemical dependency, and eating disorders.

The symptoms of unintegrated trauma are very similar to and therefore often confused with various personality or mental disorders. Common misdiagnoses may include: paranoid schizophrenic, borderline personality, bipolar personality, anxiety disorder, attention deficit disorder, clinical depression, and psychosis. While these conditions may be present in survivors, they, too, are often secondary, not primary, problems.

The list of physical problems identified as primary rather than secondary diagnosis is almost endless. Survivors may be diagnosed with or without corroborative test results. A common, although certainly not an exhaustive, list of misdiagnoses may include temporal lobe epilepsy, allergies, thyroid problems, dyslexia, genital problems, digestive and elimination tract disorders, chronic infections, skin disorders, and asthma.

Although it is important to treat all symptoms, treating the secondary diagnoses alone without addressing their traumatic source will not yield satisfactory results over the long term.

I'd been hospitalized with a deep depression three times. Once it was for three months. I am the mother of four small children, yet they kept me drugged the whole time. I was so depressed I was nonfunctional. I couldn't even talk. They gave me shock treatments that started me talking again, but it didn't lift the depression. I was always in and out of hospitals with a different diagnoses—they were always juggling medicines and would keep me drugged for months on end.   A survivor

Unless a physician or therapist has made a point of learning the signs and symptoms of unintegrated trauma, survivors may remain undiagnosed or misdiagnosed for long periods of time. A recent study showed that it took an average of seven years before a person with dissociated identity was properly diagnosed. The best indicator of possible misdiagnosis, physical or psychological, is unresponsiveness to treatment.

Perhaps the most tragic fallout from misdiagnosis is the number of survivors languishing in public institutions. It is believed that some undiagnosed or misdiagnosed survivors end up in mental institutions or in prisons. In many of these institutions survivors are being retraumatized.

SUMMARY

Accident survivors who suffered physical traumas have been treated with care, support, medical help, and kindness. This is the environment in which healing takes place. No one would dream of suggesting that a survivor of a plane crash is somehow defective—quite the opposite. Survivors of childhood trauma deserve at least as much. In a loving and supportive environment, where their pain is recognized and validated, survivors can heal.

Basics of proper treatment include getting a correct diagnosis, understanding coping strategies, establishing a safety-oriented healing environment, accessing, connecting with, and healing dissociated experiences. Unlike many other conditions, proper treatment for trauma survivors yields excellent results.

I went into my therapist's office, and I began reading to her from my journal:

> *I've lived in terror all my life and it was really exacerbated when I came into memories—my panic came to the forefront. But recently I've been on a plateau, and I'm thinking, "I'll slide back into terror pretty soon, as usual." But that's not happening. I've been on a plateau for a long time and I'm not feeling the constant terror and confusion. I remember talking to another survivor who hasn't experienced that fear in over a year—and she told me, "It's over—it's gone." And maybe that's what's happening here."*

I stopped reading and looked at my therapist. She had a kind of scrunched up look, and her face was flushed. I didn't know what was wrong. I said, "Did I say something stupid? Something wrong?" She started crying, and said, "No, it's just that when you started therapy, I didn't know if I'd ever see you like this—happy." And through her tears she said. "You're doing beautifully! You can trust that."   Jeanne

9

Recognizing the Aftereffects

I have this kind of weird visual image of my life as a car. On the outside it looks basically okay . . . it's got a good paint job and everything. But you open the hood and it's like, golly, things are held together with clothespins and duct tape, and it's like a mess, just a mess. And anyone who knows engines would say, "This is just jury-rigged! God, this is insane." And somehow it keeps running and keeps chugging and no one knows.   David Gabriel

If survivors find a way to escape, they continue in life unconsciously carrying the load of dissociated experiences. Survivors often appear outwardly normal in all respects. However, their inner world is usually a tangle of anxiety, panic, shame, and confusion. The struggle to maintain appearances and "keep the engine running" takes monumental effort. For some, just getting through each day is a battle.

I take three steps forward and two steps back, and my net gain is one step, but it took me five steps to get there. And I wonder why I come home exhausted, and why I have a pounding headache, and why does the slightest thing set my teeth on edge.   David Gabriel

Most survivors struggle to keep knowledge of the abuse dissociated. The "no one knows" usually includes the survivor as well. After all, most of us survived by not knowing.

As the body/mind tries to heal the abuse by bringing it to conscious awareness, there may be an equally strong pull to stay protected and dissociated. This internal, often unconscious, struggle takes a monumental toll.

I wake up feeling like I want to die . . . it's like your skin hurts, your heart hurts, all your organs hurt, even your brain hurts. I'm exhausted all the time. I'm always bone tired, and usually in some kind of pain.   Bea

Some survivors develop an alter to function more or less steadily in day-to-day life. This self typically has no awareness of the abuse and may be known as the host. The host, too, feels overwhelmed. In the November/December 1992 issue of *The Sciences,* Dr. Frank W. Putnam writes:

Typically, the host is depressed, anxious, rigid, frigid, compulsively good, conscience-striken . . . and suffers any number of physical symptoms, most often headaches. Host personalities usually feel overwhelmed by life, at the mercy of forces far beyond their control. In many cases a host is either unaware of the alter personalities or, in the face of all evidence to the contrary, strongly denies their existence.

COULD IT REALLY HAVE HAPPENED TO ME?

You may be feeling apprehensive, resistant, or eager to know if you are a survivor—or a combination of all three. Many survivors reason, "I know ritual abuse happens—but I know it didn't happen to me." While occasionally survivors get a "flash" of realization, in most cases it is a slow dawning. Many survivors go back and forth—one day feeling totally confident, the next doubting their own information. That's quite normal. Trust that as you are ready, you will feel more and more certain in your own truth.

A REAL MAN IS NOT ABUSED

Realization, although difficult for everyone, may be more difficult for some survivors. Male sur-

vivors may have an additional hurdle to overcome. Our society defines men in terms of power. A survivor who finds himself powerless over the abuse may feel himself wanting as a "man." This strikes at the core of our societally defined male identity. It may be easier for some to believe nothing bad happened than admit to themselves and others that they were hurt. Because it is culturally more difficult for men to admit abuse, men may also feel less supported in recovery.

There are a lot fewer resources for male survivors. It's real awful and it's real hard to find other men to connect with, to talk to. It's a lot scarier. Men are trained from day one—discouraged from creating male communities. It's a big not-allowed thing. And they often feel unwelcomed in already formed female communities. I don't believe for a second that more women are abused than men. I think that's complete bullshit. Until we see that as many boys are getting raped and mutilated as girls, and sold into pornography and sold overseas into sex slavery, until we start facing that it's got nothing to do with gender, it just becomes a cover-up. You see this lie perpetuated daily in every corner of your life. You feel invalidated, you feel like you don't exist. It's really fucked.   Adam

As increasing numbers of people get into recovery, men and women will be able to see that we are more similar than different. The pain of abuse is not gender-specific.

YOU'VE GOT WHAT IT TAKES

If you found a way to get through childhood, you've already survived the worst of it. Trust that you have what it takes to make it through recovery. You can continue to use the same creative skills and defenses you used to survive your childhood. To add to your existing survival tools you can develop new healing tools. There are other survivors, supportive friends, and competent professionals to help you through recovery.

Healing begins with recognition. Survivors' words are there to help you through. As you journey through these pages, a young part or parts of you who suffered may be hurting as you read. Be kind and gentle to yourself. Take breaks. Remember to seek comfort through your inner wisdom or your Safe Page. Stop to cry from time to time. Your anguish must be heard in order for you to heal.

I've spent so much energy trying to run away from my past. It seems like I was always running, even if I was at home—always shaking in my boots. Then I had a memory. . . . Thank God I made it through. That's when life started getting better and kept getting better and better pretty fast after that.   Jane Linn

HOW TO READ THE SIGNS

Many of the symptoms described in this chapter may feel familiar to people who are not survivors of ritual abuse. Whether a problem is severe or mild, people tend to react to difficulties in similar ways. For example, many people consume great amounts of alcohol in order to escape or medicate their own pain. While they may be suffering, it does not necessarily mean that they are survivors of ritual abuse.

Recognizing symptoms is part of a two-step process: the first step is to identify the signs; the second, to determine their cause. To heal a problem, you need to connect it with its source. For example sniffles are a symptom, not a disease. They may be caused by a cold, by allergies, or by an infection. Some survivors continue to function

with seemingly minor aftereffects. The severity or mildness of a symptom does not necessarily parallel the severity or mildness of the problem. In this chapter, survivors share their symptoms before memories or awareness of ritual abuse. Looking back, they describe how their abusive past played itself out in their life. They are neither all-inclusive (they do not represent every possible symptom) nor exclusive (there are no symptoms that point exclusively to ritual abuse.) You may recognize only one symptom. You may relate to every symptom described. The determining factor is not the number of related symptoms but their cause. For example, looking back, one survivor recognized only four symptoms before she got into recovery. However, in each instance, the problem stemmed from childhood ritual abuse. Once the cause is identified, proper treatment can begin.

You may or may not have dissociated experiences or identities. You may or may not be a survivor of ritual abuse. However, if you are reading this book, chances are you feel there is a problem you are hoping to address. The following sections and remainder of this book may help you determine the source. Reading may be especially difficult for some readers. The symptoms survivors describe represent years of abuse. It is easy to get overwhelmed. Remember to go slowly. Remember also that no matter how many symptoms you recognize, healing is possible. Recovery is a reality for many survivors. It is available to you too.

The aftereffects of sadistic/ritual abuse can generally be divided into two categories. The first set of symptoms enables *dissociation*. They describe how survivors avoid, distract from, and medicate their pain. These coping strategies help to keep knowledge of traumatic experiences at bay. The remaining categories show how the body/mind may be trying to reconnect with repressed experiences or trying to associate* them. Most survivors will have both types of symptoms, although you may have symptoms in only one group.

POSSIBLE SIGNS OF ENABLING DISSOCIATION

Before I knew I was a survivor, I was a successful, up-and-coming person in the mangement program of a prestigious business school. I had passed with flying colors and was starting graduate school. I was going to be the next guru coming out of my department. I got up in the morning and walked my dog. I worked out. I ate right. I went to school, came home, walked my dog again, worked, and went to bed. I had a fantastic relationship. Everything was, you know, perfect. I had been hospitalized occasionally for depression, but they put me on antidepressants. My life continued just perfect after that.   Alicia

The only clue to Alicia's repressed abuse is the depression. It is mentioned offhandedly, as if in passing. She minimizes its importance in her otherwise "perfect" life. This is typical of survivors who have primarily coped by finding ways to stay dissociated from their trauma. They will often make a point of describing all the evidence of their "normalcy" and downplay any indications of a serious problem.

One survivor, who had been hospitalized several times for emergency treatment and engages in severely self-destructive behaviors, looked at the list of possible indicators and said, "It sounds so dramatic. I don't do that. I want to find myself

in the ordinary, simple clues which describe me." Survivors see things when they are ready to see them. There is good reason for the timing, and it needs to be honored.

Survivors who use dissociation or repression as their main coping tool will find many ways to distract from or medicate their pain. Because children were never meant to experience such pain, survivors seek to avoid it in a variety of ways. Are you doing any of the following?

____ Use food to soothe and comfort uneasy feelings?
____ Frequently masturbate or have sex?
____ Drink excessive amounts of coffee, cola drinks, or other drinks with caffeine?
____ Become fixated on food or other "fixes" to the exclusion of everything else?
____ Go numb in front of the TV? Seek escape through the movies or reading?

As the pain continues to rise, survivors distract themselves in more compelling ways. Do you use any of the following as diversions?

____ Do you throw yourself headlong into your career? ____Studies? ____Hobbies? ____ Sports? ____Workouts? ____Competitions?
____ Do you double- and triple-book appointments to avoid quiet moments by yourself?
____ Do you fill empty moments with incessant thinking? ____Counting? ____Humming?
____ Do you create a "buzz" or "ringing" in your head? ____Do you shake your foot at exceedingly fast speeds? ____Listen to excessively loud music?
____ Do you crusade for good causes, focusing on other people's pain instead of attending to your own?
____ Are you always entertaining to throw everyone off the mark? ____Do you throw

---

* *The term "associate" is introduced and used here as a counterpart to "dissociate," rather than as Freud's clinical term "free association."*

parties? _____ Are you constantly telling jokes? _____ Do you laugh incessantly?

_____ Do you use therapy or group therapy, or are you a therapist, as a way to get close to the problem without facing it head-on?

_____ Do you overidentify with other survivors?

_____ Do you choose partners with problems, focusing on them instead of yourself?

_____ Have you been in therapy without any movement, consolidation, or relief for an exceedingly long time?

If the pain still keeps coming, survivors need more intense distractions to keep memories of their childhood at bay. Do you use any of the following as powerful antidotes?

I think dissociation can become an addictive behavior. We* would just keep creating more and more and more alters, because nobody wanted to feel feelings, and we knew how to escape it. We still do it today. I think the more addicted I became to escaping feelings, we began to create alters to handle things which are no big deal. I have people who were created just to come out and fix a flat tire on the highway.   Aimee

_____ Do you create alters as a way to escape present-day life?

_____ Do you dissociate or space out? _____ When not otherwise preoccupied, do you withdraw from your surroundings by becoming self-absorbed?

_____ Do you gamble and drink compulsively or take harmful drugs?

_____ Do you provoke arguments or conflict?

_____ Do you maintain a dizzying pace, punctuated with regular crises in your life?

_____ If you try to take time to recuperate, do you end up feeling much worse? _____ Depressed? _____ Ill? _____ Agitated?

_____ Are you unable to sleep, or need to sleep all the time?

_____ Do you have any obsessive behaviors? _____ Washing your hands? _____ Taking showers? _____ Brushing your teeth? _____ Incessant cleaning?

_____ Do you read continuously without retaining the content of what you're reading?

_____ Do you suffer from anorexia? _____ Bulimia? _____ Any other eating disorders?

_____ Do you have compulsive sex?

_____ Do you become a zealot, practicing extreme religious or physical arts in order to escape from, rather than get in touch with, yourself?

If the pain won't stay down, survivors need intensity equal to their abuse. The only thing as intense is abuse. Survivors reenact their abuse as a way to unload their unbearable, overwhelming pain. Only this time they are safe and in control. This time they're the ones causing the pain.

_____ Do you provoke violence, havoc, and crises in your life?

_____ Do you injure yourself or others?

_____ Do you have violent sex?

_____ Do you prostitute yourself or commit incest or rape?

_____ Do you obsess about suicide?

If you have been nodding "yes" to attempts to distract or medicate, you may be carrying unresolved pain. It could be anything from a repressed present-day problem such as a disintegrating relationship to long-repressed memories

---

* *Some multiples wish to give recognition to their alter selves, and so refer to themselves as "we" rather than "I." In some survivor quotes, the "we" refers to the survivor rather than to a group.*

of childhood abuse. You may also be using these means to help you stay dissociated. Until you discover your own truth, your energy will be tied up in fighting it.

I got clean and sober and made a decision to be conscious in my life. In order to get conscious, I had to get honest, because I was neither of these things.   Lynn

To treat symptoms in the first category, a survivor must recognize and control or stop the dissociation-enabling behavior(s). However, this treatment alone does not give satisfactory results until the second category is addressed. In fact, it is abusive to stop survivors' coping strategies without discovering and treating the source of their pain. Without help in understanding why they need a coping habit, survivors begin to experience unbearable pain without a means of releasing it. In time, they will either find a new coping mechanism or return to the original dissociation-enabling behavior.

If you are a survivor, you need ways to help manage your pain. However, you can begin to use your coping strategies with awareness. If you know you are dissociating, distracting, or medicating, ask yourself, "Am I ready to look? If not, is my coping strategy hurting myself or others? If so, what constructive coping method can I substitute? Can I try to substitute caffeinated drinks for alcohol, and later water for caffeinated drinks? Can I watch a movie about gambling instead of gambling?" Wean yourself of destructive mechanisms gently. It's okay to go slowly. Often the slower the transition, the longer it lasts. It also helps to have peer support (see Chapter 25).

Treating symptoms in the remaining categories (trying to *associate*) generally yields positive and permanent results. Once symptoms in these categories are resolved, symptoms in the first category (enabling *dissociation*) usually subside or even disappear, as there is no longer a need for them.

How are you feeling? If you begin to feel overwhelmed, remember to quickly exit to your Safe Page or the back pages for help.

POSSIBLE SIGNS OF DISSOCIATIVE EXPERIENCE

We had to fuck every night for the first four years of our marriage. By then my partner and I had been to a couple of therapists because by this time we were beating each other up bad; I was initiating and we were violent and I was horrible. I ripped the skin off his back, and Oh, God, it's hard to believe that I was capable of that. On the other hand, it's easy to believe how capable I was of that. So my partner made an appointment to get into counseling or we were divorcing because we couldn't keep doing it anymore. I mean, either I was going to kill him or he was going to kill me. It was just inevitable. Someone was going to die as a result of the violent and blind rages we both used to go into. So that's why I finally went to see my therapist and said, "I've never been sexually abused or anything, but my partner and I—we're going to kill each other."   Annie

Annie knew that her behavior was not normal but didn't know the reason for it. Because her early childhood trauma had been split off and dissociated, she "knew" that she hadn't been abused. However, symptoms do not exist in a vacuum. In time, Annie realized that she was a survivor of ritual abuse and was finally able to see how the repressed trauma was being played out in her life. A similar connection exists in the examples that follow.

NOTE: Some survivors may experience sexual arousal or genital sensations while reading about harmful sex, sadism, or violence. This does not mean that you are taking pleasure in these thoughts. It might mean that you were sexually abused in these ways. An abused child is NEVER at fault.

One of the things that validates my memories for me, when I'm willing to look at it, is that I get sexually stimulated when I'm having a memory about the abuse. I've even masturbated after a memory because the feeling of arousal was so overwhelming I didn't know what to do with it. And it's the body's way of telling, I think, that it was real. I know it's a source of shame. But it's also a source of validation when I'm having a hard time believing my memories.   Brice Roweland

If you experience sexual arousal during parts of this book, it may be a valid clue to your experience. Talking about it can help to heal it. It may take a little while before you feel ready to do so. Think about discussing your feelings with a therapist, a fellow survivor, or a support friend.

The following section describes possible symptoms of dissociative experience. The quotes are from survivors before they knew their histories. Again, these are neither all-inclusive nor exclusive. They are just a sample of possible signs. Keep in mind that these symptoms may indicate repressed trauma but not necessarily ritual abuse. Repressed trauma can stem from many different sources. Some therapists are beginning to suspect that some premature infants who were put on life-support systems for long periods of time develop symptoms of repressed trauma as well. Survivors of any prolonged childhood abuse ranging from incest to unenlightened parenting may share symptoms in common with survivors of ritual abuse. As before, recognition is

only the first step; the next is determining the source.

Survivors who have many symptoms in the remaining sections may appear to be less functional. However, they may in fact be closer to recovery. Since they are experiencing the body/mind's attempt at resolution, they are one step closer to healing. Many "debilitated" survivors make impressive progress once the source of their symptoms is understood.

Signs of dissociative experience can exhibit themselves through behaviors, emotions, bodily symptoms, and knowledge. Some examples below offer clues to more than one area, but they are mentioned only once. Symptoms are often extreme and out of proportion to circumstances. That's usually a good clue to possible repressed experiences.

DISSOCIATED BEHAVIORS

I remember a couple of things from preschool. I never talked. I never, ever talked. I remember a teacher came up to me over and over again and said my name and asked, "How are you today? Would you like to join us today?" For me it was like being in a fog with no way to talk through it. I remember hanging out with the bunnies a lot. I have a class photograph and I'm all by myself in one part of the picture. Everyone was on the platform at the top of the jungle gym, and I was on the bottom on a tricycle looking totally out of it.

Then I went to a Catholic school, and I remember there were three things that they wanted: one was obedience, one was self-negation, and one was silence; and I fit right in with that. For Lent I took a vow not to talk for the whole forty days, and it was like no problem. I was a very rigidly fixated kind of kid. I had patterns—patterns in the way I walked with my shoes, and patterns in how I dressed, and patterns in how I looked at things. So when my mother switched us to another school in fifth grade I was in shock. Everything was so different that I couldn't handle it. I stopped seeing colors for about six months. I remember everything was in black and white. And after about six months, I saw color again for the first time, and I remember thinking, "Oh, wow! It's red."

At the end of the year there would be a graduation ceremony for the kids in the eighth grade, and everybody in school would have to fold their hands and sit up straight in the bleachers facing the audience. One of the nuns said, "Smile and look happy during the ceremony, and the one who looks the happiest will get a prize." And I remember thinking, "I can do that." So I smiled for two hours straight. I never once stopped smiling. So all these adults would have been looking at this kid smiling the whole time, and you know how inappropriate that is. It's like this desperate act of a child who wants something. I got the prize, and I don't even remember what it was.   CeeCee

____ Were you an exceedingly obedient and compliant child?

____ Did you tend to take general statements literally?

____ Did you experience any unusual changes, such as a sudden decline in vision, a sudden deterioration in handwriting, a sudden inability to concentrate or perform?

Ritually abused children grow up in an unpredictable and dangerous environment that leaves them feeling helpless, panicked, and powerless. The panicked child grows into an adult forever trying to control their environment.

I've never been drunk or taken drugs or let anyone mess with me. I'm always in control, and I make sure everything I do is done perfectly.   Erik

The only reason things keep going is because I keep going. If I stop, my world will come unglued. Sunny

Some survivors try to gain control in undetected ways. Undetected control cannot be taken away. Others search out controlled thrills to mask their terror:

As a teen I used to shoplift sporting gear. Sometimes for thrills I used to round up the neighborhood kids and set fire to my hair.   Erik

However often, no matter what survivors try to do, they still feel powerless.

____ Are you afraid of losing control or leaving anything to chance?

____ Do you assert control by refusing food or in other self-injurious ways?

____ Do you take control through ____Stealing? ____Lying? ____Cheating ____Breaking the law? ____Refusing to follow rules?

____ Do you drive recklessly? ____Have an impulse to activate alarms without a reason?

Ritually abused children are often punished for creativity. Creative expression can reveal the secret. Sometimes the more gifted the child, the greater the punishment and humiliation. The cult-abused child may grow into an adult who loves creativity but is afraid of her or his own creative expression.

Although many artists fear the blank page or canvas, for survivors a blank page can mean terror or paralysis. I know of one survivor who teaches art, but is unable to paint himself. Many adult survivors are terrified of their own talents; many dare not express themselves.

____ Do you feel it is dangerous to express yourself?

_____ Are you afraid of your own creativity?

A cheerful child keeps adults off-guard and violators above suspicion. Cult-abused children often grow into adults who always appear cheerful.

Oh, I knew, I knew something was wrong. There was a black cloud around me. But I knew that what the Joneses thought was more important than what I thought. They had to think I was happy. I might close the door, sit under the sink, cry, and suck my thumb. But they never saw how very wrong things were, and no one ever will.   Annie

_____ Do you always smile, no matter how you feel inside?
_____ Do you feel it is dangerous to show sadness or disappointment?

How are you doing? Do you want a suggestion for a fun break? Think about jumping into puddles.

A fairly common symptom relates to sexual behaviors. A ritually abused child is conditioned to associate sex with pain, violence, torture, and death. Repeatedly manipulated into orgasm while being assaulted, a child predictably begins to associate the two. The child grows into an adult with conflict-ridden sexual needs.

I had to masturbate every night before I fell asleep. I would fantasize a lot. It was always about some fat man in power seducing an innocent child; or sex with many people, men and women, nuns and priests. Sometimes it was with dogs and snakes. I always thought that when I got married, I would go ape-nuts over sex. Funny thing is, after I got married I lost all interest in sex. The more I had it, the less I wanted it. And one day, when I

"checked in" with myself, I realized it made me feel nauseous and afraid.   Erik

Traumatized people often reenact their traumas.

I basically functioned as a crazy person. The longest job I ever held was as a prostitute, and that was for one year. It's not that I went along thinking everything was fine. But I never understood it had anything to do with the fact that I'd been abused. I just thought I was bad and crazy. Caryn StarDancer

_____ Are you confused about your sexuality?
_____ Are you compulsive about masturbating or having sex?
_____ Have you masturbated while fantasizing or had sex involving any of the following:
     _____ Children? _____ Groups? _____ Voyeurism? _____ Snakes? _____ Animals?
     _____ Objects in order to inflict pain? _____ Humiliation? _____ Bondage? _____ Violence? _____ Murder? _____ Dead bodies?
_____ Are you unable to experience affection during sex?
_____ Do you associate sex with pornography, money, or power?
_____ Do you feel self-hatred or deep shame?
_____ Are you in brutal, destructive relationships?
_____ Do you have difficulties or unusual patterns around toileting? Do you associate these with sex?
_____ Do you have either a compulsion to have sex or an aversion to sex?
_____ Are you unable to remain present and in your body during sex?

How are you feeling? Parts of this chapter may feel especially distressing. It may be helpful to reread Chapters 1 and 2 to put you in touch with your inner wisdom, reminders of safety, and strength.

DISSOCIATED EMOTIONS

As survivors heal, many talk about feeling centered. Being centered means being in touch and in tune with all of yourself. Dissociation leaves survivors feeling off-center. Here one part takes over—often a repressed, traumatized part. This part may act insistently, but the actions may often be out of keeping with the reality of a situation. For example, a survivor may spiral into shame after a chance encounter with a casual acquaintance. Another clue to dissociated feelings is that they are often at either extreme: for example, exhilaration or despair.

Often when abuse is extreme, survivors cope by arresting or dissociating their emotions. Many survivors experience emotions primarily as thoughts, without feelings. Many believe they do not have any emotions at all.

Describe my feelings? Oh, I don't know. Perhaps like a monotone vibrating in a vacuum. I never pay attention, because they never change.   Erik

I check out my body to see what I'm feeling. I know that I'm nervous by seeing my hands shake. Grace

If emotions do exist, they may exist as polar opposites—an all or nothing expression. Survivors often report feeling too much or nothing at all.

It's hard for me to know what normal fear is. I'm either numb or totally immersed in terror. Jane Linn

Some feel but are unable to express their emotions:

I've spent most of my life not feeling, then go out, get drunk, and end up in this horrible place of rage.   Dave

One survivor described how repressed emotions affected him:

I've been in AA for eleven years, and for seven of those years I wasn't feeling. I was stuck. And I just prayed for the longest time to help me feel, God, anything. And when I started to feel, man, the fucking door burst open. I've spent the last two years crying at forty-minute stretches, just deep sobbing. I gave up tissues; now I use towels. Adam

____ Are you unable to process events as they are happening?

____ Are you detached and smiling while having or describing a terrible experience?

____ Do you walk through crises as though you were walking across the street?

____ Are you aware of your feelings?

____ Do you use thinking to avoid feeling?

____ Are you afraid of spontaneous emotions?

____ Are you afraid of being overwhelmed by your emotions?

____ Do you laugh uncontrollably or at inappropriate times?

____ Are you able to identify your feelings (for example mad, sad, glad, bad, hurt, scared, lonely)?

____ Are you unable to stay with a feeling? ____ Does your shame turn to anger? ____ Does your anger turn to sadness? ____ Does your grief turn to fear? ____ Are you afraid to cry?

____ Is there little or no differentiation in your

feelings? ____Do you feel the same whether you're escaping from a burning building or making breakfast for the kids?

____ Do you react in inappropriate ways? ____ Are you ready to divorce your partner for using your toothbrush, but when your lover cheats on you, you hardly think to complain?

One of the most common dissociated feelings in survivors is fear.

DISSOCIATED FEAR

Ritually abused children repeatedly learn that nothing is safe. To stay alive means staying alert. Hypervigilance is carried into adult life, even if the abuse has stopped. Some live constantly on guard:

I slept for a year with a stick by my bed. Adam

Others live in constant terror:

I've woken up every hour on the hour all my life—especially after I had a baby, to make sure she wasn't kidnapped in the middle of the night. I had horrible nightmares. They were always running after me, always following me, always going to hurt me, and everything turned into spiders crawling all over the place.   Annie

While some survivors are constantly afraid, others are completely out of touch with fear.

Before I had memories, I was fearless. I was so out of touch with my fear, I repeatedly found myself in dangerous situations—like walking in New York's Central Park at 2:00 A.M.   Josie

____ Do you avoid all violence? ____Are you afraid to watch the news or to read a history

book? ____To watch suspense movies ____ To read mystery books?

____ Are you attracted by violence or terrifying events? ____ Do you rush to look at accident victims? ____ Are you excited by horror films?

____ Do you startle easily?

Survivors are often afraid of people.

I was afraid of being engulfed by everyone that I was around. I felt as though something was being sucked out of me. I would always leave an interaction with someone feeling like I would have to kind of catch my breath and put myself back together again.   Bea

____ Are you afraid that people may engulf or overwhelm you?

____ Are you afraid of strangers?

____ Do you feel as though people are deceiving or tricking you?

Cult-abused children are taught to look happy but are punished for being happy. Some survivors are afraid not only of bad things but good things.

Whenever I go on vacation I'll start to freak out. I'll just know that my house has burned down and that someone has come after my cats and killed them all.   Grace

____ Do you panic if things are going too well?

____ Do you have constant feelings of impending doom?

DISSOCIATED SHAME AND GUILT

Cult-abused children may grow into adults who live in fear of being found out.

I got notice that a registered letter was waiting for me. For the next twenty-four hours I was gripped with panic. I knew they'd found me out and were coming after me. I asked my husband to look inside. I could see him handing me my sentence—it was my renewed credit card. Roxana

That's another overwhelming thing. I feel people are going to figure something out about me. So there's this unbelievable level of paranoia all the time. Bea

_____ Do you feel you're an impostor who will be found out?

_____ Do you hate being pointed out? _____ Being the center of attention?

Are you afraid to look at yourself in the mirror?

_____ Are you exhausted by the effort it takes to look normal?

_____ Do you feel as if you were born guilty, and it's not a matter of *if* but *when* you will be caught?

_____ Do you feel as though you are being pursued, but don't know by whom?

_____ Do you regularly "confess" wrongdoings and feel better once you are punished?

Many survivors not only feel ashamed and guilty, but also condemned.

I stay one step ahead of the debt collectors, juggling to see which one I can fend off. I'll just get triggered into feeling that God is against me and that the entire world has been specifically designed and organized to fuck me over. Adam

_____ Do you feel as though you will never live well or enjoy success?

_____ Do you feel like there is no way out?

_____ Do you feel as though there is a conspiracy against you?

_____ Do you feel you are bad?

DISSOCIATED HATE AND RAGE

Cult-abused children are specifically prohibited from expressing anger at their violators. As survivor adults, they may be unable to give anger appropriate expression.

Everything is just knotted up inside me. It feels like my head is coming apart—like it's going to blow up in front and in back. And then the anger starts right in my stomach and then just spreads through my whole body—that tight, knotted-up feeling all the way through. And there should just be an explosion to let out whatever this feeling is. And that's when I lose control. Amy

While some survivors battle constant rage, others are completely disconnected from it.

There was a lot of politics and power plays happening at work. One of the vice presidents ramrodded through a company reorganization. A handful of executives were unfairly slotted for demotion. I was one of them. As the day of demotions arrived, the others fought and bitterly complained. I smiled through the whole thing. Erik

_____ Do you feel uncontrollable rage over inconsequential things? _____ Like seeing dirty dishes or dirty fingerprints? _____ At the sound of a leaky faucet? _____ At learning that the morning paper didn't get delivered?

_____ Are you unable to tolerate anger in others, especially children?

_____ Do conversations with your parents sometimes leave you shaking with rage?

____ Do you feel both enraged and impotent at the same time?

____ Are you unable to feel anger?

Reading through these clues is likely to bring up feelings in many readers. As a child you may have been forbidden to cry or express grief. If you're in touch with any childhood sadness or loss, it's okay to release it now. Your tears are welcome here. You can cry, scream, or rage into a pillow and no one else needs to hear.

BODILY SYMPTOMS

Repressed traumas are stored in the body. They may show up as unexplained symptoms where treatment after treatment doesn't work.

I have epilepsy, migraines, spontaneous infections, and acute pain; shingles, asthma, allergies, and menstrual problems; ear infections, sinus infections, and a lot of throat stuff . . . and just mysterious illnesses, pain and extreme fatigue . . . and that doesn't include the constant flus and colds and things that are just nameless. You don't have a name for it. You just feel sick. Katharine

____ Do you suffer from mysterious illnesses?

____ Do they recur?

____ Are doctors unable to find a solution?

KNOWLEDGE

Cult-abused children grow into adults "knowing" they are not like others and never quite feel as though they belong.

I wasn't able to function—like I was on the wrong planet. It was very difficult for me to feel like I could communicate. I could keep it up for

short periods of time on a very superficial level because I was faking it. Caryn StarDancer

____ Do you feel different from other people?

____ Do you have difficulty developing intimate relationships because of what you "know" about yourself?

The most extensive programming centers on keeping the abuse and cult activities secret. The child grows into an adult who knows enough to not know.

All my life I felt as if I had this deep secret. I just never knew what it was. Erik

Dissociated knowledge can also be expressed as "not knowing."

I had no memory of childhood at all. None. Zero. I remember moving one day when I was ten, and graduating from high school, and a date in between. That was about it. I hadn't been around. I couldn't remember my childhood because it wasn't mine at that point. I was so split off, I didn't have a childhood. Alicia

____ Do you or did you always feel as though you had an unnamed and/or unnameable secret?

____ Did this secret distance you from others?

____ Did you feel you had both a "day" world and a "night" world?

____ Have you forgotten all or parts of your childhood?

____ Are you afraid to talk?

If you are constantly on guard or in terror, if you are afraid of losing control, if you're afraid of being found out, of feeling good, of creative expression, of people and of your natural feelings, without a logical explanation, it may be a sign of dissociative experience but not necessarily ritual abuse. Connecting with repressed experiences is a process that takes time. Once the connection comes, healing can begin.

As you heal, you look back and realize how bad it was. Sometimes you didn't even know.   Bea

The next two sections contain more intense material. This may be a good time to check in with your inner wisdom. Is this a good time to go on? If not, what can you do to take care of yourself?

POSSIBLE SIGNS OF DISSOCIATIVE IDENTITY

There's lots of ways that lots of us explain it. One is that every minor decision we make is a big deal. Every time we decide to go to the store, it's like trying to convince sixty-nine people in a living room to get up and go downtown all at the same time. Every little minor decision takes a whole lot of argument and controversy before we ever get out to get anything done. That's really crazy-making, and if you don't know you're multiple, which I don't think many of us did for a long time, you wonder why everybody else has such an easy time of what you consider to be such major stuff.   Alicia

The coping mechanisms used to escape the trauma rarely, if ever, stop with the abuse. Survivors typically continue to cope with day-to-day stressors using their learned strategies. If the abuse was extreme, the aftereffects may, understandably, be extreme as well. However, these are not so much a sign of illness as a testament to your strength. Dissociative identity tells of ways in which healthy, sane children coped with insane circumstances and sick adults.

If you coped by creating helpful alters, you may have subtle or not so subtle clues to their presence. Alters sometimes peek through into your present-day life. They may go shopping, take exams, or punch someone out without your conscious knowledge. They may still be taking turns to help you cope with day-to-day life. However, as they try to get your attention, you may be feeling increasingly confused. The miracle of dissociative identity that saved you as a child may be playing havoc with your adult life.

I usually wake up in absolute terror every morning. Then we go to the closet—and argue about what to wear. Somebody wants to wear a miniskirt, somebody wants to wear a long skirt, somebody could care less if we ever wear a skirt again and we're going to wear Levis. Somebody argues that if we do that we're not going to keep our job. So we go through getting dressed, and that's real traumatic. Then we go to brush our teeth, and have to argue about which toothpaste we're going to use. And this is on a good day when we're co-conscious. Other than that, if we're not co-conscious, somebody takes control and does it, and eventually in the day somebody else has to live with something they don't like. And it's that way all day long. It's always just constant turmoil. Lots of times I can feel that there's a real argument going on and that people who are listening to that are arguing amongst themselves back deeper. And so it can be like a bottomless pit.   Amiee

I had to write three checks last night to finance the car. And it had to be done. I couldn't put it off. I felt like my whole head was cloudy. My eyesight wasn't good. I couldn't figure out whether I should put my reading glasses on or my other regular prescription glasses on. I wrote awkwardly. I kept losing the little piece of paper where you have to write how much you're sending to them—like there was another part of me sort of trying to make me not do it. Amy

I have no idea how I got my high school diploma. It looks the same as everybody else's, but God knows I didn't get it the same way, because I was never there. I always checked out. I always wondered what was wrong with me. I always heard voices and always felt just a little bit crazy, but I could always maintain control—control being the key word here. Annie

There's a lot in my life missing. I always thought I was an alcoholic who just blacked out. One night I'd been drinking. I remember someone kicked me and punched me out. I rammed my car into his trailer. The guy came out and started pounding me. I got into a terrible rage and it was blackout. Next thing I knew I'm in the hospital. I awoke at three o'clock and saw my face all beat up, full of blood. I got a sick feeling that there was something wrong with the car. If it had been an alcoholic blackout, I wouldn't have remembered the car. That's when I realized it wasn't a blackout; it was a personality switch. Dave

____ Do you sometimes find yourself "coming to" in a strange situation?

____ Do you feel confused? ____ Disoriented? ____Crazy?

____ Do you ever change subjects abruptly? ____ Sometimes even halfway through a sentence?

____ Do you have difficulty following a conversation?

____ Do you feel as though your body doesn't belong to you?

____ Do you ever feel as though your body size or shape changes? ____Becomes very large or very small?

____ Do you ever feel unreal, as though you are in a dream or in someone else's story?

____ Do you lose time? ____ Hours? ____Days? ____Months? ____ With no idea of what has happened?

____ Do you ever say something and immediately wonder "why did I say that?"

____ Do you own things you don't remember buying? ____Clothes? ____Food? ____toys?

____ Have you ever noticed marked changes in your handwriting?

____ Do you ever hear voices arguing in your head or commenting on your actions?

____ As a child, did you have imaginary playmates?

____ Have you ever referred to yourself as "we" or "us"?

____ Have you ever been accused of lying when you don't believe you did?

____ Do you dissociate in a crisis?

____ When faced with a crisis, do you ever "go inside" or blank out?

These may be signs that you have dissociative identity. The above indicators are by no means exhaustive. You may know of many other signs.

Dissociative identity is almost always an indication of severe childhood trauma but not necessarily ritual abuse. It would be important to find out what your dissociated identities hold. If you bring them to consciousness, they can be healed. Healing is discussed in Chapter 15.

If you feel that you have dissociated experiences or identities, you are not alone. There are many survivors of trauma who offer resources and support. They have written books with hints on healthy ways to cope. They have formed support organizations and launched their own newsletters to keep you informed. There are many ways that they are there for you. (See the Resource Guide.)

Take some time to comfort any inner children who may be hurting. Be gentle and kind with these parts as you get to know them. They hold a lot of your pain. Here's an idea you might like to try, or you may try an idea of your own. Find a cuddly toy, pillow, or blanket. Take these to your favorite, most comforting place. Sit with your hurting child. Take five minutes to comfort and love her or him.

I have an adult body and I say adult things. But inside I feel little children screaming—infants, toddlers, teens—pleading, "Look at me, I hurt. Tell me you love me. Feed me. Hold me, and tell me that I'm safe. Help me understand I'm not bad, and take away my shame."   Roxana

POSSIBLE SIGNS OF RITUAL ABUSE

Some survivors may relate to the signs described below before they learn they are survivors. However, sometimes survivors do not experience the signs below until they begin their recovery. Of all the examples given in this chapter, the following are most closely associated with ritual abuse. However, taken alone, symptoms are not conclusive. The key to getting the right diagnosis is connecting symptoms to their source.

SIGNS DURING SEXUAL ABUSE

For many survivors, memories of sexual abuse or incest come first. Violence during rape or incest is often a clue. Some have clear evidence of rituals in their memories.

I had done a lot of work around incest and it was just a progression. I kept going down deeper and deeper into layers of abuse. The ritual clues had been there all along, but I hadn't wanted to

look at them. In one memory of sexual abuse our neighbor and his son watched as my father just kind of used his finger to paint my body with designs of blood. I remember my therapist had said it sounded ritualistic, but I just brushed it aside. Brice Roweland

Abusers who perpetrate incest or rape do so in secret. They want no witnesses to their crime. If there were other people present during your abuse, chances are you were being abused in a cult. Your memories may be providing you with some of the following significant clues:

____ Were there onlookers during your abuse? ____Group participation or multiple violators? ____Humming, chanting, repetition of specific phrases?

____ Was there cross-dressing by the abuser? ____Into strange clothing? ____Uniforms? ____Masks? ____Robes?

____ Did the abuser use props such as ____Ropes ____Knives ____Spears ____Crucifix ____ Charms ____Feathers ____Needles?

____ Did the abuser cut marks or symbols into your skin?

____ Did the abuser draw or smear blood, feces, or urine on any part of your or their bodies?

____ Was there intentional infliction of pain during the abuse?

____ Were you photographed during your abuse?

Some survivors compartmentalize their trauma, keeping incest clues separate from signs of ritual abuse.

I had done my incest work and had a sense that there was more. Nothing in my memories hinted of ritual abuse. But I was still holding a lot of secrets that I hadn't told.   Matthew

_____ Are you keeping secrets from your therapist?

_____ Have you been working on memories of incest without significant or lasting relief?

How are you feeling? If you begin to feel overwhelmed, remember to quick exit to the back pages or your Safe Place.

CERTAIN TRIGGERS

Once a child has been traumatized, a part of her or him will forever be on guard. The event, feelings, and emotions are split off, but knowledge exists in the unconscious (see Chapter 5). It continues to act and protect a survivor from behind the scenes. This radar watches for signs of renewed abuse. Some survivors become very sensitive to reminders of the original abuse. They will have an intense attraction or revulsion to them.

It's the visceral response I go with. When I'm being triggered, my skin starts to crawl, and I start feeling really nauseated. My head starts that sick pounding. It's like I'm not safe here. It's time to leave.   Grace

Survivors may be triggered by any reminders of their ordeal.

We went to an auto show, and one of the rooms had an old vintage car on display. It was dark, all shiny, and polished up on the outside. The inside had plush velour, all tacked in. I walked into that room, turned, and shot right out of there. What I saw was a coffin.   Sunny

I always had a phobia I would lose one of my limbs. I went into a cold terror anytime I heard about sharks, or cancer, or hospitals, or anything remotely connected. I couldn't even tell anyone about this phobia, the fear was so big.   Jane Linn

I began to recognize a lot of tension and fear around people in circles; people in circles, holding hands with anything at all in the middle—a rock, or stones; or at twelve-step meetings when they put money in a basket in the middle; and especially when they were saying the serenity prayer. Adam

Listed below are things that commonly trigger survivors of sadistic/ritual abuse. Are you highly attracted to or unusually frightened by thoughts of or exposure to any of these?

_____ circles _____ chanting _____ rituals _____ groups _____ anything spoken in unison _____ candles _____ robes _____ masks _____ vestments _____ certain colors, most commonly _____ red _____ black _____ white _____ purple _____ spiders _____ snakes _____ maggots _____ insects _____ goats _____ goats' heads _____ cows _____ chickens _____ dogs _____ cats _____ house pets _____ altars _____ churches _____ chalices _____ crucifixes _____ Scriptures _____ marriages _____ baptisms _____ communion _____ funerals _____ births _____ babies _____ abortions _____ coffins _____ mortuaries _____ cemeteries _____ boxes _____ corpses _____ body parts _____ burials _____ live burials _____ suffocation _____ drugs _____ needles _____ injections _____ operations _____ shock treatment _____ hypnosis _____ psychiatrists _____ doctors _____ dentists _____ policemen _____ officials _____ priests _____ ministers _____ rabbis _____ bathing _____ cleaning _____ urinating _____ defecating

_____ writing backwards _____ bright lights
_____ fire

Some survivors are unusually tense around certain days or times of the year. The most common are during Christian holidays, especially Christmas, Easter, and Thanksgiving. In the Jewish tradition these could be Yom Kippur, Rosh Hashanah, Hanukkah, or Passover. In native traditions it could be around special holy days. In addition, many survivors feel triggered on their birthday, on Halloween, or on pagan holidays such as those that fall on or near the solstices (changing of the seasons). (See Occult Holidays.)

I had bouts of depression in March and October. At the time I had no idea this corresponded to high holidays in the cult that abused me. I was diagnosed with "seasonal affective disorder" and put on antidepressants. I coped with my seasonal affective disorder by taking medication and keeping a very tight, rigorous schedule during those times of the year. A suicide attempt, hospitalization, and a new therapist finally combined to uncover my childhood ritual abuse.   Alicia

_____ Have you noticed times of the year when you always feel tense or depressed?
_____ Do you experience unexplained sadness, confusion, or terror around certain holidays or family get-togethers?

It is common for survivors of ritual abuse to be out of touch with their body or their feelings. Please make a special effort to pay attention to both as you are reading. Stop often to notice any body aches, body chills, need to urinate, depression, fear, anger, or grief. If you notice any of these, take some time out to take care of yourself.

FLASHBACKS

Reminders of repressed trauma may sometimes trigger flashbacks. Flashbacks are usually brief visual hallucinatory events reminiscent of parts or all of the traumatic experience. They are a common symptom of post-traumatic fear. Although all survivors do not suffer from flashbacks, they are some of the most disturbing aftereffects of trauma.

Some people talk about it like a movie screen going across your mind or a picture that rotates in your mind. And for me it's not that way. My flashbacks have always been like a half-second flash of a picture. It's like you look at a picture in a magazine, then you flip the page, and it's not there anymore.   Alice

WOUNDED SPIRITUALITY

Because of the many manipulations violators use to prove to children that they are bad, cult-abused children may grow into adults with deeply wounded self-esteem and spirituality.

I feel like a broken piece of furniture that can't be repaired. I don't know what it is I'm missing because from the get-go I never had it. It feels like there's a black hole inside of me which will never be filled.   Annie

It's kind of weird for me to even think it, but some part of me has always felt as though I had been used for purposes against God. It's like my whole being, all my cells were somehow tainted. Katharine

_____ Do you feel shattered in the center of your being?
_____ Is there a bottomless hole in your core, that can never be filled?

OCCULT HOLIDAYS

Some survivors find it helpful to see a listing of occult holidays as a reference. However, different groups follow different calendars. The dates observed from group to group vary, even within the same belief system. The following calendar is a prototype representing common occult dates. It is not representative of any single group or denomination. Another version of "Common Anniversary Dates" may be obtained by writing *SurvivorShip* (see Resource Guide.)

Occult holidays may have dates in common with other, nonoccult groups. In addition, it is

SABBATS/FESTIVALS
Paganism, Witchcraft, and Satanism

January 1st (New Years Day)—A druid (spirit) Feast Day (light fires on hill tops).

January 7th (St. Winebald Day)—Animal or human sacrifice/dismemberment (If human, use a man age 15–33).

January 17th (Satanic Revels Celebrated)—Sexual (oral/anal/vaginal). Use females age 7–17.

January 20th (St. Agnes's Eve)—Diviation (see future husband). Cast spells.

February 2nd (Candlemas)—One of the Witches Sabbats (Sexual—oral/anal/vaginal). Use females age 7–17.

February 25th (St. Walpurgis Day)—Host of blood and dismemberment. Use animals.

March 1st (St. Eichatadt)—Drinking of human blood for strength and homage to demons. Use both males and females.

March 20th (Feast Day)—Spring equinox. Orgies.

April 19–26th (PREPARATION FOR THE SACRIFICE)

April 24th (St. Mark's Eve)—Divining/Herb gathering

April 26th–31st (GRAND CLIMAX/DA MUER) Corpus de Baahl. Use females age 1–25.

April 30th (Walpurgis Night–Beltane–May Eve)—Major celtic festival marked by bonfires and fertility rites (GREATEST WITCHES SABBATS).

May 1st (BELTANE-MAY DAY)—Fire festival (same as above).

June 21st (Feast Day)—Summer solstice. Orgies.

June 23rd (Midsummer's Eve or St. John's Eve)—most important time for the practice of magic-fire festival.

July 1st (Demon Revels Celebrated)—Droids Sexual Sensual Association with the demons. Use females of any age.

July 25th (St. James's Day)—Gathering of herbs.

August 1st (Lammas)—Great Sabbat. Feast of the Sun God. The beginning of autumn and the harvest season.

August 3rd (Satanic Revels)— Oral/anal/vaginal. Use females age 7–17.

August 24th (St. Bartholomew's Day)—Great Sabbat and Fire Festival. Large herb gathering.

September 7th (Marriage to the Beast Satan)—Sacrifice/dismemberment. Female under the age of 21.

September 20th (Midnight Host)—Dismemberment. Hands planted. Use female under the age of 21.

September 22 (Feast Day)—Fall/Autumn equinox. Orgies.

October 29–November 1st (All Hollows Eve)—Sexual climax, sensual association with the demons. Use any human, male or female.

Reprinted with permission from VOICES® in Action, Inc.

important to note that many occult groups, including witches, celebrate these holidays respectfully and are not involved in ritual abuse.

Some of the descriptions may contain upsetting material therefore read the listing with appropriate caution.

October 31st (Halloween)—Great Sabbat and Fire Festival. Night dead thought to return to earth.

November 4th (Satanic Revels)—Sexual (oral/anal/vaginal). Use female age 7–17.

December 21st (St. Thomas's Day)—Great Sabbat and Fire Festival.

December 24th (Demon Revels/Da Muer)—High Grand Climax. Use males or females.

PERSON'S BIRTHDAY: Highest of all holidays; involves victim and someone in authority.

SHROVETIDE (three days before Ash Wednesday): Another witches Sabbat date.

GOOD FRIDAY: Black Mass

EASTER: Children given to High Priest (rebirth to Satan).

Adding five weeks and one day to dates will present the Grand Climax to all underworld demons.

All holiday's dates change from year to year according to the satanic calendar and differs from cult to cult.

The information herein has been furnished by Officer Sandi Gallant, Believe the Children, and Dale W. Griffis, Ph.D.

_____ Do you feel that there is something awful or evil inside of you?

_____ Do you feel that it is dangerous for people to love you?

_____ Do you feel it is dangerous or forbidden for you to have children?

_____ Do you fear hypnosis, or people's stares?

_____ Are you afraid that somebody will get your mind?

_____ Do you feel as though someone is always watching you? _____ There is someone inside you? _____ They know what you're doing? _____ What you're thinking? _____ That there is no escape?

_____ Do you feel as though your soul has been _____ Lost, _____ Stolen, _____ Sold _____ Possessed?

_____ Do you feel you need an exorcism? _____ Are you afraid of being exorcised?

Self-esteem and spirituality are discussed in Chapters 17 and 22, respectively.

One of the hardest things for me to remember as I'm trying to find ways to cope is that I'm no longer four years old and helpless. Today I have power; today I have choices. Roxana

How are you doing? If you're feeling a little down, is there something you can do to take care of yourself? Calling a friend often helps. Don't be shy. It's okay to reach out.

INTRUSIVE THOUGHTS

Traumatic learning is the backbone of cult ritual abuse. It may be a survivor's most significant yet most elusive clue. By learning to recognize thought patterns that stem from traumatic learning or reenactment of trauma, you can gain control.

I don't know why I always thought I was going crazy. Cutting was a big deal—you know, like with razor blades. I used to cut . . . cut, cut, cut, all the time. And burn. Oh, God, I burned crosses in my feet, in my legs, and I've just always liked to burn and cut. And I still have razor blades around me all the time. I don't use them. I just feel safer in a room which has razor blades in it.   Annie

I'll be driving, and suddenly, for no apparent reason, I get a clear image of me driving the car off the road.   Sunny

_____ Do you have messages in your head that contradict your values?

_____ Do short repetitive phrases run through your head in response to certain situations? (For example, "I'm a liar," "It's a lie," "It's a trick.")

_____ Do phrases like "Truth is a lie and lies are the truth" and "Good is bad and bad is good" sound familiar to you?

_____ Do you regularly *report* rather than *share* information about your comings and goings to family members or violators?

_____ Do you ever feel like a robot, as though not in control of your own actions?

_____ Do you feel driven to do things that are not in your own best interest?

_____ Do you ever feel angry, self-destructive, or suicidal for no apparent reason? _____ After a visit from your parents? _____ After a minor argument? _____ On your birthday? _____ After therapy? _____ When things are going well?

_____ Do you ever have thoughts or a visual flash of hurting or killing yourself?

If there is any chance that you may harm yourself or someone else, get help now. Turn to the back pages and follow the instructions you have prepared for yourself.

Discovering traumatic learning may feel frightening. You may be feeling helpless or even afraid of yourself. You may also experience relief, which comes from understanding. Feeling frightened, helpless, or relieved is normal. You're on the right track. Awareness is the first step in overcoming traumatically based impulses. Do not act on them. Instead of responding to them, try writing or drawing them. Use the act of writing or drawing as an act of release. Once they're on paper, you no longer have to act. It also helps to share your expressions with a therapist or a support friend.

In time, you can uncover the memories that created traumatic learning and break any hold they have over you. There may be barriers to retrieving memories, but survivors are doing it and breaking free. Freedom is one of the many gifts survivors receive as they begin their healing. (For more on triumphing over harmful impulses, see Chapter 16.)

Signs of ritual during incest, certain triggers, feeling evil or possessed, and self-destructive impulses indicate a possibility of ritual abuse. You may have been nodding "yes" throughout this chapter and feeling certain in your truth. You may have been nodding "yes" but are uncertain. Periods of uncertainty are normal in recovery. Your truth will unfold in its own time, in its own way. Trust that. Whatever your childhood experiences, if this book feels healing, you can continue to benefit.

HEALING IS POSSIBLE

As life becomes unmanageable, many survivors seek help. You may be well on the road to recovery, or just uncovering your abuse. You may have no awareness of abuse, only a vague sense that something is wrong. You may be having night terrors, flashbacks, or panic attacks. Do not be frightened. This is normal. There is a way out. Wherever you are in your journey, healing is possible. There are many paths open to you. By meeting and healing the tormented child, you can heal the wounded adult. It is a difficult journey, but there are immediate rewards with each step you take. Survivors emerge stronger, more at peace, and in control of their own life.

It was both scary and a relief. Learning I was a survivor was like hearing the frightening diagnosis and knowing the cure instantaneously.   Erik

I remember people looking at me, judging me, always finding me falling short. Now I see people look at me with admiration in their eyes. People haven't changed; I've changed.   Mike

It gets better, life gets better. It does. I have no more spiders in my bed at night. I even sleep through the night now--hooray! The addiction is no longer raging like it was. I'm no longer violent and my partner and me no longer beat each other up. I haven't hit my daughter in five years. I haven't taken Valium in two years.   Annie

I still have bad days, but I would never change who I am now. Today I love myself. I trust myself and my feelings. Today I am healing.   Alicia

10

Finding Lost Parts

So many were lost
Far, far within me
In deep drifts of time,
Trapped there
By their violent flight
Through the brooding dark
Of unrealized childhood.

Excerpt of a poem by Gerald

LOST AND FOUND

Years into recovery, I began to understand that I am the sum total of my experiences or my memories. Since many of my significant experiences were dissociated, I didn't really know who I was. By finding my lost parts, I began to experience a newfound completeness inside. The difference in me "before" and "after" is profound. It's been like finding an elusive treasure hidden in forbidding grounds. But in negotiating past or through the dangers I found my greatest fortune. Today I know who I am.

The aim of ritual abuse is to fragment self-awareness and destroy self-love. The triumph of recovery is to regain both. It is a long, slow, rewarding process that cannot be rushed. During this process survivors discover and learn to love and appreciate all of their lost parts—love and appreciate themselves.

WHAT YOU CAN EXPECT

You may read through the next two chapters and identify with most of the topics described, or you may identify with very few of the experiences discussed. The likelihood of your identifying with these issues depends primarily on two things: the way in which you coped, and how far along you are in your recovery process. Some issues may be immediately relevant, others may become relevant as you get more in touch with dissociated aspects of yourself, and others may not apply to you at all.

Although recovery is challenging, its difficulty varies from survivor to survivor. Some survivors suffer primarily from post-traumatic fear, others primarily from dissociative experience, and still others primarily from dissociative identity. However, the coping strategies for most survivors lie on a continuum incorporating aspects of all three. At one end of the continuum are survivors who, although in great pain, continue to function through recovery with minimal disruption to their lives. At the other end of the continuum are survivors who are constantly suicidal, feel out of control, and need to be hospitalized. Most are somewhere in between. However, as dissociation becomes better understood and effective healing tools are developed, recovery is becoming more manageable, and hospitalizations and medications are required less often.

Most survivors develop a coping strategy that allows them to function normally in day-to-day life. If the abuse has stopped, many, if not all, of the dissociative identities may remain inactive, while a "host" self carries on. However, as survivors begin to associate their lost parts, some find that life temporarily becomes more unmanageable. "Falling apart" is an interim step in the process of recovery. This chapter discusses how to manage association more safely and productively.

Survivors typically spend a lot of energy and resources to maintain control and stability of their inner dissociated selves or parts. It may be more difficult to do so in times of stress, when you're tired, or when you are triggered by reminders of your past. To maximize personal safety and minimize disruptions, you need to take care of your needs and the needs of your inner kids as soon as you become aware of them. Self-awareness gives you better control of your life.

Ensure that you have a proper support system in place while reading through these chapters or before attempting to work through the issues described. See Chapters 1 and 2 as well as Part Six to ensure that you are getting competent help.

UNDERSTANDING LOST SELVES

The terms dissociative experience and dissociative identity may mean different things to different survivors, depending on how they coped. Regardless of whether you coped primarily through dissociative experience or dissociative identity, the trauma is usually held by a younger entity, usually a child. With dissociative experience, the child may be experienced more as an "inner child" described in popular recovery literature. She or he holds the repressed memories but is still felt to be part of the self. With dissociative identity, the child may have her or his own way of relating, experiencing, and thinking about the world, with experiences and memories and a will different from the host self. Although these dissociative identities may feel very different, they are all manifestations or aspects of one person.

The point of recovery is to develop continuous self-awareness or co-consciousness and cooperation with all of your lost parts. Parts of self holding dissociated experiences or the personalities of dissociated identities are developed to varying degrees. They have varying capacities and wishes to be treated as full human beings. Identities need to be appreciated to the full extent of their being. Their humanity cannot be recognized until and unless it is assumed to be there. Assuming full humanity of each self or part results in the most rewarding gains and deepest healing.

Beacause dissociation typically exists on a continuum, and the variations are nearly limitless, it is impossible to address every possible scenario. Survivors with Dissociative Identity generally have issues-in-common with survivors with Dissociative Experience; however, the reverse is not true. By addressing DI issues, DE issues are included. The issues described take into account the most extensive aspects of dissociation, and so will not apply to everyone. Use the sections that feel relevant to you and feel free to bypass those that don't.

RECOGNIZING LOST PARTS

The amnestic barriers that protected you as a child also act to prevent association and healing. Amnestic barriers can be very strong. One therapist who was working at a treatment center helping ritual abuse survivors come to terms with their abusive past had no idea that he was a survivor himself.

Some survivors have always known they were multiple and are quite comfortable with the idea.

I don't ever remember not being multiple, but I don't feel multiple—I mean, I do, but I don't, because it is so natural to me. I don't know what normal is. I don't know what it feels like not to be multiple.   Maya

Some survivors assumed they were like everyone else. For example, many thought that everyone heard voices inside their head. Through recovery, survivors are often surprised to learn about ways in which they are different.

I blocked out most of my childhood, but I've always known that when I wanted to remember

something, I had to stop, sit real quiet, and absorb it really deeply. Otherwise we'd never remember things. And what they tell me is that normal people don't have to do that to retain a memory. Amiee

Some survivors always had a feeling that something was not quite right. Many had a barely conscious feeling that there was more to them, but they couldn't connect with that something or express it. Learning about their multiplicity may have come as a relief.

We've been alive for thirty-five years, and three years ago a huge event happened. We discovered we were multiple. And knowing it explained a lot. It clarified a lot. We feel more at home in ourselves now.   Deborah

Some survivors learn about their multiplicity, with no awareness of ritual abuse.

We're comfortable with the way we function as a multiple. We're always working on improving things, but it's okay. So this really scares us about ritual stuff and that it probably happened. Initially the way it scared us was like "Holy Shit! I'm a multiple, what does that mean?" Then we read everything we could. And now it's the same thinking about ritual stuff—it's like, "Holy fucking shit!" We have got this programming in us, we have triggers, we have suicide triggers. I mean its really scary. And then we just thought about the way we educated ourselves about multiplicity, and now we check inside for information a lot. So we said, we can do the same about ritual stuff. So that really made us feel better. So now we are working towards diffusing the internal fear and potential internal or external harm. We're getting more expert inside—this makes us feel really good.   Deborah

Other survivors have memories of ritual abuse, but no awareness of their multiplicity. Survivors can go for years in recovery before discovering dissociated identities. Looking back, a survivor with dissociative identity remembers how it felt:

I watched the movie Sybil *and I was just horrified. I thought the whole thing was so bizarre. And I was attending a group for incest survivors at the time. Two of the women and one of the men kept repeating over and over again that they were multiple. And my whole feeling was, "Geez, I'm glad it didn't happen to me." It's pretty funny now that I look back on it, but I used to wonder what it must feel like to be multiple.   Suzzane*

Whether you are aware of dissociation or not, you may feel as though there are parts or pieces missing. As one survivor put it, "I feel as though I were a block of Swiss cheese." Recovery is about finding lost parts. As you find and heal the missing pieces, you will begin to feel increasingly whole.

IDENTIFYING LOST SELVES OR PARTS

Survivors have referred to their dissociated entities as parts, selves, personalities, alters, self-states, inner kids, and so on. Use whatever term feels right to you, regardless of which terms are used in this book. Each survivor's history of trauma is unique and different. Therefore, your internal team of alters or parts will be different from anyone else's. However, there are patterns to the types of identities survivors abused in ritual groups have found. By knowing some of these patterns, your inner kids may feel more familiar as they emerge.

The names given below to dissociated parts or selves are for purposes of general identification. However, identified or standardized names and processes are open to reprogramming by currently active violators. It's a good idea to develop your own naming system, especially if you are at all concerned about renewed abuse by your violators. Use the information in these chapters as a basis from which to create your own unique conventions and approaches to healing.

Keep in mind that your alters or parts may have split off differently than the ways described below. Remember to always trust and stay with *your own* experience. It's the only one that matters. Take whatever information applies or helps you to develop a framework for your own recovery. Do not try to "force-fit" information that does not feel right. Initially it may be difficult to know which is which. But if you stay with your feelings and intuition, your history will sort itself out in time.

THE LOGIC OF DISSOCIATED PARTS

Chapters 6 and 7 talked about cult conditioning and destructive family systems. The types of experiences described in both chapters are the types of experiences that may be dissociated. In addition to traumatic events, and personalities holding them, survivors also usually split off their most vulnerable parts, or selves, for safekeeping. These are the soft, gentle, creative, playful, and spontaneous parts.

Described below is a typical constellation of dissociated aspects or identities. It does not represent any one individual but common patterns. You may recognize some of them.

THE INNOCENT CHILD

During healing work, my friend brought up this phrase over and over—that I am sacred, clean, pure, and beautiful. That phrase went very deep and really helped me heal on some level. It helped to keep reminding my child that she was and is sacred, and that I can still contact sacredness. It's extremely important because the whole focus was to take everything that was sacred and trash it. And for us to reclaim sacred as a concept is showing that we're going to make it.   Bea

This is the child the other parts are protecting. Some survivors have a sense of an original child before the abuse, others conceptualize their innocent selves in different ways. Regardless of how the innocent child is understood, accessing innocence is healing, helps survivors feel increasingly whole, and more in touch with their self.

We don't believe in the idea of a single "original" self but think that to some degree our core is part of each personality.   Deborah

YOUNG CHILD OR PREVERBAL ALTERS

Survivors typically have preverbal or child alters. You may have four-year-old alters such as Miranda, who holds the memory of Josephine, as described in Chapter 5. You may also have dissociated preverbal parts. In these cases your body may re-create the trauma without accompanying thoughts or words. Child alters also hold abusive experiences that happened either within cult ceremonies or within the family context. Techniques used in child psychology work well in healing child alters.

Child alters are very common because the age of an identity is often related to the child's chronological age at the time of the abuse. Once created, many alters remain the same age and

perform a set function that doesn't change. Others may grow in both age and responsibilities.

Infant alters can offer profound healing for survivors. In *Treating Abuse Today,* David W. Neswald and Catherine Gould write:

> PDEs [primary dissociative experiences] will, in effect, serve as a foundation or template upon which all later (secondary) cult programming is built. . . . By associating PDEs, a survivor's primary and secondary programming may be substantially neutralized. Often a client's entire internal programming network begins to quickly unravel once the fundamental primal dissociative memories are reassociated.

By associating his PDEs, one survivor accessed a foundational alter who identified himself as "the Source." The Source was a black, evil core. The child was told, and on some level believed, that this was his basic identity. By working to transform this foundational concept, tremendous amounts of related negative conditioning began to dissipate.

Neswald and Gould warn that working with PDEs is "definitely not the place to begin practicing reassociation. . . . [It is] a very delicate process and should be attempted only after solid intrasystem co-operation and a strong therapeutic alliance between client and therapist [have been achieved]."

As always, there are tradeoffs in finding the best timing. One survivor told me:

Waiting for stable therapeutic and intrasystem alliance is an ideal that cannot always be met. Before I had that "ideal" support, the integration of my first traumatic memories helped to give me the necessary strength to deal with the horrendous shit that followed.   Caryn StarDancer

THE HOST

The host, described in Chapter 8, is the part that may have emerged over time to function in day-to-day life. She or he usually stays out more continuously once the abuse has stopped. The host may be the person reading this book or looking for help through therapy. A host is often the personality who manages the other parts. Some have absolutely no awareness of other personalities. They may be unconsciously controlling other alters, preventing them from emerging. Once hosts learn how to safely relinquish control, they become key facilitators in the healing process.

GUIDING AND HELPING PARTS

Some multiples have guiding or helping alters. They are sometimes referred to as inner self helpers, or ISHs, and are typically bright, creative, and cooperative. They usually have a working acquaintance with the inner system. Although they may not know all the answers, they may know how to get them. In other words, they may function as a sort of information broker or traffic director. They can be helpful in guiding the therapeutic process and finding ways to solve seemingly unresolvable problems. These alters often emerge early in the therapeutic process, especially if they are asked to come out.

SPECIAL-PURPOSE ALTERS

Special-purpose alters may be created to help cope with day-to-day life. These can be: the parent, the student, the cook, the gardener, etc. A common special-purpose alter is the mimic.

I remember leaving hypnosis sessions and feeling like I wasted my money. And what I found out is that basically I had, because I had alters that were created just to go in and fake being hypnotized. I

think all of us, and this includes other multiples, are people pleasers. That's one of the reasons we're multiples to begin with—so that we can act the way others want us to act. And so we would have alters for just hypnotherapists. They would imitate other alters, and they would let the therapist think that they had really accomplished something when in fact they had done nothing.   Amiee

SENSITIVE, CREATIVE, SPIRITUAL PARTS

Ritual abuse sets out to destroy a child's spirit—the combination of feelings, creativity, and will. Survivors learned how to protect these special parts by dissociating them. These specially gifted and talented personalities may be poets, artists, nurturers, singers, etc. They are often fun and delightful. Some may also be frightened. However, they have strength, fortitude, and determination. They along with the others helped the child triumph in the end.

DESTRUCTIVE FAMILY AND CULT-IDENTIFIED PERSONALITIES

Negative day-to-day learning becomes internalized, or dissociated into the unconscious. Children have no choice except to take in what they are taught. Cult families in particular force their own deficiencies on their children (see Chapter 8). After many years in recovery, one survivor realized:

I actually have a dysfunctional family within myself. I have several alters that are enraged, several that are terrified, one is a comedian—he's playful, but he also had to learn that it's inappropriate to tell dirty jokes.   Dave

These parts may or may not be dissociated, but they are damaging and counterproductive.

They are events that could not be resolved and became dissociated. They are your abusers, internalized or metaphors of your abuse. Their internal messages or voices are shaming, condemning, critical, and judgmental. They are parts who may think in extremes without room for a middle, compromising ground; selves who may medicate the pain in unhelpful ways, personalities who may be controlling, polar opposites, and so on. They may be drug addicts, bigots, prostitutes, or reminders of specific members within a cult.

We wanted to hurt people to protect ourselves. Sometimes we just wanted to hurt to see if other people hurt too. Amiee

THE PROTECTORS

Most abused children develop alters similar to Ogre, who holds a child's rage at being assaulted, deceived, and abused (see Chapter 8). They may be as mean and nasty as their perpetrators in order to protect themselves. Survivors may develop extra-violent and strong alters to protect their soft, gentle, creative parts. For some survivors these may be animals like wolves or lions; people known to a child, such as strong Uncle Charlie; or mythical heros such as Superman. However, some alters protect the child by becoming handicapped or elderly, because one child realized that "no one hurts people who are sick."

THE MAINTAINERS

The identities keeping cult messages and dogma active inside the survivor can be thought of as maintainers. Sometimes these alters are created to emerge only during cult rituals, never in the "day" world. Although they may seem hostile and to behave in opposition to a survivor's best interest, they believe it's the only way to keep the survivor or themselves alive. By "maintaining" the cult rules, no one dies. These are the parts who enforce cult commands. They may prevent a survivor from going to therapy or, once there, create havoc and confusion in order to sabotage recovery. These selves may hurt a survivor or attempt a suicide, sometimes without the conscious knowledge of the survivor. They may appear to be genuinely cult-loyal and appear to enjoy hurting themselves or others. But, like Rex, they were all created under conditions of extreme duress (see Chapter 6).

These inner kids initially almost always feel frightening, both to the therapist and to the survivor. Some identities may posture and appear threatening and so are often rejected or ignored. But it is these selves that need healing most. They are the ones who contributed so much to rescuing a survivor from unbearable circumstances and today need rescue from those circumstances themselves. After all, most of them are only kids.

ACCEPTING ALL YOUR PARTS OR SELVES

By discovering, accepting, and healing alters early in recovery, survivors are likely to experience maximum progress. One survivor found the following written in her journal:

We're thrilled that we're getting to know all the parts. We know that without all our parts there would be a depressed dead body, if that much. Maybe just a dead body. And we're ashamed to admit we feel shame about others seeing our small parts. And this makes us want to love and nurture and make amends to our small parts. Yeah, we're coming to terms with this. Deborah

Is it time for a break? If any inner people need love or comforting, this may be a good time to attend to them.

ORGANIZATION OF INNER PARTS

In the same way that various alters are created to keep outsiders from accessing the hurt, vulnerable parts, so the internal organization is constellated to accomplish the same thing. The amnestic barriers are designed to protect both the original child and her or his identities. In ritual abuse, the assaults are extreme, manipulative, and cruel. The child's dissociative system has to be able to withstand the most devious and diabolical attempts to unravel it. The internal organization of the alters and how they relate to one another can be very intricate. For example, a system may be layered. Here the external personality layers interact with the outside world, and the middle layers act as a system of messengers/interpreters, communicating with the inner layers of alters, who remain protected inside and never "come out."

It's like you pull away different layers or personalities. And it's like pulling away the people that face the world most and then others that face it a little less, and then you get some who aren't facing so much outside but more to the inside, and protecting, all protecting really one certain part. Katharine

Some survivors imagine an internal "place" where alters exist. For some it's behind an "impenetrable wall." Others describe internal worlds or geographical places. Some may have a fairyland where the children play, or a North Pole where alters who took the pain can go to have their pain "frozen."

It's like a massively intensive chess game. Certain people can jump up and across. And some really can't move at all. Others are just fakes. It's like a real complex computer system. Like a government spy ring.   Amiee

Some systems may be configured like a wheel with spokes. The selves along each "spoke" know only of the selves ahead and behind them. They may have a sense that there are more along their own spokes, but no awareness or interaction with parts existing along the other spokes. Behaviors are managed from the "hub," which maintains total awareness. The variety is nearly infinite.

It's weird. My system is organized in levels. I've gotten a glimpse of a third level. I thought there might only be two—but okay, that's fine. In the first level they were real personalities. They were very separate—would come out and live my life. My therapist and I identified one as the magazine person. Somebody I created to go to graduate school—no feelings—"We're gonna get this done. This abuse thing is getting in the way of our productivity." That's who started therapy. The second level is feelings. There are some people, but they are not as well developed. They're attached to a particular memory and only come out when I'm thinking about that memory. And I think the third level has to do with details. It appears worse because there's more of them. But everything is tinier. So they're very much easier to integrate.   Alicia

Alters that together hold a single event may be called "clusters" or "fragments." Parts in a cluster may have a vague awareness of each other but not of other parts.

Fragments usually don't have a lot that they have to do. Personalities usually have a whole story that they need to tell. So what I feel is if I only deal with somebody once or twice, they're probably a fragment. If it's somebody that keeps coming up and coming up and coming up, then they're a personality. Amiee

Some systems have safeguards to make sure no one unravels their internal logic. For example, they may take the form of a labyrinth. Parts that appear to be related to each other reach a dead end. Still others follow turns that end up going in circles. But regardless of how a system is configured, there is always an internal logic. You may have many combinations of these configurations, and other configurations not described here. Again, the variety is limited only by your own creativity. Typically, the more extensive and prolonged the abuse, the more complicated the internal organization. Extremely complex systems may result in a polyfragmented multiple. There may be no one part or self in charge. There is less continuity or awareness between the parts. In the earlier stages of recovery, alters may emerge in a state of disorientation. They may repeatedly have to be taught how to tell time, days of the week, names of their own family members, etc.

MAPPING

Typically, victim children are unaware of their own internal survival system or how it works. In addition, the amnestic barriers prevent adult survivors from knowing their own configuration of alters. Once in recovery, some survivors find it helpful to "map" their internal system—identifying the parts, their names, and how they relate to each other. However, even in recovery, many survivors resist charting.

Alters usually don't want their systems under-

stood. This is a protective mechanism. Many continue to feel threatened when "outsiders" attempt to decode their system. Some may spontaneously reconfigure their system if they feel an "outsider" is getting too close.

Some people I know have had a very aggressive approach—you know, they chart it all out and they map it all out: who is everybody, and what was their role and function. And that works for them. But for me, I don't want to know who everybody is. I mean, that may be a little overwhelming. If they come up in my life, they come up in my life. Alicia

The internal structure may be stable or quite fragile. In either case, it is important to move with a survivor's readiness to shift or unravel it. Invasive therapy techniques should generally be avoided. It is generally not a good idea for a therapist to insist that survivors name their inner people (some have no names), map their inner system, force certain alters to come out, or impose a recovery schedule. As a general rule, invasive techniques do more harm than good. Instead of breakthroughs, they may be creating internal chaos. However, it's important to recognize that each survivor is unique. One survivor commented, "my life was chaos. I welcomed directive therapy."

What feels invasive varies from survivor to survivor. If your therapist suggests something that doesn't feel right, don't do it. Instead, it is more helpful to understand and address the reasons behind the resistance.

NAMING THE DISSOCIATED PARTS

Survivors have many names for their internal constellations. Some call them a system:

I think of my inner kids as though they were part of a computer system. It feels really orderly and that's comforting.   em

Trudi Chase, who wrote *When Rabbit Howls,* called her inner people "The Troops." Some survivors refer to their inner parts as "the company"; some call them "friends"; others may call them "the team," the "group," "the community," "the cooperative," and so on. Although alters are often thought of as having names and ages, there are many who do not. Dissociated parts can be identified in any number of ways, such as "the angry one," or "the one who thinks," or "green." When different parts are "out," survivors are not always clear about who is communicating. Sometimes alters do not feel as if they have any specific characteristics. Also, as with internal organization, some alters do not like having their characteristics known.

HOW ALTERS FEEL

Although all alters want love and recognition, they will remain hidden unless they feel it is safe to be known. It's important to let changes happen in their own time and in their own way. Respect and cooperation with each alter will yield the best results in the long term. The purpose of recovery is to have everyone join the team eventually.

A lot of therapists use hypnosis, which is a form of forced regression. And what I've found since we finally have a therapist we trust is that when we walk into her office, we just go flop. Everybody jumps out and everyone wants to say what they want to say, and we really don't even need hypnosis or regression. The trust level is really important. Amiee

It may be both exciting and frightening to begin to get acquainted with your parts. For many this is an intense and awesome part of recovery. However, it's important to realize several things. Many alters are stuck in the past. They only know behaviors that got them through a combat zone called childhood. Many are not aware that the abuse has stopped. In order to protect the child, some alters had to genuinely become aligned with a cult—any sign of reluctance would have been instantly spotted. Protectors may come out still wanting to protect. Many are frightened or shy. Some may feel too damaged or fragile to come out. Others may remain mistrustful, expecting that recovery is just a trick and that coming out means being hurt once again. Some believe that recovery means losing their unique "self" and identity. Others are afraid they will be made to leave. Alters who took on unpopular jobs are afraid of being hated or rejected by the host or other alters.

If these potential problems are recognized, addressed, and neutralized up front, recovery can proceed much more successfully. Therpist Mary Ellen Holmen confirms:

Nobody has to go away. Everyone in the system can have a new job in recovery. All the personalities are important. Some can be reeducated, some can get a chance to grow up.

How are you feeling? Could you use some time out right about now? Remember to check with your inner kids as well.

PROCESS OF DISCOVERY

Many survivors first get in touch with their hurting alters, who hold painful experiences or protect fragile parts of themselves. These personalities typically hold day-to-day traumas sustained within the family and the types of experiences described in Chapter 6. Later, they may get in touch with alters that have internalized their parents, and later still alters who have internalized cult violators.

However, each survivor's order of recall follows its own unique logic. This logic is in keeping with a survivor's own internal self-protective system. Alters or dissociated experiences will emerge according to their own readiness. Much of this readiness depends on perceived permission to surface, anticipated acceptance, and safety.

It may take some time to discover your dissociated identities. There is no rush. It's not important to go quickly but to go safely and gently. You don't have to look until you feel ready. Go at your own pace honoring the needs of your inner kids, not a therapist's or anybody else's.

The unknown often engenders fear. However in most cases, once a phenomenon is studied or given a chance to be understood, it is often found that a fear is unfounded. Many survivors and their therapists, afraid of multiplicity, struggle to keep inner kids behind their protective barriers. In some instances, if a personality is trying to surface, therapists encourage the host to "take control." However, the pull to be known and recognized is the pull to become whole.

You can recover memories till you're blue in the face but not heal. When you can reach these inner children then the healing really happens. Being safe is being able to get to know these guys. And as long as we resist our willingness to accept that they're there, we deny them the right to heal. And I think the ultimate goal is when we can get to communicate with the ones who are programmed—to help them not to be afraid anymore, and not let themselves be brainwashed anymore. And that's freedom. Suzzane*

Unless and until these dissociated identities are acknowledged and welcomed as part of a survivor's experience, survivors will not have an opportunity for true healing.

GETTING ACQUAINTED

Although there's a saying, "Some things need to be seen to be believed," there's also a saying, "Some things need to be believed to be seen." This is certainly true about multiplicity. Here is one survivor's experience.

One day I went to my therapist and asked, "Do you think I'm a multiple?" and he replied, "Oh, I don't get caught up in those kinds of terms. Everyone's got different parts to their personalities." Well, about a year later I happened to be in Oregon, and entered therapy up there with a person who understood how to talk to multiples. In my first session with her, one of my inner children came out and had a voice. And the power behind that experience! Her name is the Bad Seed, and there in that office, I became the Bad Seed. Her terror had been forbidden and condemned. She was never allowed to express it until that day. She got a new name—Flower Blossom. She looked around and said, "Where am I?" I was co-conscious. It felt so strange. My body and voice experienced her fear. This experience has completely changed my perception of "looking inside" intellectually. Now I have contact in a visual and sensual manner with my inner entities. Suzzane

Usually discovering inner selves is a slow and laborious process. However, sometimes it can be quite the opposite.

A friend of ours who's multiple explained it. It's like you'll get a glimpse of something that happened and alters fall out. It's not like meeting someone new and saying, "Well, it's nice to meet you," and then they leave. It's like opening your closet and having ten or twelve people fall out and say, "Hi! We're yours."   Amiee

At the other end of the spectrum, survivors can go for years in recovery before any dissociated identities are ready to surface. You may be surprised, even frightened, to discover these seemingly independent parts. One survivor discovered his first alter after six years of working through dissociated memories of ritual abuse. The alter began to emerge over the course of several therapy sessions. This survivor had worked with other multiples in groups and took a positive attitude towards multiplicity. However, when his own alter began to emerge, his whole perception of multiplicity changed. The host, Janes, felt threatened and even terrified as this part began to take on a life of his own. Suddenly basic, everyday decisions became confused and complicated. In a reversal of circumstances, the host felt that he was going to die, as his more "authentic" six-year-old "self" began to assert his presence.

Here is an edited and abbreviated version of the dialogue between Janes, the therapist, and ultimately Jimmy, his alter:

Janes to therapist: *I've been trying to get in touch with my little six-year-old. And it's interesting—he's kinda bossy—you know, he kinda orders me around and I feel like I play a sort of victim to him. Something made me check inside, and I said, "I should be processing—*

shouldn't I?" And in a real emphatic voice he said "Yes!" You see—like making me feel stupid and guilty. Anyways I went ahead and so here's what I wrote to my six year old:

> To be part of the big me, you'd have to be part of all those horrible things that happened. And I know that you refused to be a part of those things, and so you left. And I can't believe that you would want to be part of this overwrought body, wrung inside-out with no stamina left.

And through my writing, he replied:

> I love you for what you went through for me. I'm not afraid to be with you. We'll go through whatever else needs to happen together. Thanks for remembering me. Now we have to gather up all the others so that we can be together at last.

I have this sort of feeling—like I'm all air—like I've got no substance. It doesn't feel like my center returned. I don't know what to do next. I've always known what to do—where to try to go in recovery next. But I don't feel that way right now. And he did tell me we could do this together, but I don't have any experience of doing anything with him together. And I'm afraid people won't like him, because he's not at all like me.

Therapist: *Are there some feelings there? Are those tears?*

Janes: *I just feel like there's a gulf between me and him. And I'm supposed to love and take care of him. I feel like I can't just step aside and let him take over. Because it's like he's come back to claim his body. So is this what multiplicity is like? with the co-consciousness? Is that what's going on?*

Therapist: *Sounds in the ballpark. Stay with the feelings you're having right now, and see if you can express them directly to him, talking to him. Do you feel okay to try that?*

Janes: *Well, it's like you left, and you left me to take everything on, and I did, and I did the most horrible things, because you weren't going to, because you were too full of integrity, and you were stubborn and strong. And it's not fair to just discard me as though I never existed. I did the hardest stuff, and I hung in there as best as I could. None of this is fair, and I don't even know if I like you, and it feels weird to have to die. I don't think he cares. He doesn't care about other people. He only cares about himself. At least it feels to me like he doesn't.*

Therapist: *Can you ask him?*

Janes: *Now he's all hurt.*

Therapist: *What's that hurt about?*

Janes: *He doesn't want me to be mad at him.*

Therapist: *Does he want to say anything back to you? Can you switch over? Let him talk back to you.*

Janes: *I don't know. You see I'm afraid of letting him out, because then he'll run around and do the things six-year-olds do like a real kid.*

Therapist: *What if you just pretend in fantasy that you were him, and let him speak back to you in that way?*

Janes: *Yeah—well I've never done this before so I wouldn't—this is all very new to me—except luckily I've read enough about it not to be all scared. Well—my little six-year-old is saying—*

Therapist: *Just let him talk back to you now. Just imagine that you're him, and he's doing the talking to you. Let him talk directly to the thirty-five-year-old.*

Jimmy: *Well, I'm just a little boy, and I'm really scared, and you're right, I have strong wishes and things, but I've been waiting such a long time. I've been waiting a real long time to have somebody listen and pay attention. And I couldn't come out before because of all the*

things that were happening. And I really love you for taking all those things on. I do. And I think we could work well together, and I really don't want you to be mad at me. I really want you just to love me.

The more Janes could let Jimmy speak for himself, the less threatening Jimmy felt. In time, through continued dialogue, Janes came to realize that despite how bossy Jimmy sounded, all he really wanted was to be taken care of and loved. As Janes learned to do that, the conflicts stopped.

HEALING EACH PART

Jimmy's comment "I really want you just to love me" sums up what's at the heart of healing each alter. Through love, children have their basic needs met. Many survivors feel instinctively able to console their inner children. However, some who never experienced being loved may feel lost or overwhelmed by this new responsibility. These survivors need a little help, and time to get used to love.

A common error is to concentrate on healing the cooperative parts. These parts are often already "on board" and well on the road to recovery. By leaving the difficult parts behind, a key part of a survivor may remain anchored in the past and prevent progress beyond a certain point. Some alters hold violent, angry, or destructive aspects of a child's unassimilated trauma. Because these parts hold extremes of frightening experiences, survivors and therapists alike often try to avoid them. However, it is usually these difficult parts who need healing most. In many cases accepting them restores a great amount of strength and personal power to a survivor. In addition, these apparently uncooperative parts, once healed, often become strong allies in recovery.

Every one of them has the qualities that any human being has. And every human being needs to feel that they are loved, that they are safe, welcome, and that they belong. em

MEDIATING POLAR OPPOSITES

For every extreme, polarized emotion, there likely exists its dissociated polar opposite that needs to be recognized. Caryn StarDancer emphasizes the importance of the mediative approach:

People respond to extremes of trauma with extremes of coping strategies, or polarized reactions. The result is a bipolar system of self-states who are, for example, nonverbal/verbose; dysfunctional ("helpless")/hyperfunc-tional ("workaholic"); innocent/"demonic," and so on. The healing process is one that gradually ameliorates the extremes in the survivor by moving them toward a more moderate middle. I urge survivors and therapists to keep in mind an approach based on this bipolar model. If you concentrate only on the dependent self, the independent self begins to forget how capable he or she is; if you only deal with the self who's very capable, you risk forgetting the self who's getting lost and is in pain. So in every instance it is best to remember and address both sides. Encourage the workaholic self to learn how to play. Teach the inner selves who only want to play how to do the dishes and balance a checkbook. This approach recognizes the whole self, stretches rigid roles, redefines limiting self-concepts, encourages sharing, and alleviates the load of recovery.

No matter how forbidding an alter appears, she or he is a part of us. The challenge isn't in knowing if an alter can be healed. It's in finding out how. As David Neswald and Catherine Gould write in *Treating Abuse Today:*

We thoroughly reject the notion of the "untreatable" MPD patient. As long as the patient isn't truly psychotic, there is always hope. It is up to the therapist to find the appropriate strategy for his or her particular client. If the therapist remains consistent, and is kind, direct, knowledgeable, and committed, the ritually abused MPD client stands an excellent chance of healing. This is not to say that every therapist can effectively treat every patient. . . . Those who they cannot seem to help must be referred to another therapist whose experience, demeanor, commitment, therapeutic style, and/or treatment team provides greater efficacy for the patient.

Would you like a break before reading on? Now would be a good time.

WORKING WITH PROTECTOR PARTS

These are the "Ogre" parts—little children posturing as mean and hostile villains (see Chapter 8). While initially menacing and threatening, these parts, once disarmed, are not at all dangerous. Recognizing and validating the hurt behind the anger usually disarms them. Many simply start to cry. Acceptance and nurturing heals their pain, and these originally hostile parts become transformed into regular little inner kids. In many cases, simply validating a child's pain disarms her or him. However, some alters can be very strong and violent. Here's how therapist Pat Graves connects with them:

I think it's that real soft touch that works. When I worked in the psych hospital and there were like raging alters, somebody standing on the bed, ready to hit me with a chair, I would just sit down, and I'd say, "Wow, you sure are strong. I wish I could pick up a chair like that." And it just diffuses everything. . . . It's like if you had a war, and nobody came. It's really hard to fight when there's no enemy. And so part of my philosophy is to make sure I never back anybody into a corner where there are no choices; to make sure that I don't set up battles. I step aside—because struggle only increases intensity to win.

WORKING WITH MAINTAINER PARTS

One of the more perplexing outcomes of ritual abuse is the creation of maintainer alters. These alters are motivated to keep themselves and other child parts alive and safe by following the commands of a cult. They begin to identify with their violators and over time become their loyal supporters and followers. This dynamic is a commonly observed response of victims to their captors and is called traumatic bonding. It is likely to develop in cases where the abuser holds the power of life and death; there is no escape; the victim is isolated; and the abuser shows some kindness towards his captive. A famous example is the case of heiress Patty Hearst, who appeared to "convert" to the cause of her Symbionese Liberation Army captors. It was not a conversion made by choice but an instinctive survival reaction.

Devotion, masquerading as love, springs from a place of mind-numbing terror. A survival-oriented part of a child instinctively understands that only those in power get to live. Therefore, in order to survive, victims often become desperately attached to those in power. They cannot afford to know that their "savior" is the one who is causing the abuse in the first place. By "maintaining" cult rules and devotion to the violators, everyone gets to live.

In such cases, inner kids did the job that no one else wanted. Instead of gratitude, understanding, and acceptance they may initially be rejected by the other parts. As in the case with protectors, they are usually children or adolescents. As soon as someone acknowledges their pain, acknowledges that they didn't want this job but did it anyway, and that it hurts to be rejected, especially by the survivor, maintainers begin to gradually soften, and in time they, too, come around.

The healing began when my "good" ones recognized that the "bad" ones sacrificed their original goodness in order to save the rest of us. The "good" ones returned some of the original goodness back to the "bad" ones and took back some "badness"—the responsibility, guilt, anguish, anger. This reaching out and compassion were a pivotal point in my recovery—the beginning of the end. Caryn StarDancer

It sometimes takes a little longer to convince maintainers that they're better off in alliance with a therapist and a survivor. As long as they believe survivors are not as powerful as their violators, they may not be able to change. They need to learn that violators are *not* all-powerful. They need to know that they won't die if they join ranks with a survivor. They may also need to be told that their "special status" in knowing powerful secrets is based on lies. Power comes from free choices and being true to yourself.

Chapter 16 addresses special issues that may

come up with maintainer alters. These may include suicidal or self-injury impulses or impulses to return to the "safe" familiarity of a cult. These self-destructive impulses can be overcome through understanding each alter's function and through unwavering faith in their core goodness.

11

Creating a Healing Environment

What the human mind can do is just phenomenal. And all I do is just respect that. People can control their own system, and they do it. They do their own healing. The very first thing I do is to make sure each client has a safe and cooperative way to begin their work.

Pat Graves, Clinical Director, The Life Healing Center of Santa Fe, New Mexico

Survivors have typically coped by learning to respond to threatening situations. This promotes reactive rather than proactive thinking. Recovery is about reversing the process—it means taking charge. To maximize effectiveness of recovery for survivors with many inner kids, it's helpful to have some structure. One of the most important factors affecting success of recovery is establishing a healing environment using creativity and imagination. The healing work can begin once the alters or parts can come together in safety. The ideas suggested in this chapter have worked well to promote inner safety, communication, and cooperation among the alters.

However, they may not be right or appropriate for everyone. They apply primarily to survivors coping with dissociative identity, but some ideas may be useful to survivors coping with dissociative experience as well. As you read, check in with yourself to see if these ideas fit. Remember to follow your own instincts. In time you will discover what works best for you.

There are three ideas that may be helpful in promoting safety, communication, and cooperation. They are a recovery "facilitator," meetings, and safety rules.

FACILITATOR(S)

Safety is knowing there is a part of me I can rely on.   A survivor

It's important to have some alter or a group of alters who together function as the facilitator(s) during recovery. They don't have to be adults. Responsible kids can be very effective. These identities need to know or learn how to calm scared inner children; decide when it's safe for different alters to come out; schedule recovery meetings; always be present and available; and get help in an emergency. This group's most important job is to keep you and your inner kids safe throughout recovery.

It took a while, but I finally figured out that I need to identify a responsible personality in the beginning. Just make myself grow up in some aspect and tell my inner kids, "I'm in charge. I'm not perfect. I'll screw up and do things wrong from time to time, but I won't abandon you. I'll keep trying. We'll work it out." And that's what a parent is, and that's what the system needs—a parent. Maya

Each survivor needs to decide what attributes the facilitator(s) will need to keep themselves and their inner parts safe. Basically, this self or team of selves needs to be capable, dependable, and "on call."

You can't just march in and say, "We're in recovery. You're going to tell us what you know." The most important thing was to pretend that I was in kindergarten with lots of children and they were hurt. And all I would do initially was just be there with them. Let them see me show up every day. Make them understand that I'm there for them. And in their own time, they will gradually

start coming to me and telling me things. They'll tell me everything I need to know.   Maya

Sometimes it's a therapist who initially models this parenting role for a survivor. It's important to give survivors the stability, security, and love they never experienced as children. However, good therapists will also work to gently wean you of dependency on themselves. They will encourage and help you develop those self-parenting skills within yourself. If you don't take on this responsibility, your inner parts may become dependent on yet another person who cannot be there for them constantly. Instead of helping build trust, a therapist-dependent relationship in fact erodes it, often leaving survivors feeling abandoned and betrayed.

RECOVERY MEETINGS

"Recovery meetings" help you, your therapist, and your alters get acquainted with one another. The purpose of these sessions is to help you discover your lost parts. You can try the following ideas alone; however, they work best with a qualified and trusted professional, especially until successful techniques are established.

Because you are dealing with both little children's needs and adult needs, to get communication and cooperation going you need to establish an environment that is a combination of a kindergarten and a management meeting. First, establish an internal "recovery meeting center" where your dissociated selves can come to listen and be recognized. It can be an imagined community meeting hall, your backyard, or anyplace that feels safe.

As with any successful meeting, there should be a purpose (an agenda), a time, and a moderator (this can be the host, a therapist, or the recovery facilitator). Because many of the participants are young children, they will need behavioral guidelines.

CONDUCT GUIDELINES

Since the old rules of behavior no longer apply, alters need to learn new ideas about individual and group conduct. It's a good idea to start at the beginning with very basic commonsense rules. For example, alters who are willing to "attend" (enter a survivor's conscious awareness) need to be told that they should "arrive" promptly, not interrupt while others are talking, and speak using "I" rather than "you" statements (see Chapter 20).

One survivor used to experience tremendous headaches after "community meetings," as all of his alters rushed "back home" (returned to their dissociated states) at once. He told them that they have to leave slowly and quietly, and the headaches stopped. Another survivor was besieged by the clamor of her inner parts.

I developed one of the most intense migraines I had ever had. Everyone was talking and saying things all at once, and I just couldn't handle it. It was like being trapped in a madhouse, with no way out. Finally, in desperation I called a survivor friend who suggested I talk to them and calm them down. Taking her suggestion, I told them they were all important and that each would get a chance to tell me what they had to say. The only thing was that they would have to wait till I could make time, and they would have to take turns. And once I promised to hear them out, the inner chaos stopped.   Suzzane

It's important that each alter who wishes to participate gets a chance to "check in." If they need more time than what's available, another meeting can be scheduled.

To help get internal communication going, survivors can try any number of ideas. For example, you can suggest that your alters stay in their amnestic barriers where they feel safe, but make the barriers transparent so they can watch and hear what's going on. (This means that the alter remains in the unconscious but becomes aware of what is happening in the survivor's conscious life.) If some inner kids are unable to hear, then someone can create a bulletin board to tell them what sorts of things are being decided. One of your alters can offer to keep minutes of recovery meetings, so that anytime someone forgets what happened, they can read about it in the recovery journal. Alters who are reluctant to come to community meetings can learn about what's happening in this way as well. There are many different ideas survivors have used to help their inner company develop awareness of one another.

Recovery meetings can be called on a regular basis (for example, daily, or at the start of each therapy session), or anytime something happens that everyone needs to know about. Each alter can speak for her- or himself through the facilitator(s), or another alter. If an alter cannot talk, she or he can write or draw on a notepad.

In order to encourage participation, alters who attend can get a treat at the end of each meeting. They might get coins or crayons or gold sticker stars. Older alters may enjoy a magazine. Another incentive can be to have socials or playtime after the meetings.

We have meetings at the seaside, and afterwards, those who come get to go swimming or sailing. Then, I've built a gorgeous inside home, and later the alters who want to can start to take up residence there. That way, my alters can really begin to get to know one another.   Janes

Don't worry if you do not have a distinct "inscape"—many multiples don't. A real park, your backyard, or your living room, or your Safe Place can work just as well.

Everyone is encouraged and welcome to come, provided they follow the guidelines. These new guidelines take some getting used to, and so you can expect that alters will forget from time to time. Allow your alters some leeway during times of learning and growth. However, there are some rules which must always be obeyed—these are rules you establish concerning safety.

SAFETY RULES

You can determine safety rules as a group, develop them with your therapist, or simply have the facilitator(s) decide what will work. Make them simple. Make sure they are understood by all the inner parts, and follow them without exceptions. Therapist Pat Graves found two rules that work. She explains:

I teach people to have an internal meeting where they call everybody together and people can ask me questions, cuss me out, or do whatever they want to do when they first meet me. I make sure I reassure them that I'm not trying to get rid of them. And then I start having regular meetings as a way to begin expanding the alter parts' awareness. And then pretty soon somebody will say, "Well, Cynthia here is really pissed at you." And I'd say, "Great. Let's talk about it. It's fine for you to come out and talk about it." The rules are that

NOTHING GETS BROKEN
NO ONE GETS HURT

And using those two basic ideas, I've not had

to send anybody up to the hospital because of an emergency. I had somebody the other day say she's not coming out because she can't agree to the rules. And that makes it safe, because it tells me that the alters are following the safety idea.

They know the rules—that we're working together, but we're not going to allow one of the personalities to take over and get out there and do their own thing. But that's a real tough issue that I had to deal with.   Dave

TALKING WITH ALTERS

Alters take a risk, and it takes a lot of courage for them to come forward to talk. As an alter emerges, they feel in strange territory. Their first priority is their own safety. You can support them by suggesting they ask any questions they want, and answering them as honestly as you can.

You can also encourage them by asking open-ended questions such as "Is there anything you want to tell me? Is there anything you want me to know about you?" rather than "What's your name and how old are you?" These closed questions may feel invasive if there is no relationship or trust established. In addition, alters who do not have or do not know their name/age may get an implied message that they are different from others and so feel shamed. With safety, acceptance, and permission alters will share most needed information on their own.

You can make it easier for alters to communicate by providing pencils, crayons, and writing and drawing pads for people who can't speak. Many alters are "forbidden" to talk. By using codes instead, you can help them to communicate—for example, by using finger signals (one finger may mean "yes," two fingers may mean "no," three fingers may mean "I don't know").

You can also use tapping signals (one, two, three taps) instead. You may want to establish new codes at the start of each session, to prevent tampering with signals by violators or internal identities. Additional communication ideas are given in Chapter 15.

Alters who come forward need to be thanked and acknowledged for their bravery. No matter what they say—whether it is encouraging or critical, praising or blaming, commonplace or unimaginable—each alter who comes forward deserves acknowledgment and thanks. Their messages are important pieces in the puzzle of finding your self.

Assume that every identity in the inner community is listening, whether you know of their presence or not. If information does emerge, treat it as though it is coming from an alter with a full range of human needs and feelings. This gives permission for alters to be themselves and not be concerned with rejection. Knowing they are fully accepted offers alters the greatest opportunity for building trust and healing. This open-minded approach often works best because both dissociated experiences and dissociated identities are healed through total acceptance.

THINGS TO COMMUNICATE

Once the group knows and understands the safety rules, internal communications can begin. While critical information will vary from survivor to survivor, some types of information seem generally useful to most. Most need to know what year it is and that the abuse has stopped. Some need to keep hearing it—especially if something unexpectedly frightens them.

I found one alter who calls out the date—that's his whole job—he calls out the date all the time. "Okay, everybody—It's nineteen ninety-four.

That doesn't mean it's ninety-two, it's ninety-four, not fifty-two, ninety-three and we're safe now." Suzzane

You may want to let your alters know that everyone is in recovery and the little ones need an explanation of what that big word "recovery" means. The team may need to learn about the therapist and be introduced to her or him. They may need to learn that their violators are dangerous people and that it is unsafe to continue to see them. This is also a good time to see if things agreed to in the last meeting are working out.

Those parts or selves who are brave enough to come will have feelings and reactions about the information they hear. Each alter may be affected differently. It is important to hear from everyone who is willing to talk and address their concerns and needs.

Meetings are a time when you can ask your alters for help as well. For example, you can draw a symbol and ask, "Has anyone ever seen this, or does anyone know what this means?" You can also use the recovery meetings to help in problem solving. For example, you can ask, "Can anyone tell me why some inner people are afraid of the color blue? Why is Cynthia still feeling angry? or Why won't Rex come to the meetings?"

As trust begins to build, your internal self-state can help you in many ways. In time, you can ask them if any parts in the system are still in contact with violators, and specifically if they are being reprogrammed through renewed abuse. However, alters' communications cannot necessarily be accepted at face value.

DETERMINING CURRENT CULT INVOLVEMENT

Experiences held in the unconscious have a present-tense quality. They have not yet been completed. They are still active, because they are unresolved. Therefore when inner parts or alters come out to talk, they will often talk in the present tense, as if an event is still going on. If you're listening to protector or maintainer alters, it may sound as though they are currently dangerous or still cult-active. While occasionally they may still be cult-active, most often they are not. Alters' perceptions are always based on their reality, but they may be reflecting a partial truth. It may be based on past circumstances or on information given them by violators in order to undermine the survivor. Another possibility to consider is that some alters may continue cult ceremonies on their own, without participation in an active cult. It is their way of affirming their own identity. This may or may not mean that there is any abuse going on. Caryn StarDancer explains:

> As alters who have been repressed begin to surface through recovery, some survivors experience an increased drive to become cult-active. This is understandable, since these alters are cult-identified—it's what they know and how they learned to be "safe" during their abuse. The person on the outside may not know whether or not they're cult-active. For example, a survivor may get a phone call with a message which contains a programmed cue, which evokes an alter who then goes to a cult meeting. A few hours might be lost or even a few days, but when the "host" comes back, it may only feel vaguely confusing, or as if something is wrong but he or she doesn't know what . . . and that is a chronic feeling for many survivors. There is usually a story in the mind that "explains" what happened, and it doesn't seem quite right, but those are the things you feel you don't want to question too much because you get nervous. It is also possible

that an alter is "attending rituals" only in a vivid internal scenario. These alters may not have experienced enough outside life, especially drug-free outside life, to be able to tell the difference between outside and inside reality. So people should not panic or jump to conclusions until enough information can be gathered to evaluate the situation. If it becomes apparent that the survivor *does* have an active alter, he or she has not really *changed* or become more dangerous, s/he's simply become more aware of what s/he's dealing with and what precautions need to be taken to protect self and others.

However, as soon you discover presently active cult alters, you need to deal with them, directly, as quickly as possible. You can talk to them through others initially, but the sooner you can deal with them directly, the sooner they can be brought into the fold. It doesn't work to try to change them through others. They need to see for *themselves* that they've been tricked and conditioned—anything that they hear through someone else will be filtered through their programming. If possible, it works best to find an inpatient facility familiar with ritual abuse and dissociative disabilities, and to focus the time in the unit on reaching the cult-active alter. If that is not possible, I try to help the suvivor assemble a support team who will help monitor their activities until we can talk to the cult-active alter directly, and help them realize that the cult's "power" is really bondage, and that real power is in working to keep the self system out and safe.

To help advance co-consciousness, the host and each alter might begin to keep a chart or journal, noting date, time, place, and pertinent details of activities. This can help determine whether you actually went to a meeting "outside" or "inside." While record keeping might be frustrating or tiring, it is not just helpful in promoting safety; survivors often discover that it helps them to recognize old, destructive patterns that, once identified, can be addressed.

Dealing safely with alters in a group setting is discussed in Chapter 24.

COOPERATING TO RECOVER

It is almost like a self-hypnosis, totally relaxed, they're all out. And when I first started working this step, most of them didn't know each other. And therefore, what did I have? I had all that lost time, and I went from inner child to inner child—brain compartment to brain compartment. The first two females that came out were at serious, serious odds. Early on there were only four of them, and three were pissed off with the sexual behavior of the fourth. And her behavior changed because of communication with the others.   Dave

An alter's original task had been to keep the trauma in a dissociated unconscious. Now the task is to gradually make each of the alters aware of one another. Each alter has a story to tell about what she or he did to keep the child safe. Through sharing their stories, alters develop a mutual awareness and begin to appreciate the part each played in the rescue mission.

Each alter needs to be thanked and congratulated. Whatever their part in the rescue mission, it was essential. Without participation, the rest of the system might easily have crumbled. As it is, the survival effort was a success—and now it's time to have a reunion. With each part that comes forward, a survivor experiences an increasing sense of wholeness. Each alter needs

to be welcomed back to consciousness and celebrated.

The big thing in counteracting programming is being in touch with all my alters, even the terrifying ones. Once I know who my alters are, I can set up a safety system to protect me from being pulled back into the cult.   Suzzane

Once inner parts get to know one another they become major players in the recovery mission. Each can turn their extraordinary abilities toward healing. For example, the protectors can be taught constructive defense skills and help survivors process their anger. A maintainer can now keep a survivor in the present safely and away from her violators. In this way alters can now enjoy the life they struggled to save. However, changing jobs isn't always an easy thing.

We know that some of us, or lots of us, did jobs that aren't needed anymore. Like some people's jobs involved not getting close to anyone, not trusting anyone, and those jobs just don't aid us in living the full life we want to live. So that was actually sad to realize that the jobs that people worked so hard to get good at may not be needed now or may not be helping us towards where we want to go. And there is still some mourning and grieving to do, and there's also the job of giving a tremendous amount of thanks to all those survival parts. So now, what growing up means is a choice for the parts to either heal—to operate in a thriving way—or go to sleep. That's their choice.   Deborah

Although alters typically have different personalities, motivations, and interests, they need to recognize that they are all on the same team. As the team succeeds, each alter benefits. Alters spontaneously cooperated to help save the victimized child. In the same cooperative spirit, they can learn to help heal a survivor adult. Cooperation is achieved through understanding, information, and respect for each alter's needs and wishes, much as in a warm and loving family, which these inner selves never had. Because there are so many different constellations, varieties of personalities, and possibilities, each survivor's challenges will be unique. Some survivors report very few internal conflicts. Their team seems predisposed to cooperate.

It's just so fortunate that we mostly get along. And I can't say that I really worked on getting along, since I knew about our multiplicity. I think it gets figured out internally and it just gets presented to me. So as far as functioning as a community, we've been doing great—that's with an exclamation point!   Deborah

Others are faced with challenging conflicts.

The amazing thing is it's like a relationship. The more we sit there and hiss between our teeth that we accept each other—whether we do or not— the more moderate the personalities become. The ones who couldn't do anything but scream obscenities and be real angry, now that we've said that's okay, that's what you need to do, just don't do it at three in the morning. They're becoming more moderate. They're turning into people who can go to work and function and not want to kill people and bite their heads off.   Amiee

Many survivors will have a combination of cooperative and independent-minded alters. Because many alters had roles that were polar opposites, it will take some time for the internal community to learn how to coexist and cooperate. In addition, many have to be taught ideas that people simply take for granted, such as respect for themselves and for others.

LEARNING RESPONSIBILITY

Besides cooperative conduct, some alters also need to be introduced to the idea of responsibility. With responsibility come more privileges and freedoms. Some alters learned to use the switching technique to avoid unpleasant consequences they themselves may have caused. The following example shows how alters may offload responsibility for their actions onto other more vulnerable alters.

Confrontations. I'm terrified of confrontations, and I try to leave anything that makes me uncomfortable. It's scary for me to stay, because I'm not used to that. For example, Sorita, one of my alters, started a fight with her husband one night, and she hit him and provoked him into a physical fight, and then she checked out. And what happened is he flattened her. But she left when she saw the hand coming, and Tia who's three years old got hit. And so any sort of confrontation is really scary because I never know what's going to happen with it and it's real hard to stay present for me. Amiee

In recovery, alters learn to take responsibility for themselves and their actions. If they throw a party, they have to stay "out" to clean up after the guests have gone. If they volunteer for a money-raising marathon event, they are the ones who have to run it. Changes will not happen automatically. There is tolerance and room for error. Everyone gets another chance. However, there can be no tolerance for breaking safety rules— ever. If someone is about to break those rules, someone else or a team of alters has to be prepared to stop them. If the inner team doesn't stop an alter from overdosing on prescription drugs, the whole company may have to be incarcerated in a maximum security psychiatric ward.

Some survivors have an alert team whose job is problem prevention. They will team up to stop an alter from breaking the safety rules, from self-harm, and from contact with currently active violators. However, if the inner system is not yet able to maintain safety, you need to work out a plan with your therapist and follow that.

I've heard other multiples talk about parenting—like parenting their small parts, and we don't like that at all. Nobody in us wants to be a parent—to make rules or enforce rules—yuck—all the time. So we realized that as far as responsibility, we let each part take responsibility for themselves. And this works for us.   Deborah

CHOICES AND COMPROMISES

Recovery is a cooperative effort and affects everyone. Regardless of age, job, status, or skills, each alter's needs and feelings are important. All decisions should take into account everyone's feelings. While there always need to be tradeoffs and compromises, they should recognize and honor everyone's needs—including those of weaker or more vulnerable identities.

The therapist had said something about fear just being the concern of a child part, and we felt minimized and invalidated and didn't like that at all. And I wrote in my journal, "We do have adult parts and child parts, but we won't give adult parts all the power. We're a partnership, we're a community. If a part feels strongly enough to express a concern or fear, she will be heard, and her concern listened to, respected, taken seriously, until we decide on an issue, and reach an okay answer. 'Consensus' isn't exactly the right word, but it's the closest we can think of. We are not autocrats, dictators, not even a democracy of elected parts. We don't do democracy, we don't do majority rule, we

are a community. We do not discriminate based on age or anything else." Deborah

The above ideas may or may not work for you. You may need to find other avenues to achieve cooperation with your internal identities. You may not be aware of inner conflicts and so may not have this problem. On the other hand, you may be feeling overwhelmed with uncooperative selves.

The diversity of personalities can pose unique problems. For example, one of your inner parts may be a reckless driver, another one may be a nonstop talker. Some of your alters may enjoy shopping and spending money you don't have.

Some people believe that certain alters are incorrigible, and so must be permanently severed from the system—asked to pack up and leave. I don't think that's right. As far as I'm concerned, if I ask any part of me to leave, unhealed, then I'm just releasing more unresolved problems into the world. Once I heal each of my parts, then they are free to leave, if that's what they still want. But until then, if I'm having a really hard time with an alter, I give them a choice—cooperate or go to sleep. Sophia

Remember that alters are capable of reasoning and have feelings. Instead of imposing ideas, offer them choices. If they cannot abide by the rules, then their choice is to "go to their room" and return when they are ready to behave, according to traditional discipline. If you think some identities are potentially violent, you can put them into a "breakproof glass room" where they can see and hear what is going on but cannot disrupt things. One survivor, particularly exasperated, offered her alter the choice of behaving or going into a coma. She decided to go into a coma. This will give her lots of time to do two things: to keep building her own internal strengths and keep thinking of ways to reach and heal this alter.

If there is a problem, alters can have a problem-solving committee and bring in the system experts in creativity, cooperation, good sense, and analysis. The thing to remember about multiplicity is that you contain all the answers within yourself. You only have to find them.

The following are just a few examples of the sorts of challenges faced in getting acquainted with alters and how survivors have handled them. These ideas may take time and tuning, but eventually you will find out what works for you. The keys are:

- stay in tune with your own system
- use the metaphors your identities have already established
- let your inner people take you through recovery

ALTERS HELPING ALTERS

Survivors often feel overwhelmed trying to meet the needs of all the internal selves. However, you do not have to do this all alone. You can enlist your inner parts to help each other. If you have an inner infant who needs lots of care and holding, one of your inner nurturing adults would probably enjoy helping you out. Here's how one survivor helped another survivor through a major problem.

She called up, and told me how her little alter started telling a story of abuse. And then after she got home, the little alter thought, "I'm going to get punished; we're going to get hurt." She got scared and got sick and she had to stay in bed a week. And [the survivor] says, "I need to get up, but my body is in pain. The furthest I got out of bed is to

go to the bathroom. I have tons of things to do, I have a very important appointment I can't keep this afternoon because I can't even get out of bed. I'm going to lose my job." So I said, "What can make this alter feel comfortable?" And she said, "Well, it's snowing outside; she wants to stay warm—she wants to stay in bed." And I said, "Okay, why don't you get a couple of the older alters to go let her pick a bed out, pick her favorite blanket out, get her a little electric blanket." So they brought her a "little bed," her little electric blanket and they had to build a room too with her favorite colors. And all of a sudden she's going, "Oh my God! I'm walking around here—don't feel any pain at all. I feel good. My body doesn't hurt. I need a shower, but I feel really good." I said, "Well, when you're going through body memories the alter is probably going through body memories, and she just needs to be comfortable in her little bed." Jackie Bianco

A REUNION OF LOST PARTS

Reunion is both the goal and at the heart of the recovery process. A reunion means bringing lost selves or parts back to consciousness, where each can be recognized through caring communication. It's about discovering and appreciating who you are.

REUNION VERSUS INTEGRATION

As with many other terms that continue to evolve in this developing field, the term integration may have different meanings. One definition is, "Bringing previously dissociated material into consciousness, mastering it, and making it part of accessible experiential reference and memory," as stated by Caryn StarDancer in *SurvivorShip*.

Another meaning of "integration" is merging

the identities so that a multiple becomes a "singleton." Many multiples find this idea frightening. Integration in this sense used to be the goal in treatment. However, it didn't always achieve the desired results.

We couldn't understand. Would some of us have to die? How can we heal by killing off parts? I've seen enough people die. I don't want to be party to it. Jeanne

Many multiples become frightened at the mention of the word.

To us, integration is a dirty word. There's a lot of misunderstanding about integration. The first is that everybody tells multiples and alters that they will still be there, and they will still exist when they're integrated. And that's not necessarily true. One of my alters is fearless. It's impossible for her to be integrated with anxiety-ridden kids who are three and four years old and in panic all the time, and still function as they used to. So I don't believe in total integration. My goal in treatment is co-consciousness and communication between the alters. Amiee

When forced, integration rarely takes hold.

I think if someone integrates, the minute that something that's traumatic comes up, we're going to split in every which direction and we may blow into more fragments than we were when we started. And that's been my experience with it. Amiee

Integration is only one of many possible outcomes of healing. For some multiples the goal of recovery is to learn how to function effectively as a multiple. Many experts are increasingly recognizing that the goal of recovery is co-conscious-

ness, communication, and cooperation rather than integration. Recovery should feel like a celebration and reunion.

What I felt like doing is not integrating our inner selves but integrating our outer selves—like integrating parts of my life. An important part of my life is recovery. Another very important part of our life is that we're lesbian. So we told our lesbian friend's that we're survivors of sexual abuse and multiple—and not one of them have run away. They've all been accepting. And we told our recovery friends that we're lesbian—and they're fine with that too. And we just thought that was neat that we applied the word "integrating" to this process, because people talk about integrating the inner kids, and we're integrating our outer life. And it's hard, but it's worked out really great. Janice

Our system instinctively knew what to do to survive. It also knows what is needed to heal. All we have to do is pay attention to it. The right answer lies within you. Trust your intuition and follow it.

For many survivors recovery is a blend. Some parts integrate and others remain multiple. When integration is right, it usually happens on its own and feels more like a gain, than a loss.

The way I think of it is I've got to go where they [alters] are, and I've got to walk a mile in their shoes—be with them while they have their feelings. Then they've got to be willing to come to where I am, into my life. And some of them see it and decide, "No, I don't want this." And then it's an interactional process. I go with them and then they come back here with me and back and forth. It's not like—poof! I've integrated. Typically, it involves a lot of grief. And then I realize I'm having a particular feeling or remembering some-

thing and I was still myself, and I was kind of happy and I was still myself—and I know I've integrated that part. I used to have to switch to feel. What I find is that I'm not going back—I'm there.   Alicia

Healing dissociated identities is usually an involved, long-term process. You will find additional helpful resources listed in the Bibliography marked with an asterisk.

Part Four

Association:
The Cornerstone of Recovery

12

The Process

Yes, this is hard, and yes, people get through.
Lynn

THE BASIC PRINCIPLE OF RECOVERY

As confusing and complicated as recovery may appear, the underlying principle is simple. It is the movement from *dissociation* to *association*. The process is challenging. It takes a lot of determination, courage, and heart. But trust that if you found a way to survive the abuse, you will find a way to make it through recovery. Hearing how other survivors are meeting their challenges will help you discover ways to meet yours.

Ritual abuse is the attempt to destroy who you are and redefine you in terms of your violators. A ritually abused child gets the message: *I do not exist.* Recovery is affirming the truth: *I exist.* It is

the process of discovering the "I." This means reclaiming your own experiences and so discovering your entire self. Here are the basic steps:

Reconnect the knowledge (what happened)

Complete the experience (associate your emotions, beliefs, and bodily sensations/feelings)

Affirm your wholeness (I exist) through self-expression.

Live your own life (transformation) through creativity and growth

THE BODY/MIND INSTINCT TO HEAL

The natural pull of our body/mind is towards wholeness and integration. While we are generally content to leave inconsequential information in our unconscious, there is an understandable impulse to assimilate events of consequence. If we don't integrate a significant experience, we may suffer serious negative consequences. A familiar example is the elderly husband who loses his spouse and is never seen to cry. Instead, he withdraws from his friends, falls into a deep depression, and develops various illnesses. Two years later, when he is finally able to grieve his loss, his illnesses clear up and he resumes a full existence.

The same thing occurs when a child suffers extreme trauma. As long as the significant event remains unassimilated, a survivor suffers severe problems of the type described in Chapter 9. However, once the traumatic event is assimilated, the negative aftereffects begin to disappear.

ASSOCIATION

Every survivor I have met who is making excellent progress feels the cornerstone of her or his recovery is awareness and integration of the original trauma. This does not mean that every event and every detail must be retrieved (see Chapter 15). Because survivors are not deficient but abused, their healing automatically begins once the trauma is associated.

It's a wound that goes very deep. Deep wounds have to heal from the inside out. If the outside closes up before the inside heals, the wound festers and grows worse. In ritual abuse, the Band-Aid approach doesn't work. Janes

Another survivor's experience is all too typical.

I had a nervous breakdown at fifteen. I've worked with psychiatrists, psychologists, counselors, and clergy, and none of them ever went into my history—ever. I've always been told by every therapist, "You just have to work on the 'now' stuff"—you know, now forward. Since then I have suffered horrible nightmares and migraines. I've been diagnosed with anxiety disorder and colitis. That was before I got into memories of ritual abuse. I've been with my current therapist for four years, and it's been hard work. But I haven't had a migraine in three years so I think that's really phenomenal.* Annie

Once the source of the trauma is recognized, it is equally important to integrate all aspects of a traumatic experience.

One of the things that I think is very important for anyone who is recovering and to survive as a whole person is to remember that we are mind, body, and spirit, and that all three were violated. And so there's pain held in the cells. But there's also pain held in the mind, and there's pain held in the spirit. Traditionally the triangle is a symbol of strength. So when I image my healing, I image the healing of the triangle—the mind, the body, and the spirit. Suzzane

HOW RECOVERY FEELS

As you begin recovery, you are likely to feel much worse before you begin to feel better. The cycles of feeling better and worse may continue throughout recovery, which makes sense, because survivors coped by avoiding the pain of their truth. Once you resolve to face the truth you also face the pain, the confusion, and disorientation of your childhood. However, feeling worse is a temporary phase on your way to feeling permanently better. One survivor used a metaphor for her entire recovery process. Here's how she described it in her journal.

I was living on a sinking ship with my parents at the helm. It's a ship that was always sinking, but it never sunk. I existed in expectation of the worst—hypervigilant, mistrustful, and with no sense of a future. That was my childhood.

When I turned fourteen, I tried to leave the sinking ship. The crew got furious and expelled me. I suddenly found myself overboard clinging to a piece of driftwood—wreckage from the sinking ship. I went from life on a sinking ship to survival as a castaway. Every ounce of energy I had was focused on clinging to the wreckage and keeping myself afloat. That's how I spent my adolescence.

I mastered the art of staying afloat, but something frightening was happening. I could feel dark sea creatures nipping and biting at my feet, threatening to pull me under. Days turned to nights turned to days lived in panic. I was exhausted to the limit. That's how I spent the prime of my life.

I knew I would not survive much longer. I had to confront the monsters. As I dove under they scattered. I only caught a glimspe of them, but I had a feeling of something young about them, and something about wanting help. It felt as though they wanted me—who could barely keep her own head above water—to rescue them. I had to make a decision. I would either have to keep fighting or rescue these monsters. I decided to try to rescue them. That was a turning point in my life.

As I went under again, I was terrified. I didn't want to see, touch, or hold these creatures. Utterly petrified, I grabbed my first monster and floated up for air. As I laid it on the driftwood I saw that it wasn't a monster but a little girl—in more pain than I could bear. And she had a familiar face—it was my face. And over time, in the sun and air, my little girl began to get well. Soon she was playing with me. That was my first experience of healing.

I don't know which is worse—thrashing water or diving under. They were both awful, but in time I fell into a pattern. I thrashed for as long as I

could manage, and when I could hold out no longer, I took a deep breath and would go under. Each rescue took enormous effort—every gasp of energy that I had. But as each monster was rescued and healed, I found myself growing stronger and stronger. I was in recovery.

One day I realized there was no panic—no more monsters nipping at me from below. With that the oddest idea came to me. I decided to let go of the wreckage and try to straighten up. Stunned, I found myself standing on solid ground. It had been there all along. Calmly, I began walking towards shore. My life is my own at last.   Roxana

Knowing what to expect in advance can help you recognize, accept, and heal the "monsters" as important parts of yourself. Ultimately you'll find that there are no monsters, only people or parts of us who've been hurt. Survivors repeatedly find that the monsters they feared the most are the parts inside that hurt the most. As monsters are embraced, they became gentle and docile.

ACCEPTANCE AND COMMITMENT

Recovery encompasses two concepts: acceptance *of* yourself and commitment *to* yourself. You need to accept all parts of yourself without judgment. Next, commit to healing them by recognizing and processing your feelings, thoughts, and emotions. You may be used to focusing on other people's issues, such as those of your violators or of other survivors. However you cannot heal by judging, analyzing, or blaming others. We can only fix ourselves. The how is discussed in the following chapters.

Meeting monsters is difficult for everyone. During recovery you may often feel isolated, alone, frightened, or adrift. You may feel as if you are going crazy. You may feel that your pain is beyond human endurance; that there is no end to it. You may go through periods of hopelessness and depression. You may begin to question your most cherished and fundamental beliefs. You may have to fight off impulses to injure yourself, commit suicide, or sabotage your progress. All of these are predictable reactions that may come and go during the course of recovery. However, each rescued and embraced monster brings many rewards.

THE THREE C'S

As you face your most difficult moments in recovery, it helps to remember the three C's of healing: courage, creativity, and compassion, mostly towards yourself. You will find yourself growing in courage to face the issues involved and expanding your creativity to find ways to heal your pain; and you will learn to extend towards yourself the compassion most survivors are able to find for others but cannot feel for themselves. Through recovery you will come to accept that you deserve compassion as much as anyone else.

13

Personal Safety

The more I tried to get well, the more I got shook up. All of me got more frightened and everyone around me got more frightening. And I couldn't see my way out of my terror, so I just kept crawling. I crawled my way through crisis after crisis— they call it recovery. Well, today I can look back and say, "You know, it was all in my head." But no one and I mean no one could have convinced me of that at the time.   Sophia

As survivors begin recovery, many feel increasingly unsafe. Virtually all survivors experience some degree of fear as they begin to connect with repressed cult experiences. This is hardly surprising, since every cult lesson is paired and reinforced with terror. Repressed fears come closer to the surface. Identifying them and putting them in perspective helps make recovery more manageable. It is through recovery itself that survivors begin to feel increasingly safe. You may experience all or none of the issues described. They may come up early in recovery, in the middle or final stages of recovery, or not at all. Sometimes fear you thought you'd resolved will recur.

Chapter 2 outlined ideas to help you stay safe. Regardless of how recovery affects you, you can manage most of it by being alert to and responding to your own body/mind signals. Remember to frequently check with yourself to see how you are feeling. Attend to your needs. Make sure you have your emergency pages handy to call for help. Remember to pace yourself, nurture yourself regularly, and visit your Safe Place when you need comfort.

Fear is the emotion most closely associated with self-preservation. It usually overrides emotions such as anger, joy, shame, and grief. Violators have therefore used fear as a reliable enforcer of their instructions.

> *The cult doesn't have to physically come and get us or sabotage our recovery. They have implanted so many "fear bombs" inside of us ready to detonate at the slightest infraction of their rules that we do the job for them. Until we disarm the fear through memory retrieval we will, in effect, "get" ourselves. And that's exactly the way it was planned.   em*

As survivors begin to associate their abusive past, many may hear internal messages such as, "They know I've told; It's time to die; They'll get me now for sure; I have to kill myself; I have to hurt myself, because I've told." Shortly after remembering cult abuse, you may become convinced your phone is being tapped, you are being followed, your mail is being intercepted and read. You may become suspicious of other people or other survivors. You may suspect they are cult "plants" who are cuing programmed responses within you. You may even find tangible evidence of threats. All of these reactions are understandable and common. The challenge is to unravel the past from the present. As always, the first and most important consideration is to keep yourself safe.

Remember to check with your inner wisdom. Ask yourself, "What would a child need to feel nurtured and protected?" Take care of yourself and your frightened inner kids. Once you feel safe, you are better able to examine your fears.

All fears are important because they are an indication of a real threat or they originate in issues from your past that need resolution. In either case, they are starting points for examining whether a fear requires further self-protective action. Initially it may not be easy to distinguish between past and present fears. Until they are resolved, both types of fears feel present. However, it is helpful for survivors to realize that in the vast majority of cases, fears stem from the unresolved past. This fear is neutralized through rescuing the monsters. With practice the source of fear becomes more clear.

DETERMINING THE SOURCE

In Chapter 8, I described the phenomenon of projection. This dynamic may get played out in survivors. Your own unresolved fears often get projected onto others, perhaps survivors who may say or do something that reminds you of your cult experience. For example, Nathan, a survivor in a support group, began to talk about one of his alters, Riorke, who frightened him. The other survivors tried to help him understand and resolve his fear around Riorke. However, one group member, Nancy, remained silent. She later told another group member that the account of Riorke frightened her. She was concerned that Nathan may still be active in a cult. Nancy did not share her fear about Nathan in the group. Instead, she left the group. About a year later, Nancy discovered an inner part within herself, named Riorke. In Nancy's history, Riorke's job was to keep her cult-loyal.

This type of scenario is common among survivors. Our own fears get bounced back at us through external reminders. People who provide the trigger are often not the source of your problem, only a clue that it exists. These reminders or triggers are in fact a bid for resolution, like monsters nipping at our heels. It is important not to jump to conclusions about others but rather to take time to discover the reason for your fears. It is especially important not to cast suspicion or doubt on other survivors based on your own fears.

If you are experiencing fear, first take care of your own safety needs. Next, find a safe person to talk to. Talking can help dissipate it, and it's easier to discover its source when working with others—a therapist, another survivor, or a support friend. For more information on safety in support groups see Chapter 24. For information on identifying cult-active alters see Chapter 11.

Fear is and always will be a cult's primary weapon. Examine it closely before acting on it. Survivors are often the greatest source of strength for one another. Together we gain mutual support and solidarity. Don't let cult-spread paranoia interfere with that.

INTERNAL IMPULSES

Most survivors have internal messages to keep them cult-loyal. These messages may get automatically activated as survivors try to break free through recovery. In many cases, these impulses may be internally, not externally, generated.

After reconnecting with his first repressed experience, one survivor immediately "knew" that his mother would kill him for "telling" by poisoning his food. Knowing specific details of a threat when none has actually been made may be a clue to internally generated messages. Once survivors connect with how they "know" this information, the fear is usually neutralized.

Sometimes cues may be activated by maintainer alters (see Chapter 10). If these alters are not co-conscious, the threats may appear to be externally generated. Amnestic alters may send the host threatening letters or leave threatening messages on the answering machine. By gaining the trust and cooperation of amnestic maintainer alters, recovery becomes more safe. The sooner you can determine the source of fears, the better you can take care of yourself.

Each survivor's personal safety issues are unique. Each survivor needs to check out her or his own circumstances to determine if they are physically safe. Apart from associating past experiences, there are no hard and fast rules on how to distinguish past from present threats. However, if you determine that a threat is externally and not internally generated, the following guidelines may help you to determine your current circumstances.

FACTORS AFFECTING PRESENT-DAY SAFETY

Secrecy and avoiding detection is often an overriding concern of violators. They cannot afford to get caught. They may try to intimidate survivors or their therapists in the same way as maintainer alters. However, many violators may not risk going beyond this step. Some cults may be more determined than others to get survivors to return. The risk of a present day-threat may be increased in a number of circumstances. If your violators are unstable or psychotic, there may be an increased present-day threat. If you were being groomed to assume a leadership role within the group, efforts to lure you back may be more intense. If you know highly sensitive cult information involving special secrets or have proof of illegality, you may be considered a higher risk for a cult. If you are taking steps to prosecute your violators, your present-day risks may be increased as well. In addition, the following considerations may help you to determine your present-day safety.

It helps to remember that cult violators who hurt you as a child may now be elderly and feeble. Some may no longer be cult-active. Those who are may be too consumed with their own destructive habits to enforce cult threats. On the other hand, younger, more vigorous people—such as some of your peers—may have taken their place. Therefore previously unsafe people may be less harmful today, and vice versa.

Some violators may prefer to let rebellious survivors go rather than run the security risk of disloyal members. In addition, some violators may not have been cult enthusiasts but reluctant participants who saw no way out for themselves. Some of these people may be secretly pleased to see you in recovery. Cult violators typically attack powerless children or other weak adults. Many may back off from anyone who has shown enough strength not to succumb to cult tactics.

CONTACT WITH VIOLATORS

Even though in recovery, some survivors continue to feel completely helpless and hopeless. On some level they feel as though no matter what they do, essentially nothing will ever change. There may be many reasons for this. One that is worth examining specifically is whether or not you are still being tortured and reprogrammed by your violators. Techniques to help you do this are discussed in the chapters that follow.

While not all cult violators pose a physical threat, if survivors maintain contact with their violators, the chances of coercion—overt or covert—are increased. When violators are family members or close friends, it is very difficult to break the ties. One of the reasons is because survivors have been purposely conditioned to be dependent on their violators for life. Breaking abusive ties can be as difficult as breaking any life-long pattern.

I know how very hard it is to break off with the family—even a horrendously abusive one. But to me it's like an alcoholic saying, I'm in recovery, but I can't give up the bottle. Janes

If you are financially or emotionally depen-dent on your violators, it may take some time in recovery before you feel strong enough to break abusive ties. However, in the meantime, it's important to protect your self—your feelings and your integrity—as best you can. Through recovery, you will learn how to stay with and be true to your feelings, truth, and interests—not theirs. For more discussion on safety in the presence of violator family members see Chapter 20.

MOVING AWAY

Many survivors have moved away from their violators before they had any awareness of their abusive past. It's as though some part of them was making an unconscious bid for freedom.

I had all these reasons why I had to move: I hated my job, I hated the city where I grew up, I hated the rat race, I hated the climate, I hated the geography, I hated how expensive everything was. I had all these "reasons." Well, for all this logic, I picked my new city out of a magazine—I might as well have thrown darts at a map. In retrospect, there was nothing logical about it. Something inside was compelling me to get away. It really didn't matter where I went. Josie

While moving away significantly increases safety from your violators, this may not be an iron-clad guarantee of safety. Survivors can be recontacted in new locations by longtime family friends or relatives. It is possible for survivors with amnestic alters to be recruited into new cults by people who know how to recognize and manipulate dissociated trauma victims. Therefore it is important to keep working towards association. Your most important safety guide is within yourself. Remember to pay attention to your own intuition. The more you use it, the better it gets. Someone safe for another survivor may be unsafe for you.

INFILTRATION RUMORS

Occasionally there are rumors that survivor services such as support groups, therapists, or treatment center staff may be "infiltrated" with violators. These rumors come and go. They benefit violators by keeping survivors afraid of seeking support and help. There are emotionally unhealthy people in all walks of life—at school, in church, on your sports teams, in your neighborhood. They may or may not be "plants," but your best protection is learning how to recognize them. Unhealthy people will try to enmesh you and make you dependent on them. Healthy people will respect you and encourage you to act independently in your own best interest.

If someone is making you uneasy, ask yourself the following questions: Are suspected people "disempowering" or empowering me? Do they shame me or encourage my self-esteem and self-confidence? Are they trying to control me or encouraging me to take charge of my affairs? These sorts of questions can help you decide who is safe and who is not. Apply these criteria to all of your relationships: with group members, with therapists, survivor friends, significant others, teachers, clergy, friends at work, employers, and professionals. The more you exercise your intuition, the better it gets. With practice you'll get increasingly skilled at recognizing who's healthy for you and who's not.

STEPS TO TAKE

Many survivors are relatively confident of their safety, even though some of the at-risk criteria apply to them. However, only you can determine the likelihood of present-day risks to yourself. If for any reason you are uncertain or feel there is a threat to your personal safety, take steps to pro-

tect yourself. This does not necessarily mean taking immediate action unless there is an immediate threat. Rather, it means making plans outlining steps you can take to keep yourself safe. Once the plan is prepared, you can implement it as necessary.

Your action plan should include a variety of options, from steps that are least disruptive to those that are the most secure. Survivors have taken various precautions, such as cutting off total contact with violators, especially those not in recovery, getting an unlisted phone number, installing extra locks, safety bars, safety alarm systems, monitoring incoming calls through an answering machine or an answering service. Some survivors change addresses and get a post office box to help keep their location confidential; some avoid using checks or credit cards to preserve their anonymity; some change their name and move to another area.

If you feel you need to relocate, take into account the availability of support services. Does the area have crisis centers? general support groups? survivor support groups? qualified therapists? child care? Although some survivors avoid religious organizations, it is nevertheless useful to know that some church-affiliated groups may help in crisis. Other sources include shelters for domestic violence, rape crisis centers, or battered women's shelters. Some help organizations set up for women assist men as well. You might also try some of the resource organizations listed in the Resource Guide for guidance. If these organizations cannot help you directly they may be able to refer you to the right source.

ABOUT TELLING

To tell or not to tell? That is a question that runs through many survivors' minds. Most cult messages focus on "don't tell" instructions. Survivors often feel that by keeping the silence they are insuring their own safety. However, these "don't tell" commands are not for your protection but to protect your violators. As survivors progress in recovery, many realize that their best safety insurance lies in a well thought out strategy of telling specific people.

I made a list of all my perpetrators and gave it to a trusted friend who happens to be a police-woman. I told her, if anything ever happens to me, these are the first people who should be investigated. Sunny

Some survivors were abused by groups that included or appeared to include judicial professionals, police, local authorities, etc. These survivors, understandably, may be concerned about giving information to officials. If you are concerned about the trustworthiness of certain people, your best bet may be to scatter the seeds. Alert many different types of people in different locations. Chances are good that at least some of them are reliable. You can then let a trusted friend know which authorities have your list of "suspects" in case anything should ever happen to you. This friend can in turn monitor to see which of the informed groups acted in your best interest if a problem does in fact occur. This can be valuable input on reliability or trustworthiness for the future.

The more survivors come forward, the harder it will be for violators to try to silence them. They simply won't be able to keep up with everyone. However, there is no need to declare your status, unless you feel totally ready to do so. Survivors who decide to speak publicly may experience two things: renewed fear of reprisals, followed by renewed feelings of freedom and empowerment. Here's one survivor's experience of speaking at a forum on healing:

It was a really big deal for my inner six-year-old to tell. He expected the sky to fall, the earth to tremble, and volcanos to erupt. And when he finished telling, a few people came up to me and said, "Thank you. Nice job." Nothing more than that. And it was such a huge enormous letdown, like—"Didn't they hear what I said?" It's as if I had spoken my words into some big empty hollow. But after I got over the letdown of "no rumble," I began to feel really powerful. I realized that the threats had all been in my head. Outside of my head no one cared. I was free—free to do recovery. Roxana

GENERAL SAFETY TIPS

1. Safety comes from growing increasingly strong through recovery. This means identifying sources of internal strength and calling on them often. It means having a solid support system of friends, and calling on them as needed. It also means getting in touch with your creativity and spirituality and using them for self-affirming growth and expression. By enjoying safe activities such as playing, drawing, writing, and outings with friends, survivors reaffirm safety in their life.

2. Co-consciousness is the most important safety tool for survivors with amnestic alters. Some survivors may not know whether or not they are continuously co-conscious. Signs of intermittent amnesia or amnestic alters may include losing time, having unexplained items in your possession, being greeted by people you don't know, etc.

3. Activities that occur during periods of amnesia may or may not pose a safety threat. However, this cannot be assessed until you achieve co-consciousness. Achieving continuous co-consciousness is a process that takes time. In the meantime, if you know or suspect that

you have amnestic episodes, you need to take stay-safe precautions. Work with your therapist to develop a stay-safe plan. It may include things such as calling in to a designated safe person at regular intervals, journaling your activities, limiting your social interactions to specific, trusted, and safe people, etc.

There are some things that other people might be able to do and be okay with that I can't do. I don't put myself in certain situations. I mean, even if I'm in a meeting with somebody, I don't go get into the car with them afterwards and go have coffee. I just don't do those things.   Amiee

It's a good idea to take notice of every time, everything, and everyone that makes you feel unsafe (this may include a therapist). Use the tools described in Chapter 25 and the techniques described in Chapter 15 to help you determine the source of your fears. As you work through them, you may begin to notice patterns. Recognizing the patterns will give you information to help determine your present-day risk. Your awareness will improve with practice.

4. Cults thrive by neglecting the needs of children and later keeping them in a dependent state. When survivors break away, one tactic in trying to keep them dependent on the cult is to offer them financial or emotional help.
5. To empower yourself, determine your own needs and approach people for help yourself. If you need to approach your family for help, do so on your own terms. Being able to identify needs yourself and finding ways to have them met is a step towards recovery. Remember, not everyone is going to be able to help you, and you shouldn't consider this a rejection.
6. Associate with people who are emotionally healthy and make you feel good about yourself.

7. Associate with survivors who are making good progress in their own recovery.
8. In support groups and in therapy, work only with people whose purpose is to empower you—encourage your self-esteem and self-confidence. (Avoid people who try to do things for you, or offer you "help," which is in fact making you dependent on them.)

Making these determinations improves with time. You will find that the more you recover, the easier it will be to differentiate between people who are emotionally healthy and those who are not. It is helpful to talk to other recovering survivors about their experiences with safety issues. You are likely to learn that most survivors go through varying levels of fear, but few are actually harmed or threatened.

While it is important to give all safety-related issues top priority and take safety precautions seriously, at the same time it is important to keep possible risks in perspective.

I felt pretty unsafe most of the time for two years. But I had to go through this maze of terror to figure out what was what. Recovery required internal chaos—hell. But many of the crises and emergencies were "safe emergencies." My good external support system allowed the internal chaos to occur, and sort itself out.   Adam

This perspective becomes clearer as you become increasingly adept at separating the present from the past. Until you are able to manage this yourself, work with your trusted friends, your support group, or your therapist to stay safe.

As long as you run away from fear it will chase you. Once you turn around and face it, it dissipates.   Erik

14

In the Shelter of Denial

Denial is a merciful coping mechanism which kept us alive in the past, and today keeps us from getting better.   Josie

Denial is a form of dissociation. It is altering a reality that a person cannot or will not assimilate. It can be conscious (I didn't take the cookies from the cookie jar), or unconscious (my mother is a pillar of our community; she never molested me). Denial can even persist as a coping strategy in the face of facts to the contrary. For example, during therapy, a mother shared that she had been molesting her son and wanted help to stop it. Her son had no recollection of the abuse and denied any abuse had happened.

Denial can be healthy or unhealthy. Unhealthy denial is wholesale refusal by an adult to acknowledge and deal with a problem, despite evidence that it exists. Healthy denial protects a survivor from facing a problem when the timing isn't right. Healthy denial also creates breathing space for recovering survivors. It is an adult survivor's protection from an overload of information in between traumatic associations. Therefore, it is important to respect denial during recovery as a safety management tool.

How could I get out of bed and hitch up my britches and go to work and deal with all that if I weren't in denial to a certain extent? And who wouldn't want to be in denial? It just keeps us from hurting too much all the time. It's much better to not have to deal with this stuff than to deal with it. And sometimes my denial will last a split second, and sometimes it will last for weeks. It seems to be something I'm going in and out of all of the time. So I've learned not to get down on myself too badly about it because that's a way of taking care of myself too. I now say, "Okay, just relax. Enjoy it while you can because it'll go away the next time you have a memory."   Jeanne

Survivors struggle with denial to varying degrees. Some rarely question their memories. Others question them constantly. For some, surrendering denial is the single most significant obstacle to healing. Struggles with denial can keep survivors in limbo for years.

Intellectually, I know how the programming is put in place, and I know ways to deprogram and to reeducate, and ways to acknowledge feelings and express feelings. But the denial says, "Well, you see, since you weren't abused in that way, then obviously these techniques aren't valid for you." It's just this weird box that I've got myself in and it's real tight and it's real uncomfortable.   David Gabriel

Denial usually plays a part at both ends of the 'I believe myself—I don't believe myself' continuum.

I'm not one of these people who doesn't believe their memories, but denial has been an important part of saving my behind and continues to be important as a coping mechanism. Breaking through denial has also been important in helping me make changes in certain behaviors and face the reality of my history.   Susan

Defenses allow things to remain as they were. Survivors can maintain the reality they constructed to survive. On the other hand, it also keeps them from overcoming the trauma's after-effects. Deciding when it's time to let go of denial is often a delicate balancing act.

Survivors' ability to let go can be complicated by a number of issues. Societal disbelief, as well as people invested in discrediting survivors, may intensify self-doubt. If survivors are persuaded to acknowledge abuse history before they are ready, they may spring back into denial at the first opportunity. Therefore "forced" recall may work for violators and against survivors.

HURDLES TO OVERCOME

Cult violators condition survivors to distrust their own information. Violators may purposely manipulate a victim into remembering and disclosing. During disclosure the victim is traumatized while violators pair the recall with phrases such as, "You're crazy. You are making this up. This is your imagination. You're full of crap. You're just a jerk. You're only doing this for attention." Many survivors have these messages resounding in their head as they begin to associate.

Survivors have a double trauma to associate and overcome: the trauma of the original event and the trauma that is reinforcing self-discrediting messages. After years of struggling with denial and feeling increasingly worse, one survivor finally made an agreement with himself: "Okay, I'll believe that this happened for one year." He has made enormous progress in recovery and healing since.

APPARENT CONTRADICTION

Although in rare instances all members of a family join in recovery, most often only some members choose recovery, and sometimes only one. Since most members do not seek help, they are invested in discrediting a survivor, especially if her or his memories threaten to shatter a pristine, carefully crafted reputation. In *Repressed Memories,* Renee Fredrickson writes:

When the overt and covert [family] systems are extremely discrepant, it is not only more likely that memory repression will occur but it is also more difficult to believe the memories once they are retrieved. The emerging repressed memories seem more bizarre in comparison to the overt system. Survivors must then struggle against their own crippling disbelief and overwhelming family censure.

DENIAL

Tonight
  I saw
    the
      news
   and
Heard my family gasp
  at
   the sight of a
Small battered boy
Yet if I spoke
 of
  what happened to
  my body
    as a child
They would gaze blankly
   and
Change the channel

          Suzzane

VALIDATION—A MIXED BLESSING

Many survivors long for concrete validation of their memories. The thinking typically goes, "If only I had some proof, I wouldn't have to go through this agony of uncertainty." However, when denial is a defense, concrete proof rarely eases the frustration. Initial reaction to validation may be gratitude, but within weeks, sometimes days, survivors may again find themselves struggling with denial.

One of the most interesting things I discovered in one set of my memories of being abused in my grandmother's bar was that I kept saying all the men had grease under their fingernails. When I went back there I realized that my grandmother's bar is about half a mile away from the largest oil refinery in the state. So I feel a lot of gratitude about that kind of validation. But every time a new perpetrator comes up in my memories I go into denial. And denial is a factor for me again now. Samantha

Some survivors who receive validation come to regret it. One survivor moved from the farm where some of the rituals took place when she was six years old. During association, she remembered a local library, and underneath it hidden passageways with special rooms—some used for rituals, other used for torture during programming. The rooms had bright movable lights in the ceiling. One day she returned to the town and visited the library. To her amazement, she found the passageway and the room.

I hadn't expected to find anything, so it was awesome to see that there. It was easier to deal with my memories as long as there was a possibility that it wasn't all real. The guilt, the shame, the horror are suddenly far too real. There's nowhere to hide from it. I've been far more suicidal since. A survivor

Sometimes survivors feel unable to cope with the reality of their abuse history. Although it is common for survivors to go in and out of denial, some go into denial permanently. This is more likely to happen if a survivor is reluctantly convinced of the truth about the abuse. If survivors are not ready to look, they may form even stronger defenses, and their denial may become permanent. That's why it is especially important to respect each person's pace and readiness.

Most associated traumatic memories will never be proved or disproved. However, if you're healing as you accept and assimilate your trauma, chances are pretty good that the abuse was real. The sooner you accept the truth of your associations, the faster your healing will progress.

The denial is so dominant. We can actually experience the whole thing—feel everything and remember everything and then go back the next day and say, "Nah, I imagined that. That wasn't real." That's why so many people come into recovery and then back off, like, "If I believe this then I must be crazy."   Dave

THERAPEUTIC VERSUS HISTORICAL TRUTH

In accepting your own information, do not be preoccupied with the probability of every detail. That only delays and complicates your healing. There is a difference between therapeutic truth (needed for healing), and historical truth (needed for courtroom testimony). A therapist's office is a healing room, not a courtroom. Assuming that you are working with a competent facilitator, trust that whatever information emerges has a connection to your experience.

It is important not to overreact or jump to conclusions. For example, one survivor was remembering that "Auntie Daisy" was molesting him. He didn't "see" the memory but just knew it. Over the course of therapy, as more details emerged, the survivor came to realize that "Auntie Daisy" was not his relative by the same name but the next-door neighbor, whose nickname was Auntie Daisy.

Take every piece of information seriously, without making premature assumptions. There are many ways in which defenses may both protect and confuse you. Trust your internal process and go with it, even if it means taking a circuitous route.

COVER MEMORIES

Sometimes information emerges as a cover memory. Cover memories are less painful versions of the actual event. For example, a survivor may initially remember that a babysitter molested him, unable as yet to remember the more painful truth—that it was his older sister. Cover memories may be a necessary interim step for some survivors. The sooner survivors feel supported and safe, the sooner they can get to the truth of their own experience. As survivors progress in recovery, things typically become clearer. Accepting and healing cover memories may be an interim step toward healing. Once the true event is associated and accepted, final rather than interim healing begins.

In this vulnerable early stage of recovery, it is important that survivors not undertake, or be encouraged to undertake, legal action. Informed professionals know the importance of waiting until all relevant repressed information has become conscious, and a survivor has experienced a fair amount of healing before any decisions about legal recourse are made.

RECOGNIZING PATTERNS

If you are using denial/dissociation as a protective defense, by definition you are not aware of it. Dissociation is an unconscious process and not under survivors' control. By making the process conscious, you have control over it. A step toward making the process conscious is to recognize patterns of denial. These patterns may occur before a memory, after a memory, in therapy or support groups, after validation, or after interaction with violators.

BEFORE A MEMORY

Survivors typically reject out of hand early body/mind clues and signals of emerging information. While your experience may vary, survivors usually agree that these blips, thoughts, or visual images always relay key information. No matter how difficult, they usually surface as your body/mind feels ready to assimilate them. Survivors generally agree that it's more productive to accept your body/mind signals than to spend a lot of energy resisting them—unless you're convinced that you're not ready to deal with the information yet.

AFTER A MEMORY

While some survivors simply accept each associated memory, many resist. This is understandable. Information that made your childhood unbearable may not suddenly become bearable in adulthood. Associated memories often throw you into confusion. Many survivors immediately dissociate and again repress the new-found information.

I was using the same defenses I used as a kid—repression and denial. On Tuesday I forgot Monday, and on Wednesday I forgot Tuesday. When I started remembering the incest, I told a good friend, "I think I'm an incest survivor." Then six months later, I said to her, "I think I'm an incest survivor," and she said, "But you told me that six months ago," and that was when I realized what I'm doing. It's so painful. Joan

Anytime I've ever had a new memory I've gone into some form of denial. I am one of the few survivors who has had a lot of concrete validation. There's no question at all that my grandmother was a prostitute, no one denies that. There's no question whatsoever that my grandfather was a violent alcoholic who married two prostitutes and was surrounded by the prostitute business. There's no question that my grandmother and her third husband managed a bar, and that as a child I was taken on a nightly basis to that bar to be with them. There's no question that my stepfather sexually abused me. I confronted him and he admitted that. I've had new memories as recently as two weeks ago. And always I am very guarded and I think, "Well these first fifty memories I believe are true. But maybe I've gone into this mind game where I'm fabricating things at this point, or I'm overlaying things, or I'm confusing dreams with memories." Samantha

I HEARD IT IN GROUP

Dissociated trauma has a surreal quality because it is often disconnected from emotions and feelings. Common "self-talk" includes, "I must have made it up; I probably borrowed it from someone in group; I must have seen it in a movie or read it in a book." Survivor experiences similar to yours may trigger your memory. This is common. Ask yourself, "Why was I triggered by this particular story?" Unless you are borrowing every single account you hear, and every traumatic incident in a movie or a novel, chances are there is a reason why you are being triggered by specific events.

IT'S YOUR CHOICE

Whether denial is your friend or foe, surrendering it makes for much faster progress in recovery. It's your choice.

As I go on I believe it more because I'm getting well.   Annie

It explains so much. I'm healing. I'm getting better and I'm getting my life back. I actually go to work all day and I teach a class and I do karate. I'm starting another relationship which is something that I never thought I would do again. I mean I have a life.   Alicia

15

Associating the Experience

We've all grown up with the myth that this naughty little girl opened up Pandora's box, and the demons got out. By remembering the truth and healing, survivors are rewriting the story of Pandora's box. The "demons" were miserable and dangerous because they were locked up in that box. But once they could fly, they were free to be transformed. They could become butterflies, and things could begin to grow in the open box. The best thing the little girl ever did was to open up Pandora's box so that the truth could be set free.   Suzzane

THE IMPORTANCE OF ASSOCIATION

Unassimilated trauma keeps survivors imprisoned in their abusive past. Dissociated experiences influence your decisions and actions from the unconscious, where you have no control over

them. Actress/comedienne Roseanne Arnold summed it up at a forum on healing. "You don't have a secret; the secret has you."

I was like a house built on a shaky foundation. I kept having dreams where I'd fix the plumbing, and the roof would spring a leak; I'd fix the roof, the window would jam; I'd fix the jam, and the ceiling would cave in. My inner life was in shambles.   Erik

Healing is possible on many levels. However, the deepest and most lasting healing happens when survivors rebuild the foundation of their lives. Our foundation was built on lies, hermetically sealed with trauma. To get at the lies, we need to know the trauma. Once the trauma is known, we have the power to transform and heal ourselves. This is the pivotal event of recovery.

DIFFERENCE BETWEEN MEMORY RECALL AND ASSOCIATION

Repressed experiences may begin to surface as visual flashes or snapshots, thoughts, emotions, feelings, or vivid dreams. They may come in aural form through specific words, sometimes spoken by an inner child or alter. Incidents that occurred at a preverbal age may be reenacted physically in the present. These early clues often seem to exist in a vacuum—disconnected from anything in a survivor's experience. As a result, survivors may doubt this information saying, "But it doesn't seem like a memory."

We think of memory as recollection of fully integrated and therefore conscious events. Traumatic memories are only partially experienced events, still frozen in time. In *"Psychological Trauma,"* Ivor Browne, chief psychiatrist at the Eastern Health Board and professor of psychiatry at University College, Dublin, argues that unassimilated trauma should not be called a memory but rather "unexperienced experience." In *Trauma and Recovery,* Dr. Judith Herman points out:

> Traumatic memories lack verbal narrative and context; rather, they are encoded in the form of vivid sensations and images. . . . Just as traumatic memories are unlike ordinary memories, traumatic dreams are unlike ordinary dreams. . . . They often include fragments of the traumatic event in exact form, with little or no imaginative elaboration. Identical dreams often occur repeatedly. They are often experienced with terrifying immediacy, as if occurring in the present.

When fragments of the traumatic experience begin to surface they may seem disconnected and unreal. As more and more fragments are made conscious, a picture may begin to emerge.

To the extent that all aspects of a traumatic event are associated and assimilated, the now "experienced experience" may begin to feel more like a regular memory. In cases where survivors associate rituals experienced in altered states of consciousness, the memories may continue to have an unreal or surreal quality. (For more on traumatic memory see Chapter 4.)

MEMORY ASSOCIATION

I had remembered the incest, and I asked my therapist, "Do you think there's more?" And he said, "What do you think?" and I said, "I think there's one or two more things, and it feels like it has to do with the occult." Those one or two more things have turned into eight long years of ritual abuse memories.   Janes

Janes's experience is typical. Many survivors remember other types of abuse before their ritual abuse experiences. As survivors become stronger through recovery, they may be faced with increasingly difficult material.

This material shapes what Jeanne called "my emerging identity."

My identity has been emerging with distinct landmarks every point of the way. It went from learning that I'm a partner of an incest survivor, to realizing that I was spanked too hard as a child, to becoming aware that I was an incest survivor, to accepting that I am a ritual abuse survivor, to recognizing that I am a multiple personality. Jeanne

Often the hardest realizations are not about ritual abuse, but painful truths about lost relationships or the family. Survivors sometimes discover tragedies that have never been mourned

—death of a friend or a sibling, a betrayed love attachment within the context of a cult.

Children may create illusions of a protective parent or person amidst the insanity, sometimes called a fantasy bond. Some of the final memories are of betrayal by even this guardian. It is equally difficult to admit that your parents hurt you and appeared to have enjoyed it. The final and most painful realization one survivor had was, "No one cared about me. I wasn't loved by anyone." "I didn't matter" is one of the most painful realizations; it is also a turning point in reclaiming selfhood.

THE PROCESS

I don't think anyone ever went crazy from looking at their pain. People go crazy because they won't look at their pain. It drives them crazy. I really believe that. David Gabriel

Survivors are people dedicated to reclaiming who they are. It takes the same fortitude and determination to recover as it did to survive. That resolve to make it, no matter what, is what carries survivors forward through the most difficult times. For most, memory association is the most dreaded part of recovery. Connecting with ritual abuse rarely comes as a conscious choice but as a last resort and necessity. Some survivors finally get in touch with their history while hospitalized, suicidal, or dying.

Most of us hit bottom before we're willing to look at it because otherwise it's like willingly putting your hand into the fire. Sunny

The abuse was strategically set up to convince survivors that they were isolated and that no one was ever going to reach out to help them. How-

ever, once they realize they are not alone, that help is available, and that it's okay to remember and heal, many are able to reconnect with their inner lost parts.

Many survivors remember ritual abuse while uncovering memories of incest. Some remember while in a support group. Others gain awareness in chemical dependency treatment centers, where they are sober. Initial breakthroughs are often the most terrifying experiences of recovery:

When I started having ritual abuse memories, I hadn't even heard of ritual abuse. My therapist had me do a collage of my childhood, and I had so much fear. On the back I wrote words that terrified me. I wrote, "Truth is a lie and lies are the truth." Six months later I heard the words "ritual abuse" and a cold terror swept over me. But in that moment I knew, "That's the word; that's what happened to me." Those were such hard days. I'm glad I'm past that. Jane Linn

Before retrieving a memory, many survivors experience extreme, overwhelming emotions for what seems to be no apparent reason:

I'd have this intense grief and it wouldn't be attached to an image or anything. And a day or two later I'd get one image and the intense grief, and then another image, and then I'd be suicidal; and another image and I'd be very disjointed. I used to have horrible nightmares and that's how most of my memories came through initially. Alicia

Some survivors' defenses are so unshakable that they cannot associate without considerable assistance. Association begins in various ways. Some survivors get information spontaneously:

I don't have flashbacks and I don't hear voices in my head. But I'll be driving down the road and it's like someone told me a story and suddenly I just know something.   em

However, for many it isn't a straightforward exercise of simply remembering. Unassimilated trauma may be held in many amnestic compartments or spread among different personalities. The challenge of recovery is to piece together the snapshots.

It's like trying to work a 5,000-piece jigsaw puzzle where somebody had taken the puzzle, shaken it up, and put fifteen pieces in one baggy, thirty pieces in another, and so on, and then said, you can only look in one baggy at a time.   Amiee

A survivor's first, complete memory association is often triggered by some significant life event. It could be graduation, marriage, a first job, a promotion, the birth of a baby, a child's birthday, or when someone close dies.

Sunny had just come home from the hospital with the birth of her second son. Within days she was rehospitalized after an inexplicable suicide attempt. She describes the unfolding of her first full memory of ritual abuse:

In the hospital I sat down with a poster-sized piece of paper. I took this ruler and blocked off a little square in the lower right-hand corner and prepared to draw. But first, in the inset, I drew a picture of a little baby boy with blood dripping down into a puddle underneath him. Above it I wrote "the blood of the second son" and I didn't know why. I just went into shock. I covered the corner with a book. Then I drew a huge outdoor ritual. I showed it to my therapist next day and when I moved the book, I made the connection between this ritual in the center and the picture of a baby in the corner. It was Adrian (my newborn). I was to sacrifice my second son to the cult or die.   Sunny

In an instant the entire memory was made conscious. As is typical of survivors, Sunny was prepared to kill herself rather than harm her child. However, because Sunny is a survivor, she also had the presence of mind to seek help.

With association, many survivors feel a shift within, the feeling of, "Eureka, I've got it! I know what this is." This instant recognition gives survivors enormous relief.

Well, I tell you what. Suddenly everything made sense. When I had the father incest memories, I felt like the world turned upside-down; that's when my whole reality got shook. When the ritual stuff started coming out, it was almost like the world turned back again. It was like, "Oh, my God, no wonder. Now I finally understand."   Bea

Recognition and relief are usually followed by contradictory reactions. Survivors may spiral into deep shame. Impulses to injure yourself, commit suicide, or return to familiar coping strategies may intensify. After associating their ritual abuse, some survivors experience chaos. For many, programmed messages activate:

My first ritual memory was the most horrifying experience. Now, looking back on it, I realize that a lot of it was programming. The terror, the incredible terror that came up—I was programmed that I was going to die. That they would find me and kill me if I remembered, and especially if I told. I was also frequently told that I would have to kill myself if I remembered. So not only are these horrible pictures popping into my mind, but immediately following, practically like a sledgehammer, is this thought, "I have to die now, I have to die now, I have to die."   Bea

Another common reaction is bewilderment and disbelief. Many survivors begin to question everything:

Okay, this just doesn't compute. All my life I've had fond memories of my childhood, and now this? I got so confused. It was spring at the time and I walked outdoors. I looked down at the grass which was turning green. And then I thought, "Or is it? Now I wonder if tomorrow I'll have another memory and find out that it's not green." I couldn't even trust that the damn grass was green anymore. Sunny

In time, things fall increasingly into place. The more survivors are able to assimilate all aspects of their experience, the more certain they become of their own truth. Association takes tremendous strength, courage, determination, and hard work. It is one of the most difficult but most rewarding milestones of recovery. It means looking at and accepting the unimaginable so that you can be set free of it. No matter how complex the challenge, the answers all lie within you. They only need permission and opportunity to surface.

Many survivors rely on therapy to help them safely through association. Some survivors prefer to associate alone and assimilate the information during therapy. Some survivors work effectively with each other to facilitate the process; others work on association during group sessions. Each survivor needs to decide what is right. Regardless of which approach works best, it is important to manage it. Managing the process increases safety and lessens the pain.

MANAGING ASSOCIATION

Memory association is a stressful experience for most survivors. It's a good idea to check with your doctor as you would normally do before undertaking any strenuous exercise. In addition, make sure you have a solid support system in place, as outlined in Chapters 1 and 2. The amount and type of support needed varies from survivor to survivor. Check with your therapist if you are unsure about your support needs.

The main steps in managing association include:

- establishing safety
- accessing the trauma
- integrating the information
- reconfirming safety

The next several sections address issues of safety in some detail. Feel free to skip sections which don't feel appropriate. Trust your own intuition.

LEARNING TO CONTROL ASSOCIATION

Although some survivors need assistance to connect with their trauma, many begin to connect spontaneously, sometimes at unexpected or inconvenient times. This may become an even greater problem if you lose co-consciousness. You may suddenly find yourself thrown back in time, reliving scenes, emotions, or events. You may lose touch with where you are or feel stuck in a dissociated past experience.

The first step, as always, is to learn to recognize the early signs. The sooner you become aware of them, the easier they are to manage. The beginning of unconscious association may feel something like this:

It's not a nice feeling. I don't like it. My head feels real heavy, and it flashes. Like a scene or a picture will flash. And I have no control. And then things start to disintegrate, and I'm just stepping off into the darkness. Amy

Body signals described below have traditionally been called signs of dissociation, because they dissociate survivors from their present-day reality in an attempt to reassociate unassimilated past experiences. "Association" focuses on the positive reason behind the event rather than the secondary distressing symptoms. However, because the reason for this temporary "dissociation" is an attempt at full association, the positive focus makes more sense.

The symptoms mentioned below may precede association. With practice, you will become familiar with your own preassociation signals. If you are under a physician's care, follow her or his directions. If you are doing all right without medical care, signs you can learn to notice and manage yourself include:

migraines, headaches at the nape of the neck or forehead
feeling split at the top your head
forgetfulness
losing control
feeling clumsy, bumping into things
unintentional self-injury
shallow breathing
irregular blinking
fuzzy feeling, like cotton in your head
overwhelming feelings or emotions
feeling triggered (overreacting)
feeling physically smaller/younger than you are
flashbacks
hallucinations
losing consciousness, dizziness, blackouts
feeling disoriented, losing focus

If you feel any of these happening and don't feel ready to associate the information coming into your conscious awareness, there are many things you can do to bring yourself back to the present. First of all, turn to the back page of this book and follow the emergency instructions you have prepared for yourself. If you feel this is not an emergency, but you are still associating, turn back one page from there and follow the directions for Managing Association/Dissociation. Once you feel grounded in the present and safe, you may want to try some of the ideas described below to stay safe.

Safety comes through connection with your present environment. This can be done through physical movement or touch. It is helpful to remind yourself of the current date, time, and place. It is also important to remind yourself that today, right now, you are safe. Rescue your hurting or frightened inner children by taking them to a Safe Place.

A Radix® teacher I talked with had the following additional suggestions:

Say whatever it is you're feeling out loud—"I think I'm dissociating. I feel really strange and afraid. I'm worried that I might go crazy." Then continue talking, but this time say what you will do about it—"But I have a choice about this, and I choose not to associate at this time. One of the ways that I will do that is by reminding myself that the past is not happening to me now. I am experiencing images of the past. I will remind myself that right now I am safe. I will acknowledge this by making myself a snack and a cup of tea."

Walking barefoot and breathing exercises are some of the best ways to ground yourself. Concentrate on breathing straight through the arches of your feet. Spread out your toes, and feel the texture of what's underneath—carpeting, grass, warm cement. It's very grounding to play with your toes in the sand, or any sort of textured surface, such as a shaggy carpet. If you're walking, feel each step connecting with the ground.

Picture your breath going down into your

back and into your belly, so you're breathing underneath your rib cage, and just breathe from your belly for a few minutes. Exhale all the way out, and hold your exhale for as long as is comfortable. Your next breath will be much deeper, and will help to ground you more.

Some survivors think of grounding as getting into and enjoying their own body. Turn on some music and dance (the knees bending and feeling your muscles, joints, and body during dancing is grounding). Do any body movements or exercises that are fun. Sing. Take a bubble bath. Try some bird whistles. And my favorite standby—call a friend.

Think of words that will help you feel safe, grounded, and present. Write these words or other ideas in the spaces provided at the end of the book. Take a highlighter pen and mark all the suggestions on this page that work best for you. That way you can quickly spot which technique to use, even if you're feeling disoriented.

If you need affirmation of your safety, call a friend, turn to your Safe Page, or, if you still feel unsafe, turn to the back pages and get professional help. Managing association is both an emergency and a recovery skill. Once you learn how to control association (or dissociation) you can recover on your own schedule.

Unharnessed dissociation can be like riding a wild horse. There's no control over where it goes or when it starts and stops. Once we have its reins in hand, dissociation becomes a powerful tool.
Toronto psychotherapist and ritual abuse survivor, Gail Fisher-Taylor

PREPARING FOR RECOVERY

The following ideas may take some time to set up, but they are well worth the effort. The safer you feel, the more you will be able to associate. Over time, survivors find that feeling safe comes more automatically. Dr. Cliff Morgan suggests the following:

I start and end each session at the Safe Place. I set limits, contract with the client not to hurt themselves or others and not to return to coping habits such as overeating or addictions. Once that's in place, I use regression techniques to open the memory bank; the information is processed through talking, writing, crying, storming, drawing, and so on. Then I teach the client to balance the present with the past and establish healthy boundaries. We close at the Safe Place. I help clients process ongoing memories and feelings by keeping a journal and making drawings. This material is then brought to group for processing.

Association can be a disorienting experience. Processing through one event can take several hours, several days, or even weeks. Therefore it is important to find a time and place when you are able to "fall apart." Finding this time may be more challenging for survivors with other full-time obligations such as working, parenting, or both. This is where support friends may really make a difference by offering to relieve you of responsibilities from time to time.

It became apparent within three to four months that healing wasn't going to be one tiny two hour a week time slot—that my memories were going to come up at night; that I was going to have nightmares and that I was going to not want to have sex with my lover; that sometimes at school my mind was just not going to work; and I was going to dissociate right in front of the class. A typical day then got to be struggling to get out of bed in the morning, crying as I'm trying to put on my makeup, going to work, working for maybe half a day, coming home, and, on good days, doing some healing things, like writing or drawing. Then it got to the point where it was so bad, I wasn't eating really well, not sleeping, fighting with my partner constantly, being very abusive, and my life fell apart. Alicia

As mentioned in Chapter 12, you can expect things to feel worse before they get better.

It's this contradiction: Things are getting worse—I must be getting better. I feel crazier, but there's some freedom in it. I don't have to work as hard anymore to do the impossible, like always be in control. Amiee

In addition to scheduling the time, you'll also need to have a place to "fall apart." This can be your own home, a therapist's office, or at the home of a support friend. If you're in an unfamiliar environment, make sure that the room or area feels safe. You may be triggered by a painting, or a piece of furniture, or certain colors. Discuss your fears with your recovery facilitator. Remove these items, if necessary. Once your environment feels safe, you may need special safety assurances from your facilitator. Some survivors appreciate hearing affirmations such as, "It's okay to remember now. Today it is safe. No one will hurt you anymore. I will be here if you need me. It will be okay." Once you feel secure in your environment and with the person who may be supporting you, the next step is to invite alter(s) or dissociated parts who hold the experience to listen for their safety tips.

PREPARING INNER PARTS FOR RECOVERY

The following techniques refer to working with alters, but they work equally well for dissociated experiences. One survivor developed the idea of asking all the alters who either hold or know about a particular event to come forward. Then she asks them to line up in the order in which the event needs to be known. The next step is to ask everyone who can to stay present and watch. Pat Graves explains:

> The more you have internal communication, the less concern you have about unexpected reactions. You tell the host, "It's safe and important that you stay. You can't go off to sleep. Find a Safe Place from which to watch the work that we're doing. Be an observer." If the alters could watch the abuse, they can watch the healing. Once this stage is achieved, it becomes safer for everybody.

Some inner parts are unwilling or unable to communicate. Some have been forbidden to speak. Alternative forms of communication described in Chapter 11 work well for memory association. Once initial communication is established, Pat Graves works toward interactive communication:

> Some alters may not come out, but they may be willing to talk with fingers, and so I'll talk with fingers for a long time. But then I'll start frustrating them by asking questions that can't be answered with a yes/no. And they'll finally huff out, because I'm "so stupid," you know. Or I'll say to them, "I understand that you have to do this, but I also know that underneath there's part of you that doesn't want to do it. and would like to be free. Having new choices gives you real power and freedom."

If you are unable to maintain co-consciousness, find a way to record what happens during your session. You can ask your recovery partner to report your association to you or record your session on tape.

Once guidelines or conventions are established, the next step is to give each inner person who holds the information maximum protection.

PROTECTING THE INNER CHILD

You have to look at the terror without being pushed into it. Sunny

The more protected you and your inner parts feel, the easier it will be to look at your history. You can give yourself added protection in many ways. For example, you can imagine that you are separated from the experience with an enormously thick wall. When you feel ready to look, you can peer over the wall. You can imagine yourself looking down on the event from within a cloud, where no one can see you or hurt you. You can ask that the information come only as information without visual impressions or feelings. You can use the metaphor of a VCR, where you manage the information with a remote control. With it you can turn the picture on and off, freeze it, fast-forward or replay an event, or exit to a safe channel. You can try similar ideas using the metaphor of a picture book. One survivor asks to have her memories come to her through dreams. Although this doesn't always happen, association is much easier when it does.

Before beginning to look, ask yourself, "Do I feel safe enough? If not, what else do I need? A 'magic sword'? To be 'twenty feet tall' and 'invincible'? A protector 'angel'? A 'bulletproof space suit'?"

I like to make myself very tiny—almost invisible—and pretend I'm entering the scene through a keyhole, so that no one can see me, and I can escape quickly if I have to. Roxana

Once you feel sufficiently protected, remember that you are completely safe from harm while beginning your association. You can call on your protective imagery whenever you need it to reaffirm your safety. Some survivors practice going into the past and "returning" to safety in the present, to increase their confidence.

These are only some of the many ideas survivors have used to break up traumatic events into manageable pieces. You can try these or your own ideas. Making choices on how to proceed will help you to feel empowered.

BEGINNING ASSOCIATION

Our experiences are carried in our emotions, bodily feelings, mind, and behaviors. These avenues may be activated through hallucinations, nightmares, fears, migraines, tension, anxiety, or problems with relationships. Any of the symptoms described in Chapter 9 can be the starting point for association. The tools described in Chapter 25 can be used to facilitate the process. Each avenue or trigger is like a ball of thread. As you tug on the end, it begins to unravel your experience.

You may need to take a tremendous number of safety precautions before you are ready to look at the abuse. However, there may be times when, no matter what you try, you don't feel safe enough. In these cases it may be more useful to stop and examine what underlies the fear than to proceed with memory association. Instead of battling it, try to work with it. Without withdrawing your defenses, explore them. For example, if you are drawing a blank, feeling nothing or hostile, find out what's behind the blank, nothingness, or hostility. What are they protecting? What would happen if they were removed? What color, shape, or feeling is associated with them? This way, even your resistance can help.

If someone is assisting, remember that it is your, not their process. Your support person can be helpful by asking open-ended questions—for example, "What are you feeling?" rather than "Are you feeling frustrated?" Keep in mind the information about therapists (in Chapter 23) and hypnosis (in Chapter 25). Stay with your own metaphors, and start only when you are ready.

Some survivors simply lower or close their eyes, sit still, and begin to associate. Others lie down and count back from ten, relaxing more with each count until they feel relaxed enough to remember. Sometimes a simple question such as "Does anybody in there have something they want to tell me?" will begin the association process. However, some survivors need additional help and encouragement.

R. Edward Geiselman, Ph.D., developed interviewing techniques to help young children retrieve memories with maximum accuracy. These techniques work for survivors as well. His article "The Cognitive Interview" discusses four general techniques to help jog memory: reconstructing the circumstances, reporting everything, recalling the event in a different order, and changing perspectives. In addition, it addresses secondary memory jogging techniques. For information on the article and/or a comprehensive manual on memory enhancement, see the Bibliography.

BASK INTEGRATION

Dr. Bennett G. Braun introduced the BASK model of dissociation, which has provided the framework for assimilating dissociated experiences. The acronym stands for B—behavior, A—affect (emotions, typically rage, grief, fear, shame), S—sensation (physical responses), and K—knowledge. It is important to focus on S, sensation and physical feelings, in order to help break programmed cues. Cultists typically use one or more of our five senses (touch, smell, hearing, taste, sound) to activate a message. They count on our not remembering the pain (torture, terror, threats) to keep these cues unconscious.

Once you remember the trauma, you are free of its influence. The torture or pain does not necessarily need to be physical—it may also be mental, spiritual, or emotional. You do not have to reexperience the pain in order to remember it. Sometimes a clue to repressed pain is denying its presence.

I kept writhing on the mat, my body tensed. I kept repeating, "But it didn't hurt. There was no pain." Years later I knew that I needed to believe that. Because the fact is that it hurt like hell—more than that. Janes

Survivors often have difficulty seeing faces or hearing words or chanting during association. This is sometimes a self-protective mechanism. One survivor set up a buzz in her head during rituals; she has a hard time understanding lyrics to this day. Questions that can help association are things such as, What do (I/you) feel, think, smell, taste, hear, see? What shape is it? What color is it? What name would you give it? Describe the surroundings and people. Where are you in this scene?

To dismantle programming, pay attention to

cues. These may be auditory such as words, phrases, names, tunes, whistles, patterns of knocks, and rings, or other sound; visual cues may include symbols, pictures, writing, finger or hand signals; sensual cues may include special handshakes, running a hand over your face or your forehead, touch or pressure applied to the body, often in certain patterns, contact with certain fabrics. Try to associate taste and smells. Odors/perfumes can be cues as well. If there are explicit programmed messages or instructions, it is usually important to remember the exact words.

HOW MUCH IS ENOUGH?

The healing process varies from survivor to survivor. Each person has an internal schedule that must be recognized and honored. Some survivors are able to assimilate all aspects of an experience as they become aware of it. Some survivors first need to learn most of what happened before they are able to release their emotions and feelings. Others address their current behavioral problems, discover a connection with their childhood abuse and associate the source from there. There is no right or wrong order.

Some survivors have photographic or perfect memory, recalling minute details of dissociated events. Others have a general impression or sense of what happened to them. What matters most is to associate the key, pivotal aspects of each traumatic event. This knowledge is necessary to break conditioning and find relief. Because of the sheer number of dissociated traumas, it is unrealistic that all memories will be assimilated. However, most survivors make rewarding progress by associating key events, such as those affecting critical developmental tasks (see Chapter 6).

It isn't necessary to retrieve every memory or assimilate each event separately. For example, if a cult member committed incest with you every day for sixteen years, you do not have to remember and assimilate every incident. It may be possible to work through the sixteen years in three or four years of therapy. On the other hand, a single trauma of particular significance may take many sessions and years to assimilate.

AVOIDING ASSOCIATION

Because association is so difficult, survivors may use tactics, often unconsciously, to stop the process. For example, I would often engage my therapist in a compelling discussion on days when I felt a memory coming. Another survivor used to get extremely sleepy in session before memory work. She and her therapist initially thought these were body memories of being drugged. However, after a time they realized that the survivor was also using drowsiness to avoid association.

While some survivors lie motionless as they experience deep pain, others avoid feeling the pain or even knowing that there is pain by various distractions. You may find yourself shaking your limbs violently, stop breathing, coughing, choking, making loud noises, twisting, flailing. It may be helpful to ask yourself, 'What would happen if I stopped (shaking my foot? coughing? kicking? choking?)" If you find yourself in deeper distress, then simply be aware that this is a pain-avoidance coping strategy. You do not have to stop it. However, when you feel ready, try to find out what you are defending against.

While there are many patterns in memory association, ultimately each survivor is unique. Remember to honor your own needs and intuition. For example, steady breathing facilitates association of memories. However, one survivor found she could only experience her feelings if she held her breath. When her therapist directed her to 'breathe,' she had the presence of mind to explain, "No, I need to stop breathing in order to feel." Remember, a therapist or a recovery partner is there to facilitate *your* process.

Some survivors are afraid that if they go into the past, they may not return. By practicing the association/dissociation techniques, you can feel increasingly secure in your own control over the process.

It can take two to three weeks or two to three months to process one memory. It can take four weeks to cycle through a major breakthrough. I'm in so much pain that it feels like it's never going to end. At the time it always feels like you're not going to come out. [But] what's exciting is that I'm having breakthroughs. I don't ever just go into something and never come out.   Bea

DO'S AND DON'TS

If someone is facilitating your association, encourage her or him to use and trust her or his own intuition and common sense. However, sometimes inexperienced facilitators try to stop association prematurely. Here are a few suggestions you may want to review with her or him:

- do follow survivors' leads—the decision to associate should come from survivors, not their facilitators
- do encourage survivors when they feel ready
- do not try to bring them back into the present until they ask for assistance to do so
- do not stop their pain or feelings
- do not try to "fix it"
- do not judge, excuse, or analyze—listen
- do believe what you are hearing

- do validate their pain
- do be calm; assure survivors they are safe

KEEP ALL THE PIECES

Many memories are too traumatic to surface in one session. They may unfold in bits and pieces. Many times information you associate may feel unreal, impossible, ridiculous, or insignificant. You may get a thought, a blip, or a feeling and instantly reject it. However, the more you are able to accept seemingly foreign thoughts and ideas, the sooner you will be able to understand how they fit. Every piece of information is a part of the puzzle. Keep each piece, even if it doesn't seem to make sense. Periods of uncertainty are common. Until you get and assimilate all the key parts of an event, you may experience only partial or no relief. Trust that things will sort themselves out eventually.

GO WITH IT ALL THE WAY

Although it's important to manage the association process and learn how to associate/dissociate at will, there is also a time in the association process when you've just got to "go for it." Trust in the process. As therapist Mary Ellen Holmen says:

I use the ocean as a metaphor. When you're in the middle of a memory, you're in the grips of the ocean, in a wave, and don't fight it. Go with it. Allow yourself to be pushed by this thing and pulled by this thing, because it's the natural flow. And if you just ride the wave, you'll wash upon shore. You know that your ship will be drawn and will find its way to shore, and you can trust the ocean to take you there.

WHAT TO DO AFTER THE MEMORY

Many survivors stop association as soon as they have the details of a dissociated experience. However, that's only half the goal. The second half is to transform the trauma and bring any traumatized inner kids back to a Safe Place for healing.

It's a rescue mission. I prepare to go into hell. But if someone is there to hold my hand, then I can get out again and bring my petrified kids out with me. Sophia

Check with your traumatized parts to make sure that they take back their own power. For example, imaging the use of a VCR, you can play the entire sequence backward, undoing the harm and returning your inner selves to their original wholeness. One survivor who was having flashbacks of electrocutions had his therapist "pull out the plug." Counselor Earl Moeller, formerly of Cottonwood de Albuquerque, describes the power of visualization in healing:

> People have had monsters, snakes, bugs, and evil implanted in them. I use visualization to eject those things. Angels will go inside and find a place where the spiders are and surround the place with a magic web. I ask my clients to show me where the demon is. Then I make it get really small and put it into a container and put it into a swamp. Then I draw them a picture of how I sunk him into the swamp. Sometimes we have to do it more than once with a demon. It helps to have the client actively involved in the process. Like, I'm pulling out a snake, but you need to squeeze my hand as hard as you can—and your squeezing pushes the snake out. If we pull out a snake that's been there for thirty years, then we need to replace it with some-

thing else. Otherwise the client will feel a vacuum, and the snake will come back. So we might put white light or mountain flowers in its place.

Another approach that works for many survivors is refusing to buy into cult manipulations in the first place.

My therapist never acknowledged that the stuff implanted through psychic surgery was actually in there. That would be dealing with the cult on their own terms. To level the playing field, she kept reminding me that the body naturally rejects anything foreign to itself. Jeanne

I can walk around traumatized for days if I don't take my child out of that memory and rescue her. It's like having been shattered and trying to pull all that back in to be whole again. That part of me is still stuck in those moments, and only I can get her out. When I go back into a memory I go in as an adult twice their size and yell at the people that they can never do that again. It really makes a difference. Jane Linn

Once trauma is transformed, the inner children need to be returned to a Safe Place for ongoing healing. This can be an imagined sanctuary, a children's park, safe cottage, etc. As more and more parts take up residence at an inner healing place, the amnestic barriers can begin to dissolve.

TELL IT, TELL IT AGAIN, KEEP TELLING

Once you have the knowledge of what happened, it's critical to record it immediately. It's common for unrecorded information to become redissociated. Next, you need to assimilate it. This means reversing all the old rules. "Don't think, don't feel, don't see, don't know, don't express, don't 'tell'" need to become "Think, feel, see, know, express, and 'tell.'" You need to tell what you learned by writing, drawing, acting it out. It is critical to express all your reactions. You need to break the isolation and shame by telling a trusted friend. Tell someone who loves and supports you. Tell it in group. Tell it to a therapist. Tell it to your pet. Tell it to a photograph of someone you love or to a picture of yourself as a child. Tell it to a picture on the wall. Tell it to yourself in the mirror. Keep telling the story in as many ways, and as often as you can, until you're done telling it. Then you'll know it's healed.

These are just some of the ways to help associate traumas. Remember that not all suggestions are right for every survivor. The approaches described have evolved from people trying various ideas. Don't be afraid to go with ideas that intuitively occur to you. With practice, survivors gain increasing control over their own association/healing processes. You will learn how to "schedule" your recovery times. You will be able to associate in a supportive, safe, and healing environment. After each association, you will be able to return to safety in the present. You will feel increasingly in control of your own life.

Now I do what I call memory control. I typically only do it in my therapist's office. But if I need to, I can do it on my own. The other day I was anxious, I was switching, I was fliffing all over the place. I felt like screaming, I felt like crying. It was there. So I went back and had it. I went to a quiet place and checked inside with the person who knows. Boom—she tells me. I sob and sob and sob and write it all down and feel much better. Alicia

No matter how difficult memory association is, survivors who are doing it agree that the results are well worth it.

I am grateful, at long last, that my process unfolded hand in hand with the terror, agony, anguish, despair, horror, helplessness, self-loathing, humiliation, and guilt. My suffering, since the events that precipitated it had already taken place, was an inevitable aftermath of horrific events. It makes my life make sense in the only way it can. What was done to me was ultimately senseless, but the experience of being able finally to feel it as any real child would when given the opportunity to be real returned me, literally, to my senses.   Caryn StarDancer

For additional helpful information on memory association see Renee Fredrickson's book *Repressed Memories.*

16

Getting Through the Toughest Moments

I thought recovery was about going into hell and back. I've discovered there is a place that goes deeper than the bottom of hell. But if you keep going straight through it, you come out the other side to a better place.   Janes

At various times in recovery, often before or after doing memory work, you may experience extremes of reactions: seemingly unbearable pain, seemingly impossible realizations, or seemingly irresistible urges to hurt yourself. These are predictable and temporary stages of recovery. This chapter discusses how survivors are overcoming their most difficult challenges to help you find ways to move through yours.

These difficult issues are concentrated in one chapter for easy reference. The problems discussed typically take weeks, months, or years to resolve. Reading through them in one sitting

can feel more overwhelming than hopeful. Therefore, an option is to acquaint yourself with the topics discussed and refer to them as they become relevant. The other suggestion is to read slowly, allowing time for lots of breaks. Your best choice may be to omit this section altogether.

Reading about potential problems may activate destructive impulses in some survivors. If you sense this may be a problem, read only in the presence of a therapist or competent support person. To ensure that you are supported as you read through this chapter, stop now and make note of your reminders of strength and safety (also see Chapters 1 and 2). If you begin to feel overwhelmed, remember to turn to the back page and follow the instructions you have prepared for yourself.

You will find that some stay-safe instructions

are stated more than once. Stay-safe messages are worth repeating.

RECOGNIZING THE TELLTALE SIGNS

Impulses towards self-harm often escalate in times of stress or major breakthroughs in recovery. These may come from dissociated thoughts, emotions, feelings, or amnestic alters. One of the most important skills in every survivor's recovery tool kit is learning how to recognize the moment of dissociation. This is an especially important skill in maintaining safety.

Start by simply trying to notice every time you have dissociated—how it feels. This may take a very long time, but eventually you may begin to notice it more and more. You may find yourself switching from a centered to a dissociated state, or you may be in dissociated states constantly, switching from one self-state or "compartment" to another. Try to track how this happens. Becoming aware of your dissociative mechanisms will help you begin to manage them. Managing dissociative states gives you maximum safety, protection, and significant recovery.

DISSOCIATED IMPULSES

Managing dissociative states is a long-term recovery goal. In the meantime, learn to recognize and manage dissociated impulses that could put you in danger. If you feel an impulse to sabotage yourself or someone else or do something that doesn't make sense, chances are good it is coming from a dissociated part of yourself. The impulse may feel like a message, a voice, or an urge to act against your own best interest or do something strange. For example, you may have an unexplained impulse to call your parents, even though you have broken off relations with them

and have nothing urgent to say. One survivor had to keep fighting a message to drive her car off the road. Another survivor had an impulse to walk down the streets of downtown Chicago at 3:00 A.M. She felt this instruction was coming from her higher power. Since a higher power represents a guiding presence, the instruction doesn't make sense, which is a possible clue to programming.

In addition to sensing that something doesn't seem quite right, there may be other clues to dissociated impulses. Survivors have noticed the following red flags. You may discover others as well. Learn to recognize these signs and get help in combating them if necessary.

- The impulses intensify before or after a new traumatic memory on significant cult holidays, on or around special occasions involving family get-togethers, or after contact with violators.
- The impulse feels like "automatic thinking." It pops to mind in times of stress as the answer to a problem.
- These thoughts contain not only the message but detailed "automatic" information on things such as how, where, when to act.
- The impulse doesn't make sense in context. For example, you may have an urge to sabotage a healthy relationship or say negative things about yourself to your teacher or boss.
- The impulse occurs without accompanying feelings.
- The impulse contains messages telling you to ignore people or internal selves trying to help you.

If you find yourself disoriented or in distress, find a way to walk your way through it to safety.

I wandered the streets for I don't know how long, and I hid in the corner of a wall. It was dark outside, and at some point I heard my therapist's voice in my head, saying, "What are you going to do to help yourself?" And in my head I said, "I'm going to call you." And she says "Okay, what do you need in order to call me?" "Well, I need a phone." "And what else?" "Well, I need money." The conversation continued, "Well, how much money do you need?" "Well, I think 25 cents." "Do you have it?" "Well, I think so." It's just this inner dialogue that was really helping me to get out of it.   Jeanne

By preparing and rehearsing some basic steps, you'll be able to reach help if you need it. Remember that if you don't have any money, in many places you may be able to make emergency calls at no charge or make a collect call through the pay phone operator.

REJECTING SUICIDE

One of the most difficult dissociated messages revolves around suicide. Some survivors are never suicidal, others battle suicidal urges throughout recovery. Here's how survivors are overcoming them.

Recently I'd been having a lot of impulses to hurt myself. And driving to therapy I had this impulse to saw off my head. I was really upset and crying when I got to my therapist's office, and I asked, "What kind of person has the thought that she should saw her own head off?" And she looked at me and just said, "Someone who's been severely abused."   Jeanne

Suicidal impulses in survivors almost always come from a dissociated place. They may be attempts at trauma resolution through reenactment or impulses triggered by traumatic learning

(programming). While the goal in treatment is to associate the trauma, the immediate priority is to keep yourself safe. Again, your best suicide prevention treatment is to recognize self-destructive impulses early and attend to them immediately. At times you may feel able to take care of your safety needs by following the suggestions at the end of this section. However, there may be times when you'll need assistance to keep yourself safe. This may mean taking medication, hospitalization, or more frequent sessions with your therapist. If you've ever had suicidal impulses, your first priority should be to have your "reach help" page at the back of this book completed and a ready stay-safe plan that has been worked out with your therapist.

DEALING WITH SUICIDAL ALTERS

Some of the most insistent suicidal impulses may come from maintainer alters whose job has been to maintain loyalty to violators. Although apparently hostile and daunting, cult-conditioned suicidal alters or impulses can often be quite readily convinced to join a survivor's cause. To achieve this, it is helpful to understand an alter's purpose and perspective. Suicidal alters are usually working from information based on lies and limited choices. Many suicidal alters are exclusive, all or nothing, black and white thinkers. They may be as easily convinced to protect survivors as they were convinced to try to hurt them. Caryn Star-Dancer explains: "No matter what the posturing is or what the ideas, just underneath the surface you're dealing with a terrified child." It's important to remember that survivors are motivated to recover. Seemingly destructive actions are motivated by a will to survive. When one alter seemed intent on suicide, therapist Pat Graves asked him to first contact the other alters to hear their opinions about the suicide and explain their reasons for wanting to live. The other alters helped him understand that he didn't have a right to end their lives.

No matter how impossible the circumstances, there is a way out. Cult-abused children may be taught to think in terms of total obedience or self-destruction. Information and new choices are important tools in reframing perceptions. Therapist Pat Graves explains:

Some alters don't know that if they kill the body everybody inside dies. They really don't understand that. So I start out by asking, "What will die? What or who are you trying to kill?" And once they tell me, for example, "the host alter," I explain to them, "Your perpetrators really tricked you because they told you to kill the host, and they knew that if you did, you'd die too. That's how bad these people are that you are so loyal to." You see, the alters view it as getting rid of the host but not themselves. And one of the ways I show suicidal alters what's really going on is to take a watch or a ring, or I'll have them make a mark on their hand, and then I'll have the host come out just for a minute so they can see that the watch or ring or mark is on the host's hand too. Also, if there's any alliance on the inside—like if there's an inner kid that the suicidal part really likes or believes she's protecting—I'll have that part come out too, so the suicidal alter can see that the mark and everything is on the kid's hand as well. And then I begin to explain that inside, people have different perceptions and bodies, but there's only one body that gets you out into the world. And if that body is dead, then you're trapped in there forever, and there's no way out. And when they begin to see that, I don't push the point anymore. I back

off and let them think about that a little bit. And I've never had that fail.

Suicidal maintainer alters may align themselves with whomever they perceive to be most powerful. They may first test you before coming around. In order to win them over, you need to be firm and strong. Clearly set down safety rules, and allow no exceptions. You may want to enlist the help of your inner community. Together you can work out a stay-safe strategy. You may also have several practice runs so that everyone can feel more confident in carrying out the plan.

If your suicidal impulses or alters are unable to follow your rules just yet, you may need to ask them to "go to sleep," off to a "deserted island," or into a "secure enclosure" until you feel more able and ready to work with them. (These ideas are explained in Chapter 11.)

Regardless of where impulses to commit suicide originate, and no matter how real or inevitable they feel, remember

DO NOT ACT ON THEM

Rather than acting on your impulses, draw them or write them out. You can ask yourself questions such as: Why do I need to hurt myself? Who am I trying to hurt by hurting myself? Do I really want to let my violators continue to have the power? Keep writing or drawing until the impulse passes. Call a friend to talk it out. Some survivors write stay-safe contracts.

STAY-SAFE AGREEMENTS

Every day now is still more empowering, and I come more and more into my own identity. I could see the triggers, the cues that they were using, and I just had to make a contract. That was absolutely essential. Adam

The most effective agreements are those prepared in conjunction and cooperation with all your inner selves. Some contracts are simple and straightforward; others are quite detailed. Your contract can be as short as one line or as long as three pages. However, contracts tend to work better if they are reasonable and have a starting and ending date. In times of crisis, they may need to be reaffirmed daily or weekly. At other times, monthly or quarterly agreements may work well. The following stay-safe contract from *Living with Your Selves* by Sandra J. Hocking and Company gives an example of a fairly inclusive contract. It may have ideas that will work for you as well.

In addition to contracts, survivors may find that using tangible reminders to help them stay safe works well—for example, a locket with the photo of your children or loved ones, a special stone to remind you of your strengths, a bracelet to remind you to seek help, a memento from a caring friend.

I didn't think I had what it takes, and I did. All you have to do is keep going, you know. Don't die is rule number one. No matter how much you want to die, how much it seems like the right thing to do, how bad it is, don't die, keep working on it, and you will heal. Caryn StarDancer

How are you doing? Time for a break? Now may be a good time to work out a stay-safe plan. You may want to call a support friend and work out a plan together.

MOVING THROUGH SUICIDAL IMPULSES

The earlier you address suicidal impulses, the easier it may be to overcome them. A good preventive measure is to stay in touch with your feelings as much as possible. Feelings help to keep you centered and in touch with reality—even a

painful one. If you don't address strong feelings or impulses they will build up.

Each situation and survivor is different. What works for some may or may not work for others. However, sometimes moving toward and into the impulses instead of trying to avoid them may bring the relief you seek. Survivors all too often wait too long before making this discovery.

I had been battling this urge to kill myself for two weeks. It was a constant struggle, and by Sunday night, I felt I was losing the battle. My husband was jabbering at me, and something snapped. I sat down and figured out the whole plan—when and how I would actually do it. I wrote good-bye letters to my children. And when I finally finished all the steps, I let go of the struggle and prepared to do it. I found myself in touch with inescapable feelings of hopelessness, despair, and feelings of abandonment, and with them, the desire to kill myself passed. Sunny

No matter how extreme your pain, never turn it against yourself. Have a stay-safe plan and follow it.

What I did was some really straightforward things. When I was feeling really suicidal, I had a program and I followed it rigidly. I didn't care if it required me dragging myself to a telephone. I did it. Because damn it! I wasn't going to die. I set up a schedule where people called me every two hours, or I went to stay with them. I just needed to follow my plan and I did. Alicia

Although suicidal impulses are generally in conflict with survival instincts, sometimes they may come in different guises. Sometimes violators present suicide in glorified terms. They may suggest suicide is "total freedom," especially from pain, a "noble" option, or an opportunity to

CONTRACT FOR SURVIVAL

To cover the period of _____ to
_____

I/We _____ agree not to knowingly or intentionally cause serious or fatal bodily harm or injury, including those actions which could result therein (i.e. overdose, reckless driving, etc.) to this physical, mental, emotional or spiritual body.

I/We will not knowingly kill, physically, mentally, emotionally or spiritually, ourselves or any other person or personality.

As protectors, we the undersigned, to the best of our ability, agree to intervene on behalf of our other persons or personalities who may be unable or unwilling to do so, by calling and actually reaching and connecting with the support members listed on this form.

When I call a support person, I will state that I am calling because of the contract and we will honestly address and discuss the emotions and events that led to crisis and the possible solutions and safety measures to be taken. We will continue to pursue all phone numbers, including repetitions, until the crisis is resolved.

In the event of breaking or attempting to break this contract, professional intervention may be contacted and requested.

Anyone who has reservations about signing this contract must voice them now or you are bound by this contract for the duration of the contract period.

This contract is valid past the end date until a new contract has been negotiated or all support members of the previously agreed upon contract have been contacted and agree that

relinquishment of this contract is in the best interests of the contractee.

_____
Signature of Host Personality

_____
Signatures of those who agree to intervene on behalf of the host and others in the system:

_____
_____
_____
_____
_____
_____

I object to the signing of this contract. I will discuss my reasons here:

_____
_____
_____
_____

These are the persons/agencies I agree to call:
Name and Phone Number

_____
_____
_____
_____
_____
_____

I, the undersigned support person(s) agree to provide emotional or physical support to the contractee within the terms of this contract. I understand the contractee may contact me any time of the day or night.

_____
_____
_____
_____

Reprinted with permission from Launch Press.

join with higher spirits or powers. Be especially wary of impulses to "let go" or find "the best" or "final" answer. This type of message may be especially insidious, because it may sound soothing, calming, or caring.

DO NOT ACT ON THESE IMPULSES— EVER!

Turn to the back page of the book and follow the instructions you have prepared for yourself. Your priority is to keep yourself alive and safe until help arrives or the impulse passes.

Knowing that someone cares is critical to moving through the toughest moments. A staff member at one out-patient facility told me that there hasn't been a single successful suicide by a client since the center opened in 1987. When I asked to what she attributes these encouraging results, she answered, "Because our clients know we care."

The worst time was last November. That's when I wanted to die. And it was the first time I really wanted to die, because I didn't believe that I was ever going to make it. I was having horrible memories and I tried to kill myself. What finally pulled me through was that I have a wonderful support system that I would call and I would say, "Please tell me you believe I'm going to make it." That was it. Just tell me you believe I'm going to make it. And it worked.   Alicia

It takes a lot of trust to believe that anyone could care. It's a risk to trust anything ever again. Yet I know from my experience that survivors care deeply about one another. We know that it often feels too hard to go on. But we didn't survive the worst of it in order to perish in hopelessness. We need to believe that each of us will find a way through because *we are survivors.*

Sometimes we stare so long at a door that is closing, that we see too late the one that is open.
Alexander Graham Bell

ACCEPTING UNBEARABLE REALIZATIONS

As difficult as it is to bear the feelings of being abused, most survivors find it even more difficult to know that they may have hurt others. For many it feels like the ultimate betrayal of themselves. A greater suicidal threat may come if, as sometimes happens, survivors discover that amnestic parts or selves continued listening to cult commands even while they were in recovery. For example, one survivor discovered that without his conscious knowledge, one of his alters was still attending rituals where he was being abused. Another survivor discovered that although she had left her cult, a violator was still accessing a dissociated part with instructions to "teach" her children cult dogma.

I have no idea who I am or what I'm capable of anymore. All my life, I thought I was this perfectly respectable kid, who was leading a relatively normal life. And then I discovered my abuse background. It took me forever to accept that it happened—but on some level I knew that it did. And now I hear that some survivors remain cult-active even in recovery, and they don't even know they're doing it—and I go to myself, "Well, am I doing this too?" I can no longer rule out any possibilities. Janes

It's important to be open to the truth, but at the same time, you should be certain that it is your own truth, not someone else's:

You know the power of suggestion. Survivors are shaky with who they are. They can't contain their own reality. So if someone says, "You are cult-active," they start wondering if they are, you know, even if they aren't.   Ann Seery

Once in recovery, the vast majority of survivors are able to stay safe from influences from violators, especially if they have healthy support systems in place. However, if you discover that an unconscious part of you has continued to be abused by violators, do not try to punish yourself.

SUICIDE WILL NOT FIX ANYTHING. IT WILL ONLY MAKE THINGS WORSE.

Nothing is gained. There is even more loss. No matter how unbearable the discovery, it is in fact a sign of hope. Up until now you remained in danger. Now, at last, you have a real chance for safety and a full recovery. You haven't changed as a person. You've become more aware. By making this information conscious you finally have control over it. You can, at last, take charge of your life.

SURVIVOR GUILT

This last memory I had was just the worst. I literally thought my heart would give out from the pain of it. But I also knew that it was just one more hurdle I had to overcome. I had to stay strong. I have to keep healing.   Suzzane

People who survive traumatic experiences when others died may suffer survivor guilt. In addition, cult-abused children may be made to believe that they killed or were responsible for someone's death, even if they weren't. The message accompanying each trauma is usually, "It's your fault" (see Chapter 6). As a result, cult-abused children may develop an exaggerated sense of responsibility. The guilt and

shame the child feels is usually carried into adulthood.

I ask "Why? Why was I taking lives and mine was being spared? Why did I get to stick around?" Annie

In the November 1986 issue of *Psychology Today,* Janice T. Gibson and Mika Haritos-Fatouros describe how, given certain circumstances, almost anyone can be conditioned to commit acts of cruelty. They cite an experiment in which Stanford University students who agreed to participate were chosen to simulate prison life; some were randomly designated guards and others prisoners:

> With no special training and in only six days' time, they [the study team] changed typical university students into controlling, abusive guards and servile prisoners. . . . The two groups of students originally found to be very similar in most respects showed striking changes within one week. Prisoners became passive, dependent, helpless. In contrast, guards expressed feelings of power, status, and group belonging. They were aggressive and abusive within the prison, insulting and bullying the prisoners. Some guards reported later that they had enjoyed their power, while others said they had not thought they were capable of behaving as they had. They were surprised and dismayed at what they had done.

In the above example, the changes took effect on grown volunteers aware of potential manipulations. The study was conducted by neutral researchers with no particular influence or power over the students' well-being. Despite this, the students' behavior changed dramatically within less than a week. The factors are far more stacked against cult-abused children. The manipulators are parents or adults to whom children look for direction and on whom they totally depend for survival. Responsibility for what occurs lies with the adult violator, not the victim child.

Occasionally abused children may reenact their abuse on other children. In *Repressed Memories,* Renee Fredrickson explains:

Children in the victim role sometimes act out their abuse on younger children, but this does not mean they are offenders. They are children doing what they learned to do, and they do not continue as adults in persistent patterns of sexual victimization to avoid their own pain. They also feel a great deal of remorse and guilt for their actions. Victims' responses to sexually exploiting someone else are diametrically opposed to offenders' responses.

Some survivors are concerned because they seem to have no feelings connected to memories of violating others. They may take it as a sign that they are bad. However, lack of feelings may not indicate lack of remorse but the opposite. The pain may be so great that although the knowledge comes, the feelings remain dissociated. Give them time to surface.

In Twelve Steps for Combat Veterans Anonymous, Step Seven reads, in part,

We seek the strength to complete the grieving process for those who have died . . . to finally recognize all of the feelings we have harbored for many years: anger at those who left us alone, guilt about surviving while others were killed, remorse for failing to save some of those who died, and yearnings to join those whose bodies have already been buried.

The hardest issues call for the three C's of healing—courage, creativity, and compassion. You had the courage to look—respect that in yourself. By finding ways to accept the unacceptable, you have a chance to heal. No matter how difficult the realizations, survivors are finding ways through their pain.

It felt impossible to heal from being a perpetrator. "What did we do? What did we do?" We don't really remember a lot of what we did. And we wondered if we needed to remember the bad things before we could begin the process of forgiveness. And we decided, "Yes." Because a blanket forgiveness is more like closed eyes, rationalized bullshit. And then several days after we wrote like four steps that we need to do to heal. So we wrote, "One, we need to acknowledge and remember the facts of what occurred. Two, thoroughly and compassionately determine our responsibility. Three, make amends to our sister." We weren't sure if that was going to be telling her directly or not. We decided we could make amends in absentia, because maybe if she didn't remember, it might do more harm. "Three 'B' is making amends to ourselves, and Four is eventually forgiving ourselves and our parts that actively were responsible." Gloria

Recovery means healing the shame, by telling safe and trusted others about your most difficult realizations. It will take time. Respect your own readiness. Look to support friends for acceptance and love. Take in as much of each as you can. And in time look to forgive yourself.

Most of us have done things we deeply regret. While some of them can be undone, many cannot. What we *can* do is grow through recovery. Healing demands that we grow in acceptance and understanding. As we learn to accommodate grief, rage, hopelessness, and helplessness beyond our initial comprehension, we give the word "healing" new possibilities and meaning.

We've lived in a hopeless world for too many years. Now we need to have hope.   Jackie Bianco

It's not easy. It's a lot of hard work. It's dedication. It's determination that they're not going to work me over anymore—that I, not they, are going to win.   Dave

There is order that comes out of chaos. There is hope that comes out of despair.   CeeCee

How are you doing? It might be fun to imagine the feel of healing raindrops for a break. Take as long as you like.

OVERCOMING SELF-INJURY IMPULSES

I had lived with pain for so long, I didn't know how to live without it. When it stopped, I kept doing it to myself.   A survivor

Reading about self-injury may intensify self-injury impulses in some survivors. Be prepared to resist these impulses and keep yourself safe. Although people typically think of self-injury in terms of physical injury, in a broader sense self-injury may include other acts of misdirected self-sabotage, experienced as depression, eating disorders, ruining your own career or relationships, or chronically low self-esteem. In most cases self-injury is a conditioned, learned response, manipulated by a child's violators. Sometimes a misguided, protective maintainer alter may hurt survivors because they are remembering what they were told to forget. However, impulses to injure yourself are complicated and may be motivated by other factors as well. The following describes some of them.

Violators will often tell children they have something bad inside. Cutting is sometimes an attempt to get the bad out. Some survivors feel as if they are bursting on the inside. They cut themselves to let out the unbearable feelings.

Cult-raised children are taught that if they've done something "wrong," they must be punished. Self-injury relieves and atones for feelings of guilt. Some survivors will punish themselves before a violator will punish them. This relieves the unbearable suspense over when "the inevitable" will happen to them. Others, having absolutely no control over anything consequential in their life, will injure themselves because it's the only thing they *can* control.

Survivors were told to keep the abuse secret and behave as though everything were normal. Injury is sometimes a silent way of trying to communicate a survivor's actual pain, and a nonverbal plea for help. In addition, the emotional pain survivors feel is often so great that physical injury helps to distract from the greater pain of unbearable feelings.

Self-injury can be a survivor's unconcious defense against associating painful traumatic experiences; attending to injuries keeps the focus off memory retrieval. It may also be an outlet for rage. Cult-raised children have learned that it is forbidden to express rage towards their violators. The excessive rage that survivor adults feel may be turned in against themselves. Many survivors feel totally numb and dead. Some are made to believe and feel that they are robotlike, alien beings. Seeing that they bleed reassures them that they are still alive and that they are human.

Cult-conditioned children were sadistically hurt by their violators. In addition to dissociation, the body may release endorphins and adrenaline to counteract the pain. These naturally occuring opiates may give a child temporary relief. Adult survivors may injure themselves in order to induce this form of temporary relief as well. This often becomes an obsessive/compulsive coping habit.

Some self-injury patterns are easier to break than others. Understanding the reason for a behavior is the first step in changing it. Next, survivors need to be given new information and allow themselves new choices. They may include things such as:

1. It is safer to be in recovery than in a cult.
2. I will not be punished for telling cult secrets, so I no longer need to punish myself.
3. I do not have to hurt myself to release my rage. Today it's okay to express rage toward my violators in constructive ways.
4. I no longer have to hurt myself to give expression to my pain. There are better, permanently healing ways.
5. I do not have to hurt myself to get rid of badness. I am thoroughly good, inside and out. My violators lied.
6. I do not have to hurt myself to feel my own power. Today I have options and choices. I am in control.

Where self-injury serves as pain relief, the transition may take a little longer. You will need to learn new coping behaviors. See if you can find ways to gradually free yourself of harmful coping strategies. Rather than reaching for a weapon, reach for the telephone and call your therapist or a support friend. Self-injury keeps adding to your legacy of trauma. Looking at the hurt behind the self-injury is ultimately the way out, although temporarily more painful. Release comes through remembering the original trauma and letting go of the pain by comforting and healing it.

It's getting much better, thank God. Still, some

days are hard. But it was much, much worse when I was afraid to say what was going on inside of me. Jane Linn

How are you feeling? Remember that every child deserves to be loved and your inner kids can use lots of nurturing.

MOVING THROUGH DESPAIR, DEPRESSION, HOPELESSNESS

There's this overwhelming sense that things are not going to get better. That things are hopeless. It's a real good breakdown technique. It's used frequently with prisoners of war. It's a method for breaking down someone's psyche so that they give up, and a lot of that was done to me. Fortunately, I have a part that is still hopeful and does believe that my life is going to get better. My therapist kept reinforcing that I deserve to have a good life and that things are going to work out.   Bea

Some of the hardest moments in recovery come through what one survivor aptly described as "flashback feelings of hopelessness." Our childhood lessons of "no way out" often control our adult thinking.

I feel like there's this empty, broken funnel inside which has a life of its own and no light, hopelessness, utter despair, and it's the end of the world.   Amy

Healing is achieved through expressing, and so transforming, our emotions, physical feelings, and beliefs. This includes giving expression to feelings of hopelessness.

When I'm feeling suicidal, don't give me platitudes like "This too shall pass." I don't give a damn. But what might help is knowing that some-one else has been here, and how that felt.   em

I was treading water okay there for a while and it feels as though something came up from the ocean and dragged me down to the bottom, and it won't let me up. I never experienced despair like this. I mean, I cried every night for a year and it didn't touch the last two months. I feel stuck, because I've done everything, and I can't make this stuff go away. And that caught me very much off-guard and was very confusing to me. I thought I had a spirituality that was working. I thought I had a program for living—a worldview, an idea that would sustain me a little bit in times of trou-ble. And that's turned out to be totally not the case. I was left absolutely thunderstruck and devastated, debilitated, not functional at all for the last two months. I'm unable to open my mail, unable to make or return phone calls, I'm sleeping up to fif-teen hours a day, not eating, crying for the whole day or for hours at a time.   Adam

By giving unbearable pain expression, you give it the means by which to leave.

Yesterday I had a dream about a baby deer. A hunter shot him, and it lay there. For some reason, I wanted to have that deer next to me. Finally I began to understand why. The deer is barely alive. It is in so much pain that it would far rather not be alive. But it is, and it is lying next to me. It is hold-ing the pain that I feel but cannot bear. And so I have my pain lying next to me. That's as close as I can get to it for now.   Janes

Giving expression to inexpressible pain is like a release valve on a pressure gauge. It allows the pain to leave and in time healing begins.

What really works for me is to wallow in it. Admit my very worst thoughts, which I was taught to battle and deny. And after I've put down every horrible thought in my head, I add the word "today." It's a reality check to remind me that whatever I'm feeling now is not a forever thing, even though "forever" is exactly how it feels. Sophia

The more you fight something, the bigger it gets. By embracing an unwanted feeling, you may be able to neutralize it.

Depression—sitting on the couch, I look at it. I hold it. I find myself laughing about it, dealing with it, absorbing it, and not letting it get bigger than me anymore.   Jeanne

I know it's hard, and I know it hurts, but trust that you can make it to a better place. When I last checked back with Adam, he had this to say:

I'll have to live with being a survivor for the rest of my life, but each day now I feel my psyche breathing and restoring a healing balance in my life. For the past six months I've been able to smell the roses.   Adam

This has been a very difficult chapter. But if you are trying to make it through the issues dis-cussed, then, along with the rest of us, you are heading toward a much, much better place. An excellent companion to working through the issues of healing is *The Courage to Heal* by Ellen Bass and Laura Davis.

17

Associating the Beliefs (Behaviors)

[Some] survivors have done repetitive sequences of abreactions without the opportunities to remember, review, and integrate these sequences. These survivors have contacted us because they want to know "What they are doing wrong"... why they have not been able to make the progress that they have become aware that other survivors have been able to make. I find, in almost all cases, that when survivors have the information to understand the logic and necessity of associating all aspects of their traumatic history... when they are given tools to facilitate that process... they are ultimately and often immediately relieved to get on with the painful truth.

Caryn StarDancer, *SurvivorShip*

Centered people are simultaneously in touch with all aspects of their being (beliefs, bodily sensations, and emotions) and respond to situations from a centered place. However, ritual abuse disconnects normally integrated functions, and so in recovery each of these faculties may need to be reassociated individually. The sequence of association varies from survivor to survivor. Some survivors associate all aspects of an experience in tiny (but still overwhelming) bits and pieces. Others experience emotions and feelings before connecting with the knowledge of what happened. Still others first associate the knowledge and only later are able to associate their emotions and physical feelings. Regardless of sequence, it is important to associate the knowledge and the resulting beliefs in order to be free of trauma's aftereffects.

THE IMPORTANCE OF CONNECTING

Experiences shape or confirm our beliefs. These beliefs govern our actions, reactions, and behaviors. Whereas our experiences define who we are, our beliefs define what we do.

Many recovery tools focus on expressing emotions and feelings, without an attempt to connect them to their source. When these emotions and feelings come from dissociated trauma, they are rooted in unconcious beliefs. These beliefs remain active and, until they are made conscious, cannot be changed. Once the beliefs are made conscious, a survivor has the power to transform them and can find release from the emotions and feelings connected to them. For example, one survivor found that while he really looked forward to vacations, the closer they got the more panicky he felt, to the point of getting sick. No amount of willing the panic away could stop it. Years later, through recovery, he realized that his very worst abuse happened while his family went on vacation. By associating the trauma, he understood the belief that sprang from the event—"vacations are dangerous." He was able to change his belief to "violators, not vacations, are dangerous," and the panic stopped.

FRAMEWORK FOR ASSOCIATING AND CHANGING BELIEFS

Beliefs are learned, and they can be unlearned. Changing beliefs involves a three-step process of identification, examination, and transformation. Recovery has often focused on the first two steps without establishing the third. Some survivors have had their lifelong belief systems dismantled but not replaced. Without new beliefs to replace long-held beliefs, survivors may feel something is missing, but cannot name what it is. As a result, recovering survivors frequently complain that recovery leaves them feeling lost and disconnected, "up in the air.'

Having a negative, destructive belief system may feel more secure than having no beliefs at all. Without new beliefs it may be harder to let go of the old system, and some survivors may eventually revert to it. Therefore, keeping new beliefs in focus is a key part of recovery.

BELIEFS TO EXAMINE

There are two types of beliefs that survivors need to address: programmed and indoctrinated (see Chapter 5). Programming usually refers to instructions activated through cues. Some survivors have many programmed impulses; others have very few. Because programming is reinforced with trauma, survivors are not aware of it. Programmed beliefs (I have to return to the cult) are dismantled relatively quickly once the cues, trauma, and instruction are associated.

Indoctrination, unlike programming, tends to be more resistant to change, because it shapes children's views during their developmental years. Indoctrination uses dogma reinforced with repetition and traumatic learning. Rather than a single event, it represents years of conditioning.

Typically, beliefs relating to recovery fall into one of three categories:

- Beliefs about yourself (self-esteem)
- Beliefs about the world (trust)
- Beliefs about the relationship between yourself and the world (belonging)

Beliefs formed in these three areas directly affect a person's feeling of autonomy, or personal power.

When children have their basic needs met,

they grow into healthy, happy adults. It has nothing to do with who they are. It has everything to do with how they are treated. A caregiver's face acts as a multidimensional mirror reflecting and shaping children's sense of self, as well as their sense of the world. In that reflection, infants seek to find out, "Who am I? How do I look? How does this new place feel?" These fundamental beliefs are interpreted and shaped for survivors by their violators. Children rarely question their caregivers. Instead, they question their own adequacy.

I heard a description of how children are like sponges. They just take everything in. And I thought that was a really good description of what it's like to be told really bizarre things. You just take it all in and believe it.   Katharine

SELF-ESTEEM

Children initially test and experience their power by ensuring their own survival. Their normal actions (smiling irresistibly, crying insistently), ensure that their needs are met. This reinforces the idea that they are able. Their ability ensures their survival. If they are made to feel right, children feel empowered to act. Cult-abused children are made to feel all wrong. When they cry, no one comes. When they smile, they may get slapped. Cult-abused children are often left wet and hungry for hours on end. Their efforts bring no results. They get the idea that "I don't work right" or, worse yet, "I don't exist." This idea may be specifically taught through rituals.

(The following memory describes a ritual where violators manipulate the child's sense of identity. It contains some graphic images. You may prefer to continue reading at the regular text after this quote.)

I am five years old. Mother, Mr. B., my cousin and maybe Dad took me to a dark, slimy place—it was a cold cement basement. There was a contraption there—sort of pincers embedded in the walls. They clamped these metal pincers into me, and the pincers began to pull in every direction. It's a type of torture they used repeatedly when they wanted me to lose my center and totally lose control or sense of any anchor anywhere to hold on to. As I lost my anchor, they put a liquid inside me which burned horribly. They told me that they were burning the real me. I was being completely destroyed. They "removed" the burnt "me" and began to leave. Their parting words were that I would lose all memory of who I was. And because "I" was destroyed, there would be nothing to retrieve.   Josie

As a result of rituals such as these and years of reinforcement, many survivors have difficulty connecting with a sense of self or believing that they exist.

What we discovered during some of the healing has to do with the meaning of life. We wrote, "There's a lot we don't understand. We don't know why we're here. We don't understand about life. But we are pretty sure that there is such a thing called life. And we even think that we're alive. So we'd like to try and make the best of it."   Deborah

As you progress further in recovery you may experience a stage where you begin to feel less instead of more whole. This may be a reexperiencing of an early childhood trauma around losing your identity or ceasing to exist at all.

I really felt I was losing everything that was me—disappearing, dying. But by moving into that feeling and staying with it as long I needed, it eventually passed. I never get freaked about losing "me" again.   Erik

Abused children believe, "I am being hurt because I am bad." Children who want to be good but think they are bad cannot afford to trust themselves. These children abandon their instincts, common sense, and, in effect, themselves. They begin to look outside themselves for answers.

I realized how much self-esteem I had gotten from my family-sanctioned career, even though I hated it. I realized how much of my identity was tied up with outside success. There was this hollow inside that I tried to fill up with the phrase "successful attorney."   Susan B.

Indoctrination accompanying the abuse turns children against themselves. They perceive themselves as unworthy, wrong, and hateful and are conditioned to hate themselves. Cult-abused children may grow up striving for perfection to counteract the wrongness inside. I remember one person in group saying, "I used to pray for low self-esteem, because I had none."

All children are totally dependent on their custodians. However, convinced of their wrongness, cult-raised children develop a greater dependency. They become accustomed to turning over power and may do so willingly. Many survivors feel uncomfortable when invited to act in their own interest or on their own behalf.

TRUST AND BELONGING

Cult-abused children experience a world that is harmful, threatening, hostile, and unsafe. Instead of connecting, they disconnect from their environment. Instead of belonging and feeling supported by society, they may feel threatened and unwelcome in the world. To survive, they must learn not to trust. Unable to trust themselves or their violators, they may swing between the two extremes of being too trusting or completely distrustful of others.

Violators manipulate "specialness" to separate cult children from others. While cult children are denigrated and humiliated, they are also told that they are special and different from regular folk. This serves to further alienate survivors from society; they have a sense of being somehow extraordinary. Some cling to their idea of specialness for solace. Believing that they don't belong, survivors tend to isolate themselves.

The loneliness I feel has to be one of the most desperate feelings that I have.   Amy

By letting go of being special or different, survivors can experience their commonality with other people. It is therefore important for us to affirm the ways in which we are the same as, not different from, others. It's important to realize that anyone in our circumstances would have responded the same way.

As I started recovering, I made a conscious point of looking at and being with little children. One time I was reading a story to this very bright six year old. It was a fantasy, and she got these big eyes, and said, "Really?" In that moment I realized that I could tell her anything and she would believe me. And I also understood, for the very first time—first-hand—how easy it is to manipulate little children. I wasn't bad. I was manipulated. Sophia

ABOUT POWER

Cult-abused children are often taught that they have special powers. They may be convinced that their power ensured their survival; those without power died. Unconsciously they believe that power is their lifeline. As a result, some feel they need to assume dominator/controlling positions in friendships, groups, or organizations. This unconscious need for control may ruin relationship after relationship.

At the same time, survivors may be afraid to assert their personal power, because in a cult, using power often meant somebody died. Unable to take full charge or assert their power, survivors may miss opportunities for success in life.

One blond-haired, blue-eyed survivor was told as a child that she was a "chosen" one, because of her coloring. Her power and identity were tied up in her hair and eyes. She was told that if she ever disobeyed her violators, her hair would fall out. The unspoken message was that without her hair, her value, and therefore her power, was gone. When she got into recovery in defiance of her cult, she was so anxious that her hair did indeed begin to fall out. Even though a friend pointed out the relationship between hair loss and anxiety, her inner child was in a panic, convinced that the cult predictions were right.

The following is a typical scenario of how cult-conditioned beliefs keep survivors mentally enslaved, constantly questioning their own validity.

Even though the world has told me I'm capable and competent, the basic feeling is that I'm incompetent, that I'm unworthy, and that I'm a failure, and that I will continue to fail. So I'm learning to check back with people and have them tell me that I really don't sound like an idiot ninety-nine percent of the time. And that's really helping—a sort of reality check. Bea

Trust affects relationships, especially significant relationships. The following account shows the aftereffects of destroyed trust as well as programming.

Seeing a therapist has been extremely hard—very, very difficult. As an adult, I've seen five different therapists and ended up having problems with every one of them. So I was starting with a new therapist, and I knew a number of women who had seen her, and I was basically convinced that she was a pretty safe person. I got into the sessions and sensing my uneasiness she asked, "Well, what is your worst-case scenario of what can happen?" And I said, "You could force me to do things." She said, "How could I do that?" I said, "You have guns." And instead of flat-out arguing with me or denying that she had a gun, she accepted it as a fear of mine. She said, "If I had a gun, where would it be?" And I immediately said, "In the desk." So we took the desk apart. I took out the papers and the drawers and I looked through the whole thing, and there was no gun there. But part of me thought, "You probably moved it." I looked around her office and found a number of spots where she could have easily moved it, but I didn't check those because I decided to trust her about this. And what was so fascinating was that through talking to her I ended up remembering that the therapist my parents sent me to when I was a little kid, did have a gun. I knew exactly where in the desk it was kept, and I knew some of the ways he abused me with it. So from having no memories of any gun, I eventually got very precise memories just from being specific about my fear. Deborah

The difficulty of recovery isn't about intellectually grasping that we are ordinary people who have a right to live our own life. It's in dismantling lifelong beliefs rooted in traumatic learning. One therapist told me about an experiment some researchers did with a pike and minnows. Both were put into the same aquarium. There was a glass shield down the middle, separating the pike from its natural food source, the minnows. The pike kept trying to chase its food and kept hitting the glass barrier. After a year or so, the glass barrier was removed. The pike could never again be enticed to cross the now nonexistent barrier.

After years and years of learning predetermined, unnatural ideas, survivors may become comfortable in an *unnatural* state. The image of a glass barrier becomes more real than reality. It remains resistant to change. However, most lessons you were taught, although painful, were untrue. Your caregivers never once looked to really see you. The lessons about your identity were predetermined. They had absolutely nothing to do with who you really are. And although it's painful to realize you were never seen, it helps to know this when trying to reclaim your inherited, rightful self-esteem.

My friend and I have this little banter between us. Its like, "Oops—another lie that they told us." And that's what I'd stress—is that they lie. Alicia

The more they told you that you were rotten, probably the more good you were. They had to keep proving it to you, because they were counteracting the truth. Josie

Recovery requires remembering, examining, and refuting the many lies instilled in these early developmental years. Once these beliefs and their sources are identified, they can be transformed. Each lesson, such as "You are bad," is taught many times and in many different ways. Therefore many experiences may need to be associated before a belief can be transformed.

Once we discover our invisible glass barriers (the trauma), we need to risk going through them. Otherwise, like the pike, we may live a constricted, unnatural life instead of the one that is our natural inheritance.

Every time you risk moving through the invisible barrier, it is important to affirm the truth: "The barrier has been removed. I am alive. I am safe. No one will hurt me now. Going through the barrier feels good."

You can have any kind of life you want. You may have to go through a fair amount of hell to get there—no question. But every ounce of it is worth it. Lynn

THE KEY IS SELF-ESTEEM

Beliefs formed about ourself affect our beliefs about the world, which in turn affect beliefs about belonging in it and ideas of autonomy. The key to trust, belonging, and autonomy is self-esteem which is built on two basic convictions, as explained in Dorothy Corkville Briggs's *Your Child's Self-Esteem:*

1. I am lovable: I matter and have value because I exist.
2. I am worthwhile: I can handle myself and my environment with competence. I know I have something to offer others.

In recovery, these messages need to come from two sources: from yourself and from people you respect and trust. Self-esteem comes from reparenting yourself through life-affirming messages. Self-esteem, trust, belonging, and autonomy come from life-affirming feedback from others.

ADDRESSING THE SOURCE

Self-esteem starts at the beginning of life, and that's where beliefs need to be addressed. The following technique is still experimental. Techniques that work for nontraumatized populations may have different results for trauma survivors. More research is needed. Nevertheless, the following account illustrates an important idea: Ultimately healing must begin with the building blocks of development upon which all other self-perceptions are based.

Using a pioneering approach, Dr. Foster Cline has been able to heal previously untreatable, "psychopathic" kids by reestablishing healthy bonding. A March 1993 article by Tom Keogh in the Toronto *Globe and Mail* entitled "Raging Angels" describes it as "rage reduction" therapy. The therapist assumes a parent/infant position with the child, by maintaining close eye contact and holding the child's head in the therapist's lap. The therapist encourages the child's expression of anger and discourages the child's usual defenses of intellectualization, control, and manipulation. She or he "aims to help the unattached child relinquish control that he or she has come to depend on for survival." The child "becomes enraged and finds that this rage destroys neither him nor his therapist." In time the therapist redirects the child's anger towards its source—often the family of origin. As the therapist cracks through the child's fears about expressing very intense feelings, "the child finally opens up. It is not unusual to then see the child wail and weep, like the infant he once was. This time, that infant is picked up, held, rocked, and protected."

FINDING YOUR SELF

You may have a sense of an original self, and you may not. If you do, chances are that qualities you attribute to yourself may be paired with negative associations. Survivors grow up sensing that their strengths are their liabilities; that if they ever expressed their true, talented self, people would hate them. One survivor used to look in the mirror and see a monster. As she began recovery, the monster began to fade, but the more terrifying feeling was that there was no one to replace the monster. Because survivors were never able to establish a positive sense of self, they may have no sense of themselves at all.

They stole my self and implanted shame. I know enough not to believe their lies, but if I let go of the shame, there's nothing else there to grab hold of because they perverted me at such a young age. I want to reconnect, but there's nothing to reconnect to. Adam

Many survivors know some of their inherited qualities but are afraid to claim them.

I sort of keep people from seeing the best part of me. I know it's there, but I'm not supposed to let anyone see it. No doubt I was punished any time it came out. Sometimes I feel like just a total phony, even though I try to be as honest as I can. But I'm so conditioned to hide certain parts of myself, and feel more comfortable acting wimpy than acting as strong as I really am. I hope I can get over that some day and let the strong part out and not be ashamed of it. Jane Linn

It's risky and it takes courage to be yourself. It takes a leap of faith to accept that you're okay exactly as you are. But in taking that risk, you stand to gain your self. One survivor finally realized, "What have I got to lose?"

There really is nothing bad about being yourself. This is something I should have learned by the age of two. It's something I need to keep reminding myself of. Jane Linn

You may have some sense that you are hiding your good parts, or you may have no sense of any good parts at all. In that case, start by making a list of what or who *you would like to be.*

Looking back on it, I remember often noticing certain people that I kinda thought were neat, but definitely not me. Well the things I'm discovering about myself through recovery are often those exact same qualities which I used identify as "not me." It's as though I had some sort of a genetic blueprint which attracted me to "me."   Roxana

New beliefs should be your own, not those of a friend or your therapist. They may take some time to develop and even longer to assimilate. Years of negative conditioning cannot be transformed in one instance. Aim for progress not perfection. One of the most effective ways to establish new beliefs connected to your own reality is to look at pictures of yourself at the time the abuse was happening. Reconnect with young children. Look at a baby.

When I look at a baby, I cannot imagine a single human being born on this earth who would want to perpetrate this shit. Babies thrive on love and nurturing—every single one of them.   Caryn StarDancer

Remember that you were once a baby. What would you want for a baby? How do you feel about her or him? What would you want to say to her or him? What would you want to do for her or him?

Looking at a baby may bring up negative rather than positive feelings in some survivors. That's valid too. What's behind the bad feeling? Every feeling is a good starting point for beginning your healing.

TRYING NEW MESSAGES

Start by accepting a basic truth: I AM ALIVE. I EXIST. This message may not be easy for some survivors. If it doesn't feel like a useful starting place, come back to it when you are able. In the meantime you can get some inspiration from the many life-affirming messages available in recovery literature. Below is a list of messages drawn from a framework of affirmations in Pamela Levine's *Circle of Power* and *Becoming the Way We Are.*

It's okay for me to be alive, held, fed, and taken care of.
It's okay for me to see and to be seen, to explore, and to feel my senses.
It's okay for me to grow, to think, say no, and become separate from you.
It's okay for me to dream, and hope, and create, and imagine.
It's okay for me to trust myself and decide what's right for me.
It's okay for me to take care of myself, be successful, and express my sexuality.

Start with a wish list of goals or self-affirming messages. Include a variety of ideas: specific, long-term wishes (I want to be a concert pianist), short-term wishes (I want to join a support group), and general goals (I want to enjoy fulfilling relationships). Start each affirmation with "I."

Chances are that most if not all of them will feel untrue or impossible. That's okay. For now, you don't need to believe any of them. Begin by simply reading the list out loud on a regularly scheduled basis.

Once you get used to these ideas, examine which beliefs don't feel true. Use this as a starting point for association. Find out what negative messages contradict your preferred beliefs. Keeping your new, positive beliefs in mind may give you added incentive to look at the difficult material that may be keeping you trapped in the past.

This stuff is so stuck to me, even though it's not me. But their game only works if you buy into it. If you don't play, there is no game. I'm not playing their dysfunctional game anymore. Sunny

EXERCISES TO HELP ASSOCIATE AND CHANGE BELIEFS

People cannot hold two contradictory ideas at the same time, and accepting new, life-affirming beliefs means rejecting destructive beliefs. Existing beliefs, conscious or unconscious, are usually experienced as automatic thinking. There are many ways to access these automatic thoughts. The tools described in Chapter 25 and the ideas in Chapter 15 can help identify automatic thinking. In addition, *If You Could Hear What I Cannot Say,* by Dr. Nathaniel Branden, has useful exercises to access repressed beliefs.

Once negative, untrue, or incongruent beliefs are identified, each one must be changed. Initially, the simplest way to do this is to put the word "not" into the statement.

One of the rules I use in my recovery is the law of opposites. It's simple, structural sentences that allow us to reverse our thought patterns. So if I hear "You will go crazy if you remember this, " I know those are programmed words, so all I do is say "I will not go crazy if I remember this." If you understand the logic of the law of opposites, you've got one of the keys to reprogramming, and it works in many ways. So if I got the message in my head not to talk to somebody, I would find someone safe and talk fast. If I got the message in my mind to

hurt myself, I would do something good for myself. Suzzane

You may find other helpful ideas in Steven Hassan's *Combatting Cult Mind Control.* A tool many survivors have found helpful is the Reprogramming Worksheet, developed by Caryn StarDancer and reproduced on page 219.

GETTING STRONGER THROUGH TRUTH

In addition to dismantling manipulated beliefs, look for affirmation of your positive points. Ask your friends to honestly share what they like about you. You can try this as an exercise in a support group. With permission, tape their responses. Play them back to yourself as often as you can. Anytime you catch yourself saying anything negative to yourself, stop. This is simply reinforcing the negative conditioning from which you are trying to break free. It's not that any of us is perfect. Being human gives us the right to be imperfect. It's to counteract the hundreds of thousands of negative messages already there. By staying focused on the positive, you can begin to restore the balance. Ask your friends to help you stop negative self-talk as well (you can offer to reciprocate). Equally important is to affirm your successes. For example, if you brave breaking the "don't tell" rule and experience rewarding results, affirm your accomplishment. For example, repeat as often as you can, "I told. I didn't die. It made me stronger."

Although ideally each belief would follow the three steps of identification, examination, and transformation, beliefs seem to follow their own course. There will likely be days when you can identify and embrace positive beliefs and others when you'll feel totally immersed in old negative thought patterns. With recovery, the balance will

REPROGRAMMING WORKSHEET

TRIGGER:

IMMEDIATE RESPONSE:
    Emotion:

    Message:

SHORT-TERM CONSEQUENCES:
    Emotion:

    Message:

CHALLENGE:
    Old message:

    Is this message based on fact?

    What facts refute this message?

    What facts, if any, support it?

RESULTS:
    What is the worst that could happen?

    What favorable things, if any, might happen?

NEW PROGRAM:
    What alternative thought could I try to replace the old message with?

    How might I defuse my negative emotions?

    What things can I do to replace them with positive emotions?

Reprinted with permission from Caryn StarDancer, copyright © March 1990.

gradually shift to increasingly positive, realistic, and empowering beliefs.

Recovery is simply learning that you are right. That you were born right, that your feelings are right, that your thoughts are right, that your body is right, and that your soul is right. As you begin to trust in your rightness, self-esteem is restored to you.

The best part of recovery is feeling self-esteem for the first time. All my life I wanted to feel it. I tried to feel it. I took assertiveness classes, I worked on it, I said affirmations. But it's only in remembering and healing the child inside that I have finally begun to feel self-esteem and live without constant discomfort. And that is so essential to having a good life.   Jane Linn

Keep looking to connect with your child and feel her or his rightness within you. Each step on the journey helps brings you closer to her or him. As you move through each stage of recovery, you begin to feel more and more right. Hold onto that "I am right" key. With it, locked doors will open more easily.

I will look in the mirror and say, "I'm beautiful"—just once.
I will open up to someone I trust—just once.
I will respect myself and my boundaries—just once.
Just for today, I will forgive myself for hurting others and letting others hurt me.
I will let myself feel really good for one whole minute.
I will laugh because I am alive.
I am capable of learning, growing and changing.
I am worthy of love.
I am enough.

Songs for the Inner Child by Shaina Noll has additional loving and nurturing messages to help survivors develop a positive sense of self.

18

Associating the Body
(Physical Sensations/Feelings)

For seven years I remembered, grieved, and recovered memories. Even though I was getting better and stronger, I still wondered occasionally how real it all could have been. Then one day, during body work, I suddenly felt something wet and hard right inside of me. I felt his penis moving in and out, my little body shoved back and forth. There was no more denying it. Roxana

Our beliefs can and have been manipulated. Ideas can be questioned, doubted, explained, rationalized, and changed. But our body is the anchor of our integrity. Physical sensations cannot be fabricated. When our physical feelings are associated with a repressed experience, the evidence is irrefutable.

The truth about our childhood is stored up in our body, and although we can repress it, we can never alter it. Our intellect can be deceived, our feelings manipulated, our perceptions confused, and our body tricked with medication. But some day the body will present its bill, for it is as incorruptible as a child who, still whole in spirit, will accept no compromises or excuses, and will not stop tormenting us until we stop evading the truth.*

Alice Miller, *Thou Shalt Not Be Aware*

Our bodies can bring home reality in a way that our intellect can't. When we are in touch with our selves through our bodies, we feel alive and real. We are able to have a full range of feelings, including pleasure, pain, joy, creativity, playfulness, and spontaneity. Joyful sex and spirituality are experienced through our bodies as well.

I did yoga, meditation, spiritual practices, each of which emphasized leaving my body and explor-

ing the "higher" reaches of the mind. The idea was to experience the white light, and I did. But my greatest sense of spirituality has come through working my recovery. I have had moments, still rare, when the feeling of being truly present and alive within my own body surpassed the "bliss" promised in escaping it. When I'm truly present in my own body, life has meaning, and I feel fulfilled. Erik

As a defense against pain, survivors have escaped and remained out of their body or suppressed all feelings within it. Some survivors are so out of touch with their bodies that they believe they have no feelings. (Everyone has feelings. Some people have simply learned to disconnect from them.) Others may have feelings but are unable to recognize or name them. Survivors often have little body awareness; their hands may feel disconnected from their body; they may be unable to recognize exhaustion, stress, thirst, or hunger. Because we cannot block selectively, when we block out painful feelings we block out good feelings as well. Wilhelm Reich, a pioneer in showing the relationship between expression of physical feelings and health, described this block as "muscular armor." He describes how repression holds a body rigid, as though in a suit of armor. This armor blocks out both the experience and the expression of feelings. Reichian-based and other body therapies look to soften this armor, allowing feelings to flow naturally.

PREPARING TO ASSOCIATE FEELINGS

Associating traumatic feelings should be managed carefully. Traumatic feelings take a toll on our bodies. In addition, parts of our body holding the trauma may be in a state of shock.

during trauma . . . a child begins to suffer disorientation, near shock and shock. This absence of fundamental control leads to a profound loss of ontological security bringing a sense of annihilation. To live with the fear of constantly impending annihilation, children must distance or dissociate from 1) the actual events of trauma, 2) the memories of trauma, and 3) the feelings surrounding the loss of ontological security. When children are repeatedly brought to peak arousal through stimulation that could injure or destroy them, they must dissociate from the traumatizing experiences in order to preserve the capacity to function at all.

Martin R. Smith, M.Ed., *Obedience to Insanity, 1989*

Although it is important to connect with our feelings, it is equally important not to retraumatize ourselves unnecessarily. The safety techniques discussed in Chapter 15 apply to physical feelings as well. When working with tools whose focus is to elicit feelings, and reconnect them with associated beliefs/behaviors, it is important to go at your pace, not your therapist's. If you have a medical condition which is aggravated by stress, you may need to associate feelings under the direction of a physician or even delay this part of recovery until you are physically stronger. It's important to balance the health gains made by associating and releasing trauma with the need to protect your current health.

"Neophobia, Ontological Insecurity and Existential Choice Following Trauma," by Martin R. Smith M.Ed., and Ellen T. Jones, M.A., describes a tool for minimizing trauma reassociation called Response Side Therapy. In Response Side Therapy, survivors use biofeedback to track vital signs such as pulse rate, breathing, blood pressure, skin temperature, and nervous system activation.

This promotes self-awareness and gives survivors more control over the association process. It helps survivors recognize the relationships among bodily sensations, emotions, and behaviors. Response Side Therapy also teaches survivors to soothe and comfort painful feelings thereby decreasing the difficulty of recovery and advancing the healing process.

BODY COMMUNICATIONS AND MEMORIES

In their brochure "Radix: Body-Centered Personal Growth Work" CRT therapists Dnise Dickey and Ron Andes write: "[traumatic] feelings, thoughts, movements, and sensory information [are] often blocked from the awareness and stored in the body. In this very real sense, therefore, the body *is* the unconscious." As survivors learn to pay attention, they discover that their bodies have memory, and store information. To get in touch with your body, start by simply paying attention to the ways it may be trying to communicate. Below is a list of symptoms commonly noticed by survivors. It is not meant to be definitive or exhaustive. Rather, it is a way to help increase your awareness. (Additional symptoms indicating beginning of association are given in Chapter 15.) Each survivor is unique. In time you will learn how your own body communicates.

Other signs to monitor include chronic physical problems—for example, chronic joint and bone pain, yeast infections, menstrual cramping, impotence, extreme genital sensitivity, skin irritations, hives, flushing, unexplained marks or redness, breakouts, rashes. You may be able to recognize your reactions easily. That's an important stepping stone to healing. On the other hand, you may not be aware of any symptoms or physical feelings. Keep checking inside. It may take a while before any feelings come. It helps to consciously give feelings permission to surface. Each of these symptoms is a thread toward association. A helpful reference for interpreting physical feelings is Louise L. Hay's *Heal Your Body.*

Another survivor experiences body memories like this:

Smells, oh God, the garbage can, the toilet, every smell that relates to the human body would make me nauseous. I would start to smell that thing—I guess it's death and disease and blood. So what I'm trying to say is I thought I smelled like that, and I was afraid to get close to people. Well, I was having body memories. These smells coming off my body were things that people had done to me. I had been made to lie in this stuff, I had been made to eat it, I had been made to sit in it for hours, whatever they wanted to do to me with this stuff. And I was smelling it again because my child was remembering. Now I know that. But when you're going through it, it's so crazy.   Bea

Even though our bodies cannot talk, they can communicate. For example, one survivor noticed:

I started doing Feldenkrais body movements as part of my recovery, and my teacher kept emphasizing how smart our bodies are—how you can ask them to do things, and they will. Well, one day I had terrible cramping in my foot and was just in agony. Half-frustrated, half-angry I said to my body, "If you're so smart, then tell me what I'm supposed to do now." And an idea to lean on my foot a certain way came to me, and I tried it, and the cramp went away immediately. I had never been able to get rid of foot cramps quickly before. I have a whole new respect for my body—in fact, I'm beginning to think it's smarter than my brain. Janes

Signal	*May be associated with*
feeling cold, constricted	
arching your back	
headache at the back of the neck	
gastrointestinal problems, especially diarrhea or constipation	fear or fear of feelings
need to urinate	
shallow breathing	
joint pain, arthritis, gout, especially knee or spine	
inability to make or maintain eye contact	
urge to eat/binge/purge/drink/take drugs	
increased addictive behaviors	
increased obsessive behaviors	
hold your breath	
throat constriction	
repetitive swallowing	trying to stop a feeling, memory, or experience
frontal headache	
jaw tension	
feeling depressed	
nausea	
chills, chilled to the bone	
increased nightmares	surfacing body memories
inexplicable sexual arousal	
unexplained body aches or pain	
dizziness, extreme drowsiness	
burning sensations	
extreme fatigue	
feeling confused and foggy	
deep sighing	release of accumulated emotions
inappropriate expression of emotion	
feeling hot	suppressed anger, sadness, or shame
dry mouth or diminished saliva	overtaxed system

Survivors have been able to associate body memories by talking directly to parts that are hurting or "communicating." To help get information, you can imagine breathing directly into a part of your body and waiting for a response. You can press down firmly but gently on your chest, diaphragm, or affected area to expel information. You can use any of the tools described in Chapter 26. For example,

When I start feeling pain, I write to that part of my body. I've been able to unleash quite a few memories that way. Not trying to be vulgar, or anything, but hemorrhoids were a problem with me for many, many years. Each time I had a flare-up, I'd write to that part of my body, and here comes another memory of being sodomized. And then the pain goes away. And right now, I've been free of it for five, six, months. But if it starts happening again, I know what to do to release that cell memory.   Dave

MANAGING FEELINGS

Some survivors associate a trauma without reexperiencing the original pain. It's like remembering an auto accident. You can remember that it hurt, but you might not have to feel it again in order to heal.

However, some survivors spontaneously feel the pain. If you are reexperiencing the original pain during traumatic associations, it may help to practice connecting and disconnecting from your feelings. You can try diverting your attention by going for a brisk walk or run, starting an intense discussion, or reading a book. Have your diversion tactic ready so it is available as you need it. To help moderate the intensity of feelings, you can draw, write, and act them out. These techniques may allow feelings to be associated in manageable pieces and prevent you from becoming overwhelmed.

AS FEELINGS SURFACE

As survivors become aware of body symptoms, they often don't attend to them, but such sensations are real and need proper care. If you are fatigued, rest. If you have a rash, take the appro-

priate medication. If your knee is swollen, put on a compress and don't walk on it. One survivor discounted an earache as a body memory. It was a body memory, but also an infection that spread to his throat, nose, sinuses, and chest. If you saw an abandoned child with tears rolling down her or his cheek, and a scraped knee, you would probably want to hug her or him, fix the scrape, and tell her or him things will be okay. That's what your inner kids need to hear. Taking care of what's hurting is part of the healing process. It's doing for ourselves what should have been done for us as children. Therapist Mary Ellen Holmen adds, "The things inner children need are usually very simple things: a warm bath, a cup of soup, clean clothes, a soft bed, cuddling, and quiet."

IT'S OKAY TO FEEL GOOD

Our bodies were made to experience pleasure, and our natural instincts are to pursue pleasure and avoid pain. As with everything else in a cult, reality was turned upside down. Survivors may have been conditioned to pursue pain and avoid pleasure. Enjoyment was not only forbidden but severely punished. Survivors are usually afraid of it. This belief needs to be changed. Experiencing pleasure is your natural right. It will give you more strength for healing. It is a reward after all your pain. It's both good and right to have pleasurable feelings.

To help connect with your body, try to use it consciously. Walk, noticing how your feet connect with the ground. Move freely and notice how wonderful the freedom can be. Make noise. Sing, shout, scream. See how alive it makes you feel. Breathe in and out, noticing how each inhale and exhale feels. Luxuriate in the feeling. Breathe into parts of your body that are hurting. Heal them with your breath.

You might want to treat your body to some of the following, especially after associating a difficult memory.

HEALING OUR BODIES

There are many new body-oriented therapies being explored. Therapists are rediscovering the healing properties of aromas, colors, and soothing sound. You can experiment with them to find which melodies, colors, or scents are nurturing to your senses. Baths are very healing. A bubble bath can be fun. In addition, survivors have found that combining a pound of baking soda with a pound of sea salt in bath water can be very soothing. My favorite product for releasing toxins and soaking up pain is a mineral salt bath called Masada. It is distributed from North Hollywood, California, and can be found in health food stores. Lemon water (water with a squirt of lemon), preferably at room temperature, helps to flush away bodily stress. You can drink it anytime. Some survivors drink it while soaking in a bath.

Don't forget to treat your younger selves as well.

My child deserves a chance to go play, a chance to run, and a chance to have an ice cream cone. She deserves the things she was deprived of when she was young. Writing, keeping a journal, therapy, and support groups are good, but you also need to practice playing and laughing, and learning in lots of different ways with stuffed animals and with toys. Look at it as an experience of life that we never got as children. Alice

A parting thought:

My therapist told me, "Happy animals wag their tails." So when I want to feel happy, I wag my tailbone—and my face never fails to light up. Sophia

19

Associating the Emotions

During recovery my emotions were like a golf ball. If you peeled away the white exterior, you would have found elastics so intertwined one could not be separated from the other.

Marilyn Van Derbur, former Miss America, incest survivor

Memories reflect our past, beliefs determine our future, and emotions express our present. When emotions are in keeping with existing circumstances, we feel present or centered. Centered people are able to read situations accurately and so make appropriate choices for themselves. Before recovery, survivors rarely feel present or centered. Instead, they often feel numb, out of touch, disconnected, and unreal.

When someone is startled they'll say, "I jumped right out of my skin." Well, that's the way

it is for me all the time. I live on the edge and feel empty in the middle.   Erik

Violators focus on splitting children from their emotions in order to gain control over them. Separated from their emotions, people are capable of inhuman acts. Programming cannot take hold in an emotionally associated human being. Associated emotions do not let people act against humanity.

Survivors have been conditioned to mistrust their emotions and ignore their feelings. Rather than relying on their own intuition, survivors have been conditioned to trust others instead. As survivors reclaim their emotions, they reclaim their self.

The first therapist I ever went to told me that society has had a centuries-long debate about what people should follow, their heart or their head. Since recovery, the answer is obvious. There is no conflict. Our heart should decide where to go; our head should figure out how to get there. And a healthy society should have had that one figured out as well. Roxana

ROADBLOCKS

There may be many roadblocks to associating emotions. After years of conditioning, survivors may barely know their own emotions. The words "emotions" and "feelings" are used interchangeably because it's assumed that physical feelings accompany emotions. However, this may not be true for survivors. Survivors may experience emotions primarily as thoughts, without physical sensations. They may also experience feelings such as cold sweats and shaking without connecting them with an emotion such as fear.

I was dizzy. I was nauseous. I was sweating profusely, and my hands shook. I'd never realized that I was panicked about returning home. I thought that's just the way I was. Sunny

Emotions are a blend of beliefs and feelings. To survive, children learned to rationalize away their emotions by changing their beliefs (which can be manipulated) and to ignore their feelings (which can be suppressed but not manipulated). Getting in touch with true emotions means reversing lifelong patterns—learning to trust our intuition, which comes from our gut feelings.

Certain kinds of traumatic learning may inhibit survivors' ability to emote.

(The following paragraphs describe how violators condition children to arrest their emotions. The examples may be difficult for some readers. You may wish to skip down and continue at the next section.)

Emotions are often inaccessible because of trauma. Some survivors are afraid to feel the full extent of their emotions because it reminds them of cult rituals. In cult rituals extremes of emotion may have been evoked. Survivors describe frenzied violators raging, screaming, wailing, or laughing hysterically while a victim was being abused. One survivor remembers the "murderous rage" of violators who released anger while killing a victim.

Others are unable to feel emotions because of specific traumas. One survivor used to cough violently and "konk out" whenever he tried to feel anger. He finally figured out that whenever he screamed "No!" as a child, his parents choked him into submission. Another survivor never felt angry, and saw no reason to reclaim anger. When asked why, she only knew that "It simply isn't worth it." Through association, she realized that in one ritual she had been set up to lash out. At that moment, her violators killed her baby. This survivor never got angry again. In each case, once the survivors understood the reason for their resistance they were able to move past it toward connecting with their emotions.

ASSOCIATING EMOTIONS

Associating dissociated emotions may be confusing for a while. Survivors have coped with skewed emotions for so long that distorted emotions feel normal. Many have to learn basics such as how natural emotions feel and what they are. Often it is helpful to have a recovery partner or therapist model appropriate emotions.

My therapist cried when I told her I had to put Mama cat to sleep; but I didn't cry. She gets angry when I tell her my husband goes through my purse; but I don't get angry. But it's really important for me to watch her having feelings about the things I tell her. Part of me sort of watches curiously. Another part sort of contemplates that maybe I should be doing that.   Sophia

A clue to dissociated emotions is under- or overreaction to things. You may be perfectly calm in the midst of crises and fly into a rage or panic if your spouse isn't home on time. Janes, who always appears exceedingly calm and unruffled, shared the following.

When I found the dishwasher loaded all wrong, I let out a scream so loud, I'll bet people three blocks away could hear me.   Janes

Survivors usually avoid associating emotions until they feel overwhelmed. It becomes a question of which is worse—living with unbearable tension or coping with unbearable feelings. A better approach is to schedule emotional release on a regular basis. Even five minutes a day can help.

To get emotions to flow, you can try to write, draw, or use any of the tools described in Chapter 25. Let them out a little at a time—as much as you are able to handle. This will make them more manageable and less painful. If five minutes feels like too much, start with thirty seconds, increase it to a minute, and so on. With each release, you will feel stronger, more alive, more energized, and more genuine.

Some survivors feel too much, others feel nothing at all. The key is to become increasingly aware of your reactions and coping habits.

Whenever I begin to feel, I suddenly find myself thinking instead.   Sophia

As emotions begin to connect with their source, you may not be able to complete a feeling or fully experience it. You may be aware that you feel something but not know what it is.

My feelings feel all mushed together. I wish I could pry them apart. I pray, "God, please give me a feeling—just one feeling so that I can recognize it."   Amy

Naming emotions is a learned skill that was denied to most survivors. Therefore, identifying and naming emotions may take some time. Begin to notice how you dissociate from your emotions or feelings. For example, Sophia began to notice the exact time she would begin to think instead of feeling. Once she noticed that, she was able to stay with her feelings longer and longer. Another survivor noticed all his emotions were held in his chest. There seemed to be no physical feelings from the neck up. He then began to envision connecting his head with his chest, and feelings trapped in the chest began to leave. After a phone conversation with her mother, one survivor went swimming and punched the water because that had helped to release anger after a previous phone call. But after half an hour she didn't feel any release and she realized that it wasn't anger but sadness she was feeling. As she comforted her inner selves, the feeling passed.

Although it is important to associate all aspects of a traumatic experience (knowledge, beliefs, feelings, emotions), it doesn't necessarily happen in an ordered fashion. Besides specific associations, survivors often experience general emotions.

I've been in what feels like mourning now for weeks, maybe months, and I can't figure it out. But my support group didn't think I needed to fig-

ure it out. They told me, "There's so much to be sad about. Maybe you're processing multilayered grief." Janes

Once emotions start to flow, it is important to give them full expression. Be careful not to cut off emotions prematurely, even if they are painful; it may be counterproductive.

I was in the middle of a major, very painful memory. It was about being tortured, and I was just getting to let myself know how horrible it felt. And in the moment of connection, I heard my therapist's voice, "Tell your tormentors to leave." It was so jarring. It was exactly the wrong thing to say. Erik

As emotions are associated, survivors are often astounded at the enormity of their force. Keeping traumatic feelings at bay takes tremendous energy. Once released, this energy can be used to enjoy life instead. Through association, the emotions that are often polar opposites can be mediated. Survivors experience fewer extremes such as mania or despair and feel more centered. It's satisfying to feel emotions as they are happening, even if those feelings are sad. The hard and painful work is rewarded, as survivors are able to feel increasingly alive, genuine, and complete.

BALANCING PAST AND PRESENT

It can be a challenge to establish a balance between reclaiming past emotions and creating a healthy emotional environment in the present. Caryn StarDancer suggests:

You have to honor your feelings no matter how fucked up they are, and honor your

dysfunctionality. At the same time, you have to be working to transform both. If you only pay attention to one side, you'll get messed up. So if all you do is envision yourself doing affirmations, it'll be a temporary fix, and that's it. But if you go in the other direction, which is just release your feelings, you'll identify with your illness, and that's a dead end. They're both dead ends. So the task is to honor the past, give it expression and, in spite of how impossible it may seem, look for ways to move out of those feelings.

While every survivor has unique experiences and emotions to associate, there are certain emotions common to survivors of trauma. These are fear, shame, anger, and grief. Victims of ritual abuse are left with a profound sense of terror and shame. Terror and shame generate anger in response to the pain. Underlying all the pain is grief. The challenge in recovery is to overcome the terror, break through the shame, claim the anger, and acknowledge the pain through grief.

OVERCOMING FEAR

I refer to ritual abuse as enslavement driven by fear, and I refer to recovery as a freedom movement. Suzzane

Violators rely on fear to keep their "lessons" in place. The trauma is dissociated, but the lessons learned control survivors' lives from behind the scenes. As one survivor commented, "You may not know the activity of the abuse, but you sure live the effects of it."

The key to breaking free of ritual abuse is in unraveling past and present fears. All fear feels present. Most of it is past. Janes

To help recognize and track patterns of dissociated fear, try to get a reality check. Ask support friends how they would react to specific circumstances. If you find you're overreacting, you can use the information as a starting point for association. Dissociated, projected emotions such as fear are generally intense and out of keeping with circumstances. The sooner you recognize the patterns of inppropriate reactions and specific clues, the sooner you can be free of them. Once you associate an experience, try to release all the emotions it generated, including fear. Remember to take your time.

It took me a couple of years to get over a fear about a spring-loaded trap in my brain that would explode and cut my head to pieces if I tampered with it. It protected a crystal ball, which contained cult dogma. It had been implanted by psychic surgery. My therapist kept saying, "But it isn't true. Your body would automatically reject foreign objects and would have rejected that trap if it were real." But I kept having vivid images demonstrating exactly how the mechanism would work. So I had to tiptoe past that part in my brain so as not to set it off. One day after therapy, I was driving home. Spontaneously, I saw in my mind's eye that I tossed it over my shoulder out the window, as though it were a tennis ball. At that moment I became free of it.   Jeanne

BREAKING THROUGH SHAME

I thought that the bottom of my memories was going to be terror, but I think that beneath the terror is the shame.   Samantha

Shame is absence of self-esteem. Whereas guilt suggests "I did something wrong, so I can fix it," shame suggests "I am wrong, so nothing can be done."

I feel such shame because I've done everything. I've gone to twelve-step meetings, stopped drinking and drugging, I'm not smoking, eating healthier, exercising, going to see a therapist, drawing pictures, taking time out with my kids and maintaining a strong support system, making phone calls every day—I mean, my whole fucking life is based on recovering. And I can't make it feel better. I can't find any type of relief. And so you know, it must be my fault. I just must have missed the fucking boat somewhere.   Adam

In *Trauma and Recovery*, Dr. Judith L. Herman explains:

A secure sense of connection with caring people is the foundation of personality development. When this connection is shattered, the traumatized person loses her basic sense of self. . . . When a parent[,] who is so much more powerful than a child, nevertheless shows some regard for that child's individuality and dignity, the child feels valued, and respected; she develops self-esteem. She also develops autonomy. . . . Traumatic events violate the autonomy of the person at the level of basic bodily intergrity. The body is invaded, injured, defiled. . . . Unsatisfactory resolution of the normal developmental conflict over autonomy leaves the person prone to shame and doubt.

People are born with inherited rights and abilities that are intuitively understood. Among these is the right to be loved, cared for, and protected or, failing that, the right to love, care for, and protect yourself. Survivors of ritual abuse are robbed of all these. Ritual abuse emphasizes a victim's hatefulness, vulnerability, and helplessness. The message a child gets is "There is something very wrong here." Children typically conclude, "It must be me."

Leaving nothing to chance, violators reinforce their actions with words. The resulting shame survivors may feel is profound.

A major aspect of how it feels is total self-hatred. There's a feeling of such incredible filth and dirtiness. I can't even find the words that could describe it because dirty sounds like dust on the floor. It's something like a combination of vomit and diarrhea and blood and entrails and maggots and death. And I was made to believe that all those things mixed up are what I am.   Bea

Many survivors feel a void where others feel their sense of "me."

I think that it's not so much a true void as a percieved void, because a person's value is always there. That's not negotiable. Everybody is spiritually valuable no matter what their behavior is. I think "shame" is the word that we use to describe that imagined void. And the only way to get back that sense of value is to get rid of the lies.   Ann Seery

To break through the shame, survivors need to work on regaining self-esteem (see Chapter 17). This means realizing we're human, and being human means

I DON'T HAVE TO BE PERFECT.

It's okay to have problems. It's okay to complain.

I'd been told all my life that I was just a big baby and I should stop complaining about everything. So I was able to go back and see where that idea came from—how when I cried out in pain or in need, I was called a baby and I was hurt again. My therapist helped me so much. She would

encourage me to complain. She would encourage me to talk about how tired I was and how overwhelmed I was, and it was okay. And it was just another weight coming off. I could complain. Here was someone wanting me to—who didn't think I'm a big baby. So I learned that complaining was good. Being tired was okay. All these things that I had hated myself for, just despised myself for, she began to show me were perfectly normal and okay. Bea

Because trauma breaks a person's faith and trust in the world, survivors cannot heal in isolation. As you begin to love and accept yourself, you need to risk letting safe others accept and love you as well.

Breaking through shame by reclaiming self-esteem is not a linear process but a circuitous route. There will be advances and setbacks. Sometimes the gains seem imperceptible, given all the work. But there will also be days when you'll know that it is worth it.

I guess people who haven't hated themselves can't understand how it feels or what that means, but today I love myself. And I wouldn't change that. I have perspective. I can joke, and I'm grateful.   Alicia

CLAIMING ANGER

Accepting and expressing anger is a challenge not only for survivors but for society. Although things are changing, expressions of anger toward those in power have traditionally been disallowed. Society is evolving toward recognizing that anger is a legitimate reaction.

I learned about anger from watching my two dogs. One stepped on the other's paw. She growled.

He retreated. A minute later they were playing. That was a real revelation—like, it's really so simple. And that's the way the whole thing was meant to work. Sophia

Anger can be thought of as a survivor's personal champion. Our inherited anger alerts us when our integrity is being violated. If we are hit, a natural response is to hit back. Anger gives us extra strength and energy when we are in danger or in crisis. It is meant to work as our protector/friend. Violators condition survivors to divorce and abandon their natural anger. Systematic punishment eradicates every thought of fighting back. Resistance is annihilated. As a result, many survivors feel little or no anger toward their violators.

Accumulated anger, if repressed, becomes rage. The offender is hated. Feelings of rage and hatred toward violators must be dissociated for a victim to survive. Dissociated rage projected inward becomes depression; projected outward, it gets offloaded onto others.

At times I have so much rage, I white-knuckle it to keep from showing it to my son. Sometimes I wake up angry, and he comes in when I want to sleep. If I tell him to be quiet, he makes more noise. He bangs on the wall or rollerblades across the living room floor. We keep bouncing off one another, and so it escalates, and I can't seem to make it stop. Brice Roweland

Dissociated rage tests the limits of survivors' coping skills.

My adopted daughter has just turned fourteen and she's in hormone hell. It was around Thanksgiving and I was getting ready to cook dinner. She said something and—snap!—I was gone. I wanted to murder her. I just started screaming. I lost it.

Instead of hitting her I hit the wall. I hurt myself pretty badly, but I didn't hurt her. Then I wandered the streets lost for two or three hours. Parts were switching constantly. I hid for a while behind a garbage dumpster. Jeanne

Whereas associated anger gives us power, dissociated anger takes it away. Giving expression to dissociated rage has about as much therapeutic value as striking out at air. It is likely to leave you exhausted and frustrated. Dissociated rage isn't always explosive. Sometimes it is masked and subtle. In *Of Course You're Angry,* Gayle Roselini and Mark Worden write: "Because you are UNAWARE of being angry does not mean that you are not angry. It is the anger you're unaware of which can do the most damage in you and your relationships, since it does get expressed in inappropriate ways."

The following list gives clues to possible signs of repressed anger. Do you recognize any of these?

- Physical signs of tension such as grinding teeth, chronically sore neck and shoulder muscles, a clenched jaw or fist, ulcers, or nail biting?
- Being too helpful, too accommodating, volunteering even when help is unsolicited?
- Enjoying black humor, cynicism, sarcasm, looking for every opportunity to make a joke?
- Procrastinating or being chronically late?
- Feeling depressed, overly tired, draggy, unable to sleep or needing too much sleep, always waking up tired?
- Speaking in a controlled voice, having controlled body movements?

Once you recognize dissociated anger, the next step it to connect it with its original source—your violators. That may take some time. The traumas that prevented expression of anger in the first place may need to be associated. In addition, you may feel your rage is so huge that you may "lose it" if you ever tried to express it. Some of the more satisfying, energizing, and empowering moments in recovery come from connecting with your own power by releasing anger at violators. Each release gives you more self-esteem, self-confidence, feeling of belonging, and centeredness.

RELEASING ANGER CONSTRUCTIVELY

Releasing anger is not about attacking others. It's about expressing your feelings. Recovery involves learning to honor your own truth without hurting others. There are many ways to release the physical force of feelings that come with associating rage. You can try hitting a bat or a tennis racquet against a bed. The up/down motion over your head gives good ventilation. Some survivors like to hit a phone book with a bat, or throw tomatoes against the wall—both make good anger-releasing sounds. Twisting a towel can release a lot of rage. You can also try lying on a bed and alternately hitting it with each arm, swinging outward, away from your chest.

I learned about taking anger and releasing it into a gigantic balloon, and then letting the balloon go and hit the rosebushes, and go pshhh. Alice

If you are working with a facilitator or therapist, use a pillow to represent your power. As you and your partner struggle for it, you get the satisfaction of succeeding in claiming it. (You don't need to struggle hard for this exercise to work.) You can also physically push palm to palm with your partner and learn that you can push someone away. The exercise of fighting for and reclaiming power gives your body/mind a powerful

message about new possibilities. If you have other ideas, try them. Don't forget to yell, scream, make noises to help move your anger out.

As anger is being released, it helps to verbally affirm your claimed power. You can try the following steps, adapted from Walter J. Polt's approach, called From Anger to Power.

1. State why you are angry. (I'm furious that you abandoned me in a dungeon overnight when I was only three years old.)
2. State what you wanted or needed. (I needed you to take me home with you.)
3. State what you believe, your values. (Every child deserves to be loved and nurtured.)
4. State what you choose to do. (I will heal my inner three-year-old and protect her and myself from all harmful people from now on.)

As you find ideas that work and become more familiar with the process, you may even find an immediate use for all the energy your body might release.

I've got a few in here that can really get angry. But instead of hitting their fists against the wall, and putting a hole in it or breaking a window or throwing things, dishes and stuff, I tell them, "Okay, this is how you do it. This cord of wood out there needs to be chopped; there's ironing to be done; let's make this anger productive. Let's go to it." And they do. Jackie Bianco

Connecting and working out anger is a powerful release. However, sometimes anger serves as a defense against feeling pain and grief. Until the pain and grief are identified and felt, the anger can go on indefinitely. One man was an "anger-holic" for eighteen years. His anger finally left when a therapist at a treatment facility helped him identify, admit, and feel his grief.

Here's how grief, masked by anger, may feel:

The main thing I feel for my inner kids is rage. They cause me so much pain. The last thing I want to do is rescue them. I hate them.   A survivor

Avoiding your inner kids is avoiding yourself. By connecting with them, feeling their pain, you become free of the grief and the anger. Instead of getting angry at your inner kids, maybe you could try asking them, "What hurts? What do you need?"

ACCEPTING THE GRIEF

Every survivor of ritual abuse carries grief. To many it feels bottomless. In his paper, "Silent Sorrow: Grief and Loss of Significant Others," Kenneth J. Doka writes about the impact of grief on non-traditional, secret relationships. "While grief may be intensified, resources for resolving grief are often limited. It may not be possible to utilize formal and informal support systems effectively." Survivors who break the binds of secrecy are often met with denial, and even when they are accepted, there is often a gap in comprehension.

Probably very few people can understand—I mean, it's so stupid to even say the word "loss." Because to me the word will never mean to anyone else what it means to me—ever. The amount of loss I feel in my life is a different word—it's a different concept. So I find as I go on in my recovery I talk about it less and less, because there is no word for it. Adam

Recovery gains may sometimes bring losses. Therapist Mary Ellen Holmen explains:

Recovery is like a voyage. You have to load all this stuff on board to do your recovery, and hope that you find the stuff that you need. But you may find stuff on board that you have to jettison. You get into the middle of recovery and you realize maybe the safe place that you thought you had really wasn't safe; a supportive friend in your network turns out not to be a friend—so what do you do with that? It could be a husband or a best friend who is a reenactment of some person from your past, and so you have to limit that friendship or get rid of it altogether. You might need to cut ties with a parent. Or you may find that you left port with this thing on board you didn't know you had, like an eating or drinking or sex addiction, which you'll have to jettison somewhere during the voyage. And it's hard, because a lot of times you're attached to it.

You may be abandoned by friends or partners when you tell them you are a survivor of ritual abuse. You may miss having a family. Holidays may be particularly difficult times for you. Despite the abuse, celebrating together may have given you a sense of belonging—at least somewhere. It may hurt to know that your family continues to celebrate get-togethers without you. You may grieve the loss of a normal childhood. Some survivors grieve being unable to partner or have children.

ASSOCIATING GRIEF

The dissociated grief survivors carry is usually projected or internalized. Some survivors wake up in tears for no apparent reason. Others are unable to cry. As with other emotions, grief needs to be associated before it can be released. For some the challenge is to manage grief; for others it is to feel it.

When I first started having ritual abuse memories I could not stay clean enough. I took at least two showers a day. I wouldn't take more because I'm training to be a therapist and I knew that would be compulsive. So I would allow myself two, maybe three if I'd done something where I'd gotten up a sweat. But I tried to monitor it. I tried to look at my feelings. "Okay, I'm feeling dirty. Is a shower what I really need or do I need to cry?"   Bea

To help access your grief, try peeling an onion. It'll get your tears to flow.

I was just busting inside. I knew I needed to cry, but couldn't. So I rented the movie Sybil *and soon I was sobbing hysterically. It felt so good.   Erik*

You may be getting discouraged because no matter how long and often you grieve, the pain never seems to leave. You may be spiraling into shame or blaming yourself for not doing it right. It's important to put things into perspective. A single major loss in a person's life can take one or two years to process. You probably suffered many major losses, so don't get down on yourself if the pain doesn't pass within weeks. At the same time, if you are honoring your losses, don't let others hurry you.

You run into these really militant recovery "experts" who tell you that you're choosing to suffer because you're not ready to let go, you're not ready to feel better. You know—like you're married or addicted to your pain. That's fucked.   Adam

As recovery progresses, survivors learn to come to terms with grief. For some it means accepting it as a part of their life.

Even though I will get to the point where my ritual abuse is not a day-by-day struggle, I do believe that I will be dealing with grieving on some level for the rest of my life. I think it's the human condition. I mean, I don't see how you can live on this planet and not feel grief. There are so many horrible things going on—people being tortured and abused and murdered. What I'm hoping for is to keep filling in all the little cracks with love and healing and light and connection with other people.   Bea

In connecting with emotions, we connect with ourselves and our world. By accepting what happened and feeling it, we reclaim the truth of our experience. In braving to be who we truly are, we find meaning in our existence.

Accepting grief and feeling it is a two-way street.

I was looking for ways to reconnect with my body so I tried Yoga. As I was holding the postures I felt intense emotions welling up. I couldn't let them out in a class full of strangers. When class was over I got into my car, and I prepared for that all-out sobbing sort of grief. As it came pouring through, I couldn't believe my ears. What I heard was full-bellied, magnanimous, laughter—my laughter. I realized I had not only been repressing my pain, but my joy as well.   Sophia

Part Five

Healing

20

Healing Relationships

Ritual abuse attacks a child's self-esteem, trust, and feeling of belonging. These key elements define relationships. One of the most common issues survivors have is difficulty with intimacy, social interactions, and familial relationships. Traumatized people lose their ability to retain their sense of self in relation to others. A dissociated, traumatized self or part is ever vigilant for signs of danger. As a result, survivor perceptions of present circumstances are dominated by their past. For survivors of ritual abuse, the more significant the relationship, the greater the potential danger. Fear and shame from the past may continue to influence present-day situations.

Every year or two, I'll kind of go underground. I'll want a totally new life, a new identity, a new place, new friends, new everything because I don't want people to get too close to my shit because they'll leave, and I can't handle that kind of rejection. Plus once I really start to begin to know people I start wondering if they're really who they say they are. It's sabotage and it's programming—you know, "You can't have a life or be sustained in a community." Adam

SIGNIFICANT RELATIONSHIPS

Often a survivor's most significant relationship is also her or his most troublesome one. Although each couple is different, with unique dynamics, there are certain patterns common to trauma survivors. You may be having problems with intimacy, trust, or sexual fulfillment. You may find yourself breaking off relationships, always with "good reason," when they are going "too well."

You may find yourself in a partnership bonded by fear or shame rather than love.

Survivors typically have an unusually high tolerance for unhealthy or abusive situations. They may find partners who complement their own maladaptive behaviors. Some reenact their trauma within the relationship.

I had very dysfunctional relationships, first with men, later with women. There was physical and emotional abuse. I had really violent sexual fantasies, violent fights with my partner, self-hatred, incredible self-hatred, and anxiety attacks. In the external world I was doing just fine. I was a nurse, highly functioning. No one suspected there was a problem. It was all behind closed doors. Lynn

Survivors may also find themselves in relationships that mirror cult dynamics. In their paper "'Mind Control' and the Battering of Women," Drs. Teresa Ramirez Boulette and Susan M. Andersen point out the remarkable similarities between abusive relationships and coercive cults:

"Cultic" systems, whether they are two-person relationships or larger social groups, are those that are totalistic in nature and that exercise exceptional controls over the individual freedoms of their members. . . . A cultic system can thus be identified based on the *degree* of such control simply by counting the *number* of features of psychological coercion. Those battering relationships that involve "mind control" typically possess a significant number of these features and thus merit identification as cultic systems.

The authors outline the following factors (paraphrased), which differentiate mind control

battering from other types of battering. Although the study is based on experiences of battered wives, the dynamics can apply to either men or women, and survivors may find themselves in one or both roles described. You may recognize some of these dynamics in your significant relationships:

- Physical or verbal dominance by the violator
- Isolation/imprisonment—the violator prevents the victim from getting external support by isolating her or him from friends and relatives, either geographically or emotionally
- Violator uses verbal threats or physical violence to arouse and maintain fear
- Violator blames victim for the abuse until the victim comes to blame her- or himself
- Love is contingent on obedience; a victim's feelings of anxiety and guilt are alleviated once she or he gives in
- Victim may develop a misplaced loyalty, defending a violator's actions; it is based on gratitude at not being further abused or killed
- Violator controls money and property to ensure victim's continued dependence on her or him
- Violator may be openly promiscuous while jealously accusing the victim of infidelity
- Violator makes strategically timed promises to change to ensure that the victim continues to tolerate the abuse
- Secrecy is the mainstay of the relationship, and the victim is not allowed to complain or in any way cast doubt on the violator's good character

In the same way children felt powerless to leave a cult, a victim-partner typically feels powerless to leave an abusive relationship. Attempts to do so may create extraordinary levels of anxiety, fear, guilt, and shame—dissociated emotions stemming from past traumas. Until the past traumas are associated and resolved, survivors may feel stuck.

Just as a child is unable to escape a cult without external assistance, you may not feel able to break free without outside help. If you are having difficulty leaving a physically or emotionally abusive relationship, contact a battered women's shelter for help. (Some shelters may offer battered men help or advice as well.)

MAXIMIZING HEALTHY BEHAVIORS

Survivors are often attracted to partners with a conscious or dissociated history of abuse. Having issues in common can both help and complicate the relationship. On the one hand, there is mutual understanding. On the other hand, partner interactions are often colored by past traumatic issues on both sides. It may become very difficult to sort out what's what. Because these issues cannot be instantly resolved, learning a few communication tools may help to keep things on track.

STARTING WITH "I"

A common relationship problem is projection. Thoughts, feelings, and behaviors you may not want or be able to acknowledge are assigned to your partner. "Seeing" things in other people generally means judging, shaming, or blaming them. Clues to use of possible projection are statements that start with "You. . . ."

Recovery requires that each person take responsibility for her- or himself. Once you do so, you will no longer need to assign feelings and motivations to someone else. Until self-awareness comes naturally through association, you may want to try the following techniques to help promote healthy interactions.

Communicate your problem using three steps. Start the first step with "I."

1. State the problem (I hate it when you ignore me)
2. Give specific examples (When you come home, you head straight for the bedroom and shut the door without talking to me)
3. Express your true feelings (I feel sad and abandoned); if you have difficulty identifying and naming your feelings try to keep them simple.

Avoid sentences starting with "you," "we," "let's," and "why." Bring up problems as they occur—the sooner the better. Do not let them pile up. Discuss one issue at a time. Ask for feedback, making sure your partner also speaks from an "I" perspective.

The idea is to keep more in touch with yourself. Because lifelong habits do not change instantly, you and your partner may need to frequently remind one another to stay with "I" statements. Simply state, "The idea is to use 'I' statements," or "Could you rephrase that starting with 'I'?" Avoid old patterns of "You're not using 'I' statements; you're not following the rules; you're not playing fair; you're sabotaging our relationship." As each partner grows stronger within her- or himself, the relationship becomes stronger as well.

Keep in mind that each person has her or his own recovery timetable. Respect that. On the other hand, if you're invested in recovery, and your partner wants to keep things as they were, your relationship may become increasingly strained. This may mean making difficult choices.

Recovery will help you make the right choices and give you the strength to follow through with them.

PARENTING

Parents both model and pass along behaviors. Survivor parents are usually extra-conscientious, determined to break abusive patterns suffered in their own childhood. However, parenting poses special problems for survivors. You may be feeling overwhelmed by your own inner children. You may feel you're already taking care of an entire inner family. The additional demands of parenthood can leave you feeling overburdened.

In addition, despite their best intentions, survivors often discover that they've been parenting their children the way they were parented. One survivor realized that instead of having conversations, he was interrogating his children in the same way his parents had interrogated him.

I had a sense of what was dysfunctional and what was wrong in my family of origin and I made an attempt to correct that. But many of the attempts I made were just doing it in a different way. A real obvious one that I can think of is that my father used to hit me with a belt, and I hit my kids with a wooden spoon thinking that was less damaging. Actually it was equally damaging. Ann Seery

One survivor was parenting "perfectly" but could not establish emotional contact with her children.

I knew something was wrong but couldn't pinpoint it. After years in recovery I had this flash of recognition. I kinda used to look at my kids but never really *made eye contact with them. I suddenly got it, that my kids were never really seen by me, in the same way that I was never seen by my own parents.* Sophia

Children can be triggering to survivor parents. They are reminders of a parent's own traumatic, dissociated childhood. They often evoke specific reminders of ritual abuse.

Children can be especially vulnerable to projection because they cannot defend themselves. If your parents projected their shame onto you, you may be projecting your unresolved shame onto your children.

I have a very different relationship with my son than I do with my daughter. When he was very young and I wanted him to do something, I would fly into a rage if he didn't do it exactly right—the way I wanted it done. I never understood what that rage was about until now. Now I know that my rage has nothing to do with my kids. It's my rage and I have to deal with it, not blame it on them. Janes

A common parenting problem for survivors is setting and maintaining healthy boundaries. Some are too strict, others too permissive, and some further confuse children by flip-flopping between being too strict and too permissive.

A good book for facilitating healthy communication with children is *How to Talk so Kids Will Listen and Listen so Kids Will Talk*, by Adele Faber and Elaine Mazlish. The ideas suggested apply to all healthy human interaction, from at home to the grocery store to business relationships. Keep in mind that children learn and develop self-confidence through positive guidance. Instead of saying, "Don't break the vase" say, "I know you can carry the vase safely to the table." Praise your child for the accomplishment. If you need to enforce behavioral guidelines, use discipline (let them learn the consequences of their actions) instead of punishment (for being "bad").

Recovery increases awareness of behaviors and coping techniques. Therefore, the most important legacy survivors can offer their children is to continue their own healing. A crucial part of this legacy comes from parenting your own hurting inner children. The more you apply the following ideas to yourself, the more your children will benefit.

WHAT EVERY PARENT NEEDS TO KNOW

Please, Mom, Dad

My hands are small.
  I don't mean to spill my milk.

My legs are short.
  Please slow down so I can keep
  up with you.

Don't slap my hands when I touch
  something bright and pretty.
  I don't understand.

Please look at me when I talk to you.
  It lets me know you are really
  listening.

My feelings are tender.
  Don't nag me all day.
  Let me make mistakes without
  feeling stupid.

Don't expect the bed I make or the
  picture I draw to be perfect.
  Just love me for trying.

Remember I am a child, not a small
  adult.
  Sometimes I don't understand
  what you are saying.

I love you so much.
  Please love me just for being
  me—not just for the things I can
  do.

  Parenting Pages, California Consortium to
  Prevent Child Abuse, author anonymous

And remember, the only "smack" your child needs is the one that comes from your lips.

SHOULD I TELL MY CHILDREN?

There are many variables to consider regarding if and when you should share any part of your abuse history with your children. The decision should be made in consultation with professionals. It is also a good idea to plan what to say and how to handle your child's potential reactions. Children have many tasks to master during their developmental years. To accomplish them, they depend on caregivers to provide certain basics, such as security for survival, consistency for trust, and validation of their perceptions for self-confidence. The decision about telling needs to balance all three. You should consider their need to know and readiness.

What to say, if anything, depends on the stage of your child's development. One thing you can casually do is monitor her or his level of anxiety or awareness. Children notice things to varying degrees, depending on their readiness to assimilate them. If you believe your children sense something is wrong, it is important to validate their perception. However, it is equally important not to confuse your own anxiety with theirs. The purpose of telling is to reassure rather than frighten them. Validate their perception that there is a problem, and assure them you are addressing it. They need to hear that they will continue to be cared for and safe. Let them know that your well-being is not their responsibility.

WHAT TO SAY

Ritual abuse is a difficult topic to assimilate even for adults. In addition, dissociated information emerges in stages. You may not have a complete and accurate picture, especially at the beginning. Your initial perceptions may change. This may affect what is useful to share. The problem in sharing too little is creating an atmosphere of secrecy, fear, and shame. The problem in sharing too much is giving children more information than is appropriate for them or information that is inconsistent with later realizations. Tell your truth in the least alarming terms. For example, "I am not well and so sometimes I get angry at you when it isn't your fault. But I am going to the doctor so I can get better."

Take the cue from your children. If your child doesn't respond, chances are it's not time to discuss it. If they ask questions, answer them honestly. The communication should be simple and matter-of-fact. Generally, the younger the child, the less detail is necessary. If your children seem to want more information, you might consider giving it to them in stages, with graphic and violent images deleted. Be careful not to use the opportunity to share your adult difficulties. Your child is not your confidant. Adult sharing belongs in peer support groups.

I THINK MY CHILD HAS BEEN ABUSED

Children born into generational cult families may have a higher chance of being abused, especially if family members are not in recovery. During the course of your recovery you may realize that your child had been abused by you or a cult member. You may want to tell or confess to your child. You may want to rush her or him into therapy. You may feel bottomless self-blame, remorse, and shame. Although these initial reactions are understandable, none of them may be very helpful.

Informing or confessing to your children is rarely, if ever, appropriate. Discuss the best course of action with a qualified, sympathetic therapist. While some children go to therapy readily, others may resist. Children typically form defenses around abuse as a form of self-protection. This protection is important and should be respected. If your child appears to be developing without significant problems and is resisting therapy, there may be a good reason for it. Although there may be exceptions, it is generally not a good idea to force a reluctant child into therapy.

It may be helpful for all survivor parents to explain dissociation to their children once they are mature enough. You may want to tell them that in a dissociated state you may have hurt them, and that if you did, you are sorry. You may want to let them know that you have been helped through therapy and that if ever they have difficulties with relationships, sexuality, anxiety, shyness, or expressing their feelings, therapy may be helpful to them as well. Once you've offered them information and help, leave the rest up to them. If they specifically ask or seem ready to hear more, tell them. Use your inner wisdom as a guide on what and how much to disclose.

Until your child recalls the abuse (and that may be never), find a way to make amends and restitution on your own. You can write her or him a letter and share it in group or with your therapist. Your first priority needs to be the welfare of your children. (If you discover current abuse you must take immediate action to stop it.)

You are the mirror who tells your children who they are. Your child needs a parent who loves herself or himself, not one who is guilt-ridden. Forgiving yourself is a gift not only to yourself but to your children.

The more centered I became, the more I realized how often I was projecting all sorts of untrue things onto my kids—like "knowing" their ulterior motives and "knowing" they were not telling me the truth and "knowing" they were up to no good. My son was away on a school trip, and when he returned after a week, instead of spontaneous hellos there was this formality between us that just didn't feel good at all. And then I realized I was thinking my usual judgmental thoughts. So I changed my thought from "I wonder what he was up to" to "He is good." But that didn't seem to do it. And then for some reason I thought to myself, "I am good," and as if reading my thoughts, his face broke into a smile.   Roxana

Healing happens on many levels and in many different ways. The good news about healing is that it is never too late. One survivor grew closer to her married daughter when she learned to stay centered and to use "I" instead of "you" communications. As long as this survivor remained on track with healthy communications, so did the relationship.

ONGOING RELATIONS WITH THE FAMILY OF ORIGIN

A family operates as an emotional system where each person eventually assumes a specific role to sustain that system. When parents in the system are emotionally debilitated, they force emotionally debilitating roles on the children. This is described as triangulation, and the triangular system is more powerful than any one of the members who make it up.

In *Repressed Memories,* Renee Fredrickson, Ph.D., describes the triangular family relationship of abusive and incestuous families. These patterns describe dynamics common to some ritual abuse families as well. You may be able to identify and recognize the three profiles of

offender, denier, and victim within your family of origin.

Offenders have a "high need for control and well-developed rationalization skills . . . , [are] good at projecting their feelings onto others instead of feeling emotions themselves . . . , [and] above all lack the capacity for remorse and guilt."

Deniers are "masters of offering trite phrases in response to pain. 'Don't dwell on it. Let bygones be bygones.'"

Victims are "strong," "intelligent," and "sensitive." "Victims take on others' feelings . . . including whatever feelings the offender is denying. During an act of sexual abuse, guilt, rage, and shame are dumped by the offender and absorbed by the vulnerable victim. The offender is relieved, while the victim feels guilty, rageful, and ashamed."

These roles are a "learned response to living in a sexually abusive family system." Although members may have several roles, each usually has a predominant one. There is typically one victim child per nuclear family, while siblings are either offenders or deniers. If the outnumbered victim tries to address the abuse, she or he will be met with "silencing, punishing responses by the other family members."

I DON'T WANT TO GIVE UP MY FAMILY

Survivors, like most people, cherish the idea of having a wholesome and happy family. As a result, they have often seen their families through rose-colored glasses—sometimes full-prescription strength Knowing how abusive families may be constellated may help you identify your own family patterns. This may empower you to make healthier choices for yourself.

In the face of growing associations, the question of a relationship with violator parents becomes increasingly complex. Some survivors may immediately break off all relations, but many continue to stay in contact with their violators, especially when the violators are parents. Breaking off contact entirely is a difficult step for many reasons.

For some, to take on the family is to take on society. To question the sanctity of the family is to challenge one of society's most deeply held beliefs. This may be especially true for survivors from small towns, close-knit social circles, people of color, and tightly knit immigrant communities. People of color or immigrant groups often have very close family and community ties. The expectation is that no member of the group would ever do anything to tarnish its image. In addition to possibly losing their families, these survivors also risk alienating their community.

I had been raised in a traditional Hispanic family. Strongly Catholic. There's an element of internalized oppression, coming from a minority culture. Hispanic culture, for example, is a face-saving culture. There's a real sensitivity to doing anything that identifies minorities as being less than whole, or less than able. Gerald

Survivors not raised in mainstream cultural contexts may feel completely unsupported in recovery—rejected by their own community and never fully accepted or belonging within the mainstream recovery movement. These people have additional difficulties, losses, and challenges to overcome in separating from their families.

Sometimes child alters feel a strong love and loyalty to violator parents.

Every time a new alter comes up she either adores my Mom, is indifferent to Mom, or hates Mom. That's an ongoing confusing process. I have to resolve it, but it's going to take a long time. Lots of people don't understand, number one, why I still have maybe an eight-year-old jump up and run and call, "Mommy!" or buy her a Christmas present. My husband doesn't understand that. He says, "After all that your Mother's done to you, why in the hell do you even talk to her?" I don't talk, but there's still alters in there—she's their Mom. And they love her.   Amiee

Survivors often get mixed messages from their parents.

I think my mother is multiple. I think my mother was ritually abused by an aunt who was seventeen years older than she is. But we've decided that a lot of the mixed messages and a lot of my denial comes from the fact that she has personalities who want to see me dead, and she has personalities who come up and for no reason cry and hug us and say that they're so proud that we made it through. Which fits the scenarios. She's not conscious of it and she stays drunk most of the time. Amiee

Many survivors are enmeshed with their parents and often think, feel, and behave the way their parents want or expect them to. Even if they hate it, they often keep up the expected visits.

The minute I step into my parents' house, I can feel the neuroses seeping out through the walls. I just can't wait to get out of there.   Amy

For some, no matter how bad it is, no one can replace the original family.

I had a friend who was disowned by her family, and the amount of pain that woman was in—they had a wake for her. It was like a knife in her side, and I don't want that. I don't want that feeling of estrangement from my blood family. I've tried every way I can think of to get around it. I've tried to adopt this aunt and uncle, and I've tried to kind of adopt my sister-in-law's mother. But it doesn't work. It's not the same thing.   Grace

These various issues may leave survivors simply feeling all mixed up. Although the tendency is towards exclusive thinking—"they're all good or all bad"—the reality is that people, including parents, are a blend of many qualities.

I have a lot of ambivalence about my parents. I miss them terribly during the holiday seasons, but I don't want to have any contact with them that's not honest. Because I just can't talk about the weather to them anymore. I feel a lot of anger and disgust towards my parents and I also feel a strong bond and love towards them. I want to tell them that they tortured me and raped me and that I know the same thing happened to them, too. Any contact I have with them will have that right there in the middle. I'm really committed to being as honest as I can.   Jeanne

Maintaining or breaking relations with the family of origin is a personal choice. These decisions are invariably conflict-ridden. Each option comes at great cost. Each situation is different. However, you may wish to consider the following issues in making your decision.

SELF-PARENTING

You may be looking for parenting from people who don't have it to give. If you are in recovery and they are not, you are likely more courageous and stronger than they. Your only realistic option is to give your inner traumatized children what your parents were either unable or unwilling to give. Once you give them what they need, you will be free of dependency on emotionally and spiritually disabled people, including parents. Then your choices and decisions around family relations will be more clear. John K. Pollard, III's *The Self-Parenting Program* is a helpful guide to positive reparenting.

THE QUESTION OF SAFETY

When survivors meet with cult-active family members, they run the risk of being abducted into a cult again. However, even if the family isn't active, unhealthy, triangulated patterns are all too easily activated. It is best to stay clear of non-recovering violators.

I have this cousin who lived with our family when I was growing up, and she assaulted me—raped me whenever she wanted. It was sort of sanctioned by the family—like I was her slave or something. And she used me that way. Well, one time she came up for a visit. I hadn't seen her in ages, and before I knew it, I was catering to her—asking her if I can bring her tea or wash her car or drive her into town. But even as I was doing it, I felt really weird inside. It's when she grinned that I really got it. That was the same "you're shit and I'm queen" sort of smile she used on me all the time when we were growing up. Then I realized that she was also locking me in with her look—it was the "I'm in charge here" sort of look. That awakened me. "Not in my home you're not," I thought to myself, and avoided her gaze after that. In retrospect, I think she did it unconsciously—but that was our normal and comfortable relationship. I never invited her back after that.   Janes

Many survivors were taught that their offspring belong to the cult. You may have a hands-off relationship with your own children when their grandparents are around. You may find that you automatically abandon responsibility for your own children at family gatherings that include violators. If your family was involved in generational ritual abuse and your violators are not in recovery, there is no reason to assume your children would be exempt from conditioning, given the opportunity. Your best insurance is to keep your children away from nonrecovering violators. Barring that, NEVER allow your children to be alone with them. If you are early into recovery, it may be difficult to know who is or isn't safe. Remember to check your own instincts and follow them.

I had moved five hundred miles to live away from my parents. At the time I didn't know that I had been ritually abused. A year after my move, I had my daughter. My parents announced that they were going to come and visit. From the moment they arrived I was fit to be tied. I was ready to scream at their every move in my apartment. I especially hated it when they touched my baby. Today I know why.   A survivor

If you continue to visit your family, use it as an opportunity to develop your awareness. Try to keep track of how you are feeling. If you notice discomfort, anger, anxiety, or frustration during or after visits, try to track who caused it and how. This can be valuable input to achieving safety for yourself and your children. For additional safety information, see Chapter 13.

NEW CHOICES

Some families are more toxic than others. In some cases the danger is not so much being spirited off to rituals as continued reinforcement of abusive emotional patterns. For some survivors the challenge is to develop a stronger sense of self, or boundaries around other family members. In

strongly enmeshed family relationships, it may be easier to wean yourself away gradually. Start by making different choices. (Often we are not aware that today we *do* have choices.) For example, if you have ended every phone conversation with your father by saying, "I love you," try saying something different, such as, "I'll talk to you next week," or nothing at all. No matter how tiny your changes, it's a beginning. It's often the tiniest first steps that are the most difficult to try and the most liberating.

TAKING BACK POWER

One of the hardest things for survivors to do is to assert their own rights and autonomy around family members. In many ways it's as big an accomplishment as learning how to talk. Here's how one survivor began to reclaim her power.

I was abused by my uncle who was also a sort of clown in the family—everybody liked him. Before I got into recovery, I would invite him over and never feel anything about him—either good or bad. But as I remembered and realized he'd abused me, I didn't feel so okay about it anymore, but I still kept inviting him—it was like a family tradition. Well last year he came over for my birthday and it felt majorly not okay. It was really hot in the house, and he took off his shirt, and I got triggered seeing his exposed skin. And I knew why I was triggered, but it never occurred to me to say something to him. I went upstairs and tried to journal but I just blew up instead. I couldn't go back down to face him, and so feeling utterly helpless and at my wits' end, I called my therapist. And she said, "Tell him." And I said, "Tell him what?" She said, "Tell him to please put his shirt back on." "How do I do that?" I asked. (I'm a communications specialist—you'd think I would know how to put it. But I couldn't find the words.) So we rehearsed it—my therapist and I. Finally I went downstairs and said, "Your shirt off makes me feel uncomfortable. Would you mind putting it back on?" "Oh, sure," he answered. I couldn't believe it was that simple, and my inner child felt tremendously relieved.   Josie

CONFRONTATIONS

As survivors begin recovery, many have a strong urge to confront their parents. Confrontations can give you personal satisfaction and a sense of personal power. However, if done prematurely they can have the opposite effect. For confrontations to work, you need to be clear on your motives and have realistic expectations. The main benefit of a confrontation is simply to speak your truth to your violators. It is your declaration of healing, recovery, and strength. The point of confrontation may be to declare that you are taking back your own power; it may be to declare that they have to carry responsibility for their actions from now on, because you are no longer willing to do it. As one survivor put it to her abusive father, "You can keep living your life, but from now on you're also going to take the consequences—all of them. I'm no longer here to cover up for you or carry your shame."

Before confronting your violators, think through all their possible reactions, any consequences, and your ability to live with each of them. Many survivors confront their violator parents in the hopes of validation, an admission of guilt, or opportunity to make amends. However, they are more likely to be accused of having false memory (see Chapter 4). Your parents may or may not have conscious knowledge of the abuse. One or both may be multiple. The more they abhorred their own cult involvement, the more likely it may be dissociated. They may consciously believe their own denial and have only a vague sense of the truth. Less than 5 percent of sex offenders ever admit responsibility. The likelihood that a cult violator would admit wrongdoing may be less than that.

Every set of potential outcomes will be different. Do not expect a confession. Do expect increased agitation or pressure. Ask yourself— Am I willing and able to handle things such as "You're crazy; you're making this up; is this the gratitude we get for raising you? You've always been overly emotional, how can you do this to us?" You also need to think through safety issues. Is your confrontation coming from a place of strength or programming to tell? (See Chapter 5.) Is your safety or that of your family at risk? Are you prepared for increased pressure to return to a cult, or to deal with threats?

If you feel ready to state your own truth and have no expectations in return, it's a good idea to discuss your plans with your therapist or a trusted friend. They may offer valuable suggestions. They may help you prepare for your confrontation. Be sure to have a support system in place to help you through the aftermath. Some survivors feel elated, others feel depressed, many feel some of both. However, in the long run, most survivors feel stronger and are glad that they told.

THE QUESTION OF FORGIVENESS

Forgiveness is often one of the final issues in recovery to be resolved. It's not something to be rushed. Wait for answers to come from within with the full participation of your inner kids. Your feelings about forgiveness are likely to change as you grow through recovery. In the meantime, the following discussion may help.

The traditional view of many spiritual teachings is that forgiveness gives victims freedom. Therefore, no matter what the circumstances, the forgiver benefits.

Blanket forgiveness gives freedom to some, but to some it doesn't. Some survivors feel that "forgive and forget" is advice routinely dispensed by the powerful when abusing the powerless. For many survivors, the question of forgiveness remains just that—a question. Survivors wonder things such as:

- Is anger a precondition to forgiveness?
- Is it possible to forgive someone and never want to see them again?
- Is that really forgiveness?
- Is it really ever possible to forgive such atrocities?
- Is it possible to offer forgiveness without a confession?
- If a violator denies the abuse, then exactly what and who is being forgiven?

It would be immeasurably easier on survivors if each of their violators confessed and took responsibility for their wrongful acts. However, that's not likely to happen. Some survivors wonder if forgiving people who deny any wrongdoing is largely meaningless. Others wonder if the concept of forgiving others sets the forgiver up as superior to the forgivee. The question of forgiveness presumes judgment and blame, which should be based on having all the facts; but we may not have all the facts.

Recent findings show that violators may be victims and victims may be violators. Abuse is generational. This is the first generation willing to look at the extremes of harmful consequences caused by negative conditioning. Until recently there was no permission to remember. Massive societal denial and complicity kept people locked in. It's hard to escape a cult without external assistance. Without validation, recovery tools, or support, breaking free for would-be survivors would be nearly impossible.

This is not to rationalize or excuse the abuse in any way. Ultimately every person of sound mind and free will is responsible for her or his actions and choices. Today, people have options and choices to heal. Judging and blaming may serve only to offload responsibility. Forgiveness may be an exercise in projection, where a victim sits in judgment of her or his violators without knowing all the facts. For some survivors, the question is not about forgiving others. The gift of forgiveness is the gift we can each offer ourselves.

I know enough to know that I don't know. It's not up to me to forgive anyone else. Whatever forgiveness is needed for healing is the forgiveness I can give myself.   Erik

A POSSIBLE ANSWER

It is possible to heal with or without forgiving your violators. You can heal with or without your family's participation. Here's how one survivor found healing.

I looked in the mirror and I saw the face of my mother as a young girl looking back at me, and I was horrified. I knew I had parts of her within my being. They were the most hurtful, toxic parts, and I wanted to blast her and her parts out of me. She was vicious, hurtful, unloving. But that young face, rather arrogant, was looking at me, and I noticed it was sad. And I knew my mother was anything but sad and innocent. But some part of me knew that a part of her was just a lonely, abandoned little girl, and I reached out to heal that part of her. And in that moment I felt a closing of the circle between me, her and the generations. It felt like that's what needed doing. At last the child within me starved for love and a mommy was connecting with something of goodness—with my mothers's child before her abuse. At last we were bonding.   Roxana

21

Healing Sexuality

I am having a hell of a time getting back my whole sexual being. That seems to be slowest in recovering. It involves so many bad feelings about myself, and embarrassment. You would think we wouldn't be embarrassed after all the abuse, but it seems almost worse.   Amy

Sexuality is the source of our life force and procreation—a source of energy and creativity. In other words, the source of personal power. Sex therapist Margery Noel rightly observes, "Sex is a central life event, not an appendix."

Physiologically, the sexual act of stimulation and orgasm releases tension. Orgasm can release positive tension built up through a desire to express love, or negative tension built up through mounting anxiety, shame, or hate. In other words, it can be the source of either rapture or rage. Although in principle sex is associated with love between two adults (positive tension), in practice it is often represented as war (negative tension). Dramas and commercials typically evoke images of sexual conquest: enticement and domination; deception and subjugation. The vocabulary abounds with notions of pursuit, victory, and capture. Conquerors often rape their victims.

In addition, in shame-based religions, sex is a union of two shamed people. Shame-based people do not make eye contact or communicate during sex. As a result, sex itself may become a shameful act. A common religious idea is that sex is bad.

INFLUENCES

Adult sexuality is shaped by early developmental experiences, which can be confusing for a child in our society. In *Spare the Child,* Philip Greven describes how traditional child-rearing practices form the roots of sadomasochism. He shows that it is not an aberrant but rather an inherent part of our society.

For many adults, sadomasochism in both erotic and nonerotic forms is a direct consequence of the confusion generated by the combination of love and pain in childhood, the long-term outcome of the normal assaults and abuse associated with physical punishment from infancy to adolescence. Sadomasochism provides the most direct evidence for the enduring consequences of early corporal punishments, since the sexual forms that sadomasochism (or S&M) takes mirror the earlier encounters with discipline and pain with remarkable faithfulness. . . . Sadomasochism is thus one of the most enduring consequences for coercive discipline in childhood.

Healthy sexuality is closely related to spirituality. Whereas spirituality is the experience of connectedness to and within the universe, sexuality is the physical experience of connectedness to another human being. Spiritual sexuality is the physical expression of love and union with a soul mate.

Ritual abuse, coupled with confusing societal messages about sex, has a profound negative impact on a survivor's ability to enjoy healthy, joyful sex. In ritual abuse, as in pornography or sadomasochism, sex is used to release negative tensions, very often through violence and injury to the victim. Children may be forced to have sex with adults, family members, siblings, other children, and animals. Many are manipulated into orgasm during painful rituals. They are typically forced to watch perverted sexual acts.

Ritually abused children learn to associate sex with hate, violence, pain, and power. For survivors sex may carry confusing, conflicting, and highly charged associations.

AFTEREFFECTS

Survivors typically react in one or both of two extremes: sexual over- or underactivity—even total shutdown. The confusion, pain, and bewilderment leave their mark in various ways.

I never even knew I was having sex unless I was being hurt. I'm still not sure I know how to have sex without feeling a little bit of pain. But I'm working on that. It's supposed to be nice. That's what I hear.   Annie

Many have genital-related illnesses. Some women survivors report severe pain during menstruation. Others report complications during sex, giving birth, and other difficulties.

I had bad menstrual cramps all my life. Then I got horrible endometriosis, which is a disease of the uterine lining. I was bleeding almost every day of the month and was in excruciating pain.   CeeCee

Many have gender-related confusion; for others, frequent masturbation is common as a way of releasing enormous internal stress.

GROWING AWARENESS

With recovery, survivors are able to gain awareness of their true needs and put the aftereffects into perspective.

The needs I had were for touch and nurturing and attention, but it was all confused. What I wanted was simple affection. I finally saw that in order for me to keep victimizing myself, I have to dissociate. You have to be present and relaxed for sex and pleasure. But for self-destructive addictive sexual tension, you have to dissociate—go into the past and become a victim or a perpetrator. I'm starting to understand that the power I feel when I feel sexually excited is my power and not someone else's power hurting me. It's not a domination power. It's natural power—empowerment. It's about creativity and openness and relaxation and pleasure that hurts no one. I struggled with that intensely for two and a half, three years, and finally I'm on the other side.   CeeCee

HEALING

As with all aspects of dissociated trauma, the first step is association. Here's one survivor's experience.

(The following quote describes violent, painful abuse. You may decide to skip it and continue at the regular text.)

This is embarrassing to say, but I'm going to, because it's really important. I felt like I really needed to go out and get fucked by somebody. I mean, I wanted to get gang-banged. I wanted to be hurt because I had to hurt to enjoy it. It took me everything I had not to just go out and find somebody to hurt me. It was terrible. I felt so much shame about that, so I brought it to my therapist. I mean, in reality, who wants to be gang-banged? Nobody. Nobody that has a normal life wants ten men to fuck her hard and stick things up into her. So I was wondering why I was so sick, doing this five years into recovery. My therapist told me it's probably a memory because it's so strong. We worked on one of the most horrendous sexual memories that I've ever had. There were about six people there, and my uncle said he'd teach me "you don't say 'no.'" So they just like stuck things in me—like their long, sharp fingernails. They cut my vagina and poured hot burning oil on my vagina. But the amazing thing about it was while they were doing this, my alter Sally, my sex addict, thought that it felt good. So my therapist figured out that Sally converts pain into pleasure. And if it weren't for her, I might not have survived a lot of that. My therapist was really nice to Sally and gave her a pink flower and told me I needed to be nice to her because she saved me a lot of times. So after I had that memory, I didn't feel like I needed to go to find somebody.

I've never had the romantic kind of sex, you know where there's candles and wine and stuff. And I know that it's possible. Maybe I'll never have it, but I know that I deserve it now—you know, for somebody to be gentle with me.   Annie

Once the trauma is associated, you can begin to experience deep changes from within. Recovery for survivors may mean reestablishing some very basic concepts.

I started working with this new therapist, and she says, "Try saying 'I'm a woman.'" I was like, "Why would I want to say that?" I'd spent like an hour in absolute aggravation and agitation and just antsiness trying to walk around in a circle and be in my body and go, "I'm a woman. I'm a woman walking around a room." And then it kind of kept unfolding "Okay, now I'm an adult woman, and now I'm an adult sexual woman." And my teacher was real insistent on, "You need to buy a shirt from a woman's department, instead of a man's department, or unisex." 'Cause then I could really understand that I have a woman's body. I became more female basically. So as this happened I just softened really deeply inside. I wasn't as tough as I was. My breasts grew, and that was a little shocking. So it clicked that I could actually be strong and also a woman, that there's nothing wrong with that—whew—what a relief! So I was able to have my physical strength which was real important to me, and the softer side which I always secretly liked about myself, but I didn't share. I discovered that "woman" was my life force. That's where it's rooted. It was a really humanizing kind of thing for me. . . . Emily

As in other areas of recovery, the slower you go, the faster you'll get there. By setting tiny goals (which are major achievements), you'll be able to lay a solid foundation. The rule is there are no rules, as long as you simply try to stay present in your body and your feelings. Start by trying to connect with yourself. Stay present while touching your own arm, knee, or face. How does it feel? What associations come up?

The definition of sex as intercourse and orgasm is narrow and constricting. Spiritual sex invites many expanded forms of personal expression. Some of the sexiest, most sensual moments of connection can come from simply holding hands in a fully conscious way.

Try to stay centered and present as much as possible during sex. You can start by touching your partner's hand or arm, or have her or him touch yours. Stop. Savor the moment. How does it feel? Nice? Enjoyable? If so, is there anything else you'd like to try? Do it and stay present. See how it feels and go with the flow.

If it feels scary or painful or wrong, stop and find out why. It's an opportunity to dismantle a dissociated, unhealthy foundation and build a healthy one. Sometimes you may discover you've gone a step too far only after you get there. Having a recovery plan in mind can help ease you out gently and quickly. Your recovery plan can include having safety reminders nearby, a journal and pen in case you want to write, and a tape of reassuring, comforting messages to play.

Some survivors have been traumatized so often that any touch feels painful or frightening. You may not be ready to connect with a partner. You may feel safer gently touching animals initially, because, as one person put it, "animals will never hurt or betray you." You may be able to learn safe touch by holding or petting animals while staying present in your body.

Reclaiming healthy sexuality is like restoring a once magnificent mansion. You don't do it all at once. You do it thoughtfully, attentively, one room at a time, and sometimes one tile at a time. Going carefully, respectfully, and lovingly brings the best results.

I didn't have sex for five and a half years—I mean zero. I didn't want it, and I didn't know if I'd ever have it again. And then a relationship came totally out of left field. Initially I had a little stuff come up, and maybe it will again, but I feel like I'm thoroughly enjoying sex. So there's this new experience of having a relationship that's also sexual. And it's just wonderful. There's mutual initiation, and there's an element of playfulness about it, and just no expectations. The love is really important, and there's a lot of communication. I think it's helpful that we are able to talk about sex and just take our time with it.   Susan

22

Healing Spirituality

People who are in touch with their own spirituality have a sense of inner strength and harmony that comes from being in tune with a greater life force, something much greater and more powerful than ourselves. Just as self-esteem affects our feeling of belonging within society, spirituality affects our sense of belonging in the universe. Spirituality can be thought of as "soul-esteem."

Ritual abuse is the antithesis of spirituality. In the same way that violators aim to destroy self-esteem, they aim to destroy soul-esteem. They do this by manipulating our experience of the supernatural and perverting religious beliefs.

EXAMINING SUPERNATURAL PHENOMENA

I have this fear of being able to live an ordinary life and to feel okay where I am. There was a lot of concern about losing my soul—that there's some way that my soul has been possessed, and no matter what I do, I won't be able to get it back; it's lost. And for me the issue is "Does the devil own my soul?" And out of that sense, I had to struggle with being who I am.   Gerald

Supernatural phenomena play a central role in establishing the illusion of power within ritual abuse cults. In terror, people willingly turn over power to something outside themselves. A great deal of manipulation goes into terrifying victims and directing them to put faith into other entities or their violators. In *Trauma and Recovery,* Dr. Judith L. Herman writes:

In an attempt to create some sense of purposeful action and to control their pervasive fear, traumatized people restrict their lives. . . . Constrictive symptoms also interfere with anticipation and planning for the future. Grinker and Spiegle observed that soldiers in wartime responded to losses and injuries within their group with diminished confidence in their own ability to make plans and take initiative, with increased superstitious and magical thinking, and with greater reliance on lucky charms and omens. Terr, in a study of kidnapped schoolchildren, described how afterward the children came to believe that there had been omens warning them of the traumatic event. Years after the kidnapping, these children continued to look for omens to protect them and guide their behavior. Moreover, years after the event, the children retained a foreshortened sense of the future; when asked what they wanted to be when they grew up, many replied that they never fantasized or made plans for the future because they expected to die young.

There is a lively debate between those who believe that paranormal phenomena exist and those who don't. However, there is no question that many cult displays of supernatural "powers" are simply manipulations.

I have had the experience of being able to walk into a fire and not being burned. And I can't do that now. There's programming, and there's drugs, and there's altered states. And they all play a part. People can go to a workshop and do firewalking, but they couldn't just build a fire in their backyard and walk into it.   Susan

If a child is especially fortunate, she or he may have noticed details that exposed the set-ups and manipulations used in ritual abuse cults. Such a child may develop a completely different view of the powers violators claim to have.

Once I was formally initiated they gave me my own little robe and all. I felt so proud. They told me that now I have the special power of raising people from the dead. They all assembled hastily one day to perform the body-raising ceremony. It wasn't at a regular evening ritual but in the middle of the day. They brought in a frail "dead" man on a stretcher. He was mostly naked and his skin looked grayish-blue. I was told to say, "Arise!" and as I said the word, he sat up. They all burst into a round of applause, and then everyone dispersed. It must have been their lunch hour or something. But I wasn't impressed at all. I had noticed his chest rise and fall when they brought him in. He was alive to begin with.   Erik

This survivor was not taken in by or impressed with the violators' or his own "supernatural" powers. However, the vast majority of cult-raised children live in terror of their violators' powers. In most cases they experience these manipulations as real and as shown in Chapter 6, beliefs about a cult's supernatural powers may persist into adulthood.

There was this big garage, and off to one side is this incinerator where they did cremations and things like that. So it was this cold cement floor area and there were these couples that were offering first-born babies to be sacrificed to Satan in order to move up the ranks in the cult. And each time an infant was tossed into the incinerator, the flames would just get really huge and come out of the front, because they didn't have the door closed. And it was like Satan himself was there. A giant roar came out of the furnace, and a big ball of fire came up like a wave. The flame curls came up like arms. I could always explain everything away, but I could never explain this away. I'm still not convinced it wasn't Satan talking to me and telling me that I had to bow down or die. I truly believed I saw Satan.   Christi Joy

Demonstrations of supernatural powers are even more difficult to refute if they are reinforced through traumatic learning.

They took me to my Catholic church and laid me on the altar and put a snake up inside me—in my vagina. It was the most horrible experience. First of all, I thought I was going to die because I was going to be bitten; second of all, it was just a horrible feeling moving around, and they told me that was Satan. As a Catholic I had been taught that in the Garden of Eden there was a snake who was the devil. So they did magical surgery on me. They told me that they put a snake inside of me, and that if I ever, ever thought of talking, he would bite me and I would die. But as a reminder, they wanted me to know that each month the snake would cause me pain so that I would always remember that he was there. So my entire adult life until about four or five years ago, each time I had a menstrual cycle, I thought that the snake was doing his number, and that was my reminder.   Alice

Concepts established in the early developmental years form the foundation upon which a child's view of the world is built. These beliefs, reinforced with terror, are particularly hard to reframe, because a person's interpretation of reality is invested in their being true.

If you've had the opportunity to experience magic by "walking through a solid object" and you honestly believe it happened and that it was real, you would have a whole lot of reconstructing to do. You'd have to reevaluate everything that

you've believed and try to begin to understand it in a whole different way. And I think that's where my denial comes. It is too hard to reorganize everything.   Matthew

Many survivors grow up believing evil powers have control over their lives or are trying to get them. A lot of energy may be tied up in fending off these evil forces. It is hard to break free, because the traumatic events remain dissociated in the unconscious. Even when the memories are associated, they are reexperienced as absolutely real and may reinforce a survivor's belief.

One survivor asked me, "How do you know the magic isn't real?" There aren't any studies to prove the point. However, given that much of what violators do is achieved through manipulation, why would they stop at manipulating a child's experience of the supernatural? Violators focus on altering reality to bend a victim's will to theirs. It doesn't take special skills or powers to fool a young child, and that's when most of the manipulations take place (see examples in Chapter 6).

One of the things that helps me is demystifying. This wasn't magic. This was a bunch of big people who got together to hurt a bunch of little people, and they may have said all kinds of stuff to rationalize it, but it's a bunch of bullshit. There's no explaining it, there's no rationalizing it, there's no excusing it, and it's really important for me to really demystify and disempower the perpetrators. David Gabriel

The focus of recovery is for survivors to experience *their own* autonomy or power. As long as survivors engage in activities where power is surrendered, they are prevented from regaining their sense of self. This also applies when survivors partner with people who demand they surrender their power. Through recovery, survivors become increasingly self-secure and centered. Once you know who you are, you're better equipped to decide if and when to surrender power to someone or something else.

There's a lot of weird stuff that people get into. Like I got a call from this survivor who was experiencing this energy in the room, and she and her therapist had called the devil or something, and she wanted to know how to get this entity to go up in smoke. And I said, "You don't try to burn sage to get rid of it. You just go into the entity in that room and get the memory—okay? And get to a good therapist, and get to the feelings, and get away from putting any value on psychic or paranormal." That's just the way they kept us hooked when I was a kid.   Susan

Until the early traumas around supernatural phenomenon are resolved through recovery, survivors may continue to be drawn to "magical" solutions outside themselves. Recovery is realizing that the solutions are within yourself. There is a saying, "You won't find it on the outside if you don't have it on the inside."

The only time I really feel my alters come out and try to do rituals is when all of us are in a situation where we have to recognize the limitations of being human. And we become painfully aware of the fact that we can't have the answers, and we can't control the future, and that's when the cult alters want to jump in, because they were programmed to believe that with certain rituals you could have everything you wanted, and that things would go your way if you had the power. So the majority of it is just telling them that it's not true.   Amiee

Paranormal phenomena typically influence lives of people who are open to its existence. If we let these influences take control, we are at their mercy, as we were as children. Once we gain a sense of self and safety and feel strong within ourselves, we can control and determine if, when, and what unknown forces to explore.

Every person has that ability and control. Some survivors benefit from envisioning protective fields around themselves—like a "cocoon." Others stay safe by refusing to engage in any extrasensory activities.

I'm pretty sensitive and I'm pretty intuitive. But I haven't allowed myself to open to other ways of being, so I've actually shut down these possibilities. For now I chose to be very physical, direct, and practical.   CeeCee

Once your sense of self is regained, you are in a position to sense deceit and manipulations. There is less likelihood of confusion by external influences. You are less susceptible to revictimizing by people claiming to have "the answer," when their interest isn't to empower you but rather gain power for themselves. You will know who you are and your own truth.

Reclaiming power means reclaiming all things of this earth. It's rejecting the meaning violators gave to symbols and events and assigning our own meaning to them. It means knowing that the colors red and black are neither good nor bad—they simply are. It means no longer avoiding the number six or thirteen. It means reclaiming and enjoying holidays, birthdays, solstices, and each new year.

THE ROLE OF RELIGION

People have typically considered the words "religious" and "spiritual" to be analogous, but they are not the same. Religion is the formal expression of a spiritual belief system. It reflects a society's understanding of itself in relation to the universe. Religion interprets universal events, and in so doing gives meaning to our existence. Because different cultures have assigned different meanings to universal events, there is more than one religion.

Many survivors find support through traditional religion, because it continues to give them strength. Some discover religion for the very first time through recovery. They experience the wealth and connectedness of their spiritual inheritance through community worship and prayer.

I read my Scriptures all the time and just keep praying and asking for answers.   A survivor

However, many survivors have difficulty with traditional religions for a number of reasons. Religion was perverted for survivors through deliberate set-ups and manipulations.

I was molested by a man dresed up to look like Jesus. I saw a woman dressed as St. Mary kill a baby. It's real hard to trust this won't happen again the minute I reach out to them in prayer. Jeanne

In addition, children are often convinced through ceremonies that they are evil. Many are "united" with Satan through "marriage" ceremonies or are made to bear "his" babies. Unconsciously convinced of their badness, many survivors feel unable to connect with the positive aspects of established religions.

I think I was supposed to be the daughter of Satan—and I don't mean my physical father—I mean that my father literally is Satan. This is what I was supposed to believe. And as his daughter I am supposed to take over and be Satan in this

world when he gets too old. So rituals were done in my name, because I was Satan. They killed people for me. And I felt really responsible for what was done.   Katharine

Survivors were often abused within the context of their religion not only in rituals but in day-to-day life.

Using religion as a weapon is what my mother does best. Every time she speaks, she brings God into it—like she has some sort of in with God. When she uses God, I get very fearful because I'm worried that God will punish me if I don't listen to her. I was taught all my life that if you're righteous, you'll be happy. And I've been so intensely unhappy—suicidal most of the time. I feel like there's some sort of a moral judgment against me—that others won't see that my problems are the result of my abuse.   A survivor

During recovery, some survivors temporarily suspend religious observances while trying to sort out what's what.

Some survivors leave their religion permanently. For many this is another difficult, painful fallout of recovery.

They got at every value that stood for anything. And until I reclaim everything, where the fuck do I belong? I can't just go to church. If I hadn't been abused I wouldn't have all the baggage around organized spirituality and religion that I do. There is no place for me. So I kinda limp along on my own homemade spirituality.   Susan

Others find ways to reclaim their religion:

Once a week my religious advisor and therapist work together to teach catechism to my inner kids. A survivor

FINDING SPIRITUALITY

Spirituality is being in touch and in tune with universal forces, without necessarily knowing their cause or meaning. Children have an inherent spirituality. Even though severely deprived by their caregivers, they retain an intuitive sense of goodness, love, and truth. Many survivors report that as children they connected with "helpers," "a white light," "a dove," or "angels" who got them through the worst of the abuse.

The more in touch we are with our own being and our universe, the deeper our spirituality. Many are discovering a "survivor spirituality" through soul-esteem.

If you let things be and connect with your own spirituality, then everything else works. Each of us is born with different gifts and inclinations, and the ultimate purpose is to create balance and harmony in the world. But if we negate ourselves for a "higher good," it's really for someone else's good—and that creates disharmony, both within ourselves and in the world. Then we don't know what's wrong. Saying "yes" to spirituality is saying "no" to ritual abuse.   Roxana

Many traditional religions evolved from a hostile view of the universe. A key idea was to conquer nature, earthly and human. Many things occurring naturally were labeled evil. Babies were believed to be born guilty of "original sin." Soul-esteem implies that people, plants, animals, and the universe are right the way they are. Things are unfolding as they should. The idea isn't to conquer the universe but to understand, appreciate, and love it. As a result, many survivors search for spiritual fulfillment outside the context of traditional organized worship. In their search for meaning, survivors join others in society in evolving a new understanding of our uni-

verse and our place within it. Many find meaning and strength through beliefs expressed in the twelve and sixteen steps evolved through the recovery movement.

The work I'm doing now with Al-Anon meets my spiritual needs. I have come to understand that I am powerless over people who do insane things. The dynamic I must practice is separating myself in whatever ways I need to from addicts—in my case, the abusive people in my family or elsewhere—letting them take responsibility for themselves. Then I can focus on myself and what I need. As I'm learning to set limits and demand that other people control their impulses, the universe is becoming more orderly and safe. God is not The Big Jerk in the Sky as he used to be when I was being abused by my parents, but a kind, encouraging teacher or coach, walking with me and telling me, "You can do it. You can find your way. Keep trying. I am with you."   Jeanne

Finding meaning is a process, not an all or nothing, black and white formula. It's keeping what works and retiring what doesn't.

I think it's very important to be able to recognize exclusive thinking and not be trapped by it in our recovery process. By recognizing the evil, the horror, the terrible things, the tendency is to say, "Oh, well, my life was shit. Everything I came from was bad. Nothing good happened in my life." Part of the recovery process is not to let the negative gobble up all the good. It's to recognize and cherish the good and become attuned enough to find where there was a space of goodness in our life, find out what it was which allowed us to grab a hold of the positive and keep it.   Suzzane

Here's how one survivor is creating meaning by keeping the good and adding to it.

I had a lot of Catholic religious brainwashing. And I feel it's a very sick, shame-based religion. And you're not going to get well in a shame-based environment as a survivor. But I kept something of Catholicism—my higher power. I realized that my higher power—Father, Son, and Holy Spirit—is a multiple personality. And that created a lot of sanity for me—you see, my higher power is just like me.   Dave

Some are evolving a new definition of God.

God is that internal order of being a human being. By virtue of being a human being, I have a connection to God. The one or two times in my life when I've been happy or content have been when I've been in touch with me. It's like I just reach out and touch me—that to me is about God.   Sunny

Survivors are evolving a new concept of religion.

I don't think that means church necessarily. I think that for some it may be church. But I don't think it means following some sort of official order. In fact, it's almost just the opposite. I don't feel like it's really complicated, or like there're a lot of rules. It's letting go of the official and the formal— the clutter which keeps us from discovering what's real. The grass, the bugs, the sky, the dirt—they're all part of that harmony which is reality. It's being okay with more than just me, but being okay with the rest of the world.   Sunny

Some are evolving a new concept of our soul.

I conceive of a soul as a little piece of the wholeness of life, of the "allness" of life. It's like being a wave in the ocean. There's a continuing presence of soul—at the same time that we are the wave, we are also the ocean. I think that's one of

the primal fears that we face in this world. That we're more afraid of a union with the universe than we are of the separation. One of the things that used to scare me was the thought of merging with the universe, or the source, or God and lose my identity. What I was afraid of is that I'd get lost if I saw that I'm part of the vastness. And as I began working with that, I begin to see—not only am I this wave, but I'm all of those other waves in the ocean as well. So it's not a question of losing myself. It's a question of gaining all the rest of me.   Gerald

Self-esteem brings trust; soul-esteem brings faith. Spirituality is letting go of the struggle.

Spirituality is trusting the outcome, even if it means I don't necessarily win. And me not needing to be any more a part of it than I am, and than I'm supposed to be. And with evil there's always a struggle. Evil offers you a power which says, "If you do what I want, nothing bad will ever happen to you." Spirituality says, "it's going to suck sometimes, but that's okay."   Amiee

Some people are unable to feel their connection to other beings or nature. However, everyone has had an experience of that connection, even if they are not aware of it. What we do affects others and what others do affects us. If you come into a room where there is laughter, you may find yourself smiling too. If you are treated with cruelty you may be cruel in return. If you are treated with respect, you are more likely to respect yourself and others.

Spirituality is the extent to which we are able to be in touch with the universe. Some people call it God, some feel it is represented by their ancestors, some call it a higher power, some call it the universal truth, some think of it as the natural order of things. Spirituality is about being in touch with that natural order and drawing strength from it.

Like recovery, spirituality often feels elusive and out of reach. Many survivors despair of finding spiritual fulfillment.

I've been recovering for seven years and I have never been able to grasp onto the spirituality of the program. I have tried everything I know from meditation to various religions to meeting with counselors and there has been this block in my ability to connect with a higher power. And I've never been able to understand what that was about Matthew

Children often form their concept of God through their experience of their parents. Abusive caregivers go against the rules. Therefore some survivors may need to also break the rules to undo the damage inflicted by their parents.

What finally had to happen for me is I had to feel totally fucked over by God and feel the rage, before I could get anywhere close to spirituality. Grace

To help you experience your spirituality, you can begin by trying to connect with simple things.

I felt starved for touch but was afraid to really be intimate with people. So I went into my yard and put my arms around a tree. As I opened up to

receive its touch, I could feel all of its strength surge through me. Janes

By staying open to it, spirituality will come—in its own time and its own way. It is our inheritance.

One day I was feeling suicidal, and instead I said, "Okay, I'm gonna pray." I just started praying—"I'm very thankful I'm alive"—and all of a sudden there was this feeling; the universe was very thankful I was alive too. Alicia

The spiritual way is rarely the sure or simple way. You cannot force, contrive, or manufacture it. But our spiritual connection with one another is sometimes confirmed in poignant, unexpected ways.

I was on the phone with a survivor friend and she was telling me how badly she felt that she is remembering hurting her little sister—how she'd really like to talk to her sister, reach out and heal the pain. But she couldn't do that because her little sister had never spoken about remembering the abuse. I felt a tear forming, thinking I was really moved by this story. And then suddenly I realized that I'm a "little sister." My older brother who isn't in recovery had abused me—that tear was about me. And then I began to realize that the amends this survivor was wanting to offer her little sister was being heard and accepted by me, and the pain around my brother was healing. Josie

Part Six

Resources for Healing

23

Finding the Right Therapist

The following several chapters will discuss therapists, support groups, recovery tools, and specialized treatment options. Because finding the right resources can be *the* pivotal factor in recovery, I have gone into considerable detail. There is probably more information than most people need. Feel free to skim or skip sections that are irrelevant; you may simply want to be aware that they are here in case you need them.

The characteristics defining the right therapist apply to other professionals or recovery facilitators with whom you may choose to work. Therefore, the material in this chapter also applies to Chapters 24 through 26. An important guideline is to work only with people whose focus is to facilitate *your* self-discovery and whose purpose is to empower you to believe in yourself and in your own ability to heal. Work only with people who honor, support and respect you. Never turn over your power to someone else. If someone tries to assert control, leave. This chapter will help you with all of these issues.

THE *RIGHT* THERAPIST

Finding the right therapist depends on receiving the right diagnosis and therefore the appropriate treatment. There are many *good* therapists who are not the *right* therapists for survivors of ritual abuse. And there are therapists who are incompetent and may be more detrimental than helpful. This chapter will give examples of problems survivors have encountered, how to avoid them, where to look in choosing a therapist, what qualities to look for in her or him, how to evaluate

265

your progress, how to identify and handle problems. By being an informed client, you will maximize your chances of success.

You may never have been in therapy, and so have little idea what to look for. You may have had disappointing experiences with therapists and so are discouraged, angry, even cynical. Many survivors have to budget very carefully to afford any therapy at all. You may have already spent your allotted money on therapy that didn't work.

Some survivors are simply grateful to have a person who finally gives them the attention they never received as a child. For them, good therapy simply means being recognized. And while that is important and healing, it is also important to make steady progress. Knowing how to recognize whether you are simply treading water or swimming towards shore can make a significant difference in your results.

One survivor went for four years and spent his entire insurance allotment on therapy that treated the symptoms and not the underlying causes. The therapist focused on improving the survivor's self-assertiveness skills within his marriage. When the funds stopped, treatment stopped, but the internal turmoil continued. When the survivor finally learned of his abuse background, he could no longer afford to get the appropriate treatment. This problem is far more common than not. (Luckily, this survivor has finally found the right therapist, who is also willing to work out a modified payment plan.)

Because the abuse is usually repressed, many survivors do not know of their traumatic history. They therefore do not even suspect that a therapist may not be probing for the right information. Having no idea what is wrong and no benchmark against which to evaluate good therapy, many survivors have stayed with unhelpful therapists for long periods of time:

A lot of times therapists just seem to kind of sit back and let you sink in the mud. I'd gone to therapy with one woman. I went in every week and I said, "I must be nuts. I must be making this stuff up." And she let me do this. She would have let me do this for ten years. I think if I hadn't quit, I'd probably still be saying I'm crazy. Jane Linn

Other survivors, like Dave, have worked with therapists whose lack of expertise left them feeling distrustful and embittered. Dave has given up on therapists altogether and is trying to recover on his own.

I walked out of my therapist's office several times in a different personality, and she did not recognize it. I was driving home as the memory [of my alter personality] was still going on. You know, I could have gotten into a wreck. Dave

After many years of misdiagnosis and inappropriate treatment, Annie found the right therapist.

There's something about her, and I don't know what it is, but it feels like she's there and she believes me. There's something to that. I've never had a therapist like that—ever. I wouldn't trade her for a million bucks. Annie

Qualified therapists are available, and it is well worth it to find the right one. This doesn't mean it will be easy. However, with help and guidance, you will find one who's right for you. The following information will help you avoid common problems and guide you in getting the help you deserve.

Find the therapist who knows what she's doing, even if you have to go to twenty of them to make sure you've got the right one. Jackie Bianco

There are two areas to consider in choosing the right therapist. The first is professional qualifications; the second is style/compatibility.

PROFESSIONAL QUALIFICATIONS

Identifying and treating ritual abuse survivors is not taught in academic programs. Therefore, academic degrees and therapeutic designations do not necessarily ensure the right credentials for treating survivors. Therapists skilled in treating survivors have generally received their expertise through direct experience with survivors, special courses, self-education, seminars, workshops, specialty organizations or associations, and networking with other therapists.

Treatment involves identifying and integrating trauma sustained during ritual abuse. Your therapist should have expertise in two areas: diagnosing and treating post-traumatic reactions and an understanding of ritual abuse.

TREATING POST-TRAUMATIC REACTIONS

Post-traumatic reactions most often include post-traumatic fear (PTF), dissociative experience (DE), and dissociative identity (DI) (see Chapter 8). The most complex post-traumatic reaction to treat is DI. Therapists skilled in treating PTF may not have skills in treating DE or DI. However, therapists skilled in treating DI are usually skilled in treating DE and PTF. Whenever possible, look for a therapist skilled in treating DI or multiple personality.

There are relatively few qualified therapists in relation to patient demand. As a result, knowledgeable therapists usually have a substantial percentage of trauma survivors among their patients. Some therapists limit the number of survivor clients to prevent being overwhelmed. However, others have learned how to hear extreme pain without taking it home with them. These may have a high percentage of ritual abuse patients. If a therapist claims to have no trauma survivors and a high percentage of patients with mental and personality disorders, there may be increased risk of misdiagnosis and, therefore, incorrect treatment.

Keep in mind that just because a therapist has experience treating post-traumatic reactions, it doesn't necessarily mean she or he is right for you. Some therapists are skilled in retrieving memories but cannot help the survivor integrate the information. One survivor at a treatment center was surfacing memory after memory. His therapist was proud of the success with which he was able to access repressed material. However, the therapist did not help the survivor associate the memories on an emotional, feeling, or behavioral level: "After each memory I was just left hanging there—reeling from the experience. I left the treatment center feeling retraumatized."

Some therapists are skilled in accessing repressed emotions but cannot connect them to their root cause, the original trauma. There are survivors who have been doing emotional release work for years without significant improvement. Unless full integration takes place in all aspects of our experience, the healing is not complete. It is important to find a therapist who is skilled in integrating all four areas of experience: knowledge, behavior, emotions, and feelings. In addition, some therapists are more skilled than others in recognizing and treating inner selves. It is important to validate the inner person(s) for healing to take place. You may not be a ritual abuse survivor, but if you suspect you may have suffered some childhood trauma, the same criteria apply.

UNDERSTANDING RITUAL ABUSE

Familiarity with ritual abuse helps to validate a survivor's experience and put the information into a context. Knowledge of typical cult rituals and programming provides a framework within which to process emerging material. Erik, who initially worked with a therapist unfamiliar with ritual abuse, observed:

I think survivors who are connected with other survivors are really fortunate because they don't feel so totally out there in outer space, and I felt that way for two years—me and my therapist. I had no idea what this stuff was. It was like, we're both with our mouth dropped, saying, "Can this be true?" Since then I've connected with a therapist who is dealing with other ritual abuse survivors. Now when I say stuff, she nods her head and doesn't drop her jaw. It just makes a huge difference.   Erik

It is important to work with therapists who believe that ritual abuse exists. Until recently, some therapists were reluctant to acknowledge the widespread incidence of sexual abuse. In the same way, some therapists skilled in treating trauma survivors do not believe in ritual abuse. A therapist who does not believe that ritual abuse exists will deny experiences of ritual abuse in their clients. Recovery means accessing and accepting your own truth. Therefore, work only with a therapist who believes that ritual abuse exists and that your memories are valid. At the same time, avoid therapists who believe that all post-traumatic reactions stem from ritual abuse. For example, I heard of a woman who fielded calls for a national hotline and "diagnosed" all callers as survivors of ritual abuse.

It may not be possible to find a fully qualified therapist. However, it is important that your thera-

pist have some familiarity with either post-traumatic reactions or ritual abuse. If you have to make a trade-off, check in with yourself to see what feels most important to you. Many people might say that expertise in treating dissociative identity is the overriding professional qualification. However, for me, the more important factor was knowledge of ritual abuse. What does your inner wisdom tell you? Always go with that response.

Many survivors work with therapists who have expertise in one area, and are educating themselves in the others. Fortunately, new treatment discoveries and information are becoming increasingly available. Some survivors work with a team of therapists. Each therapist in the team has different skills. Specialized skills in addition to talk therapy may include body work, art therapy, behavioral therapies, hypnotherapy, biofeedback, and dream analysis, to name just a few (these are discussed in Chapter 25). Team approaches are effective and help prevent therapist burnout.

What I want to say to somebody who is just coming into memories is don't believe the professionals, don't believe the psychiatrists. As hard as it is, believe your inner child, and find the professional who believes your inner child.   Bea

Your therapist needs to be a solid psychotherapist. In addition to established criteria of good therapy, the *right* therapist should model healthy behaviors and adopt a mentor relationship toward you. In treating trauma survivors, a therapist takes the role not of neutral bystander but of active advocate for the abused child and survivor adult. Four areas of particular importance are discussed below: autonomy, self-assessment and courage, being believed, and emotional healing.

AUTONOMY

Since the aim of ritual abuse is to take away a person's power, an essential element of recovery is to return autonomy to the survivor.

I think it is very important for people to be warned not to work with anyone who takes their power. I've seen horrible damage being done to people when their power is taken by a therapist. I met a lot of survivors and I saw a lot of people who were addicted to their therapists because they really felt that their therapist was the one who was making them well. I think the most important thing for survivors of ritual abuse is to find a process by which other people assist us in uncovering our truth and in being who we are. I can have people help me, but I would never think of letting someone take control of that process. So I think it's vital to make sure that whoever they work with are like co-workers or assistants. Therapists are a vehicle to help us through recovery. Therapy is just one of many tools.   Suzzane

Avoid therapists who set themselves up as the authority and you as the unenlightened subject. Avoid the therapist who has a hidden agenda of indoctrinating you into a new belief system, no matter how appealing the message or dogma may sound. This merely replaces one form of controlled thinking with another.

I've seen a lot of people's power taken away from them when they need it the most. I see a lot of survivors go out there needing help desperately, and so they follow anyone who extends a hand. And if that happens to be somebody that doesn't have what it takes to meet their needs and won't empower them to do it themselves, then they're really in trouble. Because then they're treated like these needy, dependent people who can't function alone, who need a therapist at their elbow telling

them which way to go, and how far to go, and when to sit down and when to stand up, and they're told that they will self-destruct if they ever take some initiative like joining a group or something like that. And with that attitude, they will take forever to recover, if they ever do.   Sunny

The purpose of therapy is to put you in touch with your own thoughts and feelings. Look for the therapist who is comfortable with her or his own power and whose goal is to empower you.

Today I have a therapist who raises me up. It's like she breathes life into my spirit. She sees the strong part of me. She sees the wholeness in me and helps me to see it too. My therapist always turns the steering wheel back to me. She gently keeps me on course as I do the navigating, and I feel empowered.   Jane Linn

SELF-ASSESSMENT AND COURAGE

Recovery means reclaiming our past and our personal truth. Most people are not survivors of ritual abuse, but many people have issues of unresolved childhood pain. Therapists who have worked through their own pain can help you work through yours. Therapists who are unable or unwilling to look at their own issues will likely keep you from identifying and healing yours.

A therapist can stop that process just by a face they make, or their body language. If they have not worked through their own stuff, if they have not dealt with their own mortality and their own abuse, at whatever level that was, then they will not be able to be with you on that level of pain. And as soon as you know that the therapist can't hear your pain, you're going to shut up.   Bea

Working through difficult issues isn't a one-time event—it's a lifelong process. Your therapist needs to stay on top of her or his own issues—recognize them and deal with them as they come up.

They can't stop and say, "I'm a good therapist now." They have to always be working their stuff and dealing with their issues and learning ways to take care of themselves better. Bea

It takes courage to go where survivors need to go to reclaim their past. Some therapists are simply afraid of working with ritual abuse survivors. Avoid them.

Therapists have been afraid of me, afraid I'll commit suicide, afraid I would go off into an alter that was a complete lunatic, afraid I would just go insane, afraid that they wouldn't be able to deal with what I said or what came up. Some would be very controlling, or they wouldn't believe me, or they'd think that I needed to be treated with kid gloves, or I'd like detonate. They communicate that fear to where I'm afraid of myself. It's important to work with therapsits who see this work as completely approachable and do-able. You can do this and still maintain dignity and respect. em

Survivors need someone courageous to help them work through recovery. Even if a therapist has worked through her or his own abuse, they may not be able to hear or encourage you to look at the extremes of yours. Here's a rule of thumb I like to use. I ask myself, "If this therapist had survived ritual abuse, would they be able to go back and look at what happened to them?" If the answer feels like a "yes," you've got the right therapist. If the answer feels like a "no," you might need to check out your assumptions with your therapist. If you're still not convinced, you may need to find a different therapist. Look for a therapist who gently encourages you to explore the source of your pain. Avoid therapists who try to direct you back to the present when uncomfortable or difficult material from your past begins to emerge.

Some people are terrified of our inner little kids' terror. These are the therapists who say they're trying to keep you safe by keeping you in the present. And they're the ones who'll tell you, "forget, forgive, and get on with your life." But it's like I can't get on with my life because I don't have a life to get on with, you know. They don't seem to get that. Sophia

THE IMPORTANCE OF "I BELIEVE YOU"

Although being believed is important in any circumstances, it is critical to the healing of ritual abuse survivors.

My [inner] child is just waiting for somebody to say, "I believe you." That child part of me is crying out to finally have somebody believe me. The last thing I need is to go to a therapist who thinks I'm making this up. Jane Linn

If your therapist is experienced in working with trauma survivors, she or he will understand the importance of believing you. In September 1985, the *American Journal of Psychiatry* published a letter by Mardi J. Horowitz, M.D., which states:

Traumatic events lead to special memories . . . which may have an uncanny quality in that the experience seems unreal. Psychotherapy of patients with posttraumatic stress disorders may usefully include efforts by the therapist to assist the patient in experiencing these memories as real.

I was remembering sexual abuse from my father before I remembered ritual abuse. At one point I asked the therapist I had at the time, "Do you believe it happened?" And she answered. "I can't believe it happened until you believe it happened." But when I told her that my sister was remembering incest too, she said, "Well, now I'm inclined to believe that it really happened." And I didn't feel good about that because I didn't know what was going on. I needed someone who did. If she couldn't believe me in and of myself and had to get it from another source, I couldn't continue. How can I tell her things? You need a therapist who believes you one hundred percent so I went and found one. Jeanne

Trauma interferes with a survivor's perception of reality. Extreme trauma intensifies denial for purposes of self-protection. Cult-abused children are conditioned to mistrust and deny their own reality, which makes it much more difficult for survivors to accept their own truth. If the therapist plays into that doubt, survivors are often needlessly delayed in getting on with healing. It is important to work with a therapist who understands that you are recalling your experience as best as you can, and that whatever you do remember actually happened or is connected to something that happened to you.

Something that's been real important to me is the validation that I get from my therapist. No matter how crazy I feel, how much shame I'm in, [how great] my level of denial, he's always just there, real strong, real positive, real affirming, and saying "I believe you. I don't think you're crazy. I don't think you're making it up." As much as I don't want to believe it, it's important for me to get that feedback. He always has reasons why he believes me. And that's powerful. David Gabriel

The therapist's role is to help the survivor heal, not to play detective. Survivors typically doubt and cross-examine their own experience more than any detective would (see Chapter 14 for more on denial). Avoid therapists who gloss over or refuse to deal with your emerging memories. A friend of mine wondered out loud in therapy if someone had committed incest with her. Her therapist's response was, "Put that thought out of your mind." Putting it out of our mind is the root of the problem, not the solution.

EMOTIONAL HEALING

Cult-abused children are emotionally deprived, even starved. Emotions and love are manipulated to control behavior. The adult survivor is emotionally numb or confused. It's critical to work with therapists who encourage you to get in touch with and express your feelings. Their offices should accommodate loud sounds—full expressions of grief, anger, or anything that comes up. They need to support and validate you. Having a caring, emotionally supportive therapist is critical to restoring emotional health.

I think the most important thing is emotional support. If your therapist can support you unconditionally on an emotional level, then you're going to get better. Because you're going to learn that something like that's possible. And that you can trust someone else in the world. Bea

Many survivors express the need for physical warmth and nurturing:

It's just really important to have a warm person, because the people in my childhood were cold. For me physical warmth is really important— somebody who hugs and feels safe in a physical manner and who can respect my boundaries, and also has good boundaries herself. There is a relationship of caring that's been really important to me. She not only helps me to contact my memories, but I come away loving myself more, and accepting my strength and my capacities.   Susan

Safe, therapeutic, non-sexual comforting can be wonderfully healing. This is a delicately balanced area, and is discussed in more detail later in this chapter.

Look for someone who trusts in your inherent goodness, supports you unconditionally, and nurtures your wounded inner child.

My [inner] child needs a therapist who believes me completely; my adult needs a therapist who believes IN me completely.   Jane Linn

THE MENTOR THERAPIST

A mentor is someone who sees great potential in a rookie (employee, player, client, student, etc.) and takes her or him under wing. A mentor has faith in you. She works with you to set goals and the strategies to meet them. She admires and develops your strengths. She effectively assesses the source of your difficulties. She observes, and gives encouragement and feedback. She allows you your experience, your pain, and your triumph. She cheers you on to victory. A mentor therapist delights in your progress and healing, and when it's time helps you gently leave the nest. The following comments are typical of a mentor/therapist.

The survivors that I know are some of the most beautiful people I have ever met. Their spirit has had to walk through fire and been burned. But there's this core there that's so beautiful and so strong from having had to survive that. It's a strength beyond anything that I've ever experienced. Because it really is spiritual abuse on a pro-

found level. There's this beauty that exists from having survived.   A therapist

Finding the right therapist may not be easy. Be prepared for disappointments and dead ends in your search. Do not let temporary setbacks stop you from getting the help you deserve. Even if it takes a number of tries, keep looking until you're satisfied you have the right one. On the other hand, be prepared to make tradeoffs. Remember that you're not looking for the perfect therapist. You're looking for an excellent therapist. Use your inner strengths and support network to see you through the "down" moments. Have on hand crisis and emergency information in case the need arises (see end pages).

The rest of this chapter will offer you suggestions for finding the right therapist. The point is not to overwhelm you with guidelines but to give you the option to pick and choose information. Give yourself permission to bypass all the suggestions and simply follow your own instincts. You may want to read only the sections that are relevant to your present situation and skim the ones that may apply at a later date.

AVENUES FOR YOUR SEARCH

There are many possible avenues you can try in finding a therapist. Here's how one survivor found the right therapist:

There was a woman in our incest support meetings. She had been with a therapist who had her on medication. She was in terror all the time and was just a mess. As soon as she started seeing another therapist, she got off the medication and started talking about memories. Her denial just seemed to drop off. And you could see visible changes. You just watched her get better week after week. There was this growth and movement that nobody else in group was experiencing. And I started thinking, "I've got to find who this therapist is she's seeing." Bea

Networks of good referrals can vary widely from location to location. One survivor found an excellent therapist through her medical insurance carrier.

[Initially] I tried a therapist who had been advertising in all the alternative, politically correct publications, and she didn't work out. In the meantime, I heard about a therapist through my insurer who was supposed to be very good with incest survivors. So I said to myself, "I think I'll just try bureaucratic techno-medicine and see what that will give me. It's on the insurance, so what the heck." That was such a radical shift. But you know, she turned out to be quite good.   Jeanne

Help can come from different types of professionals: psychiatrists, psychiatric nurses, social workers, psychologists, pastoral counselors, occupational therapists, behavioral therapists, paraprofessionals. You may get good leads from some of the following:

Referrals From Survivors

One of the best sources are referrals from survivors who are making good progress. If you don't know any survivors personally, you may be able to connect with some through ritual abuse or incest survivor support groups (see Chapter 24).

ISSMP&D

Another good source is the ISSMP&D (International Society for the Study of Multiple Personality and Dissociation), which has a membership list of professionals by city, state, and country.

Members are usually professionals familiar with treating post-traumatic reactions.

Sexual Trauma or Dissociative Disorders Treatment Facilities

Try sexual trauma or dissociative disorders treatment units at local hospitals, outpatient services, or treatment facilities centers (see Resource Guide).

Workshops and Seminars

Keep your eyes open for workshops, seminars, or professional presentations on the topics of dissociative identity, ritual abuse, sexual abuse, or trauma. Professionals attending these workshops/presentations may be qualified to help you. They may also know of other qualified therapists.

Survivor Networks/Organizations/Newsletters

Check to see if there is a local survivors' organization, twelve-step group, or newsletter. These often have potential leads. If there are none locally, see the Resource Guide for national organizations.

Local Women's Crisis/Help Organizations

Try your local battered women's shelters, rape crisis centers, or other emergency and crisis help organizations. Male survivors may be assisted as well.

Government Agencies

Try your local department of social services, department of mental health, child protection services, etc. Your district attorney's office may also know of good referrals.

Religious Organizations

Try pastoral or counseling services affiliated with various churches. These often provide counseling at minimal cost, regardless of your religious affiliation.

Colleges and Universities

Institutions offering academic accreditation in the therapeutic and educational professions often have staff that are well qualified or well connected with the local therapeutic community.

Local Chapters of Professional Organizations

Local chapters of the National Association of Social Workers, American Psychological Association, American Psychiatric Association, and American Mental Health Counselors Association may offer leads.

Your Current Therapist

If for any reason your relationship isn't working out, you can ask her or him for referrals.

Yellow Pages

Although a traditional source of leads, approach this one with caution. Yellow Pages advertising is not necessarily verified for accuracy of claims. In one town a man advertised as a hypnotherapist. His training and experience was in construction work. While it is perfectly acceptable to use the Yellow Pages as a source, be sure to verify the claims made.

ABOUT LICENSING AND CERTIFICATION

A therapist may claim to be licensed or certified. This can mean different things in different states and countries or within different organizations. If you are seriously considering using a therapist, you may want to call their licensing or accreditation organization. Verify that this therapist is a member. (If a certificate or license has been revoked for any reason, in some states the therapist may continue to practice but may not use the word "licensed" or "certified" in their advertising.) Also ask what the requirements are to obtain accreditation. You may be surprised to learn that some certificates can be obtained with as little as a one- or two-day seminar. Other

licenses/certificates have stringent qualification requirements and ongoing monitoring of their members. These usually have standards of sound practice. Some also have requirements for continuous professional education. Licensing and certification boards can offer mediation and help with resolution in case of a problem.

Some states do not have mandatory licensing requirements for therapists. Keep in mind that licensing does not guarantee the right treatment. Some nonlicensed therapists may be better qualified to treat survivors than some licensed professionals.

Once you've narrowed your choice, you may want to check several references on a prospective therapist. Although it is unlikely that references would say anything bad about a therapist, you may be able to intuit information from the tone and amount of enthusiasm or lack of it.

HOW TO PROCEED

Start with local organizations. If you are not satisfied, inquire with regional and national organizations. See the Resource Guide for survivor resource organizations that may be able to assist you. Ask each source for referrals. Ask your referrals for additional referrals. In this way you maximize your chances of getting good results.

Keep in mind that suggested resources are not endorsements or recommendations. Be cautious. A referral or even another therapist's endorsement is not a guarantee. It is important to investigate promising leads personally and make your own decision regarding the right therapist for you.

The therapist of your choice may be fully booked. Ask if you can get on a waiting list. Continue your search, but keep checking back on a regular basis, in case an unexpected opening occurs.

FEELING SAFE WHILE YOU SEARCH

You may not feel comfortable saying you are a survivor of ritual abuse when making inquiries. You do not need to identify yourself. Simply ask if the therapist works with dissociative reactions following trauma. If the therapist seems promising and asks about your background, you can say that you are an adult survivor of sadistic childhood abuse and incest. If you are asked for your name but wish to preserve your anonymity, try using only your first name, or consider using a pseudonym.

Some survivors do not like to leave their phone numbers with strangers. If this is the case, offer to call back at a convenient time. (This may not be possible where the "receptionist" is an answering machine.)

What else do you need to do to feel safe? Have a support friend present during your calls? Have your support friend make some initial phone calls? Be sure that you are taking care of your safety needs before proceeding. However, remember that responsibility for finding the right therapist rests with you.

CONDUCTING YOUR SEARCH

There is no right or wrong way to go about the search. Survivors have found wonderful therapists, sometimes without following any of the do's and don'ts. Others, like myself, regret not having had more information and guidelines.

Annie's sister was working on issues of overeating and felt they may have stemmed from childhood abuse. Annie "knew" her parents hadn't abused her, but she was having problems in her marriage, so she made an appointment to see her sister's therapist:

I thought to myself, "Right. Let's get things out on the table right now. Find out how much she costs an hour and let her know I had not been sexually abused." I had dug around inside and I know that it didn't happen to me. I had been acting out sexually since I was born, not because I was abused. No, I was just born horny. Insatiable is the word. Annie

Luckily, her sister's therapist knew that children are not born "horny"; nor are children ever to blame for sexual transgressions. The therapist knew that Annie's protest that she had not been sexually abused was a possible clue to her long history of problems. Purely by luck, Annie had found the right therapist.

Susan, on the other hand, who got a referral from a friend, had the following observation:

A lot of the way therapists have been chosen in the past has been erratic It certainly was for me. I got a reference from a friend, made an appointment, and went to him for three and a half years. That's not the way I recommend people do it. I have since found a new therapist, and I have learned that it's been really important for me to get clear on what I want, and to interview, and go about it in a professional way.   Susan

Therapists have different policies regarding initial conversations or evaluatory interviews. Some charge full rates, some charge a partial rate, some offer a limited amount of time (fifteen to twenty minutes) at no charge, and some will offer the entire interview at no charge. Ask about cost, if any, when making your initial appointment.

Most people feel awkward interviewing a therapist. It tends to be even more difficult for survivors. At one point I would never have dreamed of questioning a professional. It would have meant breaking a taboo. Their designation was proof of their credentials. Who was I to question that? Survivors are conditioned to believe that they have no rights and no power. The very idea of interviewing a therapist may bring up feelings of unworthiness, inadequacy, embarrassment, discomfort, and shame. For some it will bring up terror.

As hard as it may be to interview a therapist, it is an important part of ensuring you get the help you need. Therapy for survivors is a long, intensive, and usually expensive investment. Most people wouldn't buy a car without test driving it first. Choosing a therapist deserves at least as much care.

I met a lot of people who claimed to be good therapists and claimed to have all the answers. I was interviewing up to two and three of them a week, and I was able to talk to them one on one as equals and say, "We need to strike a deal here—do we have what it takes?" I didn't feel inferior at all, and that's something I don't think I could have done if I hadn't felt pretty good about myself coming out of the treatment center. I learned that I had a right to good therapy, and I had a right to choose someone I was comfortable with, and that I had sense enough to know what was good therapy. And so I can sit there now, toe to toe with a therapist, talk issues, talk needs, and I can judge for myself. I can stand back and say, "Well, he looks like a boob." Because normally I would not have done that. I would have thought, I'm the bozo, and he's probably right. And it was really neat. Even when I had a phenomenally bad conversation with one therapist, I felt good. I was able to tell myself, "This is a bad therapist. This person needs help. I'm not wasting my money here," and hang up the phone. And it also really helped to have a friend who supported me and didn't look up to therapists as gods. I would recommend it to other

survivors. If they're not feeling really strong in where they're at and their ability to evaluate, find a friend that will support you and say, "You have a right to feel the way you feel. You are interviewing them, not the other way around. You know what you need more than anybody else does." It doesn't matter how many degrees they have, it doesn't matter how much experience they have. If it's not right for you, if you listen to yourself, you'll know.   Sunny

The good news is that if you're interviewing the right therapist you will probably leave the interview feeling positive, hopeful, and good about yourself, even if some difficult material is discussed.

I called this woman. In our initial phone conversation I started crying because she picked up some amazing things right away. I told her I was going to school, and somehow she made the leap that perhaps I was pushing myself too hard and expecting too much of myself. I started crying at her sensitivity and the way she picked up on that. She said a couple of other things that almost frightened me, she was so perceptive. She was very sweet and supportive, so it wasn't like any feeling that there was something wrong with me. In fact, it was the opposite. It was like this total acceptance and nurturing and understanding.   Bea

If you do not feel comfortable screening a therapist on your own, consider asking a support friend to accompany you. If the therapist objects or makes you feel uncomfortable for wanting to research the relationship, then you've got the information you need. She or he is not the right therapist for you. The right therapist will welcome and encourage your questions. They will also encourage you to take care of your safety and comfort needs. Remember, you are interviewing them. You are not obliged to answer any questions that don't feel comfortable.

Once you're ready to proceed, don't feel you have to follow a prepared script. You may start with a number of questions but soon find the interview takes on a life and course of its own. You will get the best answers from open-ended questions, which require more elaborate answers. You will get minimum information from closed questions, which require a yes/no answer.

While asking the right questions can give you a lot of information, remember to pay attention to your other sources of intelligence—feelings and intuition. Remember to check with yourself. If something doesn't feel right, don't do it. Your inner wisdom is always your best guide.

A lot of people have ideas about how to interview a therapist. But I just go by my gut level. I could certainly ask all the right questions, but that's not what really matters to me.   Bea

QUESTIONS TO ASK

Following are four lists of questions that have worked for other survivors. They address areas of professional qualifications, style/compatibility, your own protection, and special needs.

In order to streamline your search, you may consider asking most of the professional qualifications questions by phone. When you connect by phone with a potential therapist, ask if they are willing to answer some questions immediately or at a more convenient time. When you have one or several promising leads, you can screen for the remaining areas in person.

A good idea to is to prioritize both types of questions (by phone and in person) in order of importance to you. This ensures that your key questions are answered in case the conversation needs to be cut short. It also means that you don't have to pay for an hour-long interview only to learn that your most important needs cannot be met.

PROFESSIONAL QUALIFICATIONS

1. What are your areas of expertise? (Look for at least one of the following: post-traumatic fear (or stress), dissociative disabilities (dissociative experience), multiple personality (dissociative identity), inner children, sexual trauma or incest, programming/deprogramming.)
2. What are your professional credentials or licensing affiliation? (Initially you may just want to make of note of this. If you decide to see this therapist in person, you may want to ask what the credentials mean.)
3. Do you have experience treating adult survivors of extreme childhood abuse? (Look for an affirmative answer. If the answer is no but this is a therapist with whom you're particularly interested in working, ask if she/he is willing to learn about the issues and treatment involved.)

I'd had a lot of encouragement from people in my support system to get someone who had experience with ritual survivors. But my feeling is that beginners can do wonderful things. As a beginner in certain areas I have done wonderful things. I knew [a certain therapist] was good with incest survivors, but I didn't know if she could do ritual, and she's been fine. I was her first one. I took tons of articles in to her which she copied and read. At one point she told me I'd given her a gift in being her first, not only because of the articles but just the way I approached working with her—giving her time to adjust and making sure that she was ready to hear my stuff before I told her something graphic. But she had solid skills already; she researched and networked on her own as well and I think I made the right choice for myself. Jeanne

4. How many trauma survivors are you treating or have you treated that fall into the above category? (It usually takes three to four clients to achieve a basic level of experience.)
5. What types of abuse have your clients had?
6. How successful is treatment with these clients? (Proper treatment yields good progress and good long-term results.)
7. How long does treatment usually last for these clients? (Be careful in evaluating this response. Length of treatment can vary tremendously depending on many different factors. However, view any claims to quick or "total" cures with skepticism.)
8. What place do the original traumatic event(s) have in the recovery process? (The trauma is the central event. Everything else comes from the trauma. Look for someone who is able to go into the past with you. The therapist should understand the impact trauma has on a developing child. Look for a therapist who will explain and normalize the experience for you.)
9. What is your course of treatment for adult survivors? (Many therapists say they can work with survivors of ritual, or other traumatic childhood abuse, but in fact are not qualified to do so. Therapists must be skilled in recognizing dissociative identity and dissociative states. Treatment means accessing and integrating repressed traumatic experiences. Therapists who look only at present-day problems may offer some skills to help survivors cope. However, this generally proves to be a short-term solution. Looking at and integrating life events impacting the original trauma provides positive and permanent results.)

10. What do you know about ritual abuse?

It's abusive for a therapist to treat a ritual abuse survivor when they don't know how it works. I was abused by a therapist who traumatized my inner people. They were surfacing memories and he just left me hanging there. That damaged a lot of trust and so it's taking me a long time to build a relationship with a new therapist. Matthew

STYLE/COMPATIBILITY

1. What experience do you have working with trauma survivors?
2. What steps would you take to educate yourself in areas that would be helpful to our work? (Treatment of survivors of sadistic/ritual abuse is a new area. Look for a therapist who will stay abreast of ongoing developments.)
3. Do you believe that survivor experiences are genuine?

There's a lot of information out there, and there's a lot of disinformation out there. Most therapists are not doing memory work. Some don't believe that these memories are real. Some are being told by "experts" in the field that this stuff is not real, but that you have to act like you believe it, because you are a therapist. Bea

Being believed is essential for recovery. Look for a therapist who understands that trauma survivors have difficulty believing their own experiences, and who will help you to believe yourself. Avoid therapists who seem uncertain or insincere or who outright doubt survivor experiences.
4. What are your fees? (If you cannot afford the cost but like the therapist, ask about other financial arrangements.)
5. How do you feel about adult survivors partici-

pating in group therapy or support groups? (Look for an encouraging response. Group therapy and support are appropriate and even essential at points during recovery.)

6. How do you feel about survivors reading literature about recovery and attending topical conferences or workshops? (Look for a positive reply. The point of recovery is to empower you to do your own healing. This means encouraging you to educate yourself and grow in every way possible.)

7. How would you handle a situation where you need to get help in dealing with a client? (Solid therapeutic practice involves ongoing consultation. Your therapist should have a supervisor, especially if they are just learning about issues that affect survivors of ritual abuse.)

8. What do you do to take care of your needs? (Survivors have developed dissociative abilities to protect them from the trauma. However, a nonsurvivor therapist can easily be traumatized during client sessions. It is the therapist's responsibility to have support systems in place to prevent being overwhelmed. This will allow her/him to give you her/his full presence and support.)

One of the questions I asked in my initial interview was, "What can I depend on you for?" I was really impressed with [the therapist's] answers. She said, "You can depend on me to get help if I need it, to process my own issues, and take care of myself." So that was really important.   Susan

9. Are you a survivor of childhood abuse or trauma? If so, what recovery work have you done? (Some therapists may feel awkward answering this question. It is inappropriate for a therapist to share current issues or personal problems with a client. However, it is both appropriate and helpful for a therapist to share a past, resolved issue relevant to the area of treatment. This helps to build credibility and confidence in the therapist. Survivor-therapists can be very effective, provided they, too, have ongoing supervision.)

10. Is it okay to cry or shout in your office? (Your therapy may involve processing intense experiences and emotions. Some therapy offices are formal and elegant. Some offices are not well insulated for sound. These may inhibit your ability to process. If the office doesn't feel comfortable, ask if there is alternative space for the work or if the present space can be accommodated to your needs.)

11. Is there a place for me to unwind if I'm not ready to travel immediately after our session? (Therapists working with survivors often have an extra room for this purpose.)

12. When are you available to see patients? Are you available outside of business hours? How long are your sessions? How frequently do you see survivor patients? How flexible are you in accommodating special needs? (Look for a therapist who is flexible, especially initially. Sessions with trauma survivors often need to be from two to four hours long. This allows time for difficult material to emerge and be properly processed. Initial therapy may bring up many issues simultaneously and so may require several visits a week. Experienced therapists understand and accommodate these needs.)

13. How do you handle emergencies? (Look for a therapist who is familiar with handling suicide and self-injury. Look for someone who is reasonably available and understands the need for having proper procedures in place. This may include giving you a home phone number or a beeper for access in case of an emergency.)

14. Have you ever had to hospitalize a client? (Hospitalization should be a last resort, such as in cases where you are in danger of hurting yourself or others.)
15. What is your policy about confidentiality? (Your confidentiality should be protected 100 percent. This means that if the therapist consults about your case, your name is never mentioned. Your history is not discussed with other survivors or with your family members. If confidentiality is broken for emergency reasons, you should be told what information has been given out and to whom.)
16. Do you have any plans to travel or be absent for an extended period of time over the next several years? (Most survivors benefit from a stable, uninterrupted relationship during recovery. Burnout is sometimes an issue among therapists working with severely traumatized clients. Look for a therapist who will be there for the long term.)
17. How would you handle termination if for any reason you were unable to continue treatment with me? (Look for a thoughtful, caring approach that takes into account transition issues. Ideally the therapist will assist in finding an appropriate new therapist.)
18. If for any reason a problem develops in our relationship, how would you handle it? (Look for a therapist who welcomes open communication and partnership-based problem resolution, or mediation.)
19. What are your religious/spiritual beliefs? (This is a sensitive issue, as survivors typically suffered religious and spiritual abuse. A therapist should never impose religious views on a client. However, a therapist should help survivors get in touch with their own spirituality. For more on this issue, see Chapter 22.)

I have concerns about spirituality. There are a lot of people who are involved in "new age spirituality," which may be another form of cult activity. I would ask about a therapist's spirituality—their idea of what it is and how it plays into the healing process. Susan

20. Do you follow any particular therapeutic schools of thought? [Avoid therapists who use the formula approach. Therapists who categorize symptoms to fit a formula often misinterpret a survivor's experience. For example, a therapist following Jung may misinterpret an emerging violent alter personality as a "shadow" aspect of a client. Some therapists may interpret dreams pointing to actual experiences as symbolic imagery. Therapists following Freudian psychoanalysis may interpret incest as an Oedipus complex. (The Oedipal theory sees a child as the seducer of the parent or adult. The child is NEVER the seducer; nor is the child EVER to blame.) Look for a nonlabeling, nonformula-oriented therapist. The best results come from a combination of therapies, and therapists who are open and flexible to various tools.]
21. What area have you selected for continuing education? What were the topics of your last courses? (Some therapists are required to take accredited courses on an ongoing basis. This is part of their licensing requirement. This is not a requirement for nonlicensed practitioners, pastors, or certain kinds of counselors. The topic of latest courses and workshops can give you an indication of a therapist's interest in trauma and abuse-related issues.)
22. Can you give me the names of two or three people who have worked with you and would be willing to offer references? (This

may not be possible due to confidentiality issues. If a therapist cannot provide ex-patient references, they may be able to provide references from colleagues or other sources.)

Remember that you're unlikely to find a therapist who meets your wish list. There will be tradeoffs, and you need to decide which ones are okay and which ones aren't.

FOR YOUR PROTECTION

Some survivors are under the mistaken impression that people in the helping professions would not abuse their position. As in all walks of life, there are abusive therapists, or therapists with poor skills. It is not always possible to catch these potentially abusive therapists in an initial interview. However, asking the questions may sometimes alert you to a potential problem. It can also alert the therapist that you are a knowledgeable client who will not tolerate improper treatment.

1. Are there any circumstances in which child/adult sex is acceptable? (The answer is NO! Child/adult sex is ALWAYS damaging to the child.)
2. Are there circumstances in which client/therapist sex is beneficial? (The answer is NO! It is ALWAYS damaging to the client.)
3. Are there circumstances in which it is beneficial to comfort a client physically? (There are circumstances when physical comforting is appropriate and healing. However, it can also lead to inappropriate physical contact.)

SPECIAL NEEDS

The above questions cover general criteria of particular relevance to survivors of childhood trauma. You may have special needs that are important to you. Listed here are some possibilities you may want to consider. Acknowledge and prioritize your special needs in choosing a therapist.

1. Is it important that I work with either a female or a male therapist? (It may be important to work with both a male and a female therapist over the course of your recovery. This may help you resolve gender issues.)
2. Is it important that my therapist share my religious values and beliefs? (For a discussion of spirituality, religion, and the supernatural as issues in recovery from ritual abuse, see Chapter 22.)
3. Do I need a therapist familiar with my cultural background?
4. Do I need a lesbian/gay therapist or someone familiar with lesbian/gay issues?
5. Do I prefer a therapist experienced in certain therapeutic approaches (for example, dream work, hypnosis, meditation, art therapy, writing)?

We have the creativity and the integrity inside us to know what we need to heal. And for each of us that will be a little bit different. You need to follow that inner intuition and not be put down by a therapist who can't handle it. Find someone who can handle it. Be as creative as you can and go for it. I think that's so important, because therapists have the idea that you sit and talk to them for one hour a week, and this is how you heal. For me that really isn't enough. So survivors need to trust what they feel and what they want, and know that they're not bad for wanting something different than what the traditional therapeutic community says is the right way to do therapy. Joan

EVALUATING THE INTERVIEW

Survivors usually have good antennae, or instincts about people. However, abuse forced survivors to shut down or ignore their intuition. Now is the time to reverse the pattern. Your intuition is your inner wisdom and protection. Trust and follow it. Your best guide is your overall feeling. However, sometimes specific questions can help you to pinpoint your response. Below are some questions you can use as a guide in determining your overall impression.

POST-INTERVIEW IMPRESSIONS

- Did the office feel comfortable? pleasant? safe?
- Did I feel safe with her or him?
- Did I feel I could develop trust with this person?
- Did I leave feeling positive and hopeful?
- Did I feel accepted and supported?
- Did I feel heard, listened to, and understood?
- Did I feel believed?
- Does this person see me as capable and worthy of respect?
- Do my inner children/parts feel comfortable with this person?
- Did the therapist seem fearful and uneasy?
- Did the therapist seem centered? Was she or he able to maintain eye contact?
- Can this person help me take the risks I'll need to take while honoring my safety needs?
- Will this person be flexible in meeting my needs?

GETTING PAST THE ROADBLOCKS

Many survivors run into roadblocks that prevent them from getting the help they deserve. Following are some common roadblocks to therapy and suggested solutions.

I CAN'T FIND A GOOD THERAPIST

If you cannot find therapists locally who have the right background to assist you, it may mean making some difficult choices. I know of survivors who have moved thousands of miles to find the right help. One survivor commutes nearly 600 miles round-trip to work with a qualified therapist.

Some areas have more qualified therapists than others. If you have not been able to find a knowledgeable therapist, you might consider long-distance therapy via phone with a qualified professional. This is not ideal for everyone but can work well, especially for survivors who have already done some amount of healing. It was through working long-distance with a highly skilled therapist that Susan discovered she was a survivor of ritual abuse.

I was in therapy [with a man] for a couple of years. One evening I had gotten about three pages of very violent physical and sexual abuse [memories] about what my mother had done to me as a child. I woke up next morning and I said, "I need to talk to a woman about this. And if I could talk to anybody in the world about this, who would that be?" And this therapist in Dallas came to mind. I had been listening to her tapes on healing and really liked what she said. So I dialed her number and made an appointment to talk to her. That was in August or September of 1988. And even though I didn't know why I wanted to talk to her, I started talking to her once a month. My appointments were only one hour long because she was very expensive and I was very poor. It was winter solstice and I called her and I said, "You know, this is the winter solstice and you can look at it in either one of two ways—as either the longest night or the shortest day. In my case it's the longest night." And in that session she asked me if I suspected ritual abuse in my history, and I said no. I hung up the phone and totally lost it.   Susan

Discovering her ritual abuse history allowed Susan to finally find the help she needed to begin a slow but steady course toward recovery. To this day Susan has never met her long-distance therapist, who was pivotal to her recovery.

If possible, try to screen potential long-distance therapists in person. Begin in-person sessions with the selected therapist. Try to have as many sessions as possible before returning to your area. Daily sessions can work very well. Continue your sessions by phone on a regularly scheduled basis. You may also be able to alternate in-person and phone sessions.

I CAN'T AFFORD THERAPY

It is worth investing in good therapy. Some therapists are willing to offer special financial arrangements for survivors who cannot afford regular payments. Some offer an adjusted "sliding" scale of fees. Check with your insurance company. They may provide full or partial coverage for certain types of therapy. However, keep in mind that free therapy may create an indebtedness and negatively affect the therapeutic relationship.

Check out all available funding in your area. Look in the Resource Guide; these same sources may know of financial assistance programs in your area. You may qualify for financial assistance or free counseling through government or other specially funded programs. Teaching hos-

pitals and university mental health clinics sometimes offer excellent services at minimal cost. Some church-affiliated programs are offered at no charge or at a nominal fee. Some rape crisis shelters may offer no-charge counseling for a limited time period or low-cost counseling for an extended period. You may be able to connect with a qualified, reasonably priced therapist through organizations such as these.

If you are filling out an application for financial assistance make a point of asking what criteria are used to determine qualification for funds. That way you are sure to include the key information. If your claim is rejected, you are generally better off to appeal it than to reapply. Chances of coverage may also be increased if the application is submitted by a physician or therapist.

The sooner you get good help, the sooner you can sustain regular employment and be able to pay your financial obligations. It is an investment in yourself. Most survivors cannot afford NOT to have good therapy.

I CAN'T FIND A THERAPIST I CAN TRUST

This is a common problem for survivors of sadistic/ritual abuse. The abuse affected our ability to trust, to seek help, and to believe that anyone really has our interest at heart. Some survivors have felt misunderstood or abandoned by previous therapists. Some survivors have been abused in therapy. Some survivors were abused by therapists who were members of their cult. As a result, they distrust and avoid therapists altogether.

One of my perpetrators was a therapist, when I was little. He was very abusive and I had no memories of it until a short time ago. And it's really hard for me to find a therapist. I'm about to start with my fifth therapist in four years. Part of it is just because therapy requires trust, and survivors in general have problems with trust. But I think it's also because I was abused by a therapist. Sometimes I feel trapped just being in a therapist's room with the door closed.   Deborah

Because of repeated betrayal, survivors sometimes begin therapy expecting to be let down or hurt. An unconscious part of us may be looking for betrayal. This is an understandable protective mechanism, but it isn't helpful to recovery. Whenever a problem occurs, it is our responsibility to look to both the therapist and ourselves as a possible source. Asking yourself some of the following questions may help to pinpoint the problem (some questions presume familiarity with the therapist):

- If the therapist felt safe and trustworthy initially, what has changed?
- Am I interpreting the therapist's remarks correctly?
- Am I being realistic in my expectations of what good therapy entails?
- Am I leaving a problem unaddressed, and so increasing chances of failure?
- Do I have a history of failed therapy relationships? Is it with therapists that initially met my key criteria?
- What specifically am I afraid of?
- Is my fear based on a past experience? What was that experience?
- Am I able to discuss my fears directly with my therapist? If not, can I discuss my problem with a support friend?
- Can I strategize with my support friend on what to tell my therapist?
- Would it help to rehearse or write out what I need to say?

You may find that your therapist did breach your trust. Use this as an opportunity to empower yourself. Take care of your needs. You may bring up the problem, and if your therapist acknowledges it and addresses it, you can move on from there. If the issue isn't being satisfactorily addressed, you may need to find a new therapist. On the other hand, you may find that the problem stemmed from a past, unresolved experience—an instance of the abuse getting in the way of recovery. Use this as an opportunity to learn how your system reacts to sabotage your progress. Work with your therapist to remove another roadblock to recovery.

Our trust was betrayed repeatedly and in many different ways. Trust may emerge as an issue more than once. The important thing is to keep paying attention to the dynamics of what is happening. Has trust been breached, or is the abuse getting in the way of recovery? The better you learn your own behavior patterns, the sooner you will be able to overcome those that have worked against you in the past.

As a note of caution, the opposite problem is also common. Some survivors shut down their feelings and, instead of using critical judgment, simply trust therapists unreservedly. While these survivors may not have a problem finding a therapist, they may, instead, stay with an incompetent or abusive therapist instead of protecting their own interests. These survivors may rationalize incompetence or abuse by making excuses for the therapist.

If you suspect that either problem is interfering with your therapy, it's an opportunity to empower yourself to address it. It may not come easily. Breaking lifelong perceptions rarely happens automatically. However, recognizing counterproductive patterns is the first step in changing them.

MY THERAPIST IS ALSO TREATING MEMBERS OF MY FAMILY

If you have family members seeking therapy as well, it is best for each member of the family to use a different therapist. (This, of course, does not include marriage counseling or family therapy.) You deserve to have the complete devotion and loyalty of your therapist. Having other family members in individual counseling with your therapist may require split loyalties of her or him.

EVALUATING THERAPY

Once you have decided on a therapist, it is important to evaluate your progress from time to time. One of the most common early problems for survivors is determining if therapy is producing any results.

Healing is a long-term process. It takes considerable time and patience to work through each issue. Until trust is established, little real progress can occur. However, trust does not happen in an on/off pattern but is slowly built up over time. For all of these reasons, it may be difficult to know if you've made the right choice in a therapist. Here are some guidelines:

Trust your intuition and instincts. If it feels all wrong, leave. Do not waste a lot of time and money confirming your gut feelings. If you're on the right track, you will generally get a sense that something is working.

There's still a lot of conditioning and some stuff that I'm carrying around in terms of self-hatred and suicidal stuff, but there was definitely something that lifted from me. That was our first session. And it was gone from that point on. I'm talking immediate relief, immediate growth. And every session after that was similar in some way. Something very serious or big would happen.   Bea

When I went to therapy before, it would be like, "Oh, here we go again . . . I get to talk about myself." But now it feels totally different. It's just intense pain. But it feels like it's going for the cure. Before it didn't feel like I was going for the cure. A survivor

If some things seem right and not others, the decision is less clear-cut. You may be feeling uncomfortable because the chemistry isn't right or because the therapist is touching on some painful but important issues. Open communication is critical, especially in the early, evaluatory phase. Communicate your needs to your therapist. Express any concerns that come up. Check out your perceptions with your therapist. See if you're reading the situation the same way. Sometimes our abuse incorrectly influences our assumptions.

If you have reviewed the above and still are not certain, try the "eight" rule of thumb. After eight weeks, or eight sessions (whichever comes first), you should have experienced some positive developments. If nothing encouraging has occurred, consider looking for a different therapist.

SIGNS OF PROGRESS

If you are working with the right therapist over the long term, you should be able to identify specific milestones and improvement. Dr. Cliff Morgan suggests survivors can monitor some of the following signs of progress:

- You are able to focus on treatment
- You begin to feel increasingly safe
- You are able to establish health/safety rules and limits and follow them
- Your suicidal and self-injuring impulses are decreasing

- You gain control of your addictions
- You no longer use avoiding or distracting behaviors as a means of coping
- Your amnesia barrier is breaking down
- You continue to access memories
- You continue to access new alters and split-off parts
- You no longer dissociate as a way of coping with trauma or stress
- Your symptoms such as nightmares, panic attacks, flashbacks, and various physical problems begin to subside
- There is increased communication among your inner children
- There is increased cooperation among your inner children
- You are reenacting your abuse less often
- Your depression begins to lift
- You no longer feel overwhelmed by the past
- You gain an awareness of your and others' boundaries
- You are able to distinguish between the past and the present
- You are able to parent your inner children

While this list is by no means exhaustive, it is a good starting point from which to monitor your progress. For a another indication, write down your list of problems and check off the ones that improve with therapy.

THINGS SEEM TO BE AT A STANDSTILL

There are times in therapy when nothing new seems to be happening. Your subconscious may be taking a break to consolidate a lot of new information. The plateau can last a number of weeks and sometimes even a month or two. However, just as students outgrow teachers, so survivors may outgrow a therapist. Therapists have skills in different areas. It is rare to find a therapist who can offer the entire range of skills needed to help survivors of sadistic/ritual abuse through every aspect of their healing. Initially, you may simply need a solid, sturdy therapist to help you stabilize and acquire some basic life skills. Many survivors are so grateful there is someone who gives them undivided attention that they may develop loyalty to a therapist who is simply there for them. But you need more than that to make progress in recovery. Once you are strong enough, you may need to move on to retrieving and processing repressed experiences. Let your therapist know if you feel stuck or ready to tackle new material. If things continue at a standstill, don't be afraid to try different therapists, but be sure you're not changing to avoid new but possibly difficult breakthroughs.

Even if you are working with the right therapist and making good progress, there may be issues preventing optimal results. You may want to monitor the following:

1. Do I feel safe to share everything with this therapist? Do my inner children or inner selves feel safe? (Safety and trust develop over time. However, monitor your progress to ensure that safety and trust continue to grow.)
2. Does this therapist model good boundaries? (Therapists should show awareness of and respect for your rights. They should respect your values and never impose their own views on you. They should discuss and ask permission to try new approaches, especially if these techniques are unfamiliar or feel threatening or invasive to you.)

My therapist wanted to do trance work. I can't close my eyes, because I see all these flashes from the past. So he tranced me with my eyes open, and a lot of inner kids felt he broke trust because he didn't ask permission to do that.   Matthew

3. If a problem develops, can I discuss it with this therapist? (If no, why not? Is it because the therapist will be displeased? Or is it because bringing up negative subjects with authority figures is painful and frightening for me?)

4. Is the therapy centered on me and on my healing? (Some therapists are distracted by the novelty of ritual abuse, especially if they have not previously dealt with ritual abuse clients. They may be overly eager to get into details that are not important to you. Some get caught up in playing lawyer, judge, and jury. They may become zealous in pursuit of "justice." Others may get fascinated with your experience. They may suggest you and they should write a book. Still others may suggest you confront or sue your perpetrators. These examples detract from the real focus: your experience. The entire focus should be on YOUR needs and YOUR healing. Suggestions about seeking justice, confronting and suing, fact-finding, or writing a book may come from you—not from your therapist.)

5. Do I feel that I must act a certain way or say certain things, and that otherwise I may be abandoned by my therapist? Do I feel I have to be a perfect client? (Therapy is not about pleasing anyone. If you feel you need to "perform," discuss it with your therapist.)

This time I've made a commitment not to do the work to please anyone. I'm going very slowly, honoring my own needs and the needs of all my inner kids. Matthew

6. How do I usually feel after my therapy sessions? (There will be times when you leave therapy in pain and bewilderment. But along with the pain, you should feel that there is progress and hope. You should feel you are learning and growing as a person.)

One survivor summarized good therapy and good therapists as follows:

It is possible to go to someone who doesn't know a lot about ritual abuse and who maybe doesn't know what to do about your memories. But they have to, number one, totally support you emotionally, and number two, be willing to hear your pain. Bea

IDENTIFYING PROBLEMS EARLY ON

Survivors have accumulated a high level of tolerance for unhealthy behaviors. As children, we had no power or support. We learned how to tolerate abuse. In time we failed to recognize it as abuse. Sometimes, even if we knew we were being mistreated, we made excuses for the perpetrator. These early experiences set us up as targets for further abuse.

Recovery means recognizing problem signals early. It is important to act immediately to remove ourselves from unhealthy situations. Listed below are some signs to monitor.

- Your therapist labels you when you disagree with him or her. (Does your therapist use words such as addict? hysteric? masochist? borderline? multiple? Labeling is useful and helpful when it explains your condition to you and helps to normalize your experience. However, it can also be used in damaging ways to put you down, control you, or take away your power.)
- Your therapist minimizes or rationalizes the abuse.
- Your therapist breaks appointments, arrives late, allows interruptions.
- Your therapist sets her/himself up as your savior, implying that only she or he can help you or that you won't make it without her or him.

- Your therapist suggests socializing—meeting outside office premises.

MY THERAPIST MUST BE PERFECT

Trauma influences relationships, particularly those with authority figures. In *Trauma and Recovery,* Dr. Judith L. Herman writes:

> The geater the patient's emotional conviction of helplessness and abandonment, the more desperately she feels the need for an omnipotent rescuer. Often she casts the therapist in that role. She may develop intensely idealized expectations of the therapist. The idealization of the therapist protects the patient, in fantasy, against reliving the terror of the trauma. In one successful case, both patient and therapist came to understand the terror at the source of the patient's demand for rescue: "The therapist remarked, 'It's frightening to need someone so much and not be able to control them.' The patient was moved and continued this thought: 'It's frightening because you can kill me with what you say . . . or by not caring or [by] leaving.' The therapist then added, 'We can see why you need me to be perfect.' " When the therapist fails to live up to these idealized expectations—as she inevitably will fail—the patient is often overcome with fury. Because the patient feels as though her life depends upon her rescuer, she cannot afford to be tolerant; there is no room for human error.

If relationship problems develop between you and your therapist, it's important to be aware of this possible source. However, it is your therapist's responsibility to recognize it and handle it.

Some unethical therapists may take advantage of survivors who are prone to idealize authority figures. These therapists may encourage dependency on themselves instead of working toward your self-reliance. It may be tempting to give over power to a caring therapist, but it runs counter to your recovery.

SEXUAL IMPROPRIETY

Although there are no data on the incidence of sexual abuse of survivors by therapists, a study by Dr. Patrick Carnes, a specialist in the treatment of sexual addiction, found that two-thirds of women suffering from sexual addiction were seduced by their therapists.

If your therapist ever makes any sexual overtures, asks if you fantasize about her or him, suggests a romantic relationship, encourages using drugs to reduce your inhibitions, or recommends nudity or sexual contact of any kind, terminate the relationship immediately. A therapist suggesting sex to her or his client is in need of therapy and should not be treating you. Report the action to the appropriate regulatory agency (see the Resource Guide).

This is a serious breach of trust. The imbalance of power between a therapist and a patient is similar to that between an authority adult and a child. Clients who have engaged in sexual activity with their therapists suffer effects similar to that reported by incest victims. It is severely damaging and can have long-term effects. What's worse, it often prevents survivors from being able to seek help through therapy again.

If your therapist hasn't made overt suggestions but you experience feelings of uneasiness for whatever reason, honor that. Look for ways to address your feelings. If you cannot discuss them directly with your therapist, try the ideas listed below under "Handling Problems." If you remain dissatisfied, look for another therapist.

Survivors have often been conditioned to

equate sex with power, affection, love, and other basic needs. It is not unusual for survivors to reenact their associations in the course of therapy. Even if the survivor suggests sexual involvement, it is the therapist's responsibility to prevent it. This applies equally to heterosexual and gay/lesbian therapists. The therapist's job is to recognize and treat sexual symptoms, not be a party to them. For survivors to reclaim self-esteem, they need to experience love without sex. They need to know that they are lovable for who they are, not for what they can offer to someone else. As survivors reclaim self-esteem and feelings of autonomy through healthy treatment, they will appreciate that the therapist did not take advantage of their suggestion and betray their vulnerability.

PHYSICAL COMFORTING

The issue of physical comforting often creates confusion. Many survivors benefit by physical comforting that was denied them as children. However, the therapist should always ask permission first. It is equally important that you exercise your personal power to say no if it doesn't feel right to you. It should feel comfortable to BOTH the therapist and the client. There are many fine therapists who do not give hugs or physical comforting. It should be ONLY for the benefit of the client. (You should feel as if you are *receiving* a hug, not that a hug has been *taken from you*.) It is never appropriate for the client to comfort the therapist, although it's okay for you to give your therapist a return hug. The therapist is responsible for taking care of her or his own emotional needs. It is NEVER your responsibility to take care of your therapist.

I know of therapists who dump on clients and get their problems into the session. And the client goes away feeling, "Oh, my poor therapist. She's having such a hard time. I really shouldn't bother her. I shouldn't tell her this stuff, or maybe I should censor it." Bea

HANDLING PROBLEMS

It is often difficult, if not impossible, for survivors to challenge a problem head-on. This is especially true with an authority figure. As children, we were systematically and severely punished for objecting to abuse. If you are having a problem in therapy, you need to find a way to discuss it openly with your therapist. Your therapist deserves to hear about it from you, not from a third-party source. This way, she or he has a chance to address it. If you are unable to do so yet, try some intermediary steps.

Discuss your problem in confidence with your support friends. Work out a strategy together. If you are frightened to implement the strategy yourself, see if your support friends are willing to speak on your behalf. However, this is only an intermediary solution. Recovery means being able to speak for yourself.

One day I walked out of therapy feeling totally angry, frustrated, and discouraged. I felt as though my therapist only ever addressed my adult self and completely ignored my inner kids. And there was this one session in particular where it was they who were talking to him, and they needed to be reassured. But instead, he gave me a logical adult reply, which didn't feel good at all. And I didn't know how to tell him or what to do. So I journaled. I let my inner kids say everything they wanted to tell him. Next session I read him their letter, and he apologized. I finally was able to get through to him. Erik

You may find it easier to put the problem down in writing. Give the written note to your therapist, or read the problem aloud to her or him. If you are uncertain about how your therapy is being handled, you might want to call another therapist or your therapist's surpervisor. She or he may help you clarify your concerns and suggest ways to bring up the matter. Your therapist should welcome and encourage you to express concerns, including negative thoughts you have about her or him. Therapists should not be offended by criticism. They should never shame you. They should show you that it is safe to talk about your problems and needs. They should help you communicate them in a constructive manner. They should respond to your concerns.

If the problem concerns sexual misconduct or breach of ethics and it is being reviewed by a board or third-party source, you should wait until the matter is settled before talking about it openly. You may, of course, discuss it while working through your pain with another therapist or your support friends. However, in fairness, these discussions should be in confidence until a proper review has been completed (see the Resource Guide for advocate agencies).

Expressing your concerns should always be a healthy growth experience. This doesn't mean that your problem will always be solved. But it should mean that when the discussion is over, you feel good about yourself, and reassured that you did the right thing.

Remember that therapists are human beings. We all make mistakes. When appropriate, survivors should recognize and accept honest errors. This should only happen AFTER discussing the problem with your therapist and being satisfied the problem has been addressed. Getting through roadblocks together can be a therapeutic growth experience.

She's human. She makes mistakes. I've confronted her and we've gotten through it. It's taught me a lot to be able to do that.   Jeanne

MESSAGES FOR THERAPISTS

Although most therapeutic conventions apply, a few considerations are unique to survivors of ritual abuse. Some survivors may need help in stopping injurious treatment of themselves or others. This can be a condition of therapy. It may be mutually helpful to reinforce the agreement with a written contract. In some cases written contracts are effective, in others, they're not.

Survivors need a lot of encouragement and permission—to remember, to have feelings, to say no. There are many things normal people take for granted that survivors need to be taught from scratch. Areas that need to be addressed are outlined in Chapter 6.

Many survivors don't have an inner sense of what normal is. After years in therapy, one survivor realized, "I have a skin. It separates me from others in the world. I don't have to take everyone in." No matter how intelligent, accomplished, and self-assured a survivor may appear on the surface, she or he invariably is hiding and protecting a lot of confusion and frightened inner children. These inner children need a loving role model and consistent parent. Maybe we expect to be let down, but maybe you can surprise us with honesty, dependability, trust, loyalty, and unconditional support, which our child never got. Firmness is okay as long as it comes with love. Here's what one therapist repeatedly tells survivor clients:

You know, from time to time I will probably say or do things that will either irritate you or frankly piss you off, not because I mean to but because that just happens between people in all relationships. I really need to hear from you when I step on your toes or hurt your feelings or even if something I do or say scares you. It's okay with me if you get mad at me. I won't get mad back. I won't hurt you or leave you if you get mad at me or tell me, "No!" Sometimes just from seeing the look on your face or the way you're sitting, I can tell you're having strong feelings, but I will still want you to say what you feel and what you think. It's safe to do that here.

If a survivor is beginning to remember ritual abuse and you are not able or willing to work with them, please don't abandon them in a panic, shame them, or make them feel bad. Let them down gently or, better yet, help them find someone who can work with them.

Nobody ever looked at us, trusted us, or believed us. We were told we were melodramatic and that we were liars. We were hurt many times for telling "lies." We don't want to be hurt anymore. Sophia

I know you may get ridiculed for believing us, but please follow your heart in this matter. If you believe me, I feel like I matter, like you're there with me holding my hand, going through this with me. If you leave it up to me to discover what is true, I feel like you've let go of my hand, saying, "I want you to get well, but you're on your own here." I've been on my own all my life. If you don't believe me, please encourage me to leave and find somebody who can.   Janes

Don't tell me, "I can't believe it until you believe it." The fact is I don't know how to believe myself. I was doubted from the moment of birth.

What I need from you more than anything else is to learn how to believe myself—something I understand most people take for granted.   Erik

A FINAL THOUGHT

As pioneers in the healing journey, both survivors and therapists are experiencing growing pains. We are all learning, making headway, experiencing setbacks, and making new discoveries together. Both parties share responsibility for the success or failure of therapy.

THERAPIST RESPONSIBILITIES

Therapists provide the environment and techniques to advance your recovery and are responsible for keeping your best interest at heart at all times. This means being honest about their background, experience, and professional credentials; educating themselves on issues relevant to your recovery; and seeking help and consultation when necessary. If they feel they cannot help you or handle the emotional pain, it is their responsibility to tell you.

SURVIVOR RESPONSIBILITIES

You are responsible for your own recovery. It is your responsibility to monitor progress in therapy, to ensure that you are receiving good help. It is your responsibility to communicate your needs and wishes to your therapist. Therapists cannot read your mind. They need your guidance in helping you. Taking care of yourself and getting the help you deserve is an important step in healing.

Even in the best of worlds there are problems from time to time. If you have taken reasonable steps to ensure good help and support, if you are going to therapy regularly and monitoring all the signs, if you are doing everything right and still having difficulties, try a change of pace. Let go and do nothing for a while. Taking breaks offers opportunities to gain perspective. And while you're taking a break you might want to do the following:

[I] call a friend, take a bath, write in my journal, hold my dog. Sometimes I need to space out. I watch a stupid movie on TV and I laugh. I get some trashy novel. I love espionage. I love it when the good guy beats everybody up—shoots everybody, makes it through unbelievable odds and wins and is alive at the end of the book. Those books give me so much happiness, because that's how it feels for me. It's me against the world, me against everybody. And there is a way, if I just keep trying like these guys who won't give up. They've been shot, they're down to nothing, and they find a way to get back up. Bea

This may be a good time to call friend, take a bath, hold your dog, or get a funny movie and laugh.

24

Peer Support

With each memory I always felt like, "God, nobody's had it so bad; nobody has lived through this kind of stuff. I must be the worst person in the world." One of the things that helped me accept what was done to me was finding out that I wasn't alone.   Katharine

Finding another ritual abuse survivor is a little like being deaf and finding someone who speaks sign language. For some, group support offers the deepest healing; for others, it is the main source of healing. You may not have been able to find the right therapist. You may not be able to work with a therapist because of mistrust or fear. Group support can make the difference between steady progress and losing ground in recovery.

Right now I'm feeling like I don't even want a therapist. I just want to share with other survivors

and validate each other and support each other; that does me more good.   Jane Linn

Groups offer survivors a Safe Place in which to test reality. You can begin to test perceptions, assumptions, and boundaries in a safe and supportive environment. By seeing others recover, you may be inspired to try your own first steps.

As a child you may have learned how groups can exploit your weaknesses and vulnerability. Where once a group exploited your vulnerabilities, today a group is touched by them. Today you can learn how to draw strength from a group. Groups allow us to build trust and survivor solidarity.

Just being with other people that had the same experience, that understood what I'd been through, I didn't feel so alone, so awful, so isolated. It was terri-

bly validating and I wasn't this weirdo person—the only one in the world this happened to.   Joan

At the same time, groups may bring up painful reminders of unresolved, repressed feelings. These unresolved issues are easily triggered by other survivors who've had similar experiences. A key factor in determining the success of a group depends on understanding factors that promote healing and recognizing those that foster problems. A healthy group environment may feel like this:

I now have a group which really works for me. It's small, secure; nothing bad is going to happen here. We have lots of spirituality and not a lot of structure. There's a basic assumption of goodness and a high respect for one another. We have a high willingness to work through difficulties. If there is miscommunication, we have the tools to work it out. In each meeting, everyone gets a chance to talk, and everyone can do what they need to do, and we'll stay as long as it takes. Sometimes we go for four hours. Some of the most gratifying moments happen when somebody comes in with this insurmountable problem, and everyone puts in a piece of advice and you walk out with a wealth of information and always a solution. It may not solve the whole problem, but it puts you in a good place. It's just great how together we help get one another unstuck.   Jeanne

By knowing what's healthy and recognizing what's not, you will be able to make better choices and take care of yourself. The remainder of this chapter addresses issues that promote successful interaction of survivors in groups and identifies potential problems. This includes types of groups available, formats that work, choosing a group, deciding to join, monitoring, safety, and how to start a group.

TYPES OF GROUPS

A facilitated group is guided by a therapist qualified in running group therapy. There is usually a fee for facilitated groups. For some, this is the group therapy of choice, if it is available. However, often there is no qualified available therapist. Sometimes therapists unskilled in handling survivors attempt to facilitate groups. These may be more harmful than helpful.

I was a multiple put into a group with singletons and made to feel different and ashamed. I was told things weren't working right because I wasn't working right. It turned out be their lack of knowledge all along. The therapist wasn't willing to make room and special consideration for me. So I ended up shamed and traumatized and it's taken me a long time to try group again.   Matthew

Nonfacilitated groups are not guided by a paid professional. They may rotate facilitation, have an informal leader, or share responsibility equally. There is usually no charge for nonfacilitated groups. Everyone shares in the responsibility for success. While these may take more effort, they offer a good opportunity to develop facilitating skills and build self-confidence.

Both facilitated and nonfacilitated groups may have a variety of formats. Open groups are open to any person who wishes to come, provided she or he fits the profile defined by the group. The group may or may not screen potential attendees. Members have the opportunity to meet a greater number and variety of survivors in open groups. Information shared tends to be broader in scope but not as in-depth. Regular attendance is generally not mandatory. This is both a benefit and a potential problem. Some survivors find irregular attendance disruptive. In addition, safety concerns are more likely to occur in open groups.

The first group I ever attended was an open group. Sometimes over twenty people would show. That was amazing to me—that there were so many survivors. It was like connecting with kids who grew up in the same neighborhood, but you didn't know each other then. For the first time in my life, I instantly felt I belonged! Josie

Closed groups generally have a set number of members that remains unchanged week to week. Regular attendance is usually a requirement of membership. Admission of new members is discussed and mutually agreed on by the group. Potential new members are generally screened. Closed groups usually foster closer relationships among group members. Members are more likely to discuss in-depth, sensitive issues.

Open and closed groups can be all women, all men, or mixed. Single-sex groups generally offer a higher comfort level to members. They allow men an opportunity to address issues of masculinity and gender-specific damage to their self-esteem. Women are able to work on issues of defining and embracing their feminine selves and empowering themselves and can deal freely with sexism. Mixed groups offer an opportunity to work through opposite gender issues, which most survivors need to address; they also help survivors realize ways in which we are all the same. Mixed groups work best when members are already well into recovery.

Most groups follow a format. Some are highly structured; others may be more informal. Highly structured groups generally provide a higher level of safety. Unstructured groups give more opportunity for spontaneity. As a general rule, the less experienced the group members, the greater the need for structure.

Most groups start with a check-in (introduction) of each member. Some groups limit check-into a maximum of five minutes per member.

After check-in, the facilitator generally picks members to begin more extensive processing. In nonfacilitated groups, the members may share according to their needs and the time available.

In some groups, check-in is followed by an open discussion format. Members are free to speak and exchange experiences at random. In other groups, members take turns sharing their experience about a specific topic, such as overeating, depression, anxiety, fear, relationships, isolation, intimacy, therapy, etc.

Isolation is the deadliest thing for recovery. If we go hide in the corner, who are we telling? Nobody. We can get a lot sicker staying hidden by ourselves. We need to get out there and let people know that we made it, so others will make it too. Dave

FORMATS THAT WORK

The most critical ingredient to the success of a group is following principles of sound practice. The following guidelines are some of these:

1. Have a group charter that includes a statement of purpose, format, and ground rules; ensure that each member is aware of what these are. (See the Resource Guide for organizations which can send you relevant information.)
2. Read the guidelines at the start of each group, or monthly at a minimum.
3. Ensure that each group member is in individual counseling.
4. Each member should have a clear understanding of what to expect from group.
5. Each member should understand their individual rights and responsibilities.
6. Each member should be free to leave the

group. To minimize disruption, the charter should offer guidelines on how to do so.

7. The group charter should include a procedure for handling grievances and problems.

8. Each person must agree not to injure her- or himself or others or to commit suicide while a member of the group. This may be done verbally or in writing.

9. Have the name and phone number of each member's therapist, in case the need arises.

10. Although group members may help in case of special circumstances, each group member is responsible for taking care of her or his own therapeutic and safety needs.

11. Have guidelines to address safety issues in group.

12. Everything that is discussed in group stays there. Members must be assured of total confidentiality.

13. There may be exceptions when confidentiality should be broken for safety reasons, as for example a suicide threat. Each member must be informed when and under what circumstances confidentiality may be broken.

14. When a member is absent, neither they nor their issues should be discussed by the group. There should be no gossip, either in or outside of group.

15. The group must decide with what level of processing they are comfortable. It is a good idea to initially share only present-day concerns. Reporting of repressed experiences or processing repressed experiences should generally be done in facilitated groups. The exception would be in groups where members are highly experienced in healthy group interaction and the majority have done a lot of personal recovery.

16. Do not assume you know what happened to someone else.

17. The purpose of group is to witness and vali-

date one another's experience. Members should focus on their own feelings when offering feedback; they should not judge, criticize, psychoanalyze, give direction, or impose values on others. In communicating, use "I" statements; avoid "you" statements whenever possible.

18. Group members should be aware and respect one another's boundaries at all times.

19. If you feel you want to offer advice or observations on material being shared, you may want to ask for permission. Some survivors may not appreciate feedback.

I remember once in group giving another survivor what I thought was very insightful feedback. And the therapist said to me, "Now repeat everything you said, only this time substitute "I" for "you." As I repeated what I had said, I realized that all those great insights actually applied to myself. Roxana

20. Group members are partners in healing. Offer each other the same emotional support you would expect to have from your therapist.

21. Have group agreement about how to handle feedback.

22. Survivors are sometimes unclear as to what is appropriate to bring to group. If you have no pressing issues to discuss, ask yourself, "What is causing me a problem right now? What am I feeling right now?" If you stay with the "I" statements and with your OWN experience, you will generally gain maximum benefit from group.

23. No drugs or alcoholic beverages are ever appropriate before or during group meetings.

24. Ritual abuse survivor groups meet for two

to four hours. Two to three hours is most common. A good rule of thumb is at least half an hour per member who is working through an issue. Anything less does not allow time for difficult material to emerge or be processed. Some processing can take an hour or more.

25. Survivor groups do not benefit from the standard twelve-week format often adopted for other types of group therapy. It may take twelve weeks for survivor members to begin to establish safety and trust with one another. A facilitator should be committed to long-term, continuous group processing. If group is ended prematurely, survivors may feel abandoned or betrayed.

26. Each meeting should have a designated facilitator. In facilitated groups this would be the therapist. In nonfacilitated groups the role can be rotated. The facilitator ensures that the guidelines are being followed; that members are sharing feelings rather than opinions; that each member has an opportunity to speak; that the discussion stays on topics related to recovery.

27. Have quarterly meetings scheduled to address special issues. At these meetings, review the group's charter to ensure that it continues to reflect the needs of the group. Make appropriate changes, if necessary.

Knowing how to process in group takes practice. What is appropriate in one group may not be appropriate in another. People will make mistakes. The important thing is to recognize and address digressions early. Be careful not to shame anyone. The best approach is to simply restate the guideline in question.

Because I was abused, I didn't know how to behave in a more functional way. But I want to

spend the rest of my life as a functional being, having relationships with other people, having boundaries, behaving in a way that doesn't bring tons of shame. And the only way I can do that is to just stay in recovery and keep going to meetings and keep getting support. Today I have those choices. So it gives my recovery a lot of meaning. Brice Roweland

CHOOSING A GROUP

The decision of if and when to join a group usually takes shape over some period of time. You may have no idea where to begin looking for a group, or you may be feeling confused by the possibilities. You may wonder if you're ready for a group of ritual abuse survivors. This section will help you review various options to help you make choices that feel comfortable.

Different groups have different characters, so I suggest people try a number of different groups and a number of different times to make sure they feel really at home. That's how it evolved with the OA [Overeaters Anonymous] group. There's people there with a lot of recovery. It's a warm group. It's helpful to me, even though I can't talk about some of the [ritual] things I want to talk about. Susan

Many survivors feel a need to share their experiences with other ritual abuse survivors who can really understand what it's like:

When I first started having ritual abuse memories, my buddies (in a nonritual abuse support group) were very sincere. They were very genuine when they said they would be glad to listen to whatever is going on with me. And I know they meant it. But I couldn't do it. One of the reasons I

couldn't do it was that I needed to tell it to someone who knew, not to someone who was just supportive. Jeanne

For some survivors the ideal group is facilitated small (five to seven members), flexibly structured, and members are survivors of ritual abuse. Some additionally may prefer a group where members have a similar abuse history, and are at a similar place in their own recovery. However, more likely survivors will have to make some tradeoffs. Keep in mind that the most important criterion for success is a *well-run group,* whether it is facilitated or unfacilitated, specifically comprised of ritual abuse survivors or other profiles, open or closed, structured or unstructured.

It's not important that they be ritual abuse survivors. I'm still getting what I need out of the group. I get emotional support and acceptance. And it's got a great facilitator. She's hot, she's funny, she's sweet, she's real, she shares a little bit of her own stuff but doesn't dominate the group. She keeps things on track. She deals with people's feelings as they come up. She doesn't let people get left by the side. Bea

TWELVE-STEP GROUPS

Twelve-step support groups exist for many survivor-related issues: Alcoholics Anonymous, multiplicity, Incest Survivors Anonymous, Survivors of Incest Anonymous, Overeaters Anonymous, Narcotics Anonymous, Adult Children of Alcoholics, Debtors Anonymous, Sex and Love Addicts Anonymous, Al-Anon, etc. In addition, twelve-step ritual abuse support groups are being formed in some cities.

Twelve-step groups have a charter based on twelve principles of recovery. They are structured on a formula that works, have operated successfully for a substantial period of time, and are well represented throughout North America. However, survivors have mixed reviews about their suitability for issues of ritual abuse.

Some survivors are strong supporters:

If [ritual abuse] is there, why not go ahead and face it? You don't have to do it alone. Any twelve-step program helps you get firmly based in what the recovery process is. My recovery comes from working the twelve steps with my inner kids. Dave

Other survivors are equally enthused at discovering twelve-step support groups:

What's exciting about recovery for me is that I can find tools that work and help me to be free and strong. I think that going to a [twelve-step] group was vital for my recovery because in that group I learned not to cross-talk, not to interrupt, to be able to express myself, not to fix other people's feelings, which is what I'd done all of my life. It was my first experience with sharing in a way where I wasn't commanding, controlling, and fixing but sitting and honestly listening to other people. Suzzane

One survivor had this to say:

I love the certainty. The system works. It's excellent in helping to establish boundaries, and there are never any surprises. We hate surprises above everything else. Deborah

Other survivors find the twelve steps difficult in some respects:

It helped a lot with the incest stuff. I did the whole workbook. It got me in touch with a few things, but [all of] the twelve steps don't really work for me . . . like saying I'm powerless. That could work really well for alcoholic men, or men in general. But it doesn't help when I'm trying to recover from being powerless. Women have been denied rights and power for so long that we need something to help build us up. We don't need to deflate our overblown egos, because our egos have been squashed. And then there's the moral inventory of our wrongs. I'm Catholic, and it's not like I haven't run all my sins through my head too much anyhow.   Jane Linn

Some survivors have difficulty with the "no feedback" guideline. Ritual abuse survivors often need positive feedback about having shared, and assurances that their feelings and experiences are acceptable. This guideline can create difficulties if it hasn't been explained:

I think I disagree with this no feedback stuff. Sometimes people say stuff that needs to be responded to. I told one group how bad I felt and I didn't know that there was no feedback or cross-talk. I felt like I got the silent treatment. I thought that everybody must be agreeing with me, that I must be the worst person in the world. Katharine

Some survivors have developed new formats adapted from the twelve steps. Psychologist Charlotte Kasl developed sixteen steps that seem to work well for some survivors (page 302).

Keep in mind that every group, whether twelve-step or another format, develops a unique identity. It is determined more by the attitude and character of the members than by format. More important than format is a member's maturity, kindness, commitment, and integrity.

Regardless of which format works for you, remember that the purpose is support, self-discovery and empowerment. Recognize and avoid charismatic people who appear to be guiding you, but in fact are taking your power.

There may not be a single group or format that meets all your requirements. That's quite common. Consider joining several groups to address your recovery needs. You may want to start with groups that are well run and well established, and deal with related issues such as sexual addiction, eating disorders, alcoholism, anxiety, money management, etc. The idea is to learn how healthy groups function and develop effective communication skills. Next you can progress to a group dealing with incest issues, and when you feel ready to do so, you can join a group dealing specifically with ritual abuse. Since ritual abuse issues tend to be more complex, it is especially important that people in the group have good group interaction skills.

To join or start a twelve-step group or for a copy of the twelve steps write ISA or SIA (see the Resource Guide). If you need additional leads on finding a group, ask your therapist or try other organizations mentioned on page 274. In addition, check your local want ads. There may be information on people looking to start various support groups. Keep in mind that ritual abuse support groups usually don't advertise. These are usually found through word-of-mouth and networking with other survivors.

Try not to prejudge or dismiss a group prematurely. Follow up leads in person. Give a promising group five or six tries before making a commitment. Let inner wisdom be your guide.

DECIDING TO JOIN

The idea of joining a support group may make you feel excited and hopeful. At the same time, you may feel vulnerable and afraid. Maybe no

SIXTEEN STEPS FOR DISCOVERY AND EMPOWERMENT

1. We admit we have the power to take charge of our lives and stop being dependent on substances or other people for our self-esteem and security.

   Alternative: We admit we were out of control with/powerless over ____ but have the power to take charge of our lives and stop being dependent on substances or other people for our self-esteem and security.

2. We come to believe that God/The Goddess/Universe/Great Spirit/Higher Power awakens the healing wisdom within us when we open ourselves to that power.

3. We make a decision to become our authentic selves and trust in the healing power of the truth.

4. We examine our beliefs, addictions, and dependent behavior in the context of living in a hierarchal, patriarchal culture.

5. We share with another person and the Universe all those things inside of us for which we feel shame and guilt.

6. We admit to our strengths, talents, accomplishments and intelligence, promising not to hide these qualities to protect other's egos.

7. We become willing to let go of our shame, guilt and any behavior that prevents us from taking control of our lives and loving ourselves and others.

8. We make a list of people we have harmed and people who have harmed us, and take steps to clear out negative energy by making amends and sharing our grievances in a respectful way.

9. We express gratitude to people who have been kind or loving to us, and remember to acknowledge our many blessings.

10. We learn to trust our reality and daily affirm that we see what we see, we know what we know and we feel what we feel. When we are right, we promptly admit it and refuse to back down.

11. We promptly admit to mistakes and make amends when appropriate, but we do not say we are sorry for things we have not done and we do not cover up, analyze or take responsibility for the shortcomings of others.

12. We seek out situations, jobs, and people that affirm our intelligence, perceptions, and self-worth and avoid situations or people who are hurtful, harmful, or demeaning to us.

13. We take steps to heal our physical bodies, organize our lives, reduce stress, and have fun.

14. We seek to find our inward calling, and develop the will and wisdom to follow it.

15. We accept the ups and downs of life as natural events that give us lessons for our growth.

16. We grow in awareness that we are sacred beings, interrelated with all living things and, when ready, take an active part in helping the planet become a better place for all life.

one will like you. You may feel uncomfortable having group attention focused on you. You may feel afraid of having to share in a group of strangers. Being in a group may bring up feelings of shame, or worries about doing it wrong. Your inner children may feel frightened about having to cope with a new situation. Maybe you'll feel unwelcome or that you don't belong. At the same time, you may be afraid that joining a group of survivors means you are admitting to being one.

Your feelings are perfectly normal. If you could ever share your feelings with other survivors in the group, you would be relieved to learn that most experience the same fears.

The city I came from had a twelve-step meeting for anything. But in this new city there just weren't that many, and I was going to mixed meetings with men and women, and I didn't like that. The format was different and they read different things at the beginning. We met people and it was hard to do, because they weren't the same people as in my previous city. And so of course none of the people were the right people. We were ready to point out every way in which it was different—even criticizing it for the vegetation outside the building. But part of me, the inner parts, needed it, so we kept going back. Every time, I kept thinking, "I don't have anything to say." I'd sit down and other people would start talking, and all of a sudden I would have three or four things I wanted to say. And once I got over the resistance of my new city not being my old town, it was the right meeting and they were the right people. And it was even okay for those types of trees to be outside the meeting place. But it took a year. It took time.   Deborah

Often people are uncertain if they belong in a group. One woman who suffered from anxiety attended a ritual abuse support group for three years without any memories of abuse. She kept saying, "I don't belong here. It's time to leave and get on with my life." But she kept coming back. Most of the group members were okay with that. They told her that if the group was helpful to her, she was welcome, with or without memories. One day, she shared that her mother had died. A week later, she began having memories.

As difficult as it may be to make it to the first meeting, chances are you'll feel much better by the time you leave. And if everything doesn't go smoothly, that's okay too. Sometimes getting comfortable takes time. Sometimes it's not the right group. Sometimes it's the right group but not the right format.

One of your best allies in finding the right group is good information. It will help you develop realistic expectations. You will learn to recognize the difference between healthy and unhealthy interaction. Being well-informed means being able to make the right choices for yourself.

ISSUES TO MONITOR

A group is a highly complex system. Its success is affected by many factors. Among them are group behavior, group dynamics, and member profiles. It takes considerable skill and experience to run a healthy, effective group.

It's important to understand how to function in group. It adds to the safety. It's not just a matter of having group experience, but having skills. There's people with a lot of experience (in groups) but I don't feel comfortable with their skills.   Susan

As with any group interaction, problems may arise. The best way to address potential problems is to expect them. Assume they are going to come up, and have systems in place to handle them.

Problems pertaining to the group should be worked through in the group. Problems between two individuals should be resolved between those two individuals. Sometimes the distinction isn't clear. In that case, check with your facilitator, a survivor experienced in group problem solving, or a trusted friend.

It is human nature to avoid problems or confrontations. However, the sooner you recognize and handle a problem, the easier it is to resolve. Each time you work through an issue together, the group will grow stronger and more resilient. Unexamined problems will undermine, weaken, or even cause the demise of the group.

EQUAL OPPORTUNITY TO PARTICIPATE

Ensure that each member in the group has equal opportunity to share and examine their own issues. There may be some members in your group who seem to be in crisis week-to-week. While occasionally one member may take up the entire meeting working a problem, it is important to monitor that everyone's needs are being met over the long term.

New members may be shy or reluctant to express their needs. It is common for survivors to think such things as, "I don't want to take too much time"; "I don't think they can handle what I have to say"; "They'll hate me if I tell them the truth"; "They won't believe me"; "I'm not as badly off as some of the others, so I shouldn't take up time." Other times survivors test the group by thinking things such as, "If they really cared, they would ask me to speak." Be sensitive to these possibilities, but at the same time respect people's decision to decline participation from time to time.

Survivors further along in recovery may defer to newcomers who seem to have a more immediate need. If advanced or knowledgeable survivors do not share regularly, they may lose interest in coming to group. The group then loses the benefit of their experience.

TAKING CONTROL

Some survivors feel safety in taking control. A group member may be doing this unconsciously by criticizing another group member, by polarizing group members over an issue, by always leading the discussion, or by trying to impose her or his own views on the group. There are also more subtle ways of taking control, such as selectively sharing information.

There was one person who wasn't really forthcoming to people and telling them what was going on—or telling me a little bit and telling another person another little bit—and I sensed more and more that I knew less and less.   Jeanne

These members need gentle reminders about group guidelines. Remember to address problems early, before they get out of hand.

FAMILY MEMBERS

Because more than one family member is often in recovery, you may have to make a decision about having several family members in the group. This can be validating to the family members. However, it could polarize the group. In addition, recovery issues may become confused with family issues.

BOUNDARIES

Members are responsible for their own processing and their own feelings. Be careful not to take on others' issues or problems.

I don't have to be sponge, taking in someone else's stuff. It's about me. I can be a mirror.   A survivor

USING GROUP FOR THE WRONG REASONS

Some people use group meetings as another means by which to distract from their own issues. They begin the recovery journey and then seem to get stuck at the first oasis.

I know of people who have been in twelve-step group for many years. They'd just be there, hanging out, smoking and drinking coffee with the boys and girls. They joke about their abuse issues or their abuse like it was funny. There is nothing funny about anybody being sexually abused or abused in any form, yet to them it's funny. It's an excuse not to really look at their own stuff.   Dave

KNOWING WHEN IT'S TIME

Some groups have a natural life cycle. It could be six months or several years. Others go on indefinitely. If your group has outlived its purpose, do not struggle to keep it going. Acknowledge the benefits you received and have a farewell party.

It's hard to believe that it's possible for survivors to heal each other without the professionals. But I think it's possible. I've developed this really tight friendship where no matter how much shame, or no matter how awful the memory, she's the first person I call, and I feel understood. I always feel better. Jane Linn

SAFETY

One of the main inhibitors to survivors getting the group support they deserve is fear. While in rare instances there may be real danger, for the most part survivors respond with dissociated fear. The more the group works with repressed experiences rather than present-day issues, the greater the likelihood that some members will experience uneasiness. As survivors work through their dissociated fear, they will feel increasingly safe, both in group and in day-to-day life.

We were ritually abused in groups, so any concept of a group setting is going to trigger fear. And facilitators are not necessarily the answer, because many facilitators are incompetent and do not know what to do about group process. They end up allowing abuse to happen in the group.   Bea

Safety is a complex issue for survivors in general, and not exclusive to group interaction. Chapter 13 discusses factors that may affect survivor safety. Read Chapter 13 now if safety is an issue for you in your group.

POSSIBILITY OF AMNESTIC MAINTAINER ALTERS

Infrequently a survivor may have an amnestic maintainer alter who is still in contact with violators and being abused in rituals. This issue is addressed on page 156. The alter may in some cases try to recruit group members to join her or his cult. Caryn StarDancer suggests the following:

The person on the outside may not know whether or not they're cult active. This is when they get far enough to even ask the question. Until they get far enough in recovery to ask the question, you may have a risk factor in a group setting, so groups need to take measures that recognize this possibility without stigmatizing or scaring off a survivor from seeking recovery. For example, have guidelines for contact outside of group . . . concentrate on recovery strategies and processing feelings rather than talking about rituals, chants, or dogma. In groups there are almost always going to be "cult alters," but the crucial question is whether those alters are actively engaged with perpetrators in the present. It is possible that a person is being managed by a real perpetrator in the present, one who periodically uses them (e.g., for prostitution, sex, or crime) or who is reprogramming them (e.g., to recruit other survivors). If the group guidelines recognize this possibility in advance, the survivor is given a way to recognize and address the problem if it arises. . . . It does not force a person to quit, or lie, or condemn themselves unnecessarily.

If a member is discovered to have a cult-active alter, do not judge, blame, or run from her or him. Now is when they really need your support. This is not so much a sign of danger as a breakthrough in safety. Breaking away from violators is after all a goal of recovery. The steps to take are discussed on page 157.

MAKING IT WORK

There are differing opinions as to whether it is possible for survivors of ritual abuse to meet safely in groups, especially nonfacilitated groups. I have personally had experience with seven ritual abuse survivor groups. Three were facilitated, four were self-administered. The most successful and the least successful of the seven groups were facilitated.

Because survivor antennae are finely tuned, if you are experiencing discomfort in group there is usually a good reason for it. It may relate to a current situation. If so, be sure to take care of your safety and protection. However, more likely, it stems from past, repressed trauma. It is important to identify and resolve the source of your apprehension.

If you begin to feel uneasy around another member, work with your therapist or the group to help determine why. Very often, fear of others points to repressed issues within ourselves or within one of our inner children: Regardless of the source, present or past, recognizing and overcoming the fear will significantly advance your recovery.

The most important rule concerning anxiety is to address it as soon as possible. Once fear takes hold, it feels present and real and may provoke a chain reaction within the group. The longer it goes unaddressed, the bigger it grows. The sooner it is addressed, the less damage it will do.

It's really important to be aware that people [could be] projecting, interpreting, and judging each other. Switching could also be a factor if there's multiples in the group.   Susan

If you are afraid, probably the last thing you want to do is tell the group. Yet by examining fear, survivors learn to manage and control it. Addressing fear becomes easier with practice. Start by telling the group that you are experiencing it. Speak only of your own feelings, using statements beginning with "I." Do not use "you" statements, accusing someone of "making" you afraid. (See page 241 for more information on constructive communication.) Next, let the member who has triggered your fear respond. She or he, too, should speak only using "I" statements. Often, these opening statements reveal observations that need to be examined. Once examined, they often lead to an early repressed traumatic experience activated by something the member has said or done. Once identified, the problem can be resolved.

If you do not feel comfortable addressing the fear yourself, discuss your concern with another group member. You can also ask if the group would be willing to invite a facilitator to help work through the safety discussion. A knowledgeable facilitator can offer excellent guidelines that the group can use to work through future safety issues. If safety is not worked through within the group, it guarantees the demise of a healthy support system.

I was in an open group where there was suddenly an influx of about ten new people, and it was around the time of year when many survivors get triggered. So some of the original members started to freak out, and I watched as that group fell apart. And I recognized that some of the newer people were being targeted in the group, and some unsafe things were happening, and no one would talk about them.   Bea

It is important to only work in groups where each member feels safe to you. Keep in mind that fears may be unfounded. Do not target, scapegoat, or shame another survivor. Remember that we've all been through enough. Above all, be gentle and kind with one another. As a general guideline, the higher the recovery level of each group member, the lower the level of fear.

Ensuring safety may mean making tradeoffs in areas of spontaneity, flexibility, and subjects addressed. Some factors that may increase safety include closed groups, structured meetings, sharing only present-day issues, uniformity (all male or all female members), maturity, no members meeting outside of group, and having a *skilled* facilitator.

Expect that issues of safety and fear will come up—maybe sooner than you think. When another survivor and I started our own support group, I was prepared to handle fear if it should ever come up. Was I surprised when it surfaced in our second meeting! Had I not had experience in getting through this hurdle, our group would never have made it to the third.

Because it is hard to think clearly in the midst of experiencing fear, it is important to decide in advance how to address fear in your group. Write it into your charter. Find a way to follow your own guidelines, even if it is difficult to do so.

Survivors in the early, emergency stages of recovery should work in a facilitated group with a highly skilled, knowledgeable therapist. If no facilitated group is available, it may be preferable to wait until your situation has stabilized before joining a group. However, it is important that you have a support system in place to see you through this difficult period (see Chapter 1 for more on support systems).

GROUP INTERACTION WITH MULTIPLES

If a survivor is a multiple, it is common for her or his inner children to become frightened during group interaction. The frightened child personality may take control and begin to act on her or his fear.

I had tried to be in group before, but I had always switched personalities and somebody would be too afraid and I'd end up running out and disrupting the group. So for a long time [eight years], I couldn't be in a group.   Katharine

The issue of inner children and alter personalities should be discussed, agreed to, and written into the charter of the group. It is important to discuss group issues in, not outside of, group. Again, survivor experiences vary. Some believe firmly that survivors should stay in their "executive" adult during group interaction, especially in nonfacilitated groups.

It's really important for people to be able to stay in their adult. I don't think that peers should be interacting with each other's child personalities. It's not appropriate for me to take care of your child. It's not appropriate for you to want or let me do that. And in terms of group safety, the skills to relate within a group situation are not in the realm of a child but in the realm of the adult. Susan

Others believe that interaction of inner children in a group setting can be both safe and healing.

I have had good results with pretty intense situations in some groups—like child alters coming out and needing lots of support and attention, or one of us having a memory right there in group. These situations have been very healing for everyone. It has to be pretty "seasoned" survivors, however, with lots of knowledge and experience. The group I am in now is small, and is safe for "kids" to come out or feelings to get intense, and we don't need a facilitator, as long as we keep checking in with each other. Bea

There are groups especially for multiples in which inner children are allowed to come out and interact with other members of the group. The key is to have the presence or co-consciousness of the "executive" adult. It is the adult's responsibility to address any fears and calm inner child alters.

Doris Bryant, Judy Kessler, and Lynda Shirar, authors of the *The Family Inside,* recommend the following:

We believe that support groups for only multiples should be structured yet noncon-

trolling. Activities and conversation must be directed by a therapist to assure that the group functions to provide support and does not become an arena for therapy work. We believe that abreactive work is not appropriate for a group of multiples.

I had tried a lot of different groups . . . there was always some tension and some awkwardness. I always felt like there was some element of pretending to try and fit in. Then I learned about an off-shoot group of the self-help incest meeting for multiples. I heard women share about multiplicity. With these women it felt like I could just talk, and they were accepting us. I feel very grateful that that existed because it really saved me from a lot of pain. I just feel really grateful that this whole movement is going on now. Twenty years ago, I probably wouldn't have been healing from my abuse, just suffering its effects. Deborah

Safety is served best when survivors are able to keep things in perspective. Always take care of your present-day safety needs first. However, keep in mind that on balance, survivors are caring, compassionate people. They are generous and steadfast in their support of one another. Working through apprehension together allows us to triumph over our past. Triumphing over anxiety strengthens group bonds and group healing. A well-run group offers survivors some of the most rewarding experiences in recovery.

I get emotional support and acceptance. Just by walking into that room, I'd feel safe for the first time all week. It's like, "I'm okay here." I can say anything I need to say right now and nobody is going to censor me or be embarrassed or think that I'm off the wall. The group has somehow made it very safe to be myself . . . to share my stuff, to hear their stuff. These people understand. Bea

Support group interaction is a growing field. We are all learning as we go along. This means encountering challenges and difficulties. Being aware of potential problems will help you avoid them or recognize them as they come up. Conquering difficulties will help you develop your personal power. Trust your instincts. If something doesn't feel right, it probably isn't. While it takes time to adjust to a new group, you should feel comfortable after five or six meetings. If you continue to feel uneasy, talk to your facilitator, a safe group member, or a support friend for help in pinpointing the source. Next, if appropriate, address the problem in group. If the problem isn't or can't be resolved, look for another group.

IF YOU WANT TO START A GROUP

As more is being understood about the effects and treatment of ritual abuse, increasingly better programs are becoming available. One of the most encouraging trends is toward survivors helping survivors. Recovery meetings that used to be provided at expensive treatment centers, hospitals, or through professionals exclusively can be equally well provided by survivors for survivors. As survivors empower themselves in their own recovery, they become less constrained by lack of financial resources or qualified professional help.

Many survivors feel the need to be part of a ritual abuse group but cannot find one to join. I met a survivor from a rural area who wanted to start one but was afraid. She was afraid she wouldn't do it right; that all the responsibility for its success would rest with her; that things might get out of hand and she would be blamed. Still the need for group support prevailed.

Though her fears are understandable, there is every reason to believe she will succeed. There are many ritual abuse support groups, both facilitated and nonfacilitated, working effectively. Each started with one or two people recognizing a need and taking action. These groups prove that ritual abuse survivors can overcome the abuse. They can and do come together for mutual support and healing. One survivor who helped start a group observed:

They just took the bull by the horns and said, "By God, we're going to do it." And they have done it. They're still together and they're going great. And it was so wonderful to see people stop needing hand holding, stop thinking that they're these fragile things that are just going to come completely unglued if there's not a therapist standing there to tell them what to do. And I think that's probably the most empowering thing they could do.   em

You can tailor your own group any way you want. Some groups offer not only support but fun.

I've been thinking all along that I needed some support in my life for continuing to do healing art work. I've been talking to people about it and all of a sudden it just—boom—came together two weeks ago. The right people, the right time. We found the time to meet, and we've met twice. The first meeting we talked about what we were feeling and what we expected out of the group. And one person brought out some art work. It was really bonding and wonderful for her to put that out. We had an incredible time. I shared a memory, and I got a lot of support around that. So this group is going to be ritual abuse memory work with art. And I think it's going to be really good.   Bea

If you want to start a group, the following suggestions will increase your chances of success:

- Make it clear that each member shares equally in the success or failure of the group.
- Use the charter of an existing, well-functioning group as a starting point for developing your own.
- If nobody has group experience, attend several different support groups in your area to gain experience in group process and group interaction.
- Initially, stay with current problems and your present, day-to-day issues, and follow recommendations on maximizing safety.
- As with every aspect of recovery, let inner wisdom be your guide.

Other sources for starting and choosing groups are Mike Lew's *Victims No Longer,* a booklet by VOICES® in Action, Inc., called *How to Start Your Own Self-Help Group,* and self-help organizations. (See the Bibliography and Resource Guide.)

25

Self-Discovery Tools

It's vital that survivors work with people who know what they're talking about, and be receptive to tools that are helpful in our recovery. Each of us can find those tools if we open ourselves up to looking for them.   Suzzane

Everything we need to heal is right inside us—we only need to reach it. The pain and the means to heal it are contained within our body/mind. This chapter describes only some of the many and varied avenues available for healing. These tools can be used in many different ways. You can use them to manage emergency states, to access repressed experiences, to help assimilate traumatic material, and to tap into the beauty and joy within yourself. These tools are like the wheels of your recovery. They move you forward at your own pace, but you can stop them and even roll back to rework already covered ground as needed.

If you are using these tools to access repressed experiences, you may want to do so in the presence of a support person (be sure to read Chapters 1, 2, and 15 first). Some survivors can only access repressed material in the presence of a therapist; others can access memories only when *not* in the presence of a therapist. Check with yourself to see what would work best for you. Trust your inner wisdom and follow it.

The following pages describe only a handful of tools that are helping survivors heal. You will probably hear of others as well. The important thing is to know how to choose the right tools, learn how to manage them, and evaluate their effectiveness for you. Not every tool is right for every survivor. Furthermore, different tools are useful at different stages of healing. You may feel drawn to try certain techniques. Trust that. Other techniques may seem wrong, frightening, or even like reenactment of your abuse. Trust that too; do not pursue them. You may want to review this chapter from time to time and check to see what feels right as you progress in your recovery.

My therapist encouraged me to journal with my nondominant hand. When I initially tried this method, it brought up so much repressed material that I became wary of using it. I remember telling my support group, "I don't mind writing with my left hand, but I don't do it, because you just never know what it's going to turn up." The group laughed because that is, after all, the whole point of the exercise. However, several years later I thought I'd give it another try. Now I find it invaluable in processing my feelings. I write for fifteen minutes with my left hand daily. This helps to access and release accumulating feelings before they overwhelm me. Today I no longer experience the total bodily shutdowns that used to paralyze me.

Working with some tools is like doing major root canal surgery on the psyche. You want to be working with a competent and safe therapist.   Jeanne

MAXIMIZING EFFECTIVENESS

In my intense desire to heal, I pursued every tool that sounded promising. There was no shortage of enthusiastic claims. Over the course of about eight years, I have tried behavioral therapy, psychotherapy, dream analysis, Jungian analysis, writing, hypnosis, art therapy, Radix®, holotropic breathing (also called rebirthing), group therapy, psychic warfare therapy, ropes course, anger release workshops, rolfing, sand tray, body work, eye movement desensitization and reprocessing (EMD/R), and, most recently, acupuncture Feldenkrais. (Most are explained later in this chapter.)

From this experimentation I learned several things. Any number of tools can work effectively. What matters most is not the tool but tailoring it to work for a survivor. It's important to work with people who feel healing and are aware and sensitive to post-traumatic reactions. An effective tool may access several dissociated aspects simultaneously: knowledge, feelings, emotions, behaviors, and inner parts. Too many practitioners are trained in only one aspect and ignore the others or prevent them from surfacing. Many therapists work with behaviors but don't deal with the emotions that are connected to them. Some focus on the knowledge but not on how it affects the body and feelings. This leaves a survivor with "half-baked" results. One survivor went to a practitioner who specifically advertised herself as a holistic therapist (dealing with mind, body, and spirit). However, when feelings started to come up, the survivor was asked to restrain them so as not to disturb neighboring office occupants. Another survivor's experience is all too typical.

I got the opportunity to go to massage school. Everything that was in my body got triggered during that six-month training—all that touch, all that breathing. And I was really a wreck by the time that class ended, because I had no idea what was happening to me. I had all these feelings but no context for them.   CeeCee

Even more important than the ability to fully integrate each aspect of our being is know-how in using a tool with trauma survivors. If you are using these tools with professionals, it's important that they understand post-traumatic reaction.

I had to figure out what to do next. I heard about a body-centered psychotherapy, and that's where I learned about a recovery milestone—safety.

The number-one premise of this therapy is that a client doesn't have to work until she's safe. And it's the therapist's job to make it as safe as possible and find out what the client needs to make it safe. The whole world lit up for me. Because I hadn't known it, but at that moment I realized that no place had ever felt safe for me before.   CeeCee

Although therapy may be difficult, even painful at times, the tools should be used to release trauma, not accumulate more of it. Some survivors release very little repressed material during the course of a session. Others may release significant amounts of trauma with a minimal amount of treatment. What's important is to work with any repressed material as it surfaces.

In the earlier stages of recovery, many survivors are not in touch with their own bodies. They may not be aware that they are being retraumatized. Many are so used to extreme pain that they may not recognize it as abnormal. There are tools being developed to help survivors monitor their responses. One of these tools is called response side therapy and is described in the Resource Guide.

Once overwhelmed, the body/mind develops defenses to prevent a repeat occurrence. Over time, if a particular tool is not applied therapeutically, it may cease to work.

My therapist was able to get through to repressed material by "tricking" my defenses. She told me to imagine myself in a cloud, and sinking into it, so that I would become totally relaxed. As I did that, she'd ask a question, and I'd blurt out a startling response. These answers were usually painful and unexpected, but they also always gave me great relief. However, the same trick would never work twice. In the following session, when I was told to relax into a cloud, instead of relaxing, I found myself tensing up. Each session, the thera-

pist had to come up with new and different ways to "trick" me.   Jacques

Although tricking our defenses can sometimes produce gratifying short-term results, in the long term they are counterproductive to the goals of recovery. The purpose of recovery is to restore safety, trust, and control to survivors. Any approach that ignores our internal communications or needs will reinforce the abusive conditioning we are trying to overcome. Survivors have been tricked enough. Our defenses are our protection and must be respected.

My therapist explained to me that I cannot integrate or heal as long as the abuse is being reenacted and I dissociate. So each week I'd stay a little longer on the mat and do the breathing, which helps to release tension. But when I would start to dissociate, we'd end that part of the session. She trusts that I dissociate when I can no longer handle it, and she has no interest in pushing me past the point where my body is saying, "That's enough." She said, "We will not do reenactments here." She was very clear about that. So it probably took about four to six months of hard work, of learning to stay in my body. But she taught me skills—like not only knowing what it felt like when I was out [of my body] but how to come back in.   Lynn

Again, it's important to recognize and validate different approaches that work for different survivors. One survivor read the above quote and commented, "If my therapist had worked this way, I'd still be at square one—stuck with everything exploding unexpectedly at home."

The goal in therapy should be not only to release trauma but also to help survivors integrate repressed or dissociated material as it emerges. In addition, it's important to acknowledge present issues and their connection to the past. Repressed material doesn't need to be forced. It will often emerge spontaneously once the time is right. This may depend on any number of factors. The most common ones are trust, safety, and total acceptance—permission to feel or remember *anything* that comes.

As repressed material tries to surface, it's okay to give it a nudge—to remind survivors that they are safe, give them encouragement, and praise them for being brave enough to look. Otherwise, it's important to let repressed material emerge in its own time. That usually produces the best results. If repressed material begins to emerge towards the end of a session, a therapist should not stop the process because "time is up." This can be very painful for a survivor. It simply dredges out the trauma without healing it. There is no therapeutic value in that. (If a therapist cannot stay with you, they still need to make provisions to help you process the pain on your own.)

It's important that a practitioner move at *your,* not *their* pace. Some survivors want to move slowly and carefully; others prefer to just go for it. Whatever your preference, trust that it's the right approach for you. Good communication is also important. Even therapists who understand trauma reactions may not intuitively know when and how much pain is surfacing for you. Therapists need to know if you are experiencing any bodily, emotional, or mental discomfort. The right therapist will stop the procedure and process the pain or otherwise attend to your needs. In this way, survivors learn that events are controllable, safety is manageable, and trust is possible for them. In time, they will be able to go further, retrieving greater and greater amounts of repressed material, knowing that they are in charge and safe.

The recovery process is—you feel your feelings a little bit and then back off. Like the first time I

felt fear. I'd feel it and I'd back off. Then one night, all of a sudden I was able to feel it entirely and stay with it. I took just as much as I could handle—and only then did I back off. I was able to contact four inner children. One by one, we pieced together the whole memory. Then the pain and fear around that incident were gone for good. Dave

In summary, to maximize the effectiveness of recovery tools, work at a pace that is right for you (if unsure what's right, start slowly and gently), pay attention to your bodily responses, attend to your needs, and, if you are working with a professional, use only a qualified practitioner experienced with trauma survivors.

CHOOSING THE RIGHT TOOLS

The important thing in deciding which tools to use (aside from their availability in your area) is to go with your own intuition. Most survivors find that if they check with themselves, they will have a more enthusiastic response to some tools than to others. Some, such as hypnosis, for example, may feel downright wrong. That's important information. Listen to your intuition in guiding your decisions.

I am not dependent on any one person, tool, or treatment plan. It takes being tuned into what works and what doesn't. And for us that takes a lot of practice. I didn't have that skill, because all my life, I made things that didn't work for me work— if that makes sense. So it takes a lot of careful thought and conscious effort to see—this works; okay, I'll use it. This doesn't work; I won't use it. I no longer feel obligated to somebody or something to keep using things which don't work for me. Suzzane

There are a great number of tools being used effectively to manage, retrieve and process repressed trauma. The following is a description of some of these. They are generally grouped according to their access avenues: creativity, body, inner children, etc.

Some of these avenues can only be accessed with a practitioner (rolfing, body work); others can be accessed on your own (writing, sand tray). If safety is an issue, have a support friend on hand while you try a new tool. Regardless of avenues used, it is usually healing and beneficial to share your work with your therapist or a support friend. It is also helpful to review your work on your own—over and over again, until it is healed.

CREATIVE AVENUES

Many survivors used creative means to escape overwhelming trauma. It is also through creativity that many survivors are able to heal themselves. Creative avenues are among the most accessible, most effective, and least expensive tools of recovery. Two writing and art, will be discussed in some detail.

WRITING

In *Journal to the Self,* Kathleen Adams, M.A., describes writing as "The 79¢ therapist." Some survivors have been unable to write or draw because of abuse around this form of self-expression; they may start with other avenues. (You can try to use other avenues to help overcome the barrier.)

Journaling
Journaling is simply recording something. The act of putting feelings down in writing helps to express and release them. Journaling is also useful in recording memories. Very often, repressed material is quickly forgotten again. Having a record helps to keep it in your sphere of awareness, where you can continue to process it as you are able. It is also a wonderful form of validation. I remember recording a particularly difficult memory in 1988. Shortly after retrieving it, I forgot all about it. About a year later, it felt as if new information around that 1988 memory was emerging. It seemed to be the tail end of the original experience. Again, I recorded it in my journal. To see how the two memories fit, I looked up the 1988 memory. I was surprised to find the memory in its entirety—including the tail end that I thought was new material—all recorded there. What surprised me even more was that I described the event the second time around in almost exactly the same detail. I knew I couldn't have made up the same experience exactly the same way twice. It had to be real. That was important validation to help counteract self-doubts, which nagged at me during various stages of my recovery.

AUTOMATIC WRITING

Automatic writing is known by many other names: stream-of-consciousness writing, free writing, free-association writing, intuitive writing, and so on. This is one of many tools to help you access repressed feelings or experiences. Here's how it works.

Sit in an undisturbed area with a notepad and set a timer for ten minutes. (You can gradually increase the time, depending on what works best for you. Some people suggest writing for at least thirty minutes or longer.) Without paying any more attention to the time or anything else, start writing whatever comes to mind. You can start with a feeling, an idea, a word, or a visual image—anything at all will do. Throw any writing rules you've been taught out the window. What you write doesn't have to be spelled right, doesn't have to be grammatically correct, doesn't have to be logical, doesn't even have to make sense. It's important not to stop for any reason—especially not to think, judge, analyze, figure out, criticize, or censor anything. (There'll be plenty of time to do that later.) Don't let your pen leave the paper. If you have nothing to say, just keep making a mark until something else comes along. It's perfectly all right to write whatever is happening, such as "I have nothing else to say. I don't know why I'm doing this. Nothing about this makes sense." The key is to just keep writing, without stopping, until time is up. The less you think about what you're writing, and the faster you write, the better. When you're done, you may find some important information has in fact emerged.

NONDOMINANT HANDWRITING

Another way to access repressed information or process difficult feelings is to do automatic writing with your nondominant hand. If you are right-handed, write with your left, and vice versa. It will feel very awkward at first, but with practice it will become much easier. Survivors are often surprised at the wealth of information this can yield.

It took me over a year to overcome my writing block. I was going to a support group, and one of the women in the group kept saying, "Write with your left hand. If you want to recover, write with your left hand." Every time I went, she would say that. Finally, one day I sat down, and I said, "Oh, this feels so stupid." Then I started writing with my left hand. When I did, that's when I tapped a part of my hidden awareness. I realized that they

[the perpetrators] put a lot of energy into stopping us from writing. I also know it's worth the energy to break that block.   Suzzane

DIALOGUE

A rich and fascinating source of information comes from a writing technique called dialoguing. It can be used for a wide variety of purposes. One of the best uses is to get in touch with your inner, repressed parts or alters. If you are feeling distressed and don't know why, start a dialogue with yourself in the following manner. Write a question with your dominant hand, such as "I am feeling very angry. Can somebody inside tell me why?" Then switch hands and, using the rules of automatic writing, write out your reply. Continue the "conversation" by switching hands back and forth until the problem has been worked out. This is a great way to help access experiences that are controlling and creating difficulties in your present-day life.

You can use the technique to solve problems, "dialogue" with a person in your present-day life, and find a creative solution in a faltering relationship. You can dialogue with your body, your inner wisdom, your emotions/feelings, with a block or resistance, and so on. Dave unblocked his body pain through this technique (see page 224).

AUTOBIOGRAPHY

Sit down, and without thinking about it, write out your life story. You don't have to be precise, and what you say does not have to make sense or be logical. Just write anything that pops into your mind. Write your life story from birth to the present. Be sure to include blocks of time about which you do not have any conscious memory. Don't censor or judge anything. Keep writing until you have a feeling that your story is complete. (This does not have to be completed in one sitting.) You can write your life story many times, with both your right and left hands. When you're done, you can use what you've written as a basis for uncovering repressed material.

I wrote two life stories—the one I knew and the one I didn't know. The one I didn't know was powerfully healing.   Sophia

A variation is called guided autobiography. Here a therapist assigns a topic, such as power, sex, money, childhood, help, etc. For example, the exercise may be "How was grief expressed in your family?" You write an autobiography around that subject. One survivor was told to write her life story around money. Here's an excerpt from her journal.

Money was always a big deal in my family. Father worked three jobs to make sure we had enough, but he seemed to always need more. Mother counted pennies. If she sent us shopping for something like bread and a single cent of change was missing, she would go crazy—sort of stark raving mad.

These are just some of the many writing techniques that survivors have used successfully to work through recovery. You can write on your own, during the course of therapy, or join other survivors in writing workshops. *The Journal to the Self, The Courage to Heal Workbook,* and *If You Could Hear What I Cannot Say* are some of the many books available to help you explore writing as a healing tool (see Bibliography).

ART

One of my therapists had suggested I read *Boundaries of the Soul.* In the middle of the book, I found patient self-portraits. They intrigued me. Although I had never done one, I had a very clear idea of how I would draw myself. I did it right there and later showed the drawing to my therapist. My face was a circle. My mouth was a narrow rectangle with overlapping, zipperlike clenched teeth. Through the portrait I had drawn a large X. Underneath it I wrote the words "Clearly Forbidden." I saw the look on her face as she said, "I had no idea that this is how you felt," and I realized that the drawing was significant.

Knowing nothing about art interpretation, I had no idea that my self-portrait spoke volumes—not only by what was there but also by what was omitted. Art is a powerful access tool to repressed material. It is especially useful when trying to connect with preverbal or preschool inner children, who may not know how to talk or write.

Like writing, art is easily accessible. All you need is a pencil and paper. But it can be lots of fun as well. You can use all of your creativity to express yourself. You can use crayons, you can cut out shapes from paper or pictures from magazines, you can glue on strings or sticks or colorful, shiny things and make a collage. You can use any medium—clay, paints, crayons, papier-mâché. You can draw or sculpt self-portraits or anything at all that comes to mind. Some survivors have found making masks wonderfully self-expressive and healing. You can try variations such as drawing with your eyes closed or with your nondominant hand.

MUTE DIALOGUE

Another variation of art therapy is called mute dialogue. You have a silent conversation with questions and answers in order to associate a repressed experience. You can start by simply making a mark on a piece of paper with your dominant hand and responding to that mark with another mark or picture, with your non-dominant hand, as if carrying on a conversation. This can be done alone, using alternating hands, or with a therapist.

The best part is that no artistic ability or experience is needed. However, be sure that you are working with a qualified art therapist who is familiar with signs of ritual abuse. You can also join art therapy groups or workshops. Here you get the added benefit of being able to share your work in a supportive and healing environment with people who can validate your pain.

BODY AVENUES

I had done touches of psychoanalysis. The therapists would try to lead me into verbal and intellectual stuff, and that never got me anywhere. I just kinda felt functional on the surface, but totally dysfunctional on a really deep level. The only thing that could break through that was therapy which had to do with my body. And that's what Radix® has done for me. I've been feeling terror for five years now, and I'm really tired of it, but it's obviously not out of me yet. But today I can recognize it. I have all sorts of subtle ways that it starts to vibrate through me, and today I can go, "Hmmm . . . I'm scared. Okay, I know what this is and what to do about it." Grace

Much of our trauma and experience are stored in our bodies. Our body is a repository of infor-

mation. Recent findings indicate that the mind likely resides in the entire person, including the body. There appears to be both memory and intelligence at a cellular level. However, our bodies, unlike our intellect, cannot be manipulated. For example, we can alter our perceptions intellectually in order to help us cope. This can be done through rationalizations (a battered husband consistently claiming, "She didn't mean to hurt me. It was an accident") or through dissociation. However, cellular knowledge is incorruptible. It cannot be altered, manipulated, or changed. The information coming from our bodies is irrefutable. If your body has retained unresolved pain, has scars, or reenacts an event, you can be certain that the pain, the injury, or the event happened. Bodies simply communicate what is.

Healing the body and the trauma it holds is an important aspect of recovery. However, many survivors cannot tolerate being touched, even years into recovery. That's all right. You don't need to try body avenues unless and until you are ready to do so.

Some survivors may feel a sense of elation and inner calm after treatment. Others may experience extreme fatigue up to three days after body work sessions. This may occur even if there has been no physical discomfort during the treatment itself. Sometimes the fatigue does not begin until one or so days after the actual therapy. These are usually signs that treatment is taking effect. It's important to mention them to your practitioner. The real proof is gradual and steady improvement. If a technique that is supposed to invigorate you consistently leaves you feeling sick or depleted and there is no medical cause for the reaction, you need to consider the possibility that the treatment is retraumatizing you.

Recognizing the body/mind connection in Western culture is a relatively recent development, and techniques in the field are rapidly evolving, changing, and expanding. Body work varies according to the method/modality used and the interpretation/execution of the practitioner. The techniques mentioned below are only a few of the many methodologies being used today.

RADIX®

Radix is a neo-Reichian growth work that strives to restore the inherent balance of emotion and expression within each of us. It is based on the theory that if a person is blocking pain, pleasure is also being blocked. The blocking of anger leads to the blocking of soft, loving feelings. If fear is being blocked, we are also blocking our capacity to trust. This blocking process is often not in our conscious awareness and therefore is addressed on a body level in order to bring it to consciousness. Radix education is taught in individual, group, and workshop sessions and encourages a student/teacher relationship as opposed to a patient/doctor relationship.

Radix is an effective technique for accessing and/or containing feelings, and many survivors experience great release after therapy. However, it is important to go at your own pace and maintain ongoing communication with your teacher to prevent being overwhelmed. Try to find a teacher who is willing to explore the source of your feelings. Otherwise, you may need to supplement Radix work with memory association work.

There are a variety of techniques and therapies that promote overall fitness and health. These are not necessarily designed to access repressed trauma, and they may not bring up any repressed material for you. However, any exercises that use movement, breathing, or other techniques to release bodily tension or correct

bodily alignment have the potential to release long-held trauma or feelings. You may have been working with some of these techniques for years without noticing anything unusual. However, once survivors begin recovery, many become far more sensitive. Therefore, if you are currently using or decide to try any of these, be aware that repressed issues may surface.

Listed below are some therapies or techniques that have released memories for survivors. Unexpectedly released memories, although sometimes frightening, also provide an opportunity to begin your healing. However, if they are released at an inopportune time or place, they may need to be contained. If you are not ready or unable to process them, you can make a choice to temporarily repress them again. You can simply decide to put them away; if that doesn't work, try the suggestions in Chapter 15 or the end pages.

MARTIAL ARTS

Martial arts teach Oriental self-defense or combat skills such as karate, aikido, judo, kung fu, and tai qi (formerly tai chi). Although any tool can be used in any way, martial arts are generally used to promote body awareness, to release anger and reclaim power. Martial arts also stress proper breathing, centering, and balance. Be cautious of "masters" whose aim is to solicit followers. Recovery is about self-empowerment, which comes through following your self.

I'm a very spiritual person, and I believe that a higher power has really taken care of me and landed me in karate school, where most of my support system comes from. It's no coincidence that it happens within a context where you're trying to merge the mind and the body and the spirit. I would recommend martial arts to every single survivor. You face everything. I've had to face my ability to injure someone, and I have to face that I'm vulnerable to somebody else—it doesn't matter who or what they are. I'm vulnerable. I have to face that. That's good.   Alicia

ROLFING

Rolfing works with the deep fascia (connective tissue that binds the body's muscle group). Using deep massage, it restores the body's natural shape and its relationship to gravity. A treatment usually involves ten one-hour sessions with a certified practitioner. Rolfing often brings up body memories, and most practitioners are comfortable with witnessing a client's feelings, although they may not facilitate connecting them with their source.

FELDENKRAIS

Feldenkrais uses the relationship between bodily movements and the ways in which we think, feel, and learn. It follows infant movements which use our inherent genius to organize the body for graceful, effortless movement. Unlike some techniques which stress "pain and strain for maximum gain," Feldenkrais adopts the "radical" idea that the body responds best to pleasure. It encourages playfulness. Feldenkrais elicits the body's intended reflexes allowing it to move more freely, fulfilling its promise of evolution. As one Feldenkrais teacher put it, "It lets the baby go back to Eden, as if it had not been betrayed."

YOGA

Yoga is a series of exercises that promotes body/mind health and harmony. It is based on a series of postures called asanas, for toning body muscles and releasing tensions. Yoga may also include a daily practice of meditation. Some sur-

vivors have told me that they enjoy all the exercises but are unable to do the meditation without getting in touch with repressed material. While it's true that self-discovery tools sensitize us more to our past traumas, they also equip us to overcome them.

I always stayed away from meditation until I got into recovery, because I was afraid to do it. I was afraid that meditation would open up a channel that somebody could step into and take my power—which is what the cult used to do—so that is a real fear. Now, as an empowered person in recovery, I realize that I can be in control of that process. I have the ability to allow or not allow in anything. So meditation now is something safe. I use it to get in touch, and it's an enormous tool for getting to what's inside.   Suzzane

TRAGER®

Trager® allows people to explore their physical self through the medium of motion. Since emotions are held in the body, these movements help to release trauma and replace constricted feelings with free, light, good feelings. Through *Trager,* students discover the joy of having positive "in-the-body" experiences.

ACUPUNCTURE

A key objective of acupuncture is to strengthen one's "wei chi" (protective vital energy). Once the wei chi is strengthened it can help bring up deep-rooted stagnant energy caused by trauma. These deep-rooted energetic imbalances interfere with proper organ functioning and relate to chronic pain syndromes typical in survivors.

It's just phenomenal how well it works. When I'm lying there, getting acupuncture or massage or something, I allow my energy to flow and move and breathe and I meditate while I'm getting the treatment. It makes it that much more effective. Suzzane

INNER CHILD AVENUES

Because traditional cult training is done largely in the early years, many of the dissociated experiences are held by child inner parts or alters. Therefore, any treatment used with traumatized children proves very successful with survivors. Sandplay, or sand tray, is based on the principle that almost all children are drawn to play in the sand. A sand tray is a child-size tray (about 20 by 30 by 3 inches) filled with sand and hundreds of miniature toys of every imaginable variety. You can make your own using a cake pan or Tupperware. As a survivor plays, her child alters can enact their own dramas. It is one of the most accessible of all communication means. It doesn't require the ability to write, draw, or even to speak. It often allows the survivors to bypass the "don't tell" programmed injunctions. As they manipulate the toys, they are able to experience some measure of power and control that they didn't have as children. This offers possibilities not only for retrieving repressed information but for gaining mastery over it (see Chapter 17 for more on reclaiming power).

GUIDED AVENUES

The preceding sections describe tools that often access information spontaneously. However, from time to time there is repressed material bottled up inside and seemingly no means of accessing it. In those instances, guided avenues help the material to surface. Guided avenues are usually therapist-assisted.

PSYCHODRAMA

Psychodrama is a spontaneous acting out of a scene or an event. As with writing and art, it's an effective way to access and work through emotions and feelings and to bring forward new, significant information. Psychodrama can be done one-on-one during the course of a therapy session or in a group setting. A survivor can play several parts and carry on dialogues between various inner parts (similar to the dialogue writing technique). In a group setting, a survivor can assume a part assigned by the therapist. You may be asked to do a soliloquy, where you express thoughts and feelings you have not been able to express directly to another person. A lot of pent-up feelings can be both discovered and released in this manner. Psychodrama can be effectively combined with other tools, such as music, dancing, and art.

I started with a psychodramatist, and I got someone to read programming to me out loud, and that froze me all over again. I was back at square one, because here's a man sitting there reading this to me. And the therapist said, "All right, what are you going to say to that? Talk back." And I did that and then we got to where I could do that comfortably. Then we added a cloak, and the man sat there in a cloak and read my programming to me. Back to square one. I was frozen all over again. And then I got so that I could counter the programming that way, and then we added black candles in a circle. Back to square one. And now I've gotten so that I can be really cheeky with it. It doesn't control me. It still hurts to know that they did that kind of stuff to me, but I can counter it more quickly now, more spontaneously.   Joan

DREAMS

Dreams have traditionally been used as a tool to access the unconscious. Because repressed, dissociated traumatic events are stored in the unconscious, dream analysis can be an important access tool. However, dream material referencing your trauma may sometimes be interpreted as symbolic rather than rooted in actual experience. It is most effective when the therapist is familiar with typical practices of ritual abuse. A helpful guide to interpreting dreams is *Dreams, A Portal to the Source* by Edward C. Whitmont and Sylvia Brinton Perera.

For me, dreams have been highly significant, and they were my first indication that I was a ritual abuse survivor. They're a sort of turnpike—a shortcut to what I'm all about. They may not give me a literal representation, but they point to what happened. I find I can handle my memories a little bit better if they come to me as dreams. So I ask to have my memories in a dream, and sometimes they come.   Jeanne

ROPES COURSE

A ropes course is a little bit like an obstacle course and consists of wooden beams, ropes, ladders, pulleys, etc. A person is given a physical challenge to complete. Some challenges are relatively manageable—climbing a rope ladder. Others feel nearly impossible—walking a tightrope twenty feet off the ground. The point of the exercise is not the physical accomplishment but understanding the emotional significance of the event.

Survivors may get in touch with fear, issues of trust, premonitions of failure, feelings of shame, and so on. The purpose is to help them work through each of these and to reinforce within themselves feelings of ability, self-confidence, and trust. Ropes courses can be simple or elaborate.

The elaborate ones are generally used in treatment centers or other, more formalized treatment settings.

It's a communication exercise among other things—communication and trust. The hardest thing for survivors is to ask for what we need—to ask for help. And we'd get stuck and we wouldn't think that we'd have the right to ask for help. But just before you started, the facilitators had the group get around you and you have to ask them out loud, "Are you there for me?" And some of us could barely choke out the words. I haven't been allowed to ask for someone to be there for me. One woman had to have everyone look away from her before she could even ask the question. But my experience was that I could ask it and I could look at people and when they said, "Yes, we are," it went right through me, all the way down to my legs. I felt those people being there for me. So that was really good.   Bea

There are many other types of guided avenues as well. Any one of the tools mentioned in this chapter can be used in guiding survivors toward accessing lost parts of themselves. Don't be afraid to experiment. Combining different tools and ideas can be very effective. You don't have to use these tools only for healing; you can use them to have fun. Many survivors form their own support groups structured around writing, art, or other avenues.

PROBLEMATIC TOOLS

Some tools used in treating ritual abuse survivors need to be reevaluated in light of recent findings, namely hypnosis, exorcisms, and EMD/R.

HYPNOSIS

Hypnosis can be a powerful healing tool, but it can also be misused. It was often used in cult rituals for purposes of programming and manipulation, and as a result some survivors make good subjects. An abusive therapist can exploit this susceptibility for her or his own purposes—e.g., to manipulate thoughts or feelings, reconstruct or suggest memories, or implant suggestions and instructions not related to therapy. If you suspect unethical hypnotic practice, stop seeing the therapist immediately and report her or him to the appropriate organizations (see the Resource Guide).

You can ensure your safety during hypnosis if you are able to maintain conscious awareness or co-consciousness. If you are unable to maintain co-consciousness, ask to have the sessions videotaped or ask to have a support friend present. This will help ensure your protection and give you access to the retrieved material.

It's probably a good idea to try other avenues first; only if they prove unsuccessful should hypnosis be considered. In certain jurisdictions, information retrieved under hypnosis may not be admissible in court.

PSYCHIC WARFARE/EXORCISMS

Exorcisms are ceremonies performed to free a person of evil spirits. They may sound appealing to some survivors, who indeed may feel "possessed." For example, Josie went through a period in her recovery where she was feeling possessed by a wild animal. All she wanted was to get rid of that horrible feeling. She asked her therapist if it wouldn't just be easier to do an exorcism. Her therapist did some research and learned that although short-term exorcisms may seem to "cure" a person, there seem to be no appreciable long-term results.

A survivor's internal conflict, confusion, and pain stem from traumatized alters. Exorcisms do not address the root cause of the problem and so do not offer permanent relief. Effective treatment involves learning each alter's story and healing the traumatized, split-off parts (see Chapter 11). Trying to exorcise inner alters can sometimes have seriously negative consequences.

EMD/R

Eye movement desensitization and reprocessing (EMD/R) is a relatively new tool. As the name implies, it uses eye movement to process trauma trapped in our body/mind system. Researchers hypothesize that EMD/R operates on the same principles as the rapid eye movement (REM) dreaming state, which is believed to discharge daily accumulated tensions. Some therapists believe it is another form of hypnosis.

Early reports seemed especially promising for trauma victims. However, it appears that initial studies were not done on survivors with dissociative defenses. Ritual abuse survivors who have tried EMD/R are reporting mixed results from enthusiastic to disastrous. There are as yet no data on long-term effects.

EMD/R, like hypnosis, has the potential to be a powerful tool. It is important that survivors use it as carefully as possible. Here is one survivor's experience:

As the therapist finished the first exercise, a tremendous amount of emotions came through. I was still in the midst of experiencing them intensely when she was ready to continue with the next round. Because of several retraumatizing experiences with other therapists, I had the sense to tell her, "No. I need to finish processing this set of emotions before I can go on." So instead of more EMD/R, we talked. That was really helpful. I know that if I hadn't spoken up, I would have left the session traumatized. As it was, I had all I could handle. However, EMD/R has been working great. My therapist always checks with me now, to see if I'm ready to continue.   Janes

Another survivor had this experience:

I tried EMD/R and I loved it. I was surfacing memories but feeling no pain. I would leave my sessions feeling euphoric. Every time I was feeling bad, I started to look to EMD/R as the solution because of the high that I would get. I also started back on some of my past coping habits, like I started drinking again. Then suddenly it's as though my whole system crashed. I found myself in terror, paralyzed with grief, just as I had been in early recovery. I felt very small and helpless. It was

scary. I think it's because I wasn't processing my feelings. We all look for the easy cure. But "euphoric" memory retrieval doesn't do it. It took me a very long time to regain the growth that I had achieved before EMD/R.   Jane Linn

As victims, we had no tools, no help, no chances for healing. We were forced to follow others' rules and directions—no questions asked. As survivors, we have options and choices. Today we have the power and responsibility to ask questions that will ensure the right choices.

I look at my survivor friends and they all have honesty, determination, courage. And I don't know if that's what people see in me. But I know that I have this attitude—I'm going to do whatever it takes to heal.   Mike

26

Specialized Treatment Programs

Specialized treatment programs can offer intensive focus on recovery, allowing survivors to work through a large number of issues in a relatively short period of time. This chapter will discuss the types of specialty programs currently available, from hospital inpatient treatment to intensive treatment with a team of therapists.

Because treatment for survivors of sadistic/ritual abuse is still largely in its pioneering stages, specialty approaches are evolving at a fairly consistent rate. Other types of treatment programs may become available. It pays to stay abreast of new developments, and not rely on dated information.

Survivors' experience with specialized treatment programs have ranged from excellent to dismal. The following two survivor stories illustrate this point.

My therapist had a suspicion that I might have had incest, and so when I tried to commit suicide we were trying to find a residential treatment center. But my insurance would not cover that. So I ended up having to find some place that was a certified psychiatric hospital—a nuthouse. That's how it looks on all the insurance forms and my medical records. They say "psychiatric hospital." They don't say treatment center or trauma center or anything else.

When I got there, there was this cab service which the hospital contracts to bring patients to the trauma unit. A little old man comes to pick me up and by this time I'm absolutely panic-stricken. I'm thinking, "This was a mistake. I've got to get out of here. But where am I going to go?" And as we're driving this little guy goes, "A sweet little girl like you doesn't have any problems, does she?"

We get to the hospital and I get all these forms to sign myself in—"commit yourself voluntarily," it says. And I'm reading, "Restraints won't be used unless absolutely necessary either to prevent harm to yourself or to others. . . ." So I sign all the forms. Then the worst part of the check-in comes. I go to the room and the nurse goes through all my stuff. They take away what they call your "sharps," which is anything. I mean, if it was a powder case and it had a mirror they took it, nail files, the razors to shave my legs, my prescription medicine that I take every day. They keep the blow dryers and anything you could potentially harm yourself with. It felt like I was in jail.

The windows don't open, the whole floor is locked—you can't get out. And they put you on SVC—something like "Strict Visual Contact"—where you have to be out in the open. You even have to take the staff along when you go to eat, and that annoyed the hell out of me. I really hated that. I really need to be alone, especially when I'm freaking out.

I guess I wasn't a basket case, so they took me off SVC after a couple of hours. But as soon as they did, I went to my room and just stayed there. That was Saturday night.

Sunday night they were having this big meeting. All the folks—the patients and staff members—kind of sit down and post where they're at, and what's up for the week. About 9:30 P.M., somebody happened to notice that I wasn't there. This staff lady came up—she was really nice—and found me. I was sitting on the floor between my bed and the wall with my teddy bear, just crying and hiding. It was like, "I don't want to be here. Let me out of here." And she started talking to me, and I hadn't eaten the entire time, and so she said, "You don't have to come to the meeting." After everybody left, she took me out to the kitchen and helped me dig out something to eat, and sat and talked. After that, I felt better.

Arriving on the weekend was really hard because there was nothing going on. Monday was a bit better because they started their classes and their groups. And once things got started, it was different.

The very first thing, at eight o'clock, was what they called ST, the sexual trauma group. There were about fifteen people and four counselors in each group. I had been warned that it could be hard, because people share memories. So I sat down, and the very first thing that happened was an extremely multiple, extremely ritually abused person started going into a horrific memory. And I had no idea what to make of it. I mean, she had drawings, and I'm looking at them, and I wasn't overly shocked. But I'm thinking, "Is this real? This isn't real!" and I'm getting really nervous. When she finished, the director of the unit, who happened to be one of the counselors in our group, said, "I just want to tell everyone to absolutely believe what she said. It's real. It's true. It happened." And as soon as he said that, my heart just kind of fell to my shoes. But I stayed real calm, and I don't remember anything else about the group.

By Wednesday, I had an individual session with the therapist who had been assigned to me. I was with her each afternoon. And then in between we had group, art, experiental therapy. We had a ton of little groups about John Bradshaw—type stuff—you know, facing shame, identifying dysfunctional patterns, how to develop healthy patterns, lots of instruction sort of thing.

I was pretty uptight now that I think about it. I didn't draw in art, I didn't talk in group, I sure as hell didn't move in movement class. I would just stand there like a stone, thinking, "There's nothing wrong with me. I don't need to be here. I'll be damned if I'm going to move." I was just frozen.

I didn't have any memories. In therapy, it was like, "Well, what do we do? Just sit and stare at each other for an hour?" And finally my therapist said, *"What I want you to do is just think about your childhood, just come up with an image."*

It was the next day when suddenly the ritual abuse stuff came and it hit me like a ton of bricks. But once I'd had that memory, it was like, "Okay, now at least I know what I'm doing here." It was this kind of relief, because, well, there is a reason why I almost shot myself, I'm not just nuts. At least this is something I can tackle and I can fix. It gave me hope that I can feel better. And then I started working on it full-fledged.

The counselor I worked with was really wonderful—completely accepting, completely believing. She would go anywhere with you, do anything with you. She was not afraid of anything that I came up with. She never acted shocked.

She wasn't detached and cold either. She was very much there for me. I was able to talk to her and tell her that if they ever used restraints on me, that would be the end of me. You know, "Please don't let that happen." And she didn't, and she told the rest of the staff about that too.

She was completely on my side. She didn't treat me like a patient but like a person. She never made me feel like I was some weak, messed-up individual. Her standpoint was that, "Yes, there were these horrendous problems, and yes, you have things to work out, but you certainly are able to do that. You're a functional, intelligent human being and we just have to get through this stuff. There's no reason why you can't deal with it." She taught me not to be afraid of it.

She trusted me to say what I needed to say or do what I needed to do to be safe. She didn't try to tell me what my process should be. She let me discover it.

I found that she really gave me a good start. The whole hospital staff was like that. They treated you like you were a perfectly capable, fully functional adult. You need a little help, you know. You need to know your limitations—but they were really good about helping us to find those limitations and helping us to identify when we needed extra help. They were really empowering—that's the word for it.

It set the tone for my whole recovery. I'm really glad I had my first memory in a treatment center. I didn't have to go through a lot of wondering and puzzling: What is this? What's happening to me? Why am I doing this? Is this real? Is this not real? What do I do about it?

It was all right there. It was like, "It's a ritual abuse memory. Now we know why you're here and what to do." I came out of there thinking, "Yes, I'm a ritual abuse survivor, so I'll deal with it." Not, "Oh my God! I'm an RA survivor—What am I going to do now?"

That alone cut light-years out of my recovery. If I had been in a less competent treatment center, I don't think I would have done nearly as well. It aimed me down the right path so that I knew where I was going. I think I got a really good start because these people helped me believe in myself and helped me see how the process works. I didn't know it at the time, but that was the most valuable part of my hospital experience.   Sunny

Although it was frightening for Sunny to trust an institutional facility, it turned out to be a productive, empowering experience. She was treated with love, dignity, and consideration. She was believed. She was not forced into participation or punished for expressing her needs. The treatment team helped Sunny to connect her suicidal impulses with her traumatic childhood experiences. She improved as a result of the treatment. These are indicators of being in an appropriate treatment facility.

However, the names "treatment center" and "psychiatric hospital" are not guarantees of proper treatment. Joan had quite the opposite experience.

I was terribly depressed after my parents died in January, only I didn't even really know it. By June people said, "They've been dead six months now. It's time for you to sell their house. You've had enough time to grieve." Because I always did what I was supposed to do, I put it up for sale and it sold right away. It panicked me because I was in no way ready to deal with it or let it go. I didn't want to touch their stuff, I didn't want to have anything to do with it. The night before I was supposed to go up there and pack their stuff, I overdosed. It wasn't that I wanted to die, it was just a way of screaming for help—"I can't tell you what's wrong, I can't tell you why I don't want to go, but I can't do this." I made a decision to go into a psych hospital, thinking erroneously that I would get good care. We had insurance, so of course the hospital was glad to see me. I got a lot of therapy. In art therapy I was drawing guns and knives and cages and stuff like that, and I was getting in trouble. I was told, "Get on with your life. You're just depressed over your parents' death." I was self-mutilating and one day I cut myself and wrote "Mommy" on the wall in blood. Nobody said, "Finish the sentence. What is it that's so horrible that you want to draw it in blood?" I drew my family's house, colored it in with my own blood, and I got into a lot of trouble for that. I got threatened with the state mental hospital. It was like now I was the bad patient. I overdosed twice while I was in the hospital, ran away once. I was pouring boiling water over my head, I had a third-degree burn. I was screaming my story and they wanted me to shut up. I was seeing a psychiatrist in the hospital and he put me on antidepressants, which I wouldn't take. I said, "I am here just for therapy. I'd really rather not take medication." And he said, "I would recommend antidepressants, but you don't have to take them, but then what's the point in your being here?" It was like a subtle threat that if you don't take the medication, you can't stay. And I was so desperate, I didn't know

what else to do. I took them for a while at a lower dose, and I got to the point where it did lift my spirits a little bit. Then he did a blood test and found that it wasn't in the therapeutic window, or whatever they called it, and he wanted it to be more concentrated. I said, "But I think this is enough." He increased the dose to where my family said, "You act and talk drugged." I didn't feel good either. And it's so parallel to my childhood. It didn't matter what I thought or felt or wanted. He was controlling me. So they shut me down. They were doing the same thing the cult did to me—"Be quiet or you're going to really get it." I got drugged. And a lot of double messages: "Show your feelings." So I'd lie there and cry or I'd stand there and be angry, and I'd be in trouble and be told, "Now calm down. Be a good patient." And I thought, "Wait a minute, this is a psych hospital. I came here to find out what was wrong with me and get help. And you guys aren't helping me." But I was still vulnerable enough to believe I was somehow the bad patient. So four months later, when my insurance ran out, I was "well." Isn't that interesting. I did a serious overdose where I was on a respirator and I nearly lost my life. I came out of it, and that was decision time for me. I saw a friend who was also a therapist, and I said to him, "I can't go on like this. My life has been too screwed up. It hurts too bad. I can't keep trying to kill myself. So I'm going to fight this. I'm going to find out what's going on, and I'm just going to walk into it, whatever it is, and if I die, I die. But I'm going to die anyway if I keep on like this." So that was a decision to heal, and I am so stubborn. Once I made that kind of decision I have only kept going forward. It was May of 1986 that I changed therapists to the one I'm still with, and he's been very helpful. Joan

If you feel you are being abused in treatment, trust your feelings. If you are being medicated or drugged instead of treated, if you are disbelieved, if you are not encouraged to safely vent the full force of your feelings, if you are talked at instead of listened to, make arrangements to leave. It may be scary to try to leave on your own. Call a support friend or a trusted therapist and enlist her or his help. You deserve good treatment.

A survivor's treatment center experience, especially at the beginning of recovery, can have a significant impact on the difficulty, the course, and the success of the recovery journey. A *qualified* treatment facility offers survivors an all-in-one recovery "tool kit": excellent therapists, properly run support groups, and introduction to various recovery vehicles (discussed in Chapter 25). However, treatment centers are not necessarily the answer for everyone.

The idea of going to a treatment center is difficult for many survivors. Some have been hospitalized and treated for psychiatric disorders, although they are perfectly sane. Survivors have been put in restraints, given shock treatments, drugged, and otherwise medicated by staff not familiar with post-traumatic reactions, especially multiplicity. Many survivors are chronically afraid of medical help because of programmed set-ups. Some have been put into institutions for trying to disclose. One survivor tried to tell of his abuse by an uncle at the age of nine. His father pronounced him "crazy." The child was locked up in a psychiatric facility and given shock treatments to cure him of his "delusions."

Some survivors have been to treatment programs and received little or no relief. This may be because they were not ready to uncover abuse memories. It could also be because the staff was not properly trained. It could be because a maintainer alter personality took the program. One survivor in crisis was checked into a treatment center. He had an alter whose job it was to convince everyone that nothing bad had happened.

The entire treatment time was spent denying any abuse.

Whatever your circumstances, if you feel a treatment program may benefit you, the information in this chapter can help to make it a positive event. Getting into a supportive, caring, therapeutic environment may help survivors overcome unfortunate past experiences. Even if you find a center that is not ideal, as long as the staff is competent and caring you can still benefit.

I tell survivors that it's okay to go into a hospital program if you need time and space to work on your recovery issues. We've been programmed to believe that if we ever got put in a hospital we'd never get out. If you go to a hospital program you're crazy. But I really want to say that it is okay to go and spend that time, and after your first experience you'll see that it is very healing and it does help. I went through this treatment program. There were eighteen men and me. Now I realize that it was like being with eighteen of my [abusive] fathers for thirty days, and it was horrible. Yet there were a lot of good pieces I got out of it. I learned how to do journaling. I learned how to write. I learned how to take one day at a time, and even though I'd heard that before, I didn't know how to live it, feel it. To turn it over to God. I started learning it was okay for me to take time for me.   Alice

INPATIENT TREATMENT PROGRAMS

Many survivors, like Sunny, find themselves in inpatient treatment in response to a crisis. Luckily, Sunny found an excellent program that helped her cope. However, finding a good program from scratch takes some research. It is especially hard to do so while in crisis.

A lot of time, emotional investment, and financial resources are tied up in treatment programs, and it is well worth your while to make sure you will receive the benefits you expect. Ideally, programs should be used as a supplement to an existing, ongoing recovery effort. Facilities are differentiated on the basis of availability and interaction with licensed medical staff—doctors, psychiatrists, nurses. They are typically not differentiated based on specific treatment programs such as cancer rehabilitation, sexual trauma, dissociative disabilities, chemical dependency, and so on. If you don't have a condition that requires medical care, your primary criterion should be the effectiveness of the program rather than amount of medical attention. The following section discusses treatment center options and questions to consider before deciding on a program.

There are basically four types of inpatient treatment facilities. Each category may be known by other names in addition to those shown. Also, there are variations on the four main types of facilities listed. These would offer some combination of the treatment and programs described.

Admission policies for ritual abuse survivors vary. Some centers will take survivors who admit themselves. Others will only take referrals from a therapist. Some may help you find a qualified therapist in your area if you don't have one.

ACUTE HOSPITAL CARE

Acute hospital care (the phrase "chronic care hospitals" is often used interchangeably) meets licensing requirements for a psychiatric facility. This usually includes maximum staff, maximum safety, and maximum security. The unit may have locked doors, restraints, and soundproof rooms. (Leading treatment programs for survivors of ritual abuse are moving away from using locked premises and restraints.) A psychiatrist and support staff are on hand at all times. Patients are examined daily during physician rounds. The hospital may have units focusing on special issues such as depression, dissociative disorders, or ritual abuse. All meals and living needs are provided.

These are the most expensive of the various treatment options. In some cases they are used primarily to stabilize, not treat, a survivor. The typical stay in acute care facilities tends to be seven to fourteen days. However, as in Sunny's case, it could be much longer.

RESIDENTIAL TREATMENT CENTERS

Residential treatment centers, also known as therapeutic residential centers or skilled nursing facilities, are licensed facilities with professional staff available at all times. The psychiatrist and medical doctor on staff see patients as needed rather than on scheduled rounds. Patients participate in an ongoing program of individual and group therapy led by trained professionals.

Typically, patients remain on the premises twenty-four hours a day. Meals and daily living needs are provided by the treatment center. This leaves patients free to spend the majority of their time in treatment or processing.

These facilities are not as secure as acute care hospitals. They typically don't use restraints, don't have soundproof rooms or locked doors, and are potentially not as safe for people in extreme danger of hurting themselves or others. They may specialize in certain programs, such as chemical dependency, sexual trauma, dissociative disorders, or ritual abuse.

Residential treatment centers are less expensive, per day, than acute hospital care. The typical stay in residential treatment centers is twenty-eight to thirty-five days.

EXTENDED CARE FACILITIES

Extended care facilities, also known as health-related facilities, intermediate care facilities, or community treatment houses, are licensed facilities with fewer professionals on staff or on the premises. They may have a visiting or consulting physician. They usually have an established treatment program, and may specialize in certain areas.

Extended care facilities are less secure than residential treatment centers. Residents have more come-and-go privileges.

These facilities provide survivors with a transition from total-care treatment to independent living. Residents may be responsible for making their own meals and taking care of their daily needs. This means less time is spent in counseling, treatment, or one-on-one therapy. The programs are usually less intensive and less structured than in residential treatment centers. However, ongoing processing and recovery are still the focus of the program.

Extended care facilities are generally less expensive, per day, than residential treatment centers. However, the stay is usually considerably longer, from three to six months.

HALFWAY HOUSES

Halfway houses are licensed residential facilities with minimum professional staff and minimum security. They may have a consulting professional on staff or ready access to emergency facilities. They provide a transition from treatment-oriented facilities to fully independent living. Residents are generally free to come and go, are helped and encouraged to find employment, and are usually expected to prepare their own meals and take care of their daily needs. There may not be a treatment program offered.

Halfway houses are usually the least expensive of the four residential treatment options. The typical stay is three to six months.

NONRESIDENTIAL TREATMENT PROGRAMS

Hospitals often have outpatient treatment, which allows you to live at home while attending the program. Many of the programs parallel the format of inpatient programs. You can inquire at your local hospital or at hospitals offering good inpatient programs for survivors.

In addition, there are many variations on the above formats. For example, a team of therapists at the Restoration Therapy Center in San Mateo, California, offers a three-week intensive program. The survivor has two sessions of individual therapy a day, in the morning and in the afternoon. This approach does not work well for everyone, but many survivors who have tried it have been pleased with the results. You may discuss the approach or have other suggestions to review with your therapist.

If you have an idea, don't be afraid to explore it. It may not only work for you but provide a good alternative for others as well.

CHOOSING THE RIGHT PROGRAM

Until recently, most inpatient programs for survivors were offered through acute hospital care and residential treatment centers. There were very few extended care facilities specifically for dissociative clients and ritual abuse survivors. However, as the need for other formats is being recognized this situation is changing. Therefore it may be more useful to understand how to identify a qualified treatment facility than to know the names of specific ones.

Factors to consider in choosing the right facility include safety considerations, your personal commitments and responsibilities, cost and availability of local resources, amount of time spent in individual and group therapy with qualified staff, and length of the program. Inpatient treatment facilities generally offer the most support.

It was wonderful to be there because I wasn't responsible to my husband or to my kids. I didn't have to work. I didn't have to worry about meals. You're in this totally supportive, structured, predictable environment which has everything you could ever want. You can have tantrums, you can cry, you can just laugh hysterically, and you have that kind of freedom to just work out whatever it is that's going on. I literally had to do nothing but show up. And some days that wasn't easy. But I needed a place where I could let go and just completely release, and really get to the feeling and stay with the feelings, even if that meant that I couldn't do anything else except choke down some oatmeal in the morning and tie my shoes. em

If your area does not have qualified therapists or a support network for survivors, consider starting with a treatment center. In addition to supportive, knowledgeable therapists, you will have valuable group interaction with other survivors. This can help you to both validate and normalize your experience. Many close friendships develop at treatment centers.

If you are not in crisis and have a recovery program that works for you but wish to concentrate on it in a supportive setting, extended care or halfway facilities might be best for you.

If you don't wish to be away from your friends and family but want intensive focus on your recovery in order to move through some difficult material, an outpatient intensive treatment program may serve your needs best.

SOURCES OF REFERRALS

Treatment facilities and programs are listed in the Resource Guide. Good sources of referrals are your therapist or other survivors who were pleased with their treatment programs.

Treatment centers themselves may be an excellent referral source. If a center cannot assist you, the staff often has the inside track on which facilities have the best reputation. Some may even assist you in finding the right one.

There are special referral services that help match patients with the right center; the fee for the service is usually paid by the treatment center. Although referral services may offer you excellent advice and direction, keep in mind that they may have a secondary interest in directing clients to certain treatment programs. Services have sometimes been known to misrepresent the nature of a program or a facility in order to sign up patients with their clients. In addition, some facilities are more focused on making a profit than providing the best care. These facilities may have sophisticated marketing programs and pay therapists and doctors for referrals, even though it is illegal to do so. If possible, also try to get information from clients who have had recent treatment at the facility you are considering.

FINANCIAL CONSIDERATIONS

The cost of a program varies directly with the amount of services required and medical supervision provided. In general, as mentioned earlier, inpatient hospital care is the most expensive and halfway homes are the least expensive. However, some insurance programs only cover hospital care, so your least expensive treatment may in fact be a hospital.

If you do not have insurance, determine which

type of facility would best meet your needs. Are you in crisis? Do you need round-the-clock surveillance? Are you able to function on your own? The cost of treatment can range from thousands of dollars a day in a hospital to less than a hundred dollars a day at an extended care or a halfway house facility.

Some treatment facilities offer payment plans; you don't have to pay the entire cost up front. If you have no financial resources, you may qualify for state-supported programs. Some state agencies retain a number of "beds" at certain facilities for state-sponsored care. Check with your local government mental health office for information. For more on financial help see page 285, "I Can't Afford Therapy."

MAXIMIZING SUCCESS OF TREATMENT

The success of a program generally depends on three key factors: 1) finding the right facility; 2) good ongoing communication between the treatment facility staff and your therapist; 3) having a support program in place after discharge, for ongoing recovery.

FINDING THE RIGHT FACILITY

Referrals are only the starting point in finding the right treatment facility. A good experience for one survivor is not a guarantee of good results for others. A high recommendation from a therapist or facilities referrals agent does not mean successful treatment either. Individual needs vary. In addition, the following factors may affect the success of treatment:

1. Staff turnover in treatment facilities can produce varying results. For example, a leading psychiatrist set up a dissociative disorders treatment unit that developed an excellent reputation. The doctor left, but the hospital still offers the program. It may be quite different today under new directorship.
2. Physician expertise may be inconsistent. For example, psychiatric hospitals have attending psychiatrists. One patient may have had excellent results with a particular psychiatrist. However, you may be attended by another psychiatrist with no training or experience in trauma-related symptoms.
3. Bed availability. A hospital may have a dissociative disorders unit, but if it is full, you could be placed in the general unit. In that case, you may not be getting the specialized treatment you expected.

Some facilities have an excellent reputation based on an individual therapist. Other facilities have an excellent reputation based on the specifics of their treatment program. Generally, treatment that is program-based rather than individual-based offers more consistent results. However, both factors—the therapist and the program—are relevant to a successful outcome.

It is important to distinguish between a *program* and a *track*. A program implies a focused treatment plan for a specific condition. A track implies that a certain condition is treated but is not the focus of a treatment plan. For example, a ritual abuse track at a chemical dependency treatment center may mean that you are acknowledged as a ritual abuse survivor. However, the focus of treatment is getting you clean and sober, rather than healing memories of ritual abuse. Treatment centers generally specialize in one or several programs. They may have many tracks. All things being equal, always choose a facility with a program for trauma survivors rather than a track.

QUESTIONS TO ASK

If you are considering a treatment facility, you or your therapist should ask to speak to the program director or one of the therapists. This may give you some indication of compatibility between you and the personnel. In addition, you can ask to speak to a person in admissions, to the administrator, or to the clinical director concerning the facility and cost information. You can ask some of the following questions, or use your own list.

- In what type of treatment programs do you specialize? (Look for survivors of ritual abuse; second best is dissociative disabilities, multiple personality, or sexual trauma.)
- Are these programs or tracks?
- Could you describe your program? (It should be similar to that mentioned in Sunny's story.)
- What types of trauma survivors have you treated successfully? What percentages in each category?
- Do you have family counseling programs?
- Do you believe that ritual abuse exists?
- Is there anyone I can call for a reference? (Ideally, get the names of two patients for a reference; second best may be a reference from their therapist. It may not be possible to obtain patient references for reasons of confidentiality.)
- Are you covered by any insurers? (Ask specifically about your insurer. If your insurer does not cover the program, ask if they know of another treatment center that might be covered by your insurance.)
- What is the cost?
- Do you have term payment plans?
- Do you have an after-care follow-up program?
- Is there communication between your staff and my therapist throughout my stay?
- Is there any assistance in finding me competent therapy and ongoing support upon discharge?
- If you have special dietary needs, inquire about diet as well.

Adam did his homework before choosing a treatment center. Even though his circumstances are difficult, he was grateful for the experience. Here's a part of his story.

My grandfather, who was in the cult, left me thirteen thousand dollars when he died. I spent a lot of years saying, "When I get happy, I'm gonna know how to spend the money and invest it for my future so that it can grow. But I was living in my truck, and I was unable to work. I was severely debilitated—just having freak-out memories and night terrors. Incredible, intrusive hallucinogenic type of stuff. I didn't have any health insurance. And I thought to myself, "Maybe if I just spend this money, then I can have a life." And I spent the whole fucking thing on treatment, because I was dying. So, I cross-referenced [information] a lot and got a lot of different resources and talked to lot of different people in order to find a residential facility that treated satanic ritual abuse and to know that it was a Safe Place. Because, especially ritual survivors, when our stuff starts to emerge, and we start to realize that it's real, we totally lose it. So it has to be a place that we know is safe, and that's an individual thing. That was the extent I was willing to go to, and I'm broke now. I don't have anything. But I don't give a shit, because I know what happened to me and I know my truth and I know who I am and I know why I've lived my life the way I have. The whole thing makes sense. Adam

ONGOING COMMUNICATION

It is critical that there be ongoing communication between your therapist and the treatment center staff. Your therapist may be aware of subtleties of your behavior that will maximize treatment results. Knowing which modalities of treatment you respond to best can advance treatment results as well. Finally, some survivors may have alters or selves who come out to take therapy or treatment programs. If a defensive alter takes the treatment, the inner community may not benefit from the program. Good communication during treatment can usually prevent these types of problems.

ENSURING FOLLOW-UP HELP

It is important that you have an ongoing recovery program upon leaving treatment. Survivors who make excellent progress in treatment centers often regress upon discharge. Without a good recovery program in place, many feel lost. For others, the focus is shifted to coping with their daily routine. Some may stop processing altogether. Without ongoing therapy, survivors may find themselves in crisis again.

Try to make arrangements for ongoing therapy while still at the center. If this is impossible, make it a priority upon discharge. Your treatment center may have a continuing care coordinator who can help. If not, the staff may have referrals or potential leads.

The only complaint that I really have is that there is no transition back to the real world. It's like you check out, and there you are, on your own. I didn't know anything about ritual abuse when I left for the hospital, and I returned thinking, "Wow, how am I going to re-create the treatment center in my home town?" And I hadn't a clue. And so I did a certain amount of backsliding because I got slapped in the face with reality and didn't have a bridge. It felt kind of cold. Like you walk out the door and it slams behind you. Sunny

Few experiences in life are perfect, and treatment programs are no exception. A frequently heard complaint has to do with administrative problems and lack of internal communication. But, all in all, survivors can forgive the problems because of the support and healing they received. Sunny is contemplating a return visit.

I would love to go back, just to be able to get into that kind of environment where I can completely let down. I'm really interested in testing my wings. You know, how is my judgment? Do I do boundaries better? Am I getting it? Do I know when something doesn't feel right? Are my alarms going off sooner? Can I judge a relationship better? Can I size things up? It would be a good way to kind of stand up against a growth chart and see where I am now—measure myself against myself. It helps to remember where I was, to recognize the changes in myself, and to say, "Here are the hurdles that I overcame and the things I don't even think about anymore.   Sunny

27

Hopes and Dreams

Whatever else they took from me, they never got my humanity—my hopes, my dreams, my heart, and my spirit.   Janes

The human spirit is driven by hopes and dreams. Ritual abuse is anti-hopes and anti-dreams. Yet despite every effort, our violators could not destroy either. Hopes and dreams chart the course of our recovery, and it is through recovery that they are fulfilled.

As challenging as the last few years have been for survivors who shared their stories in this book, they have been years of growth and changes. As we connect and give one another validation, we discover that we are the ones who are strong. We not only survived but are taking responsibility for our lives. We are breaking free of the lies and healing the pain.

In connecting with one another, survivors give each other strength. The combined strength we gain in joining hands is far greater than that of our violators, because truth is on our side. We are a catalyst for change in this world, not by shouting slogans and carrying signs but by quietly and simply recovering.

Survivors offer deep healing for one another. Each of us has been there. We know how hard it is to believe ourselves. We know how hard it is to think well about ourselves, and to believe that we deserve the good things in life. But we are able to see how true it is for other survivors.

To believe these truths about ourselves, it helps to first hear them from trusted others. Survivors can be mirrors of integrity and strength for one another. We can give each other messages that we needed to hear but never got from our violators: that we are good because we were born innocent; that we are beautiful because we are alive; that we are capable because we survived; that we belong on this earth because we are human. Once we can accept these truths about ourselves, we will find that the world is a good place.

The time for healing is now, and we can make the most of it. An Oriental proverb says, "A journey of a thousand miles begins with the first step." All it takes is that first step. Even if it's a tiny step, everyone can begin. And those who begin can make it because today is a good day to start.

TODAY IS A GOOD DAY

Today is a good day to make a commitment to yourself. It's a good day to join a creative healing group or to start one. Today is a great day to say "No!" to someone who is hurting you or taking your power. It's the right time to stop living your life to please your violators. It's time to stop seeing yourself through their eyes. Today is a good day to stop unhealthy coping habits and begin to take care of yourself. As one survivor put it, "There is a healthy way to have a bad day."

Today is a good day to connect with the joyful things of life—nature, animals, sunshine, and flowers. Maybe it's time to climb to the top of a deserted ridge and yell to the universe. Cry out your grief; express the pain. The earth can absorb it, even if no one else can. Then shout of your hopes and dreams. The winds will carry your message to those who need to hear it so you can be helped along the way. Reclaim your voice. Let it sing.

Today is a good day to smile at yourself in the mirror and say, "I'm pretty; I'm handsome," and to tell each of your inner kids the same thing. Check in with them often. Take care of them. Appreciate them. Start by remembering their hopes and dreams. What were they? To be a ballerina? a fireman? a doctor? a fairy princess?

Today is a good day to make dreams come true. Find a way to give your child her or his dream. Take a dancing lesson. Take a ride in a fire truck. Volunteer for the Red Cross. Maybe your nicest friends can throw you a party and tell you how really special you are.

Your inner kids are a source of creativity and strength. Once you help them make their childhood dreams come true, they can help make your adult dreams come true too.

RECOVERY, HOPES, AND DREAMS

At my very first support group of ritual abuse survivors, each person introduced her- or himself. One woman said her name and added, "I want everyone to know that recovery meetings are productive and achieve concrete results." With that she stood up, and an afghan unfurled from her lap. She had knitted it during recovery meetings. Her introduction was amusing but also true. For me the tangible result of recovery was the writing of this book.

The pattern of growth and movement that has become so clear was first experienced by pioneering survivors who showed all of us how we, too, can make it.

I was asked to exhibit my art at the first national conference on ritual abuse in 1989. There I met another survivor-artist named C.R. et al. As we got to know each other, we discovered that, unlike anyone else we had heard or met at the conference, we both had psychotic experiences as a result of our abuse. We both felt pretty alienated and isolated because no one was talking about that level of symptomatic reaction. We had never met anyone else who had been through ritual abuse, psychosis, and recovery, so we really hit it off. When we talked, one of the things we shared as a common interest was doing something like a newsletter. We both knew a lot about recovery, but we both felt that much of our recovery had been like looking for a black cat in a dark room, because there wasn't any information—no one had been talking about ritual abuse prior to that time that we knew of. Very few people were talking about multiplicity—especially the way it really was, rather than how others thought it was. Very few people were connecting the experience of psychotic breakdown with trauma, yet we knew we had gotten through it in spite of being close to dying a few times. We felt that we would have really benefited by having had a newsletter— something that came regularly to our houses, since we had been shut in at times, and "crazy."

So we just did it. We got a business license and all the other necessary permits. I had a video writer, and we got rubber cement, scissors, and paper and along with a lot of trips to the photocopy center, that's what we used to put it together the first year or so. I drove to San Francisco, and we put it together on her kitchen table. We called the newsletter SurvivorShip.

When I first "went public" as a survivor, I thought a lot about whether I would be identifiable. I knew it was a scary thing. I went through embarrassment and I went through terror. It was very tough. For the first two years I worked on it as a major issue in therapy—the impact of the role I had taken upon myself. How to wear it and not have it distort me, yet not have what I present become distorted either. To make a very clear statement that all I'm saying is that we can make it.

My struggle was with the burden of responsibility, and I would say that's ongoing. It's just that the terror isn't there anymore. That was the initial thing. Once I had some experience with being public, I went from terror to fear, then from fear into a gigantic feeling of responsibility, and I've never gotten rid of that. But if I were to lose that, I'd

quit, because I'd be afraid of making more mistakes if I lost track of how much is at stake for survivors in early recovery. Also, I don't think that doing something valuable in life comes without an equal measure of responsibility.   Caryn Star-Dancer

Although recovery is a difficult path, it is the rewarding path of meaning. Jane Linn credits recovery with finding a loving, nurturing, sexually fulfilling relationship.

It's the best part of recovery. It's even better than I imagined. It's so nice to have someone who's good for me. For the first time I'm so happy.   Jane Linn

Katharine is completing a master's program and looking forward to a new career; Jeanne is fulfilling her childhood dream to launch a project in the creative writing field; Susan, Bea, and Joan have completed academic studies for professional designations and are each beginning careers in their chosen fields; David Gabriel has enrolled in a university and studying towards a degree. Christi Joy is making up credits toward a degree in order to pursue her master's program. She has plans to open up a healing retreat. Amy completed updated studies to resume her former career; Gerald changed jobs and Sunny got a promotion. Both got good salary increases. Alice is making a long-term career change and developing her own business to provide resources for survivors and their families. She has a goal of creating a survivor's healing center. Deborah has started transition planning for a long-term career change as well. CeeCee has rolled back hours spent in her practice in order to pursue her interest in the creative arts field. Those are changes about which I know. There are probably others about which I don't know.

These changes don't come easily. But the hard fought gains are yours to keep and will be with you each day going forward from here.

I love to do the big art pieces—I dream big. I've been able to get the big jobs without even trying and ask the big price without feeling nauseated. My business is going better. More creative expression. More income. My relationships are much better; there is more love and support. Even my garden is more productive. So the important external things have improved. But it's the peace and love I feel within myself that is the best part of healing.   Jane Linn

As survivors continue to heal, they have this to share.

I am able to make decisions about my life which in the past were too scattered or felt hopeless. I have the tools to work through the memories and diminish their debilitating impact on my life. I have regained a sense of safety and love in the world. I have been able to regain my innocence and my humanness.   Sasha Trillingham

I have days when I'm in a memory, but I don't fight them anymore. And if I don't fight, I'm fine in the long run. So it's kind of coming full circle, and I feel like now I'm in a better place than I was. I describe the feeling as happy sad. I guess some people would call it bittersweet. I look at the tremendous losses that I've had, to get to who I am today, and they've been bad: my family totally, close ties with several siblings, a relationship with a person I dearly love, my status at school, my career. But I wouldn't give it up for the world, if I had to change who I am today.   Alicia

My abuse no longer dominates my existence. What dominates now is being a person. I'm a wife and mother. I want to be a good grandmother and, if I'm lucky, a good great-grandmother. I'm looking forward to old age. And I have this major goal—I want to be a cool old lady.   Caryn Star-Dancer

Sometimes I was really sorry that I had to face all this, but I never stopped going forward because I felt that the only way out is through. And in the beginning it felt like the light at the end of the tunnel is an oncoming train. But I've now come to the point where it's like—it's a rainbow. Recovery is no longer the focus of my life. I'm not so driven by it anymore. I want to focus on my children, I want to focus on my friends. I want to play. My life is very different now. There's hope, there's joy.   Joan

Whatever else you are doing, include recovery in your life. For some this means making an appointment with a therapist, for others, it's making an appointment to go have fun. Each of us has had lots of practice learning how to survive but little practice knowing how to live and enjoy life. If you have three meals a day and a roof over your head, you no longer need to focus on surviving. Focus instead on thriving—on living *your own* life.

For every disconnected feeling of terror, despair, and hopelessness, there is a memory that can free you from it. Learn to live with hopes and dreams instead of shame and terror. They make for much better company.

BE STRONG IN YOUR TRUTH

Violators cannot live with the truth; survivors cannot live without it. There are those who still, once again, are poised to invalidate and deny us. If we don't assert our truth, it may again be relegated to fantasy. But the truth won't go away. It will keep surfacing until it is recognized. Truth will outlast any campaigns mounted against it, no matter how mighty, clever, or long. It is invincible. It's only a matter of which generation is willing to face it and, in so doing, protect future generations from ritual abuse.

Your truth is your strength. When you speak it, you will find that you are supported and validated. Don't be afraid to be who you are. Every time you comprise your own integrity, you compromise your strength as well.

Remembering and healing helps to restore the balance of decency in the world. The harmony we generate within ourselves is felt by others as well. Every step of healing brings new hope for all survivors, and recovering survivors renewed hope for healing in this world. Some people might have thought that it couldn't be done, but we are doing it.

Nothing can stop me from doing this—nothing! I got stopped all my life. There ain't nothing going to stop me from doing this now. Annie

May your healing journey continue, and may it follow the call of your dreams.

Resource Guide

The following organizations offer literature, resources, and referrals. They address survivor-related issues such as incest and trauma, but not necessarily ritual abuse. This is not a comprehensive list and it is not meant as an endorsement or recommendation of any person or group. Please keep in mind that many survivor organizations are run on a voluntary basis and may not be be staffed full time. There may also be turnover in organizations from time to time. When writing for information, it's a good idea to enclose a self-addressed stamped return envelope.

CRISIS HOTLINES
(Staffed 24 hours a day, 7 days a week)

UNITED STATES

1-800-4-A-CHILD (1-800-422-4453): Child-Help USA/IOF Foresters National Child Abuse hotline. Crisis counseling for children or adult survivors. Also offers referrals for sexual abuse treatment programs, reporting suspected child abuse, shelters, advocacy, mental health, legal aid, and various national organizations. Literature on prevention of child abuse available upon request.

1-800-448-3000: Boys Town National Hotline for children and families in crisis.

CANADA

416-863-0511 or TDD 416-516-9738 (for the hearing impaired): Assaulted Women's Helpline. Twenty-four-hour crisis line for women in the metro Toronto area who have been assaulted at some point in their lives. Cannot accept collect calls, but will help long distance callers, and refer them to local services in Canada whenever possible. (If calling the TDD number for the deaf, you will be asked to leave a message, and someone will return your call.)

1-800-668-6868: Kidshelp Phone/Jeunesse, jécoute: Canada's only national bilingual twenty-four-hour, toll-free, professionally staffed telephone helpline targeted specifically to Canadian children and youth. Provides professional counseling, education, information, and referrals.

SUPPLEMENTARY

Also check the inside page of your phone book for possible local twenty-four-hour crisis numbers. Likely sources are rape crisis, sexual assault, family violence, and child-abuse prevention numbers. For referrals to other or local crisis hotlines in the United States call the following during regular business hours: National Victim's Center Infolink, 1-800-FYI-CALL (1-800-394-2255).

MULTISERVICE RESOURCE ORGANIZATIONS

RITUAL ABUSE

Believe the Children
P.O. Box 268462
Chicago, IL 60626
(708) 515-5432

A grassroots nonprofit organization founded in 1986 by parents of children abused in day care centers. Focus is on educating the public about sexual and ritual abuse. Provides resource materials, information, and support for child victims of ritual abuse and their families. Referral services for survivors and survivor advocates. Publishes a quarterly national newsletter; sponsors an annual conference; speaker's bureau. If calling, you will be asked to leave your name and phone number and someone will return your call.

Los Angeles County Commission for Women
Ritual Abuse Task Force
383 Hall of Administration
500 West Temple Street
Los Angeles, CA 90012
(213) 974-1455

An educational and referral organization of professionals from the fields of mental health, law enforcement, and clergy serving together with adult survivors and parents of child victims to study and define ritual abuse and foster awareness in the community. Annual conference and training; speaker's bureau. Has drafted "Guidelines for Establishing a Ritual Abuse Task Force" to help establish ritual abuse task forces in other states. Authored an excellent thirty-page report, "Ritual Abuse: Definitions, Glossary, The Use of Mind Control." Available for a $5.00 donation. Free for survivors.

Real Active Survivor
P.O. Box 1894
Canyon Country, CA 91386-0894
Phone: (805) 252-6437
Beeper: (818) 587-1461
Fax: (805) 252-9146

A Christian outreach organization providing therapy, support, education, and safety for survivors and their families. Offers intensive therapy weekends, informational workshops, support groups, retreats, and speaker's bureau. Also provides a listening line (not a crisis line) offering support to survivors 9 A.M. to 9 P.M. Monday through Friday.

SurvivorShip
3181 Mission #139
San Francisco, CA 94110
Phone: (707) 279-1209 (business calls only)
Fax: (707) 279-4103

Forum on survival of ritual abuse, torture, and mind control. Bimonthly newsletter. Up-to-date, reliable information on survivor issues. Workshops, seminars, professional consultations. Write for listing of available articles on ritual abuse and recovery issues. Include self-addressed stamped envelope (SASE). Confidential penpal and referral services for members.

GENERAL

California Consortium to Prevent Child Abuse
Metro Centre
1600 Sacramento Inn Way, Suite 123
Sacramento, CA 95815
Phone: (916) 648-8010
Fax: (916) 648-8007
1-800-405-KIDS (1-800-405-5437; available to
   California residents only)

An educational, nonprofit, statewide organization of 30,000 individuals and organizations dedicated to the prevention of child abuse in all its forms. Serves agencies, professionals, and other working programs to prevent child abuse through education, advocacy, public awareness, and early intervention training. Does not handle individual cases.

Hope and Help Recovery Resource Center
17 Hayden Street
Toronto, Ontario M4Y 2P2
Canada
Phone: (416) 922-2900
Fax: (416) 966-2748

A registered chatrity providing support, information, referrals, education, peer support groups, facilitated support groups, peer counseling, and counseling. Offers a twenty-four-hour telephone-answering-machine service. Sponsors an annual conference for survivors. Located above "That Other Bookstore," (Canada's comprehensive recovery bookstore) offering a wide selection of recovery literature as well as free brochures/pamphlets on recovery issues.

Incest Survivors Resource Network International (ISRNI)
P.O. Box 7375
Las Cruces, NM 88006
(505) 521-4260

An educational resource organization for professionals founded in 1983 in New York City as a Quaker peace witness. Also offers networking and resources for adult survivors of mother–son incest. Operates a national and international helpline staffed by incest survivors. Calls are received 2 to 4 P.M. ET, and 11 to 12 P.M. ET, Monday through Saturday.

International Society for the Study of Multiple Personality and Dissociation (ISSMP&D)
5700 Old Orchard Road, First Floor
Skokie, IL 60077-1057
Phone: (708) 966-4322
Fax: (708) 966-9418

A nonprofit professional association organized to promote research and training in the identification and treatment of MPD and allied dissociative states. Provides professional and public education and serves as a catalyst for international communication and cooperation among clinicians and investigators working in this field. Membership is open to mental health professionals and other interested parties. Journal and newsletter; membership lists; spring and fall conferences; local chapters; and study groups.

Monarch Resources

P.O. Box 1293
Torrance, CA 90505-0293
(310) 373-1958
1-900-988-9896 ext. 764

Nonprofit clearinghouse of information on ritual abuse, incest/sexual abuse, and dissociation. Recovery literature/articles for survivors, partners, supportive parents, and professionals. Resource packets, referrals, bibliographies, audio/visual materials, etc. Professional consultations, workshops, seminars, support groups, public education and advocacy, conference planning service, and speaker's bureau. Nominal fee for written materials. Send SASE with inquiries. Call the 900 number above for recorded information on hotlines, resources, support groups, clinical messages, books, etc. Two dollars per minute; average call, 2 minutes; entire message 4–5 minutes. Available twenty-four hours a day.

Multiple Creations

1238 1st Street
Brandon, Manitoba R7A 2Y6
Canada
(204) 725-2741 (support and business line)
(204) 725-2301 (alternate line)

A trimonthy newsletter providing a forum where MPD/DD survivors share their thoughts and feelings about being multiple or dissociative and about the recovery process from abuse. Referrals,

resource library on MPD/DD, and abuse issues; educational services for mental health professionals and lay persons through seminars, speaker presentations, and workshops. Support line calls accepted twenty-four hours a day, seven days a week. Cannot accept collect calls, but will talk to long distance callers.

The Sidran Foundation

2328 W. Joppa Road
Suite 15
Lutherville, MD 21093
Phone: (410) 825-8888
Fax: (410) 337-0747

A national nonprofit organization devoted to advocacy, education, and research on behalf of survivors of catastrophic trauma in childhood. Operates Sidran Press and Sidran Bookshelf to publish and distribute books, tapes, and educational materials about dissociative disorders for academic, professional, and lay audiences. Sidran's PsychTrauma Infobase provides extensive nationwide information services on a state-by-state basis, maintaining constantly updated lists of treatment providers, publications, organizations, support groups, etc. Offers educational workshops, development and funding of research, and support of a low-cost treatment / training demonstration clinic.

Survivors Reaching Out

P.O. Box 899
Citrus Heights, CA 96511
(916) 967-0424 (business and crisis line)

Nonprofit organization for adult survivors of extreme childhood abuse and their families. Services include twenty-four-hour crisis line (when not staffed, calls are recorded via answering machine and returned at the earliest opportunity). Provides referrals, resources, a and variety of support groups for women, men, partners, family members, and support group facilitators. Conferences, workshops, public education, and special programs for survivors with multiple personality.

VOICES® in Action, Inc. (Victims of Incest Can Emerge Survivors)
P.O. Box 148309
Chicago, IL 60614
(312) 327-1500 or 1-800-7VOICE8 (1-800-786-4238)

Forum for male and female survivors for resource literature. Offers special interest groups a nationwide letter writing support forum. Organizes annual international and regional conferences; task forces; chapters; and newsletter.

NEWSLETTERS/BIBLIOGRAPHIES/ PUBLICATIONS/EDUCATION

Cavalcade Productions
7360 Potter Valley Road
Ukiah, CA 95482
(707) 743-1168 (in California)
1-800-345-5530 (outside of California)

A video production company dedicated to developing educational materials for professionals, survivors, and the public. Topics include understanding trauma, including ritual abuse, the aftereffects, and healing. See Bibliography for selection of video topics.

Children's Institute International
Marshall Resource Center
711 South New Hampshire Avenue
Los Angeles, CA 90005
Phone: (213) 385-5100
Fax: (213) 383-1820

Private, nonprofit organization serving abused/neglected children and their families. Specializes in the treatment and prevention of child abuse and neglect. Multilingual and multicultural staff of professionals. The Marshall Resource Center is a library specializing in treatment and prevention of child abuse and neglect containing articles and a detailed bibliography on ritual abuse. Open to survivors, partners, and professionals by appointment.

The Healing Woman
P.O. Box 3038
Moss Beach, CA 94038
(415) 728-0339

A national, monthly, twelve-page newsletter for women survivors of childhood sexual abuse. Includes self-help articles, survivor writings, research news, journaling exercises, book reviews, and resource listings.

Incest and Ritual Abuse Library
Multicultural Women's Centre
114 South Street
Freemantle 6160
W.A. Australia

In Search of Healing
The Magazine of Recovery from Sexual Abuse
The Survivor Press
P.O. Box 30702
Albuquerque, NM 87190
(505) 880-8683

A quarterly magazine with informative articles, in-depth interviews, and topical humor about every aspect of recovery from sexual abuse. Also includes an anthology of survivor/prosurvivor writings and art. Aesthetics and diversity are given respectful treatment. Features the Green Pages—a regularly updated national resource directory; and The Network, a communications section. Queries and/or reader submissions welcome. Sample issue, $5.00.

Many Voices
P.O. Box 2639
Cincinnati, OH 45201-2639
(513) 531-5415

Bimonthly newsletter providing an information exchange for professionals and survivors with multiple personality and dissociative disabilities. Call or write for *Mending Ourselves,* a book on healing the trauma ($12.95, plus shipping and handling). Also publishes an annual Resource Guide to MPD/DD treatment, education, and support.

Men's Issues Forum
The M.A.L.E. Survivor Newsletter
P.O. Box 380181
Denver, CO 80238-1181
(303) 693-9930
1-800-949-MALE (1-800-949-6253)

A bimonthly newsletter published by M.A.L.E. (Men Assisting Leading and Educating, Inc.). M.A.L.E. is a national nonprofit organization dedicated to healing male survivors of childhood sexual abuse. For a complimentary sample copy call the 800 number above.

Pathways
238 Lakeshore Road East
Oakville, ON L6J 1H8
Canada
Phone: (905) 338-1055
Fax: (905) 338-8901

Bimonthly Canadian magazine of wellness and recovery exploring holistic health practices and recovery from a range of life circumstances including abuse, addictions, as well as related ill-

nesses. Includes a consumer listing of helplines, self-help meetings, community and government agencies. Call or fax for subscription information.

S.O.A.R. (Survivors of Abusive Rituals)
P.O. Box 1776
Cahokia, IL 62206-1776

Bimonthly newsletter providing a forum for survivors of ritual abuse in which to express feelings and share stories. Articles, bibliographies, and resource lists available to subscribers.

Society for the Investigation, Treatment, and Prevention of Ritual and Cult Abuse
P.O. Box 835564
Richardson, Texas 75083-5564
Phone: (214) 235-0399
Fax: (214) 235-0529

A forum for health, mental health professionals, attorneys, law enforcement officials, media representatives, clergy, and other interested parties. Newsletter.

S.O.F.I.E.
(Survivors of Female Incest Emerge)
P.O. Box 2794
Renton, WA 98056-2794

A bimonthly newsletter for men and women who were sexually abused as children by a woman or women.

Treating Abuse Today
The International Newsjournal of Abuse Survivorship and Therapy
2722 Eastlake Avenue East
Suite 300
Seattle, WA 98102
Phone: (206) 329-9101
1-800-847-3964
Fax: (206) 329-8462

A comprehensive bimonthly publication focusing on a broad selection of timely and relevant editorials relating to treatment of sexual abuse. Offers the Resource Database, an IBM-compatible computer diskette with extensive annotated bibliographies relating to abuse; rosters of national, regional, and state organizations; and state crime victims compensation agencies with names of people to contact. Fifteen dollars or free with a two-year subscription.

Vis-À-Vis

Family Violence Program
The Canadian Council on Social Development
55 Parkdale Ave.
P.O. Box 3505
Station C,
Ottawa, Ontario K1Y 4G1
Phone: (613) 728-1865
Fax: (613) 728-9387

A free, national quarterly newsletter dedicated to actively supporting and promoting the work of those directly involved with preventing family violence. Provides news from the Family Violence Prevention Division of Health Canada, calendar of events, dialogues, and survivor viewpoints and resources.

Westord Institute

1563 Solano Avenue
Suite 344
Berkeley, CA 94707
Phone: (510) 527-9969
Fax: (510) 527-3014

Sponsors comprehensive educational programs for professional audiences on the long-term effects of abuse and trauma, and issues of empowerment. Audiotapes available on treatment of MPD, trauma in children, and special considerations in working with survivors of ritual abuse.

Does fund-raising in support of survivor organizations.

SELF-HELP/COUNSELING/ SUPPORT ORGANIZATIONS

The following organizations address survivor-related issues, but not necessarily ritual abuse. Most address issues of childhood trauma or incest. Keep in mind that organizations have different approaches/philosophies. A listing is not a recommendation, but a starting point for your personal assessment. Guidelines for evaluation are given in Chapter 24.

American Association of Pastoral Counselors

9504 A Lee Highway
Fairfax, VA 22031-2303
Fax: (703) 352-7725

A professional association of certified pastoral counselors providing leadership, standards, and credentialing for the involvement of more than eighty faith groups in mental health care and counseling. The association provides clarity in pastoral counseling practice and training criteria for religious institutions in pastoral counseling ministry and coordination with other mental health professions. Counselors not familiar with trauma issues will refer clients to qualified help. Write or fax requests for local referrals.

American Self-Help Clearinghouse

St. Clare's-Riverside Medical Center
Denville, NJ 07834
(201) 625-7101
TDD (201) 625-9053 (for the hearing impaired)

Provides a directory of national self-help organizations and self-help clearinghouses in the United

States and Canada. Booklet with guidelines on starting a self-help group.

Incest Survivors Anonymous World Service Office

P.O. Box 17245
Long Beach, CA 90807-7245
(310) 428-5599

A nonprofit twelve-step/twelve-tradition organization. Local self-help support groups. Information on starting a self-help group. Packet of recovery literature. Include a SASE with inquiries and specify that you are a survivor.

1-800-TRY-NOVA (1-800-879-6682):

National Organization for Victim Assistance (NOVA) is a nonprofit, public interest, membership organization based on volunteer efforts and individual contributions. Provides twenty-four-hour crisis counseling, local referrals, and follow-up assistance to all victims of crime, including rape and incest. Offers professional development and training to allied professionals across the country. Newsletter.

Parents United International Inc.

P.O. Box 608
Pacific Grove, CA 93950
Phone: (408) 646-1855
Fax: (408) 646-1054

A national self-help organization with local chapters. Guided self-help in a group environment and counseling by therapists for all family members of sexual trauma including offenders, victims, nonoffending parents, and survivors.

Rainbow House

P.O. Box 1261
Taylor, MI 48180
(313) 295-7144

A clubhouse run by persons with dissociative disorders. Serves as a "sanctuary" for survivors receiving treatment for MPD or DD-NOS. Offers art therapy, music therapy, and general support meetings for a modest fee. Also a resource center.

Survivors of Incest Anonymous International (SIA)

P.O. Box 21817
Baltimore, MD 21222
(410) 433-2365

Organization based on the twelve-step philosophy of recovery. Resources for survivors over eighteen years of age looking to start or join support groups. Introductory packet of recovery literature. Support groups nationwide. Penpal referrals. Send SASE with inquiries.

ADVOCACY ORGANIZATIONS

Stop Abuse by Counselors (STOP ABC)

P.O. Box 68292
Seattle, WA 98168
(206) 243-2723

National client advocate organization. Recommends avenues of recourse if you've been abused by a therapist. Networking, extensive resource materials, speakers, and guidelines in choosing a therapist.

MASA (Mothers Against Sexual Abuse)

503 S. Myrtle Avenue
Suite 4
Monrovia, CA 91016
Phone: (818) 969-0404
Fax: (818) 305-5190

National nonprofit organization to protect children through advocacy, legislation, and education on the epidemic of child sexual abuse. Offers support groups and legal referrals/assistance for survivors and parents of abused children. Develops public and media awareness through Public Service Announcements, conferences, and training. Does court monitoring and monitors legal developments and legislation for survivor advocacy issues. Chapters nationwide.

NOW Legal Defense and Education Fund

99 Hudson Street
New York, NY 10013

Information on the legal rights of adult survivors of child sexual abuse. Packet of information on legal issues, and local referrals. Written requests only please.

National Center for Missing and Exploited Children

2101 Wilson Boulevard, Suite 550
Arlington, VA 22201
1-800-843-5678 (staffed twenty-four hours a day; seven days a week)
Business line: (703) 235-3900

A private, nonprofit organization working in conjunction with the U.S. Department of Justice. Spearheads national efforts to locate and recover missing children and raise public awareness of how to prevent child abduction, molestation, and sexual exploitation. Call or write for free publications/flyer for an extensive listing of literature including pornography tip line brochure, as well as topics addressing issues of child care such as safety, child protection tips, selecting babysitters, or day care, etc. All calls to the 800 number are taped and you will hear a message advising you of this.

The National Center for Redress of Incest and Sexual Abuse

1858 Park Road, NW
Washington, D.C. 20010
(202) 667-1160

The Center for Redress is assembling a national constituency to address the legal needs of survivors of incest and sexual victimization. Is working to establish a comprehensive network of attorneys, develop educational outreach programs, launch a national effort to support heightened media awareness, and get support for litigation of test cases under civil law. Offers a year's subscription to *Moving Forward* to contributors of $50 or more.

TREATMENT FACILITIES

The following list is intended as a starting point for evaluating an appropriate treatment facility for survivors of ritual abuse. This is not a comprehensive list of available treatment options and is not intended as an endorsement or recommendation of facilities listed. Staff turnover or changes in specialization can dramatically impact the effectiveness of treatment. It is important to evaluate a potential facility independently. Guidelines for evaluation are given in Chapter 26.

ACUTE CARE/RESIDENTIAL TREATMENT CENTERS

Akron General Medical Center
Trauma & Recovery Program
400 Wabash Avenue
Akron, OH 44307
(216) 384-6793

Charter Hospital of Dallas
Dissociative Disorders Unit
6800 Preston Road
Plano, TX 75024
(216) 618-3939

Charter Peachford Hospital
2151 Peachford Road
Atlanta, GA 30338
(404) 455-3200

Columbine Psychiatric Center
8565 South Poplar Way
Littleton, CO 80126
1-800-942-2734

HCA Dominion Hospital
Abuse & Dissociative Disorders Recovery Unit
2960 Sleepy Hollow Road
Falls Church, VA 22044
(703) 538-2827

Institute of Pennsylvania Hospital
Dissociative Disorders Unit
111 N. 49th Street
Philadelphia, PA 19139
(215) 471-2058

Ivy Lea Manor
1379 Park Western Drive
S. 310
San Pedro, CA 90732
(310) 832-8511
1-800-428-9906

The Meadows
P.O. Box 97
Wickenburg, AZ 85358
1-800-621-4062

National Center for Multiple Personality &
  Dissociation
23700 Camino del Sol
Torrance, CA 90505
1-800-645-3305

Northwestern Institute
450 Bethlehem Pike
Fort Washington, PA 19034
(215) 641-5300
1-800-344-6947

Pocket Ranch Institute
P.O. Box 516
Geyserville, CA 95441-0516
(707) 857-3359

Quakertown Community Hospital
Eleventh Street & Park Avenue
Quakertown, PA 18951
(215) 538-4575
1-800-858-8876

River Oaks Psychiatric Hospital
1525 River Oaks Road West
New Orleans, LA 70123
(504) 733-2273
1-800-733-3242
1-800-366-1740

Rush North Shore Medical Center
Dissociative Disorders Program
9600 Gross Point Road
Skokie, IL 60076
(708) 933-6685

Sheppard & Enoch Pratt Hospital
6501 North Charles Street
P.O. Box 6815
Baltimore, MD 21285-6815
1-800-627-0330

The Center for Trauma & Dissociation
4400 East Iliff Avenue
Denver, CO 80222
1-800-441-6921

Two Rivers Psychiatric Hospital
5121 Raytown Road
Kansas City, MO 64133
(816) 356-5688
1-800-872-7049 (in state)
1-800-225-8577 (out of state)

EXTENDED CARE, HALFWAY HOMES, AND OTHER TREATMENT OPTIONS

The Life Healing Center of Santa Fe

P.O. Box 6758
Santa Fe, NM 87501
(505) 989-7436

A halfway-house setting offering individually tailored therapy modeled on treatment center programs for survivors with multiple personality or dissociative difficulties. Promotes healthy group interaction creating an emotionally supportive "family" environment for clients. Experienced team of therapists and consulting psychologists/psychiatrists conduct individual and group therapy. Partial scholarships available to qualified applicants.

Response Side Therapy

8540 Sepulveda Boulevard
S. 1117
Los Angeles, CA 90045
Phone: (213) 933-9451 (Martin R. Smith, M.Ed.)
or: (310) 417-8481 (Katharine B. Thompson,
    RN, MN, MFCC)

Response Side Therapy incorporates the use of biofeedback in addressing the cognitive disrup-

tions, emotional distress, and physical pain which make up the foundation of traumatic dissociation and PTSD. This active approach guides and directs both the client and the therapist in a precise manner to bring about sufficient soothing, comfort, and control so that the conscious feeling and rational choice is possible. By utilizing objective physiological measurements, retraumatization, flooding, etc., during therapy are kept to a minimum.

Restoration Therapy Center

19 11th Street
San Mateo, CA 94402
(415) 572-2710

Provides intensive therapy for those dealing with childhood abuse/neglect, inner child healing and recovery, and ritual abuse. The intensive approach (usually three weeks with two extended sessions per day), allows for uncovering and healing deeply repressed inner child wounds. Therapy is provided by a male/female therapy team. Housing available for out of town clients.

Safe Harbors

2325 West Victory Boulevard
Burbank, CA 91506
(818) 845-0729

An intensive five-day residential workshop available nationally and internationally for survivors of sexual abuse, incest, ritual abuse, torture, and child pornography/prostitution. Professional consultations.

Women's Living and Support Systems

P.O. Box 1182
Redwood City, CA 94064
(415) 366-9936

A long-term care facility for women who have not responded to traditional mental health treatment of dissociative disorders, eating disorders, or any other complex condition. Support and advocacy for women's issues. Staff psychiatric nurse works with team of consulting medical doctors, psychiatrists, and psychologists to tailor an individualized treatment plan for clients.

Selected Bibliography

Note: A double asterisk (**) indicates resources of potential interest to ritual abuse survivors in general. A single asterisk (*) indicates references that may be of special interest to some survivors. Contact information for some of the organizations mentioned in the Bibliography is given in the Resource Guide.

*Adams, Kathleen, M.A. *Journal to the Self: Twenty-two Paths to Personal Growth.* New York: Warner Books, Inc., 1990.

Adler, Jerry, with Rosenberg, Donna. "Dr. Bean and her Little Boy." *Newsweek,* April 13, 1993, p. 56.

Allan, John, and Berry, Pat. "Sandplay." *Elementary School Guidance and Counseling,* 2, no. 3 (April 1987): 300–306.

Alpert, Judith L. "Retrospective Treatment of Incest Victims: Suggested Analytic Attitudes." *Psychoanalytic Revue,* 78, no. 3 (Fall 1991).

Andes, Ron, CRT, and Dickey, Dnise, CRT. *Radix: Body-Centered Personal Growth Work.* Santa Fe, NM: Radix Center of Santa Fe, 1993.

Ash, Stephen M., Psy.D. "Cult-Induced Psychopathology, Part I Clinical Picture." *Cultic Studies Journal,* 2, no. 1 (Spring/Summer, 1985): 31–89.

**Bass, Ellen, and Davis, Laura. *The Courage to Heal: A Guide for Women Survivors of Childhood Sexual Abuse.* New York: Harper & Row, 1988.

*Baugh, Michael, L.C.S.W. "God as a Multiple Personality: Reflections on Spirituality and Ritual Abuse." *SurvivorShip,* IV, no. 1 (January 1992): 2–4.

*Beahrs, John. *Unity or Multiplicity.* New York: Brunner/Mazel, 1981.

Beck, Melinda; Springer, Karen; Foote, Donna. "Sex and Psychotherapy." *Newsweek,* April 13, 1992, p. 53.

Bennetts, Leslie. "Nightmares on Main Street." *Vanity Fair,* June 1993, p. 42.

*Bentley, Judith J. "How to Choose a Therapist: A Checklist" (1985). Available through VOICES® in Action, Inc.

**Beyond Survival.* Special issue on ritual abuse, 2, no. 2 (1989).

**Blume, E. Sue. *Secret Survivors: Uncovering Incest and Its Aftereffects in Women.* New York: Ballantine Books, 1990.

Bodden, Jack L. "Accessing State Bound Memories in the Treatment of Phobias: Two Case Studies." *American Journal of Clinical Hypnosis,* 34, no. 1 (July 1991): 24–29.

**Boulette, Teresa Ramirez, and Andersen, Susan M. " 'Mind Control' and the Battering of Women." *Community Mental Health Journal,* 21, no. 2 (Summer 1985): 109–17.

**Bradshaw, John. *Bradshaw On: The Family.* Deerfield Beach, FL: Health Communications, Inc., 1988.

*Brain, James L. "The Filthiest Show in Town: Sex and Death." *The Australian Journal of Anthropology,* 1, nos. 2–3 (1990): 180–91.

**Branden, Nathaniel, Dr. *If You Could Hear What I Cannot Say: Learning to Communicate with the Ones You Love.* New York: Bantam Books, 1983.

*Braun, Bennett G., M.D. "Multiple Personality Disorder: An Overview." *The American Journal of Occupational Therapy,* 44, no. 11 (November 1990): 971–76.

*Braun, Bennett G., M.D. *Treatment of Multiple Personality Disorder.* Washington, D.C.: American Psychiatric Press, 1986.

*Braun, Jerome. "Pressuring Institutions and Flat Personalities." *The International Journal of Social Psychiatry,* 29 (Winter 1983): 313–17.

Breslow, Norman. "Locus of Control, Desirability of Control and Sadomasochists." *Psychological Reports,* 61 (1987): 995–1001.

*Briere, John. "Studying Delayed Memories of Childhood Sexual Abuse." *The Advisor,* 5, no. 3 (Summer 1992): 17–18.

*Briggs, Dorothy Corkville. *Your Child's Self-Esteem.* New York: Dolphin Books, 1965.

Brown, Dee, M.A. *Satanic Ritual Abuse: A Handbook for Therapists.* Blue Moon Press, P.O. Box 300308, Denver, CO 80203-0308, 1994.

*Brown, Dee. "Observations Regarding the Experience of Survivors of Ritual/Satanic Abuse." Presented at the California Consortium of Child Abuse Councils Conference, February 20, 1987.

Brown, H. Jackson. *Life's Little Instruction Book.* Nashville, TN: Rutledge Hill Press, 1991.

*Browne, Ivor. "Psychological Trauma, or Unexperienced Experience." *ReVISION* 12, no. 4 (Spring 1990): 21–34.

*Bryant, Doris; Kessler, Judy; Shirar, Lynda. *The Family Inside.* New York, London: W. W. Norton and Company, 1992.

Bugliosi, Vincent, with Gentry, Curt. *Helter Skelter.* New York: Bantam Books, 1974.

*Burgess, Ann Wolbert, R.N., D.N.Sc.; Hartman, Carol R., R.N., D.N.Sc.; McCausland, Maureen P., R.N., M.S.; Powers, Patricia, R.N., M.S. "Response Patterns in Children and Adolescents Exploited Through Sex Rings and Pornography." *American Journal of Psychiatry,* 141, no. 5 (May 1984): 656–62.

Burmeister, Claudia. "Satanism as a Form of Organized Evil." *SurvivorShip,* IV, no. 1 (January 1992): 10.

Campbell, Beatrix. "Children's Stories" (Why Was the Ritual Abuse the Nottingham Children Reported Disregarded by Police?). *New Statesman and Society,* 3 (October 5, 1990): 15.

Campbell, Joseph, with Moyers, Bill. *The Power of the Myth.* New York: Doubleday, 1988.

*Casey, Joan Francis, and Wilson, Lynn. *The Flock: An Autobiography of a Multiple Personality.* New York: Knopf, 1991.

Castanenda, Carlos. *Journey to Ixtlan: The Lessons of Don Juan.* New York: Pocket Books, 1972.

*Cavendish, Richard, and consultant Rhine, J.B. *Encyclopedia of the Unexplained.* New York: Penguin Books, 1974.

Chain, Steven, L.C.S.W. "EMDR: A New Treatment Procedure for Trauma and Phobias." *Men's Issues Forum,* 4, no. 1 (1993): 1–2.

The Children's Aid Society of Hamilton-Wentworth vs. D.C., H.C., and M.R. Transcript of Unified Family Court in the Judicial District of Hamilton-Wentworth, March 30, 1987.

**"Children at Risk" (video). Ukiah, CA: Cavalcade Productions, 1991.

*Clark, John G. Jr., M.D.; Langone, Michael D., Ph.D.; Schecter, Robert E., Ph.D.; Daly, Roger C.B., M. Div. "Destructive Cult Conversion: Theory, Research, and Treatment." American Family Foundation, Bonita Springs, Florida, 1981.

*Coates, James. "Mormon-Affiliated Group Linked to Rituals of Devil Worship, Occult." *Chicago Tribune,* November 3, 1991, section 9, p. 1.

*Cohen, Barry M; Giller, Esther; Lynn, W. *Multiple Personality Disorder from the Inside Out.* Baltimore, MD: The Sidran Press, 1991.

Cole, Nancy J., Psy.D. "The Dynamics of Fear." *The Center for Trauma and Dissociation,* I, no. 2 (June 1993).

*Collings, Mari. "Reasons Not to Kill Yourself." For reprints write *SurvivorShip.*

**"Coming Home: Recovery from Satanic Ritual Abuse" (video). Shrewsbury, MA: Grace Productions, 1992. (Also available through Cavalcade Productions.)

**Cook, Caren. "Understanding Ritual Abuse: Through a Study of Thirty-three Ritual Abuse Survivors From Thirteen Different States." University of Colorado at Boulder. For reprints write Ritual Abuse Project, 5431 Auburn Blvd., Suite 215, Sacramento, CA, 95841.

*Crewsdon, John. *By Silence Betrayed: Sexual Abuse of Children in America.* Boston, MA: Little, Brown and Co., 1988.

"Criminal Offenses: 5/12-33. Ritualized Abuse of a Child." *720 Illinois Criminal Statutes (720 ILCS) 5-12-21,* p. 1036, 1993.

Crivillé, Albert. "Child Physical and Sexual Abuse: The Roles of Sadism and Sexuality." *Child Abuse and Neglect,* 14 (1990): 121–27.

*"Current Statistics." CHILDHELP USA, P.O. Box 630, Hollywood, CA, 90028.

"Dahmer." (TV journalism transcript.) "ABC News Day1One," April 18, 1993. Transcript source: Journal Graphics Inc., 1535 Grant Street, Denver, CO, 80203.

*Daraul, Arkon. *A History of Secret Societies.* New York: Carol Publishing Group, 1961.

Davant, Charles. "Letters—(re:firewalking)." *Newsweek,* August 9, 1993, p. 12.

*Davis, Laura. *Allies in Healing.* New York: HarperCollins Publishers, 1991

**Davis, Laura, and Bass, Ellen. *The Courage to Heal Workbook,* Third edition. New York: HarperCollins Publishers, 1994

Davis, Wade. *The Serpent and the Rainbow.* New York: Warner Books, 1985.

Dawson, Judith. "The Vortex of Evil." (Children's Own Evidence of Ritual Abuse, Torture and Murder in Nottingham [England] and the Social Workers' Clash with the Police.) *New Statesman and Society,* 3 (October 5, 1990): 12–14.

De Sade, Marquis. *Justine, Philosophy in the Bedroom, and Other Writings.* New York: Grove Weidefield, 1965.

Dell, Paul F. Ph.D. "Violence and the Systemic View: The Problem of Power." *Family Process, Inc.,* 28, no. 1 (March 1989): 1–13.

Dimock, Peter, L.I.C.S.W., M.S.W. "Characteristics of Adult Males Sexually Abused as Children," 1989. Reprints available from Peter Dimock, 401 Groveland Ave., Minneapolis, MN, 55403.

Dimock, Peter, L.I.C.S.W., M.S.W. "Guidelines for Interviewing the Male Sexual Abuse Victim," 1989. Reprints available from Peter Dimock, 401 Groveland Ave., Minneapolis, MN, 55403.

*Dimock, Peter, L.I.C.S.W., M.S.W. "Recovery for the Male Sexual Abuse Survivor: Critical Steps in the Healing Process," 1989. Reprints available from Peter Dimock, 401 Groveland Ave., Minneapolis, MN, 55403.

Dickey, Dnise, and Andes, Ron. "Body-Centered Personal Growth Work." *Radix® Brochure,* Radix Center of Santa Fe, NM.

*Doka, Kenneth J. "Silent Sorrow: Grief and the Loss of Significant Others." *Death Studies,* 11 (1987) 455–69.

*Driscoll, Linda N., and Wright, Cheryl, Ph.D. "Survivors of Childhood Ritual Abuse: Multi-Generational Satanic Cult Involvement." Department of Family and Consumer Studies, 228 AEB, University of Utah, Salt Lake City, UT, 84112.

Durant, Will. *The Story of Philosophy.* New York: Simon & Schuster, Inc., A Touchstone Book, 1926.

Eisler, Riane. *The Chalice and the Blade.* New York: HarperSanFrancisco, 1987.

*Eisler, Robert. *Man into Wolf: An Anthropological Interpretation of Sadism, Masochism, and Lycanthropy.* Santa Barbara, CA: Ross-Erikson, Inc., 1978.

Ellenson, Gerald S. "Disturbances of Perception in Adult Female Incest Survivors." *Social Casework: The Journal of Contemporary Social Work,* 67, no. 3 (March 1986): 149–59.

England, Lynn W., and Thompson, Charles L. "Counseling Child Sexual Abuse Victims: Myths and Realities." *Journal of Counseling and Development,* 66, no. 8 (April 1988): 370–73.

Eyer, Diane. "The Battle Over Bonding." *U.S.A. Weekend,* May 7–9, 1993, pp. 4–5.

*Faber, Adele, and Mazlish, Elaine. *How to Talk so Kids Will Listen and Listen so Kids Will Talk.* New York: Avon Books, 1980.

*Faller, Kathleen Coulborn. "Can Therapy Induce False Allegations of Sexual Abuse?" *The Advisor,* 5, no. 3 (Summer 1992): 3–6.

*False Prophets of False Memory Syndrome" (video). Ukiah, CA: Cavalcade Productions, 1993.

Fauntleroy, Gussie. "Don't Call It Love." *The New Mexican,* November 12, 1993, p. C-1.

Favell, Judith E. "The Treatment of Self-Injurious Behavior." *Behavior Therapy,* 13, no. 4 (September 1982): 529–54.

Fenichel, Otto, M.D. *The Psychoanalytic Theory of Neurosis.* New York: W. W. Norton & Co., 1945.

*Fike, Laurita M. "Childhood Sexual Abuse and Multiple Personality Disorder: Emotional Sequelae of Caretakers." *The American Journal of Occupational Therapy,* 44, no. 11 (November 1990): 984–90.

*"Finding a Therapist for Persons with Multiple Personalities or a Dissociative Disorder." Available from ISSMP&D.

*Flanigan, Mary Beth. "Client Bill of Rights for Psychotherapy." Available through VOICES® in Action, Inc.

*Flanigan, Mary Beth. "Signs of an Unhealthy or Abusive Therapist or Therapy that Isn't Helpful." Available from VOICES® in Action, Inc.

**Fossum, Merle A., and Mason, Marylin, J. *Facing Shame*. New York: W. W. Norton & Co., 1986.

Frankl, Victor E. *Man's Search for Meaning*. New York: Washington Square Press, 1959.

*Fraser, Sylvia. *My Father's House: A Memoire of Incest and Healing*. Toronto: Doubleday Canada, Ltd., 1987.

**Fredrickson, Renee, Ph.D. *Repressed Memories: A Journey to Recovery from Sexual Abuse*. New York: Fireside/Parkside Books, 1992.

Fremantle, Francesca, and Trungpa, Chogyam. *The Tibetan Book of the Dead*. Boston, MA: Shambhala Publications, 1975.

*Friesen, James, G., Ph.D. *Uncovering the Mystery of MPD*. San Bernardino, CA: Here's Life Publishers, Inc., 1991.

Galland, China. *Tara and the Black Madonna*. New York: Viking Penguin, 1990.

Garfield, David, M.D., and Havens, Leston, M.D. "Paranoid Phenomenon and Pathological Narcissism." *American Journal of Psychotherapy*, XLV, no. 2 (April 1991): 160–71.

Geiselman, R. Edward, Ph.D. "The Cognitive Interview." *SurvivorShip*, V, no. 1 (1993): 6–8.

Geiselman, R. Edward, Ph.D., Fisher, Ronald P., Ph.D. *Memory Enhancing Techniques for Investigative Interviewing: The Cognitive Interview*. Springfield, Il: Charles C. Thomas Publisher, 1992.

*"General Dynamics for Survivors of Childhood Trauma." Reprints available from Monarch Resources.

*Gibson, Janice T., and Haritos-Fatouros, Mika. "Education of a Torturer." *Psychology Today* (November 1986): 50–58.

*Gil, Eliana, Ph.D. *United We Stand*. Walnut Creek, CA: Launch Press, 1990.

*Goodwin, Jean M., M.D., M.P.H. "Sadistic Abuse: Definition, Recognition and Treatment." In press for *DISSOCIATION Journal*, VI, nos. 2–3 (in press).

**Goodwin, Jean M., M.D., M.P.H. *Rediscovering Childhood Trauma*. Washington, D.C.: American Psychiatric Press, 1993.

Gordon, James S., M.D. "The Cult Phenomenon and the Psychotherapeutic Response." *Journal of the American Academy of Psychoanalysis*, 11, no. 4 (October 1983).

**Gould, Catherine, Ph.D., and Cozolino, Louis. "Ritual Abuse, Multiplicity, and Mind-Control." *Journal of Psychology and Theology*, 20, no. 3 (1992): 194–96.

**Gould, Catherine, Ph.D. "Signs and Symtoms of Ritualistic Abuse in Children," 1992. Available from Catherine Gould, 16055 Ventura Blvd., Suite 714, Encino, CA, 91436, (213) 650-0807.

Greer, Germaine. *The Female Eunuch*. Toronto, ON: Paladin Grafton Books, 1970.

Gregory, S. S., "Children of a Lesser God: The Surviving Kids of Ranch Apocalypse Offer Shocking Details of Life with David Koresh." *Time*, May 17, 1993.

*Greven, Philip. *Spare the Child: The Religious Roots of Punishment and the Psychological Impact of Physical Abuse*. New York: Vintage Books, 1992.

Grossman, William I., M.D. "Pain, Aggression, Fantasy, and Concepts of Sadomasochism." *Psychoanalytic Quarterly*, LX (1991): 22–51.

*Hart, Kenneth E, and Hittner, James B. "Irrational Beliefs, Perceived Availability of Social Support, and Anxiety." *Journal of Clinical Psychology*, 47, no. 4 (July 1991): 582–87.

**Hassan, Steven. *Combatting Cult Mind Control*. Rochester, VT: Park Street Press, 1988.

*Hay, Louise L. *Heal Your Body*. Carson, CA: Hay House, Inc., 1982.

Hayes, Kate F. "The Conspiracy of Silence Revisited: Group Therapy with Adult Survivors of Incest." *Journal of Group Psychotherapy, Psychodrama, and Sociometry*, 39, no. 4 (Winter 1987): 143–56.

Heilbrun, A.B., Jr., and Seif, David T. "Erotic Value of Female Distress in Sexually Explicit Photographs." *The Journal of Sex Research,* 24 (1988): 47–57.

"Hell Night." (TV journalism transcript.) "ABC News Primetime Live," October 23, 1993. Transcript source: Journal Graphics Inc., 1535 Grant Street, Denver, CO, 80203.

**Herman, Judith L., M.D. *Trauma and Recovery.* New York: Basic Books, 1992.

*Herman, Judith Lewis, M.D. "Adult Memories of Childhood Trauma: Current Controversies." (Position paper presented at the Annual Meeting of the American Psychiatric Association, May 26, 1993.)

*Herman, Judith Lewis, M.D., and Schatzow, Emily, M.Ed. "Time-Limited Group Therapy for Women with a History of Incest." *International Journal of Group Psychotherapy,* 34, no. 4 (October 1984): 605–16.

*Herman, Judith Lewis, M.D., and Schatzow, Emily, M.Ed., Women's Mental Health Collective. "Recovery and Verification of Memories of Childhood Sexual Trauma." *Psychoanalytic Psychology,* 4, no. 1 (1987): 1–14.

**Hill, S., and Goodwin, J. "Satanism: Similarities Between Patient Accounts and Pre-Inquisition Historical Sources." *Dissociation,* 2 (1989): 39–44.

*Hochman, John, M.D. "Miracle, Mystery, and Authority: The Triangle of Cult Indoctrination." *Psychiatric Annals,* 20, no. 4 (April 1990):179–84, 187.

*Hocking, Sandra, J., and Company. *Living with Your Selves: A Survival Manual for People with Multiple Personalities.* Rockville, MD: Launch Press, 1992.

**Hollingsworth, Jan. *Unspeakable Acts.* New York: Congdon and Weed, 1986.

Horner, Thomas M., Ph.D. "Rapproachment in the Psychic Development of the Toddler: A Transactional Perspective." *American Journal of Orthopsychiatry,* 58, no. 1 (January 1988): 4–15.

Horowitz, Mardi J., M.D. "The Unreal Real and the Really Unreal." *American Journal of Psychiatry,* 142, no. 9 (September 1985): 1131.

How to Start Your Own Self-Help Group. Available through VOICES® in Action, Inc.

**Hudson, Pamela S., L.C.S.W. *Ritual Child Abuse: Discovery, Diagnosis and Treatment.* Saratoga, CA: R & E Publishers, 1991.

*Hurley, Thomas, J., III, and O'Regan, Brendan. "Multiple Personality: Mirrors of a New Model of Mind." *Noetic Sciences Collection: Ten Years of Research, 1980–1990.* Sausalito, CA: Institute of Noetic Sciences, 1991.

*"Identification of the Ritually Abused Child" (video). Ukiah, CA: Cavalcade Productions, 1989.

Jilek, Wolfgang G. "Altered States of Consciousness in North American Indian Ceremonials." *Ethos,* 10, no. 4 (Winter 1982): 326–43.

*Johnston, Jerry. *The Edge of Evil: The Rise of Satanism in North America.* Dallas, TX: Word Publishing, 1989.

*Jones, Richard W., and Peterson, Linda W. "Posttraumatic Stress Disorder in a Child Following an Automobile Accident." *Journal of Family Practice,* 36, no. 3 (February 1993): 223.

*Kahaner, Larry. *Cults that Kill: Probing the Underworld of Occult Crime.* New York: Warner Books, 1989.

Kane, Steven M. "Holiness Ritual Fire Handling." *Ethos,* 10, no. 4 (Winter 1982).

*Kasl, Charlotte Eliza, Ph.D. "Dear Therapist, I Want You to Know . . . " *Through the Voices of Survivors of Childhood Abuse,* March 1986. For reprints, write Castle Consulting, Inc., P.O. Box 1302, Lolo, MT 59847.

*Kasl, Charlotte Eliza, Ph.D. "The Role of Addiction and Spirituality in Recovery from Childhood Abuse." *International Congress on Rape: Jerusalem, Israel,* April 1986.

**Kasl, Charlotte Davis, Ph.D. *Many Roads, One Journey: Moving Beyond the 12 Steps.* New York: HarperCollins Publishers, 1992.

*Kassorla, Dr. Irene. *Nice Girls Do.* New York: Berkley Books, 1980.

*Keogh, Tom. "Bad Kids Raging Angels," *New Age Journal. The Globe and Mail* (Toronto), March 6, 1993, p. D5.

Kinsella, Warren. "Satanism Suspected in Unsolved Kidnap Cases." *Calgary Herald,* March 7, 1987.

*Kluft, Richard. *Childhood Antecedents of Multiple Personality.* Washington, D.C.: American Psychiatric Press, 1985.

*Knight, Stephen. *The Brotherhood.* New York: Dorset Press, 1984.

Koch, Kathleen, and Jarvis, Carolynne. "Symbiotic Mother–Daughter Relationships in Incest Families." *Social Casework: The Journal of Contemporary Social Work,* 68, no. 2 (February 1987): 94–101.

Lacks, Hazel, E., C.S.W., C.A.C. "Anger and the Recovering Substance Abuser." *Alcoholism Treatment Quarterly,* 5, nos. 3–4 (1988): 37–52.

LaVey, Anton Szandor. *The Satanic Bible.* New York: Avon Books, 1969.

LaVey, Anton. *The Secret Life of a Satanist.* Los Angeles, CA: Feral House, 1990.

*Lew, Mike. *Victims No Longer.* New York: Harper & Row, 1988.

*Lifton, Robert, J. *The Nazi Doctors.* New York: Basic Books, 1986.

*Lifton, Robert, J. *Thought Reform and the Psychology of Totalism: A Study of "Brainwashing" in China.* Chapel Hill, NC: The University of North Carolina Press, 1989.

*Lifton, Robert J. "Cult Formation." *Cultic Studies Journal,* 8, no. 1 (1991): 1–6.

*Lindsey, Carol J., Ph.D., B.C.S.W. "Ritual Abuse in Health Care." *SurvivorShip,* IV, no. 10 (October 1992): 6.

Loewenstein, Richard J., M.D. "President's Message." *issmpd NEWS,* December 1992, pp. 1–2.

Loftus, Elizabeth. "The Malleability of Memory." *The Advisor,* 5, no. 3 (Summer 1992): 7–9.

Long, Haniel. *The Marvelous Adventure of Cabeza de Vaca.* Clearlake, CA: The Dawn Horse Press, 1992.

**Lovern, John D., Ph.D. "Spin Programming: A Newly Uncovered Technique of Systematic Mind Control," 1992. For reprints write John D. Lovern, 2141B W. Orangewood Ave., Orange, CA, 92668-1941. Written requests only please.

Luckstead, Orlin D., and Martell, D. F. "Cults: A Conflict Between Religious Liberty and Involuntary Servitude?" *FBI Law Enforcement Bulletin* (April/May/June 1982): 1–15.

**Marron, Kevin. *Ritual Abuse.* Toronto: Seal Books, 1989.

Martin, John D.; Blair, Garland E.; Nevels, Robert M.; Brant, Mary M. "A Study of the Relationship Between a Personal Philosophy of Human Nature (Good or Evil) and Self-Esteem." *Psychological Reports, 1987,* 61 (1987): 447–51.

**"Mastering Traumatic Memories I, II, III" (videos). Ukiah, CA: Cavalcade Productions, 1992.

McCann, John, M.D., and Voris, Joan, M.D. "Perianal Injuries Resulting from Sexual Abuse." *Pediatrics,* 91, no. 2 (February 1993): 390–97.

McCann, John, M.D.; Voris, Joan, M.D.; Simon, Mary, M.D. "Genital Injuries Resulting from Sexual Abuse: A Longitudinal Study." *Pediatrics,* 89, no. 2 (February 1992): 307–17.

McCann, John, M.D.; Wells, Robert, Ph.D.; Simon, Mary, M.D.; Voris, Joan, M.D. "Genital Findings in Prepubertal Girls Selected for Nonabuse: A Descriptive Study." *Pediatrics,* 86, no. 3 (September 1990): 428–39.

McCarty, Loretta M. "Mother-Child Incest: Characteristics of the Offender." *Child Welfare*, LXV, no. 5 (September/October 1986): 447–57.

McKay, Barbara, M.A. "Uncovering Buried Roles through Face Painting and Storytelling." *The Arts in Psychotherapy*, 14 (1987): 201–8.

**Mellody, Pia, with Miller, Andrea Wells, and Miller, Keith J. *Facing Codependence*. New York: HarperSanFrancisco, 1989.

Mellon, Charles David, M.D.; Barlow, Carrolee; Cook, Joshua, D.O.; Clark, Lincoln D., M.D. "Autocastration and Autopenectomy in a Patient with Transsexualism and Schizophrenia." *The Journal of Sex Research*, 26, no. 1 (February 1989): 125–30.

*Miller, Alice. *The Drama of the Gifted Child*. New York: Basic Books, Inc., 1981.

*Miller, Alice. *For Your Own Good*. New York: Farrar, Straus & Giroux, Inc., 1983.

**Miller, Alice. *Thou Shalt Not Be Aware*. New York: A Meridian Book, 1984.

*Miller, Jesse S., Ph.D. "The Utilization of Hypnotic Techniques in Religious Cult Conversion." *The Cultic Studies Journal*, 3, no. 2 (1986): 243–50.

Moore, Thomas. *Dark Eros: The Imagination of Sadism*. Dallas, TX: Spring Publications, Inc., 1990.

Moriarty, Anthony R., and Story, Donald R. "Psychological Dynamics of Adolescent Satanism." *Journal of Mental Health Counseling*, 12, no. 2 (April 1990): 186–98.

*Morinis, Alan. "The Ritual Experience: Pain and the Transformation of Consciousness in Ordeals of Initiation." *Ethos*, 10, no. 4 (Winter 1982).

Naipaul, Shiva. *Journey to Nowhere: A New World Tragedy*. New York: Simon and Schuster, 1980.

Nallan, Gary B.; Kennedy, Karron; Kennedy, Kimberly. "Retrospective and Prospective Memory Coding in Humans." *The Psychological Record*, 41 (1991): 79–86.

Necromonican. New York: Avon Books, 1977.

**Neswald, David W. M.A., M.F.C.C., in collaboration with Gould, Catherine, Ph.D., and Graham-Costain, Vicki, Ph.D. "Common 'Programs' Observed in Survivors of Satanic Ritualistic Abuse." *The California Therapist* (September/October 1991): 47–50.

**Neswald, David W., M.A., M.F.C.C. "Working With Primal Dissociative Experiences in Adult MPD Survivors of Satanic Ritualistic Abuse." Paper presented at the Fifth Annual Western Clinical Conference on Multiple Personality and Dissociation, April 10–12, 1992, Costa Mesa, CA.

**Neswald, David W., M.A., M.F.C.C., and Gould, Catherine, Ph.D. "Basic Treatment and Program Neutralization Strategies for Adult MPD Survivors of Satanic Ritual Abuse." *Treating Abuse Today*, 2, no. 3 (1992): 5–10.

**Noblitt, Randy, Ph.D., L.C.D.C. "Cult and Ritual Trauma Disorder" (video), 1991. Center for Counseling and Psychological Services, P.C. 2060 N. Collins Blvd., S. 105, L.B. 9, Richardson, TX, 75080, (214) 235-0399.

**Noll, Shaina. *Songs for the Inner Child*. Corta Madera, CA: Backroads. 1-800-767-4748.

Otani, Hajime, and Hodge, Milton H. "Mechanism of Feeling of Knowing: The Role of Elaboration and Familiarity." *The Psychological Record*, 41 (1991): 523–35.

Pagels, Elaine. *The Gnostic Gospels*. New York: Vintage Books, 1981.

*Painter, Susan Lee, and Dutton, Don. "Patterns of Emotional Bonding in Battered Women: Traumatic Bonding." *International Journal of Women's Studies*, 8, no. 4 (September/October 1985): 363–75.

Patten, Sylvia B.; Gatz, Yvonne K.; Jones, Berlin; Thomas, Deborah L. "Posttraumatic Stress Disorder and the Treatment of Sexual Abuse." *Social Work* (May 1989): 197–202.

*Peck, M. Scott. *People of the Lie.* New York: A Touchstone Book, 1983.

Pennebaker, James W., and Beall, Sandra Klihr. "Confronting a Traumatic Event: Towards an Understanding of Inhibition and Disease." *Journal of Abnormal Psychology,* 95, no. 3 (1986): 274–81.

Pennebaker, James, W.; Kiecolt-Glaser, Janice K.; Glaser, Ronald. "Disclosure of Traumas and Immune Function: Health Implications for Psychotherapy." *Journal of Consulting and Clinical Psychology,* 56, no. 2 (1988): 239–45.

*Perry, Nancy W. "How Children Remember and How They Forget." *The Advisor,* 5, no. 3 (Summer 1992): 1–2.

*Pia, Jacklyn M. *Multiple Personality Gift: A Workbook for You and Your Inside Family.* Saratoga, CA: R & E Publishers, 1991.

**Pollard, John K., III. *The Self-Parenting Program.* Deerfield Beach, FL: Health Communications, Inc., 1992.

**Polt, Walter J. "From Anger to Power: A Process for Those Who Suppress Anger," 1983. Reprints available from Walter J. Polt, 1713 Harzman. S. W., Albuquerque, NM 87105, (505) 242-3333.

*Putnam, Frank, W. *Diagnosis and Treatment of Multiple Personality Disorder.* New York: Guilford Press, 1989.

*Putnam, Frank W. "Altered States: Peeling Away the Layers of a Multiple Personality." *The Sciences,* (November/December 1992): 30–36.

*Ragazzi, Catherine, R.N. "Understanding Ritual, Part 1: The Abuse of Ritual." *SurvivorShip* (October 1990): 1–3.

*Ragazzi, Catherine, R.N. "Understanding Ritual, Part 2: Ethics and Ritual Abuse." *SurvivorShip* (September 1991): 5–7.

Randall, Tom M. "Is Supernaturalism a Part of Authoritarianism?" *Psychological Reports,* 68 (April 1991): 685–86.

*Raschke, Carl A. *Painted Black.* New York: Harper-San Francisco, 1990.

Regardie, Israel (selected by). *Gems from the Equinox: Instructions by Aleister Crowley For His Own Magical Order.* Las Vegas: Falcon Press, 1988.

Rhodes, H. T. F. *The Satanic Mass.* Secaucus, NJ: The Citadel Press, 1974.

**Ritual Abuse Task Force, Los Angeles County Commission for Women. "Ritual Abuse: Definitions, Glossary, and the Use of Mind Control," 1989.

*"Ritual Child Abuse: A Professional Overview" (video). Ukiah, CA: Cavalcade Productions, 1989.

*"Ritual Crime: Guidelines for Identification" (video). Ukiah, CA: Cavalcade Productions, 1986.

*Robbin, Sandy, M.D. "EMD/R Revisited." *Survivor-Ship,* V, no. 2 (1993): 16–17.

Robbins, Rossell Hope. *The Encyclopedia of Witchcraft and Demonology.* New York: Crown Publishers, Inc., 1959.

*Robinson, Robyn, Ph.D. "EMD. . . . A Breakthrough in Therapy." *The BULLETIN of the Australian Psychological Society* (April 1992): 4.

Rogers, Martha L., Ph.D. "Evaluating Adult Litigants Who Allege Injuries from Child Sexual Abuse: Clinical Assessment Methods for Traumatic Memories." Presented at Fourth Annual Meeting of the American Psychological Society, San Diego, CA, June 20, 1992.

Ronningstam, Elsa, Ph.D., and Gunderson, John, M.D. "Identifying Criteria for Narcissistic Personality Disorder." *American Journal of Psychiatry,* 147, no. 7 (July 1990): 918–22.

Rose, Elizabeth S. "Surviving the Unbelievable." *Ms.,* III, no 4, (January/February 1993): 40–45.

*Roselini, Gayle, and Worden, Mark. *Of Course You're Angry.* New York: Harper & Row, 1986.

Ross, Colin A., M.D., F.R.C.P.C. "Epidemiology of Multiple Personality Disorder and Dissociation." *Psychiatric Clinics of North America,* 14, no. 3 (September 1991).

*Ross, Colin. *Multiple Personality Disorder: Diagnosis, Clinical Features, and Treatment.* New York: Wiley, 1989.

*Rossman, Martin L., M.D. *Healing Yourself.* New York: Pocket Books, 1987.

Rothman, Stephen. "Heart of Darkness." *Changes* (May/June, 1990): 34.

**Ryder, Daniel, C.C.D.C., L.S.W. *Breaking the Circle of Satanic Ritual Abuse.* Minneapolis, MN: Comp-Care Publishers, 1992.

*Sachs, Roberta G., Ph.D. "The Role of Sex and Pregnancy in Satanic Cults." Paper presented at the Fourth International Congress of the Pre- and Perinatal Psychology Association of North America, August 5, 1989.

*Sachs, Roberta G. "The Sand Tray Technique in the Treatment of Patients with Dissociative Disorders: Recommendations for Occupational Therapists." *The American Journal of Occupational Therapy,* 44, no. 11 (July 1, 1990): 1045–47.

Safron, Claire. "Dangerous Obsession: The Truth About Repressed Memories." *McCall's,* June 1993, p. 98.

**Sakheim, David K., and Devine, Susan E. *Out of Darkness: Exploring Satanism and Ritual Abuse.* New York: Lexington Books, 1992.

**Sanders, Emily. *Multiple Personality Disorder: Selected Bibliography and Resource Guide for MPD and RA.* Somerville, MA: Peace by Piece, 1992.

Saravay, Stephen M., M.D. "Parallel Development of the Group and Its Relationship to the Leader: A Theoretical Explanation." *International Journal of Group Psychotherapy,* 35, no. 2 (April 1985): 197–207.

*Sargant, William. *Battle for the Mind.* Garden City, NY: Doubleday & Co., 1957.

*Saywitz, Karen J. "Enhancing Children's Memory with the Cognitive Interview." *The Advisor,* 5, no. 3 (Summer 1992): 9–10.

**Schnoebelen, William. *Wicca: Satan's Little White Lie.* Chino, CA: Chick Publications, 1990.

*Schreiber, Flora Rheta. *Sybil.* New York: Warner Books, 1973.

*Schwartz, Lita Linzer. "The Historical Dimmension of Cultic Techniques of Persuasion and Control." *Cultic Studies Journal,* 8, no. 1 (1991): 37–45.

Shapiro, Laura; Rosenberg, Debra; Lauerman, John F. "Rush to Judgement." *Newsweek,* April 19, 1993, p. 54.

*Sexton, Daniel A. "Dynamics More Often Associated with Sexual Abuse Survivors." Reprints available from Daniel A. Sexton, Director of SOAR (Survivors of Abuse in Recovery), P.O. Box 989, No. Hollywood, CA.

*"Significant Others" (Demystifiying Multiple Personality) (video). Ukiah, CA: Cavalcade Productions, 1990.

Singer, June. *Boundaries of the Soul.* Garden City, NY: Anchor Books, 1973.

Smith, B. J., L.M.S.W. "Believing Heals." *Survivor Times,* no. 1 (1993): 5.

Smith, Joseph, H. "Rite, Ritual and Defense." *Psychiatry,* 46 (February 1983): 16–30.

**Smith, Margaret. *Ritual Abuse: What It Is; Why It Happens; How to Help.* New York: HarperSanFrancisco, 1993.

**Smith, Martin R., M.Ed. "Post-traumatic stress and the loss of ontological security: Overcoming trauma-induced neophobia in adult children of alcoholics." In B.G. Braun (ed.), *Proceedings of the Fourth International Conference on Multiple Personality/Dissociative States,* 1987. Chicago: Department of Psychiatry, Rush University.

*Smith, Martin R., M.Ed. "Obedience to insanity: Social collusion in the creation and maintenance of dissociative states." In B.G. Braun and E.D. Carlson (eds.), *Proceedings of the Sixth International Conference on Multiple Personality/Dissociative States,* Oct. 13, 1989. Chicago: Department of Psychiatry, Rush University.

*Smith, Martin R., M.Ed. "The Addictive Nature of Perpetrators of Ritual Abuse." *SurvivorShip,* III, no. 5 (May 1991): 1–3.

*Smith, Martin R., M.Ed., and Jones, Ellen T., M.A. "Neophobia, Ontological Insecurity and Existential Choice Following Trauma." *Journal of Humanistic Psychology,* 33, no. 4 (Fall 1993): 89–109.

**Smith, Michelle, and Pazder, Lawerence, M.D. *Michelle Remembers.* New York: Pocket Books, 1980.

*Song of the Wind. "Information for Survivors Who are Considering Emergency Psychiatric Hospitalization." *SurvivorShip,* V, no. 3 (1993): 4–5.

**Spencer. Judith. *Suffer the Child.* New York: Simon and Schuster, Pocket Books, 1989.

*StarDancer, Caryn. "Demonic Possession: One Survivor's Perspective." *SurvivorShip,* I, no. 2 (October 1989).

*StarDancer, Caryn. *Returning to Herself: Poems of Restoration.* Kelseyville, CA: H.P.L. Publishing, 1989.

**StarDancer, Caryn. "Assessment and Identification of Intrafamilial Childhood Ritual Abuse: A Cautionary Statement," 1989. Training Presentation Accompanying the "Childhood Indicators of Intrafamilial Ritual Abuse" list. Available from *SurvivorShip.*

**StarDancer, Caryn. "Dear SurvivorShip. . . . Some Frequently Asked Questions," 1991. Available from *SurvivorShip.*

*StarDancer, Caryn. "Providing 'Theraplay' for the Children Inside," 1990. Reprints available from *SurvivorShip.*

**StarDancer, Caryn. "Recovery Skills for the Dissociatively Disabled, Part 1: Recognition; Part 2: Identification; Part 3: Reprogramming," 1990. Available from *SurvivorShip.*

*StarDancer, Caryn. "Childhood Indicators of Intrafamilial Ritual Abuse" (1990). Available from *SurvivorShip.*

*StarDancer, Caryn. "Recovery Issues: Self-Mutilation." Reprints available from *SurvivorShip.*

*StarDancer, Caryn. "The 'F' Word: Functional Multiplicity as a Viable Alternative to Fusion." *SurvivorShip,* III, no. 9 (September 1991): 16–17.

**StarDancer, Caryn. "Understanding Cult Alters." *Survivorship,* III, no. 11 (November 1991): 10–13.

*StarDancer, Caryn. "Triggers." *SurvivorShip,* IV, no. 3 (March 1992): 2–5.

*StarDancer, Caryn. "Dancing with the Serpent." *SurvivorShip,* III, no. 8 (October 1992): 2–4.

*StarDancer, Caryn. "The Basics: Working in a Total Treatment Context." *SurvivorShip,* IV, no. 12 (December 1992): 2–3.

**StarDancer, Caryn. "Sibylline Shackles: Mind Control in the Context of Ritual Abuse." *SurvivorShip,* V, no. 2 (1993): 4–8.

*StarDancer, L. J. *Turtleboy and Jet the Wonderpup: A Therapeutic Comic for Survivors of Ritual Abuse.* Kelseyville, CA: H.P.L. Publishing, 1989.

*Steward, Margaret S. "Preliminary Findings From the University of California, Davis, Child Memory Study: Development and Testing of Interview Protocols for Young Children." *The Advisor,* 5, no. 3 (Summer 1992): 1, 2, 13–15.

*Stratford, Lauren. *Satan's Underground.* Eugene, OR: Harvest House Publishers, 1988.

*"Successful Ritual Abuse Prosecutions." Available from Cavalcade Productions, current through April 1993.

*Suedfeld, Peter. "Torture: A Brief Overview," *Psychology and Torture*. Hemisphere Publishing Corp., 1990. Reprints available from Monarch Resources.

*Summit, Ronald C. "Misplaced Attention to Delayed Memory." *The Advisor,* 5, no. 3 (Summer 1992): 21–25.

*"Symptoms of Ritualistic and Sexual Abuse," 1988. Reprints available from Believe the Children.

Te Paske, Bradley. *Rape and Ritual: A Psychological Study.* Toronto: Inner City Books, 1982.

*Terr, Lenore C., M.D. "Childhood Traumas: An Outline and Overview." *American Journal of Psychiatry,* 148, no. 1 (January 1991): 10–19.

**Terry, Maury. *The Ultimate Evil.* New York: Bantam, 1989.

*The Troops for Truddi Chase. *When Rabbit Howls.* New York: Dutton, 1987.

*Thomas, T. *Surviving with Serenity: Daily Meditations for Incest Survivors.* Dearfield Beach, FL: Health Communications, Inc., 1990.

Tobacyk, Jerome. "Cognitive Complexity and Paranormal Beliefs." *Psychological Reports,* 52 (1983): 101–2.

*"Treatment of the Ritually Abused Child" (video). Ukiah, CA: Cavalcade Productions, 1989.

**"True/Not True: When Memories Can Be Trusted" (video). Ukiah, CA: Cavalcade Productions, 1993.

*Utain, Marsha, and Oliver, Barbara. *Scream Louder: Through Hell and Healing with an Incest Survivor and Her Therapist.* Deerfield Beach, FL: Health Communications, Inc., 1989.

**Van Benschoten, R.N., M.Ed., M.A., S.C. "Multiple Personality Disorder and Satanic Ritual Abuse: The Issue of Credibility." *Dissociation,* III, no. 1 (March 1990): 22–29.

*Verny, Thomas, M.D., with Kelly, John. *The Secret Life of the Unborn Child.* New York: Dell Publishing Co., 1981.

Wagner, Mahlon, W., and Ratzeburg, Fredrick, H. "Hypnotic Suggestibility and Paranormal Belief." *Psychological Reports,* 60 (1987): 1069–70.

*Ward, James S., Rev. "Ritual and Healing: The Liberating and Rehumanizing Resources of the Church for Ritual Abuse Survivors." Presented at the Healing Institute on Ritual Abuse at U.C. Berkeley, CA, January 20, 1989.

*Warnke, Mike. *The Satan Seller.* Plainfield, NJ: Logos International, 1972.

*West, Granger E. *Good Grief.* Philadelpia: Fortress Press, 1962.

*Whitfield, Charles L., M.D. "Co-dependence: Our Most Common Addiction—Some Physical, Mental, Emotional and Spiritual Perspectives." Codependency: Issues in Treatment and Recovery, special issue. *Alcoholism Treatment Quarterly,* 6, no. 1 (1989): 19–36.

*Whitfield, Charles L., M.D. *Healing the Child Within.* Deerfield Beach, FL: Health Communications, Inc., 1989.

Whitmont, Edward C. *The Symbolic Quest.* Princeton, NJ: Princeton University Press, 1978.

*Whitmont, Edward C., and Perera, Sylvia Brinton. *Dreams, A Portal to the Source.* New York: Routledge, 1989.

*Williams, Linda Meyer. "Adult Memories of Childhood Abuse: Preliminary Findings from a Longitudinal Study." *The Advisor,* 5, no. 3 (Summer 1992): 19–20.

Wright, Lawerence. "Remembering Satan—Parts I & II." *The New Yorker,* May 17, 1993, and May 24, 1993.

York, Lyle. "When a Therapist Hides Abuse Under the Cloak of Respectability." *Santa Fe Reporter,* November 18–24, 1992, pp. 7–8.

**Young, W.; Sachs, R.G.; Braun, B., et al. "Patients Reporting Ritual Abuse in Childhood: A Clinical Syndrome; Report of 37 Cases." *Child Abuse & Neglect,* 15 (1991): 181–89.

Index

Stay Safe Pages

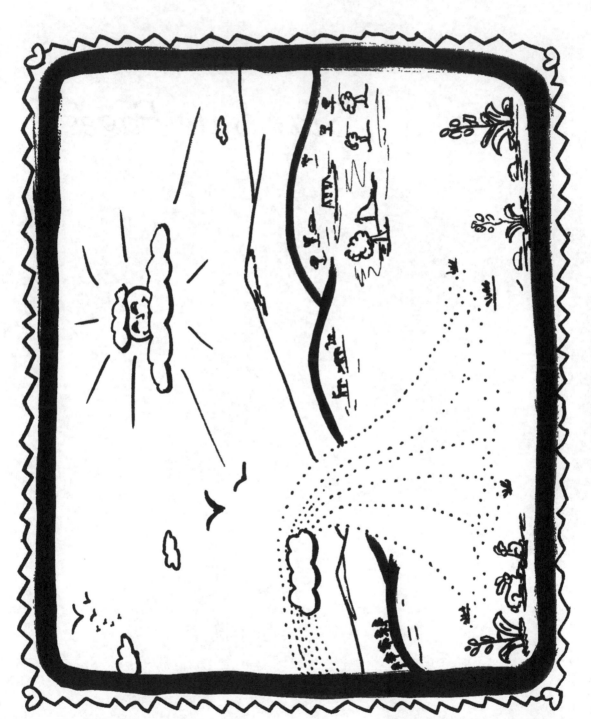

RAINBOW PLACE

(for description see page 17)

MANAGING ASSOCIATION/DISSOCIATION

1. I AM SAFE.

THIS IS_____
     (fill in the year)

I AM _____ YEARS OLD. I AM A BIG PERSON. I CAN PROTECT MYSELF.

_____

_____

_____

2. BLINK HARD. BLINK AGAIN. DO IT ONCE MORE AS HARD AS YOU CAN.
   MAKE TEA. DRINK IT.
   CALL A FRIEND.
   EAT A SNACK
   JUMP UP AND DOWN WAVING YOUR ARMS
   LIE DOWN ON THE FLOOR; FEEL YOUR BODY CONNECTING WITH IT. KEEP YOUR EYES OPEN.
   HOW DOES IT FEEL? DESCRIBE IT OUT LOUD TO YOURSELF.
   MAKE EYE CONTACT WITH YOUR PET. NOW HOLD IT.
   CLAP YOUR HANDS.
   BREATHE DEEPLY. KEEP BREATHING. PAY ATTENTION TO YOUR EVERY BREATH.
   HOLD A STUFFED ANIMAL, PILLOW OR YOUR FAVORITE BLANKET.
   ALTERNATELY TENSE AND RELAX SOME MUSCLES.
   NOW "BLINK" WITH YOUR WHOLE BODY, NOT JUST YOUR EYELIDS.
   MOVE YOUR EYES FROM OBJECT TO OBJECT, STOPPING TO FOCUS ON EACH ONE.
   WASH YOUR FACE.
   GO OUTSIDE FOR SUNSHINE OR FRESH AIR.

_____

_____

_____

_____

For more ideas turn to page 189.

INSTRUCTIONS

1. Fill in the blanks and write in other statements that can remind you of safety.
2. The ideas in part two have helped survivors stay grounded and safe. Some may work better for you than others. There is additional space where you can write in your own ideas. Use a highlighter pen to highlight statements you want to see first if you are feeling disoriented. That way you can spot them quickly when needed.

PREVENTING INJURY, SELF-INJURY, OR SUICIDE

1. I PROMISE TO KEEP MYSELF SAFE UNTIL HELP ARRIVES.
   I WILL NOT HURT OR KILL MYSELF.
   I CAN DO IT. I KNOW I CAN.
   NO MATTER HOW HORRIBLE I FEEL, THIS FEELING WILL PASS.
   MY INNER CHILDREN NEED ME.
   I WILL FIGHT THE FIGHT, SECOND BY SECOND, MINUTE BY MINUTE.
   I AM STRONGER THAN THE IMPULSE.
   I WILL ASK MY INNER WISDOM FOR HELP.
   I WILL CONNECT WITH MY SAFE PLACE.
   I WILL OVERCOME THIS. I AM ALREADY DOING IT.
   IF I TELL SOMEONE WHAT'S HAPPENING, HELP CAN COME.

2. There are people who care about me. They are hoping I will make it through this difficult time. They don't want me to bear this alone. I can call one of them. Together, I know that we will do it. I will call someone now.

   _____

   _____

3. I can write or draw or talk about my impulses instead of acting on them. I can keep writing or drawing or talking until the impulse passes and I am safe.

   _____

   _____

4. I will reward myself for triumphing through crises by

   _____

   _____

5. For more support I will reread this page, read the other Stay Safe Pages, or Chapter 16.

INSTRUCTIONS

2. Fill in the names of special inner kids, your children, friends, partners, therapists (past or present), survivor friends, family members, pets, etc.
4. Write down how you might reward yourself for triumphing through the crisis.

REACH HELP

1. EMERGENCY OR CRISIS HOTLINE PHONE_____ DIAL_____

2. TELL THEM

_____
(your name)

_____
(your address)

_____
(your phone number)

3. CALL YOUR TWENTY-FOUR-HOUR SUPPORT FRIENDS OR THERAPIST

_____
(name)   (number)

_____
(name)   (number)

_____
(name)   (number)

_____
(name)   (number)

_____
(name)   (number)

4. CALL THE AMBULANCE AND CHECK YOURSELF INTO A HOSPITAL

_____

_____

5. TURN BACK ONE PAGE AND CONTINUE READING.

INSTRUCTIONS

1. Look inside the front cover or first pages of your local phone book. Find the most appropriate emergency number for your area. Many areas use 911. Or you may prefer to use a national crisis hotline (see the Resource Guide). Call the number you plan to use, and know what to expect before entering it. Recheck it periodically. The "Dial" space is for preprogrammed numbers, in case you have automatic dialing.
2. Fill in the information requested.
3. Fill in names of people you could call in an emergency.
4. See the front page[s] of your phone book, or call your nearest hospital, and enter ambulance or hospital emergency numbers.